The Wireless Mobile Internet

The Wireless Mobile Internet
Architectures, Protocols and Services

Abbas Jamalipour, Ph.D.

WILEY

Other Wiley Editorial Offices

John Wiley & Sons Inc., 111 River Street, Hoboken, NJ 07030, USA

Jossey-Bass, 989 Market Street, San Francisco, CA 94103-1741, USA

Wiley-VCH Verlag GmbH, Boschstr. 12, D-69469 Weinheim, Germany

John Wiley & Sons Australia Ltd, 33 Park Road, Milton, Queensland 4064, Australia

John Wiley & Sons (Asia) Pte Ltd, 2 Clementi Loop #02-01, Jin Xing Distripark, Singapore 129809

John Wiley & Sons Canada Ltd, 22 Worcester Road, Etobicoke, Ontario, Canada M9W 1L1

Wiley also publishes its books in a variety of electronic formats. Some content that appears
in print may not be available in electronic books.

Library of Congress Cataloging-in-Publication Data

Jamalipour, Abbas.
    The wireless mobile Internet : architectures, protocols, and services / Abbas Jamalipour.
        p. cm.
    Includes bibliographical references are index.
    ISBN 0-470-84468-X (alk. paper)
    1. Wireless Internet.   I. Title.

    TK5103.4885 .J35 2003
    004.67′8—dc21

                                                                          2002191086

British Library Cataloguing in Publication Data

A catalogue record for this book is available from the British Library

ISBN10: 0-470-84468-X (H/B)
ISBN13: 978-0-470-84468-7 (H/B)

to Zohreh, Soroush, and Sepehr

Contents

Table of Contents

Preface

As a regular course instructor on the subject of the Mobile and Wireless Internet in the past few years at major international conferences, companies, and universities, and as a researcher in this field, I was always struggling to find comprehensive literature that could give me all the knowledge that I required for my research in this important field. In recent years, many books on the subject of GSM, CDMA, UMTS, and cdma2000 for cellular networks and many others on the subject of data communication network, Mobile IP, cellular IP, and IP mobility for transferring IP technology to the mobile environment have been published by the experts from industry and academia. I had the opportunity to read almost all those books and also survey through numerous relevant technical papers published in the proceedings of international conferences, magazines, journals, and transactions. On the one hand, the cellular-type books have mainly explained the physical and link layer concepts of the wireless cellular systems, both 2G and 3G, with a little conceptual description of the network and even less information on how cellular systems could build the underlying infrastructure for future wireless Internet. On the other hand, the Internet-oriented books have focused on Internet network architecture, reference models, and mechanisms for migrating the IP technology into the mobile world with very little assistance from the cellular research community. Technical papers, either survey and tutorial or research-type ones, could give only specific information in a limited number of pages. Finally, I came to the conclusion that whilst each individual text in the literature has a lot of information to offer the researchers in the field of wireless and mobile Internet, none of them could be used as a comprehensive knowledge-based text, especially related to networking issues, by the researchers. Therefore, I came up with the idea to write a book, the one you have in your hands right now, that could become the first complete literature for the wireless Internet.

The majority of the contents and structure of *The Wireless Mobile Internet* have been developed during the many courses I have taught on the topic of wireless and mobile Internet in the past few years. The order of chapters and their respective contents have been modified over and over according to the feedback I have received from the course attendees. The background knowledge that the course attendees had on this topic was very diverse; they were among new researchers in the field, university postgraduate students and professors, engineers and R&D managers from governmental agencies and telecommunications industries. Accordingly, their feedback to my course contents and the presentation format was also very diverse. As a result, much of the original content has been deleted and many new things have been added in each chapter because I discovered I could write a text that could target a broad range of prospective readers. I came to the conclusion that I needed to include all materials required to understand the topic and I also needed to describe some primary issues. Using this strategy, which was completely based on the feedback, I am very pleased to see that *The Wireless Mobile Internet* has been completed in a very appropriate, logical and modular format, and most importantly, that it covers all the necessary materials. I really appreciate all those who helped bring this book to this shape

The Wireless Mobile Internet is written such that it is neither an industry-oriented nor an academic text. The contents of this book will be of considerable interest to both academic researchers and to the people in the concerned industry. While some chapters in *The Wireless Mobile Internet* describe the standard activities and the current status of the wireless IP, other chapters detail network models and specific techniques that are usually approached by academic researchers. This combination, I believe, has a very significant effect in directing wireless IP developments to the right path, as I experienced during my many years of working with the industry and higher education institutes.

The Wireless Mobile Internet is organized such that it can cover a broad range of audiences starting from senior-level undergraduate university students to postgraduate students, research engineers, system developers, and professionals. *The Wireless Mobile Internet* is also structured such that individual parts of it could be used as a text for specialized courses on the subject of wireless IP. The first part, which includes Chapters 1 to 4, provides a comprehensive text on the definition of wireless Internet and its enabling technologies. The second part consists of six chapters, and discusses basic requirements and issues toward the realization of wireless Internet. The last part, including three chapters, provides more advanced topics on wireless Internet and its generalization on a global basis. The book as a whole, therefore, can be used as a comprehensive text on the subject of wireless mobile Internet, its requirements and implementation, whilst its parts individually can be customized and used as the text for a more specialized course in the field. Details on the contents of these three parts are included in the final section of Chapter 1.

Acknowledgement

During the course of this project, I received invaluable help and encouragement from many people and I must acknowledge their role here. Many research results included in *The Wireless Mobile Internet* have directly come from my research at Sydney with my postgraduate students. Jade Kim, my former PhD student, now a research engineer at Ericsson Research in San Diego, California, has provided a lot of input for the contents of chapters on traffic modeling and traffic management. My PhD student, Tracy Tung has composed most of the materials on mobility and location management in Chapter 8. Since I consider the role of mobile ad hoc networking in future wireless IP networks to be very important, I asked my friend C-K. Toh, a former professor at Georgia Institute of Technology, GA, now the director of research at TRW Systems, California, who is an expert in the field of mobile ad hoc networking, to write a chapter on this topic for my book. His kind contribution on advanced topics in mobile ad hoc networks is presented in Chapter 12, after a short introductory section from me.

The people who attended my short courses on mobile and wireless Internet are the anonymous reviewers for this book, and without their invaluable feedback I do not know how *The Wireless Mobile Internet* would have been structured. Raymond Steels, the chairman of Multiple Access Communications Limited, who has been working on telecommunications systems for many years, encouraged me on this project during a meeting at Calgary, Canada. I cannot forget the help I received from the organizing committee of many international conferences such as IEEE Global Telecommunications Conference, IEEE International Conference of Communications, IEEE Wireless Communications and Networking Conference, IEEE High Performance Switching and Routing Conference, IEEE Vehicular Technology Conference, TR Labs Annual International Conference on Wireless Communications, and others during the period between 2000 and 2002 that helped me explore my ideas on wireless Internet in my tutorials included in their technical programs. My lecture notes in those tutorials became the main source for composing *The Wireless Mobile Internet*.

I would like to convey my appreciation to the staff at Wiley Chichester, who helped me publish this book. I would especially like to convey my thanks to the editors Sally

Mortimer and Birgit Gruber, who have helped me patiently through the multi-year period of this project, which has been delayed because of my numerous duties both at the University and outside. The comments from anonymous reviewers who have checked the contents of this book, requested by Wiley, were really helpful. I would also like to acknowledge the great work by Wiley cover designers and others in the editorial team.

I am very grateful for the encouragement and patience displayed by my family members, Zohreh and my boys Soroush and Sepehr, during the long days and nights I spent working on this project, despite the fact that I was using their share of my time to write the book. Soroush's and Sepehr's passion and enthusiasm for the Internet exhibited the great need for having a book on the subject of wireless Internet and assured me that when they grow up, Internet will serve them no matter where they would be and what they would be doing. Their generation will hopefully get the benefits from the technology introduced in *The Wireless Mobile Internet* and similar books that will be published in future.

I would also like to thank all the people who have in any way been involved in making this project a reality. I hope that with *The Wireless Mobile Internet* I am able to provide at least a small share in enhancing the knowledge on this profoundly important topic and that the readers find *The Wireless Mobile Internet* useful in their research for many years to come.

Abbas Jamalipour
Sydney, 2002

Part I

The Wireless Internet

CHAPTER 1 AN INTRODUCTION TO THE MOBILE INTERNET

In this chapter, fundamental trends toward the realization of wireless Internet have been identified. These trends include those within the telecommunications technology as principles and those within the Internet community. Several statistics have been provided to justify the need for wireless Internet implementation and related field studies. A general understanding on the requirements of wireless Internet has also been included in this chapter. The chapter ends with an outline of the book in order to simplify a customized selection of chapters for a particular course and for a selected group of audiences.

CHAPTER 2 WIRELESS CELLULAR DATA NETWORKS

In this chapter, major initiatives to the wireless Internet, mainly within the framework of the second-generation wireless cellular networks, have been introduced. An attempt has been made to describe the related materials in a general format as details of network architecture, and access technologies of the cellular systems will be introduced in the next two chapters. Whilst recent second-generation systems have provided some sort of data services and Internet capabilities to their mobile users, they cannot be a substitute for a system that offers full Internet services to mobile users. However, understanding these architectures is very important during the design process of an advanced wireless Internet system.

CHAPTER 3 CELLULAR MOBILE NETWORKS

In this chapter, network architecture of the 3G system UMTS have been described. UMTS is the successor of the 2G cellular network, GSM, which has been very successful in getting the largest geographic and population number share in the worldwide cellular telephony market. As an intermediate system enabling the most evolutionary developments toward the UMTS system, GPRS is considered as an important development. GPRS is the packet service designed on top of the GSM network in order to provide data services at higher rates than GSM to mobile users.

CHAPTER 4   MOBILE NETWORKS OF THE FUTURE

In this chapter, we complete our discussion on third-generation wireless systems that we have started in Chapter 3. The core and access technologies considered in the other 3G standard, cdma2000, will be described and compared with those of UMTS. We will see how cooperation of the two systems would provide a solution to the wireless mobile Internet in future. We will look at the wireless networks beyond the third-generation networks. Several proposals from industry and academia for the next-generation mobile networks will be investigated. Finally, a functional layered architecture for the future mobile Internet will be proposed in this chapter, which will pave the way for the detailed discussions in the second part of this book.

1

An Introduction to Wireless Mobile Internet

The wireless mobile Internet, which was a dream just a few years ago, is now progressing so fast that it could revolutionize the whole framework of the telecommunications industry. The wireless mobile Internet is not just an extension of the Internet into the mobile environment giving users access to the Internet services while they are on the move. It is about integrating the Internet and telecommunications technologies into a single system that covers all communication needs of human beings. With the extensive progress achieved during the last decade in wireless access technology, switching and routing in the Internet, and sophisticated hardware and software design, such a comprehensive Internet technology would no longer be a dream but a practical reality. Whilst the first cellular-based mobile Internet services provided users with flavors of an actual wireless mobile Internet system, there is still a need to research more to achieve the systematic goals of this network. In this chapter we will review the main related telecommunications technologies and then give some statistics on global trends toward wireless Internet. These trends include those within the telecommunications technology as principles and those within the Internet applications. A general understanding of the requirements of wireless Internet is also included in this chapter.

1.1 TELECOMMUNICATION TECHNOLOGIES

Wireless has been the most significant technology breakthrough among all human achievements in the past few decades. Barely twenty years ago, it was very difficult to assume that telecommunication services can be provided to people irrespective of their geographical

The Wireless Mobile Internet: Architectures, Protocols, and Services.   Abbas Jamalipour
© 2003 John Wiley & Sons, Ltd   ISBN: 0-470-84468-X

location and while they are moving around, but now for many people it is very difficult to imagine life without continuous availability of communications using a mobile phone. Telecommunications technology has indeed completed its biggest improvement in just a few years so that sometimes its future growth is doubtful. What would be the next breakthrough in this fast-growing industry? Is there still anything that we can add to telecommunications? Where will be the end of the telecommunication industry's progress and when will that end come?

1.1.1 Telecommunications: Wired, wireless, and cellular

Telecommunications services started with voice communications; the most natural requirement of human beings is to talk, no matter where they are, at the same location or thousands of miles away from the person they want to talk to. Invention of the wired telephony fulfilled this natural desire and has been considered as the most significant breakthrough of its time. This enormous breakthrough, however, needed 75 years to get its first 50-million users for the wired telephony network.

Radio technology started a new era in telecommunications history with the invention of the electromagnetic wave. Replacing wires with space as the medium for transmission of communication signals brought new ideas for the emerging telecommunications. Researchers started work on improvement of communication techniques so that more information could be sent on air. New coding algorithms have been developed so that a better quality radio signal could be received. Analog modulation schemes have been invented so that more users could access the same frequency spectrum and could share the available bandwidth resources. Radio and television broadcasting started their dominance in the user market all around the world. In particular, television brought in new media for connecting people in a visual manner, more desirable than the voice-only service, and satellite communications made it possible to transmit radio and television signals in just a few seconds to all parts of the world. Even these breakthrough inventions needed some time to get sufficient popularity. Broadcasting radio received its first 50-million users in 35 years, and the popular television required 13 years for the same number of subscribers. This was just the start of wireless communications.

1.1.1.1 Multiple access schemes

As people started using telecommunications resources at such a rapid pace, researchers started working on methods that would enable the efficient sharing of these resources. They found out from the beginning that telecommunications resources are limited, whether you use wire or radio frequency (RF). Multiple-access schemes thus started to be developed. Discussions on different multiple-access schemes can be found in all classic communication texts such as References [1–4] and in more specialized literature [5–13]. Frequency modulation (FM) gave the idea of sharing the frequency among many people so that they send their signals at different frequency bands. As a result, frequency division multiple access (FDMA) schemes have been invented. In FDMA, as shown in Figure 1.1a, each user is granted with a small fraction of frequency or channel within the available frequency bands. A small amount of frequency spectrum is allocated between each pair of

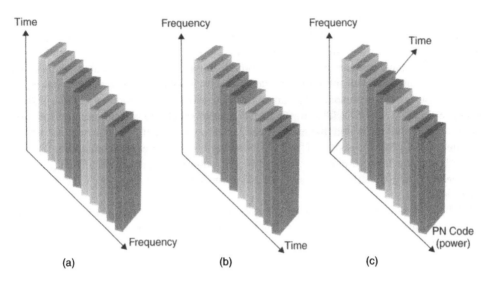

Figure 1.1 Telecommunications resource allocations through different multiple-access schemes: (a) FDMA; (b) TDMA; and (c) CDMA

adjacent frequency channels as guard-band, to reduce the interference from adjacent channels. First wireless systems, including satellite systems, used FDMA as the main method of accommodating many users. One reason for this selection was that FM is more robust to the nonlinearity, and thus the satellite's analog amplifiers could operate at their highest gain range where the amplification is no longer a linear process.

With the invention of digital communications and analog-to-digital conversion methods, it has been understood that dividing the time domain into channels while all users share the same frequency spectrum would be a better option than FDMA. Therefore, the time division multiple access (TDMA) scheme has been invented, allowing multiple users to use the whole available frequency band, but by sending their respective information at different periods of time, namely, *timeslots* as shown in Figure 1.1b. Each pair of adjacent time slots is separated with a short time period as guard-time, to reduce the interference from adjacent channels. Pulse code modulation (PCM) has been a great achievement in completing this era of digital communications sending smaller amount of information, but sufficient to retrieve the sender information, over the shared medium. The PCM itself finds its development through the invention of Nyquist's sampling theorem. TDMA and FDMA both are categorized as contention-less protocols as users' transmissions are scheduled in either the time (TDMA) or the frequency (FDMA) domain, and therefore there is no contention in accessing the channel by users, as, for example, can be experienced in an Aloha multiple access scheme [8].

More recently, code division multiple access (CDMA) schemes came to be used as commercial techniques in sharing the wireless channel resources [9–12]. In a CDMA system, users' signals occupy all the frequency spectrum during the entire transmission period, but these signals are distinguished from one another according to the specific code assigned to each user, as shown in Figure 1.1c. At any given time, a subset of the users in the system can transmit information simultaneously over the common channel to corresponding receivers. The transmitted signals in the common spectrum can be distinguished from one another by the superimposing of a different pseudorandom (or pseudonoise, PN) pattern, called a *code*, in each transmitted signal. Thus, a particular receiver can recover the transmitted information intended for it by knowing the PN pattern, that is, the sequence used by the corresponding transmitter. The most popular form of CDMA is direct sequence CDMA (DS-CDMA), in which DS spread-spectrum signals occupy the same channel bandwidth, provided that each signal has its own distinct PN sequence. As we will see later, DS-CDMA is used in UMTS (Universal Mobile Telecommunications System) FDD (frequency division duplex) mode [14–18], whereas in cdma2000 [19,20], another third-generation (3G) cellular system, a multicarrier CDMA, is used (see Chapters 3 and 4 for details).

CDMA can be considered as either a contention-less or contention protocol, depending on the situation of the channel. A CDMA scheme is a contention-less protocol if the number of simultaneous transmissions on the channel or the level of multiple-access interference is under a given threshold in which all the transmissions can be handled successfully by the system. It is a contention protocol if the level of interference is above the threshold, which results in contention and loss of all simultaneous packets on air. For this reason, CDMA is referred to as a power-limited system, limited by the total power of interference from other users, different from TDMA and FDMA, which are bandwidth-limited systems.

1.1.1.2 Cellular mobile communications

Progress in radio communications, multiple access schemes, and coding algorithms brought the means for the implementation of mobile communications for personal users. So, the new era of Personal Communication Services (PCS) has started. At the same time, progress in electronic design and manufacturing made it possible to put many of the developed communication algorithms on a small electronic chip. All these achievements paved the path for mobile communications. Popularity in the use of mobile communications for voice conversation and the enormous progress in very large-scale integrated (VLSI) circuit technology forced the price of mobile communications and devices to go down dramatically during a short period of time. Therefore, even radio and television were considered as the most attractive telecommunication services, and the mobile communications found a new record in attracting the first 50-million users in just 12 years.

In the PCS systems, the concept of cellular structure has been included in order to achieve higher spectral efficiency by reusing a same frequency band in a cell far enough from another one using the same frequency band. In a seven-cell frequency reuse pattern shown in Figure 1.2, for example, the total radio spectrum allocated to the cellular communication service is divided into a maximum of seven subbands. While neighboring cells use different subbands, the pairs of cells that are far enough could use a same-frequency subband, as shown in the figure. Each number shown in one cell in this figure means a separate frequency subband used in that cell. The current cellular mobile communications systems all use a similar concept as shown in the simple example of Figure 1.2.

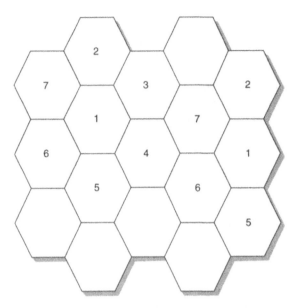

Figure 1.2 Basic concepts of cellular mobile communications and frequency reuse

The cellular concept discussed here can be used in FDMA systems, so the same sets of frequency bands can be used more than once in groups of cells far enough from one another. It can be used also in CDMA systems so that the multiple-access interference from users of adjacent cells is reduced, resulting in higher system capacity. It can be used in TDMA systems to provide a higher capacity system, accommodating more users, through combination of TDMA and FDMA techniques.

1.1.2 Internet: Fixed, wireless, and mobile

By that date, broadcasting using radio and television and voice communications using wired and mobile phones were considered as the complete set of services for the telecommunications industry. This was the case until personal computers (PCs) became available, replacing many traditional office and home equipments. Invention of hypertext transfer protocol (HTTP) and hypertext markup language (HTML) brought the Internet as the new media for telecommunications. PCs have been connected to each other and have started exchanging information data. Soon people found out that the computer and the Internet could replace many traditional means of communications that they knew until then, including the radio, the television, and even the telephone. The dramatic decrease in the price and the huge increase in the processing capability of personal computers made it possible that anyone could have a computer at home and then connect it to the Internet. The services provided by the computer and the Internet were so exciting that the Internet created a new record by attracting a 50-million market, that is, in just four years. Figure 1.3 illustrates the market achievement of the different telecommunication technologies discussed above.

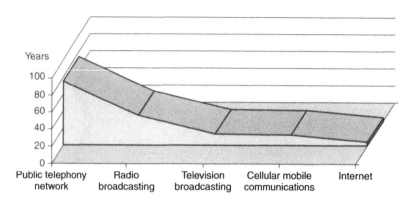

Figure 1.3   First 50-million users market period for telecommunications technologies

It seems that we achieved all that we could not even imagine just a few decades ago. We have good voice and video transmissions in our offices and on the road and can get any up-to-date information from the Internet with a click of a mouse. Then what is left? The answer is simple when we think about the progress in telecommunications. When voice communications could become mobile, why should the Internet access be restricted to geographically fixed locations. If the Internet plays an important role in our daily life, why should we not be able to use it whenever we want and wherever we want. So the mobile Internet is the next step (albeit a huge one as we will see soon) in the development of the telecommunications industry, and this book is all about it.

Mobile Internet in general is defined as an architecture in which a user can have access to the global Internet network and its usual services regardless of the current point of attachment to the network. Such definition implies that the mobile Internet is much broader than the wireless Internet. In wireless Internet, the user physical connection to the network is composed of wireless medium through RF channels. But mobile Internet provides access to the network through not only the radio channels but also through a wired network such as Ethernet and dial-up connections wherever available. An example of wireless Internet is the wireless local area network (LAN) in which an access point is the base station serving several mobile computing devices in an indoor environment and within a limited geographical area and connecting them through a wireless LAN server to a wired LAN and eventually to the global Internet. The mobile Internet however may include the wireless LAN as one of its several segments. A user in a mobile Internet network may be connected to the Internet through high-speed Ethernet access and at another moment may change his connection to a wireless LAN through a wireless LAN access card and then be connected to the cellular network through a cellular modem. Different from a nomadic user who has to disconnect from one network (for example, Ethernet) before connecting to another network (for example, wireless LAN or dial-up), a user in a mobile Internet network moves around, and his connection is changed seamlessly without any connection interrupt.

Realization of the mobile Internet is not as straightforward as what we have experienced in voice and telephony communications. There are many parameters in the way of such realization that could make it very challenging. In the case of voice communications, the problem was merely (at least in the beginning) to make a means of transmission of analog in nature signals using electromagnetic waves. As long as the communications can be established within a reasonable delay and the voice is recognizable, there would be no complaint from a subscriber using the mobile voice service. Short interruption or signal corruption in voice communications is acceptable to the human ear, and as long as the signal-to-noise ratio (SNR) of the received signal is above some flexible level, the signal can be regenerated at the receiver and delivered to the speaker. For the data communications such as the Internet, however, even very short interruption in data transferring could damage the whole data file and may be difficult to recover. Therefore, there is a need for more research and development until a reliable mobile Internet network is available. In this book, we will explain the requirements for realization of wireless and mobile Internet and detail current activities and progress in cellular wireless systems and similar telecommunication segments.

1.2 TRENDS TOWARD WIRELESS INTERNET

Before introducing technological requirements and worldwide activities for mobile and wireless Internet, in this section we try to explain why such a network is needed in the first place. The logical question that arises is "what are the evidences that a mobile Internet network is necessary as being part of the global telecommunications infrastructure" and must be answered before trying to solve the problem of how to realize it. The discussion given here, thus, more or less continues the introduction given in the previous section but with several statistical figures.

1.2.1 Access technology: Fixed and mobile

In order to understand the need for mobile and wireless Internet in the near future, it is wise to look at the trends in telecommunications in the past few years and how the industry has evolved from its first years in a comparably short period of time. The first significant trend that is visible in the telecommunications industry is the change from fixed access communications to mobile communications. It is not necessary to go back to the very old days to understand this trend. As shown in Figure 1.4, the increase in worldwide subscriber number for fixed telephone lines has been very smooth since 1996 at around 650 million and it would reach one billion by the year 2005 [21]. The graph illustrating this increase has shown signs of saturation or a very small increase after the year 2005. On the other hand, the increase in the number of mobile subscribers, shown on the same figure, is exponential with no sign of a stop or a slowing down of the increase rate. The figure illustrates a very natural and easily understandable phenomenon; that is, people want to have at most one or two fixed telephone lines at home used by the whole family but prefer to have one or two mobile phones for each member of family, for example, one for business and one for personal use. Continuous decrease in the cost of mobile handsets

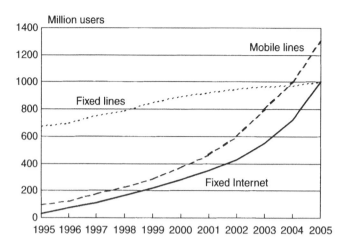

Figure 1.4   Increase in user population in fixed and mobile communication systems

and mobile usage charge tariffs is also accelerating this increase to an unknown future. Maybe the only slowing parameter in this trend would be the limited available spectrum in the future to be shared by billions of users.

The growth in the number of fixed Internet access is also shown for comparison [21,22] in Figure 1.4. As observed from this figure, Internet growth has a very similar pattern with the mobile cellular network market growth. Mobile Internet services, as we will see in Chapter 2, have been started in the second phase of the second-generation (2G) cellular networks, such as the General Packet Radio Service (GPRS) [23–25], the successor of the worldwide Global System for Mobile communications (GSM) cellular network [26]. If we add the number of users of such mobile Internet services with the fixed Internet figures, we will even see a sharper increase.

1.2.2   Increase in Internet usage

Although the Internet has been in place since the 1980s, its usage was limited to file transfer, remote access to computers, and simple mail transfer in the form of a file transfer until 1995. The Internet has started gaining popularity after the invention of HTML and HTTP, that is, the starting age of web browsing. Figure 1.5 shows the Internet growth usage over the last two decades. The web browsing has really revolutionized the Internet and is considered as the main factor in the popularity of the Internet. After invention of web browsers such as Netscape and Internet Explorer, and new email management programs that include browsing capabilities, ordinary people without a deep understanding of the computer could use PCs connected to the Internet in their daily lives, and thus a huge increase in the Internet subscription happened. The wireless Internet will be the next revolutionizing factor in the Internet usage growth, as it will provide freedom with respect to the user location and access to the Internet. In the near future, every mobile

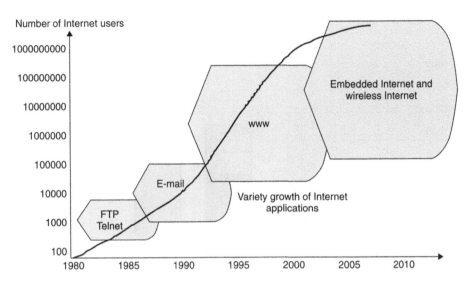

Figure 1.5 The exponential growth in the Internet usage

phone, refrigerator, air conditioning system, and other household appliances will have an Internet protocol (IP) address and will be connected to the Internet. The new usage of the Internet, called *embedded Internet*, will boost the usage of the Internet in fixed and mobile domains, generating billions of new virtual subscribers. Although the Internet started as a communication means for people, it will soon connect devices and connect people and devices. All these will require major enhancement in the Internet infrastructure and the new segments. Wireless Internet will play a major role in providing the access to these new users and devices.

1.2.3 Telecommunication services for everyone

Mobile cellular users are distributed very evenly in all parts of the world. Although this has happened for the voice communications, it would most probably be the case for mobile Internet and thus it shows that the scalability feature of the Internet will not be damaged when it becomes mobile. Figure 1.6 illustrates the worldwide mobile subscriber distribution since 1995 with an expectation for up to year 2010 [18]. The Asia Pacific region with China and other populated countries will have a major share in global mobile communications. The Internet usage is also considered to have similar distribution because of the number of people who live in this region, and thus many multinational companies consider China as the main market for future Internet. North American and European Union countries occupy the second major part of the mobile market, and other countries in Middle East and Africa show major growth for mobile usage. The figure shows a huge market in all parts of the world for the wireless Internet if a reliable and affordable network can be implemented.

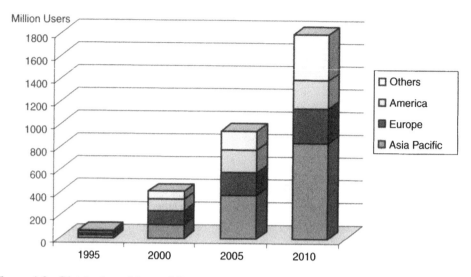

Figure 1.6   Distribution of the mobile communication subscribers around the world

1.2.4   Mobile cellular technologies coverage

Looking at the mobile cellular technology distribution worldwide, shown in Figure 1.7, we see a major part occupied by the GSM. (Cellular technologies will be explained in Chapters 3 and 4.) The advanced technologies used in the GSM network as well as the security and the portability provided by this system utilizing the subscriber identity module (SIM) made it one of the most successful mobile systems in the world compared to its counterparts in Japan and in the US. We will review these technologies later in the book, but here we want to emphasize the potential role of the GSM in future wireless mobile Internet. The successor of GSM, GPRS, has started some mobile Internet services, and 3G systems will use the GPRS as the core network. The future of mobile and wireless Internet thus will be very much related to the success of the GSM and its successor networks.

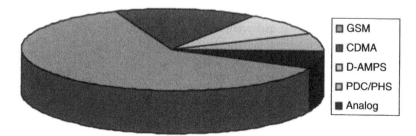

Figure 1.7   Worldwide distribution of mobile cellular technologies

1.2.5 Telecommunication traffic: voice, data, and multimedia

Figure 1.8 illustrates another trend in the telecommunications industry, that is, a service change from voice service to data service. The popularity of the Internet in recent years has been the main influence on this trend. On the one hand, the traffic load generated by the voice users had a very smooth and almost flat increase over the past few years. On the other hand, new multimedia and Internet applications, including email, web browsing, Internet telephony, and Internet videoconferencing, are pushing more data traffic into telecommunications networks in an exponential rate. In several developed countries in the world, the data traffic load has already taken over the voice traffic. In many situations, techniques such as voice over IP has made it possible to send voice information over the Internet, making the data and Internet traffic to increase even more rapidly. 500-million Internet subscribers are generating the major part of the traffic load of telecommunications networks. When the mobile Internet finds its role in the telecommunications network, this rate will increase even more rapidly. Current 2G systems such as GSM that provide short message service (SMS) have already shown huge data traffic generation from mobiles. It is expected that the 3-million mobile data users will increase to 77 million by the year 2005, that is, a 70% annual increase [21,22,27]. The traffic load on future communication networks will be composed of mainly data, and therefore new traffic management techniques are required to handle that traffic. We will discuss these important issues in realization of mobile and wireless Internet in the second part of this book.

1.2.6 Mobile internet traffic

The mobile Internet applications consist of not only those applications that have a mobile nature but also the traditional wired Internet applications. This makes another accelerative

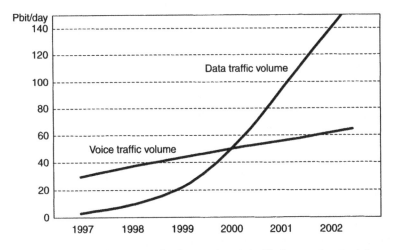

Figure 1.8 Changing the telecommunications network traffic from voice to data

factor in the wireless mobile Internet compared to its successor, the wired Internet. Mobile video and audio conferencing and navigation services are, for example, included in the wireless mobile Internet list of applications, which is already flooded with numerous applications that have migrated from the wired Internet network.

By the discussions and statistics provided previously in this section, it should be clear that the future of telecommunications networks will be very much dependent on the Internet, as the Internet will occupy the major capacity of the network. Data communications and, in particular, the Internet is the determining factor in future telecommunications networks, and the mobility provided by the wireless technology will be desired enormously. The mobile Internet will thus be the main topic before the researchers in the academia and the industry. Implementation of a mobile Internet network will not finalize these researches because the quality of service (QoS) for the telecommunications networks in general and for mobile Internet in particular need to be provided in future networks. We will discuss QoS and other important topics throughout this book.

1.3 WIRELESS INTERNET REQUIREMENTS

As we proceed through this book, each chapter discusses details of requirements and specifications of an efficient wireless mobile Internet network. In this section, we will go through a few general requirements of wireless Internet. Therefore, in this section we try to answer the question of 'what would be an ideal wireless Internet and what aspects should be included in such an architecture?'

1.3.1 Extension of Internet with mobility features

Mobile and wireless Internet, as its name specifies, should provide a seamless transition from a geographically fixed domain into a mobile environment. By seamless transition, we mean that there should be no sensible change for a user who is connected to the Internet while moving from a fixed domain into a mobile domain. In a broad sense, this could be the case even when a user moves from a wireless network domain to another one. In technical terms, the Internet access for the user should be independent of the access technology used for the Internet services.

Let us simplify this definition by an easy example. Although the current computer operating systems (OS) and the Ethernet do not support more than one Internet access at any instant, imagine that your computer is connected to an Internet service provider (ISP) through a 100-Mbps 100-Base-T Ethernet [1] card of a wired LAN and an 11-Mbps IEEE802.11b wireless LAN [28–30] card simultaneously. The backbone network of both is assumed to be the same, for example, a bus LAN. Your imaginary (or ideal) OS is assumed to be capable of choosing between the two connections in accordance to the connection speed, for example. So when you are sitting in front of your desk in your office, your computer OS chooses the 100-Mbps Ethernet and ignores the alternative wireless LAN connection. Now you are going to a meeting. You unplug the 100-Base-T cable from your computer and then your computer OS switches all your Internet connections to the wireless LAN. Assume that while this physical movement is happening, you are in the middle of downloading a large file from an FTP (file transfer protocol) server. If the process of downloading is continued without any interruption and you really have not felt the change of speed between the two connections, we can say that your connection has seamlessly transferred from one access network to another. The main point of being seamless here, of course, is the fact that the FTP session has not been interrupted while you moved from one (wired) domain into another (wireless) domain. But if the change in the downloading bit rate is not sensible for the Internet user as a human being, then the process is even more seamless.

The example above should clarify the difference between a seamless mobile Internet system (that this book is all about) and a nomadic Internet. A nomadic Internet user in the previous example has to unplug the 100-Base-T cable, insert a wireless Internet card and reconnect to the Internet. If there was an ongoing FTP connection, for example, it has to be interrupted and restarted after changing to the new network connection. All data transferred before the network access interruption will be lost. Therefore, there is a clear difference between the two cases. We will not discuss the nomadic Internet in this book. The above example could be extended to the case that the Internet access is provided partly through cellular mobile networks.

1.3.2   Internet connection specifications and QoS

The example given in the previous section of one computer and two Internet accesses should clarify some of the changes required in the realization of the mobile Internet. We mentioned connection speed as the determining factor in choosing between available connections by the OS. Indeed, this is the case in any seamless transition from one access network to another. In a mobile Internet system, the user should not feel a dramatic change in the QoS for the application currently being used. The most humanly sensible quality measure is the connection speed or data bit rate, which is logically, followed by the delay requirements. We will discuss QoS parameters comprehensively in Chapter 5.

1.3.3   Change in Internet protocols

The simple example given above shows a major change in requirements for the protocols that govern the Internet. Change in protocols goes into all layers of the network protocol stack. Link layer (Layer 2) has to be modified in order to concurrently establish two or more connections via different access networks supported by the physical layer (Layer 1). This change in the link layer protocol has to be incorporated with the computer OS so that, for example, two Internet connections can be set up and maintained at the same time.

At the physical layer, mobile devices have to be equipped with multiple interfaces to different access networks (wired such as Ethernet cable and dial-up modem as well as wireless such as wireless LAN, infrared, and cellular modems). The physical layer has to include several interfaces to Layer 2 in order to manage the best connection to higher layers, and if one connection cannot provide the required quality to the application, a combination of two access networks can be granted.

At the network layer (Layer 3), IP needs major changes so that it can handle the routing and other tasks of the network layer in wired and wireless environments. Mobility of the Internet IP address should be accommodated into the future mobile Internet. Signaling requirement of the IP layer protocol has to be simplified to provide more spectrum efficiency in future wireless access network. IP addressing and global address translation between heterogeneous networks must be performed in protocol change at Layer 3.

The transport layer on top of the IP layer may be considered as the main part of the modification for future mobile Internet networks. The legacy design of this layer for wired networks avoids efficient use of the radio channel capacity and thus major modification and extensions are required at the transport layer with dominant transmission control protocol (TCP) and user datagram protocol (UDP). Chapter 9 will discuss these changes for IP and TCP protocols.

1.3.4   Authentication, authorization, and accounting

In a mobile Internet, the mobile user does not see any difference between the currently available service providers at a given time and location, and it is assumed that a user may access the Internet regardless of his point of attachment to the network and the supporting access and core networks. Therefore, a system for the authentication and the authorization of users when moving across different networks must be established.

Authentication provides the proof of identity of a user to the network that the user is going to access. This process is usually performed through an authentication function procedure. Authorization certifies what type of services may be provided to an authenticated user. Therefore, it is not sufficient that a user is in a capacity to connect to a network but the user has to be subscribed for a list of services that he is going to receive from the connecting network. Accounting, as the third A in the network AAA (authentication, authorization, and accounting), provides a history of what and when a user used a particular service while connected to a network.

In the existing communication networks, every service provider keeps a database for its users and their profiles in order to perform the related AAA procedure. In some situations, two or more service providers might share a common database or have access to their partner providers' databases so that some type of portability of users among these networks is possible. In the future mobile Internet, however, this database is required to become more globally available so that users can easily switch their access networks and still can get appropriate services from the Internet and be charged accordingly. Maintaining the database in an efficient way and with minimum conflicts among different service providers will be important issues that are to be resolved before a mobile Internet can be realized. Billing and charging users for the services they have used by appropriate operators are among issues involved in this process. The system must be designed also to prevent the release of personal information to unauthorized entities and the misuse of the services by users who are not subscribed to receive those services.

1.3.5 Resource management

Mobile Internet is going to stay among different telecommunication technologies and hence need to share the limited available resources. A sophisticated resource management thus would be vitally necessary to share these resources among all coexisting technologies. Resource management schemes such as bandwidth managements, admission control, congestion control, and so on will guarantee reliable performance of the network as well as a fair allocation of resources to all eligible users. We will address this issue in several occasions within the chapters of this book.

1.3.6 Changing the network architecture

The current network architectures used in either the wired Internet or the cellular networks would not be appropriate and efficient for future wireless mobile Internet, even if we assume that the cellular networks will provide the major infrastructure of the mobile Internet. In recent years, many literatures have discussed this issue and how it is possible to change the network architecture to be utilized for the mobile Internet [31–37]. One major issue is making the core network independent of the underlying access technology. In Chapter 4, we will discuss this issue in detail and provide some solutions from the industry as well as other related research communities.

The exponential increase in both the Internet and the wireless cellular domains is expected to produce a huge market for the wireless Internet as a technology that covers existing and new subscribers of both the technologies. This expectation is shown in Figure 1.9. By that

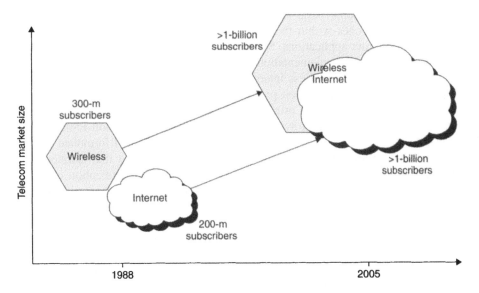

Figure 1.9 The wireless and Internet growths

time, the wireless should become an integrated part of the Internet and not just another access technology for it.

1.4   OUTLINE OF THE BOOK

This book is organized so that it could cover a broad range of audiences including senior-level undergraduate university students, postgraduate students, research engineers, system developers, and telecommunications managers. Different set of chapters of this book could be used as a text for different course levels, targeting the subject of wireless IPs. The first part, which includes Chapters 1 to 4 provides a comprehensive text to the definition of wireless Internet and its enabling access and core network technologies. The second part, consisting of six chapters, discusses basic requirements and issues toward the realization of wireless Internet. The last part, including three chapters, provides several advanced topics on wireless Internet and its generalization on a global basis. The book as a whole, therefore, can be used as a comprehensive text on the subject of wireless mobile Internet, its requirements and implementation, whereas its parts individually can be customized and used as the text for a more specialized course in the field.

Each chapter has a final section summarizing the main topics discussed in it followed by additional conclusions to those topics. A complete set of references cited within the text at the end of each chapter provides the reader access to the most relevant literature. A list of all abbreviations given throughout the book is provided at the end, which can help the reader in locating the meaning of numerous abbreviations used in related literature. To simplify customizing this book for different target audiences, a summary on each chapter is provided in this section.

In the first chapter some basic trends toward wireless Internet have been identified. These trends include ones within the telecommunications technology as principles and ones within the Internet applications. Several statistics have been provided to justify the need for wireless Internet implementation and related filed studies. A general understanding on the requirements of wireless Internet has also been included in this chapter.

Chapter 2 starts the discussion on practical wireless Internet architectures by reviewing the most promising solutions originally created over the second-generation wireless cellular systems and more recent systems such as Wireless Application Protocol (WAP) and Japan's i-mode. The discussions provided in this chapter could formulate the future wireless Internet architectures so as to avoid the drawbacks and the shortcomings of the predecessor systems. A summary of who is who in the standardization of telecommunications networks and the Internet has been included in the chapter to introduce appropriate locations that the reader needs to search for relevant information for wireless Internet.

In Chapter 3, a comprehensive review on the third-generation UMTS family has been provided after introducing its predecessor systems including GSM and GPRS. The UMTS will have a major role in the establishment of underlying technology for future wireless mobile Internet and hence such a review is considered as significant for the subject of this book.

Chapter 4 completes the discussion started in Chapter 3 on third-generation systems, by first looking at the cdma2000 system and giving a comparison of that system with the UMTS. A new trend toward harmonization of 3G systems has been followed and then the proposed functional layered network architecture for future wireless mobile Internet has been presented.

In Chapter 5, as the start of the second part of this book, the quality-of-service requirements and establishments in telecommunication systems and in particular for mobile networks has been presented. QoS progress in both Internet and cellular networks has been reviewed in this chapter. This chapter could be also considered as a self-complete literature on QoS for telecommunications networks.

Chapter 6 looks at the traffic nature in telecommunications data networks and future wireless Internet systems. Mathematical representations of several traffic models used in different telecommunications systems have been presented.

In Chapter 7, traffic management techniques have been discussed as a major contributor to the solution of the problem of limited telecommunication resources. In particular, admission control techniques have been described with numerous numerical result presentations.

Chapter 8 outlines the mobility characteristics in wireless networks. User mobility patterns and models have been discussed in detail. The problem of finding a user within a network in order to achieve an efficient network management, usually referred to as location management, has been detailed in this chapter together with a comprehensive discussion on paging schemes in mobile networks.

In Chapter 9, the selection of an appropriate transport protocol for future wireless Internet has been addressed. The traditional TCP has been reviewed first to give the reader some fundamental aspects in performance evaluation of the transport layer protocol. This discussion has been followed by up-to-date activities toward implementation of transport protocol over the error-prone wireless channel, detailed discussions on one of the modification techniques for transport protocol, and several numerical results and discussions.

Chapter 10 looks at the IP as the enabling function of the future wireless Internet systems. After describing the existing IP and its next-generation model, the issue on how the fixed-IP address allocation of the Internet needs to be modified to migrate into the wireless Internet has been discussed.

The third part of this book begins with Chapter 11, in which some Internet perspectives for the future wireless Internet have been outlined. The chapter discusses the initiatives from the cdma2000 core network for such wireless Internet realization.

Chapter 12 provides a concise but comprehensive discussion on wireless LANs, the mobile ad hoc networking using the wireless LAN, and future challenges within the mobile ad hoc networking, as partial implementation of the wireless Internet.

Discussions on advanced topics for wireless Internet have been finalized in Chapter 13, in which the globalization of mobile Internet has been addressed through the usage of satellites. The chapter starts with a comprehensive discussion on narrowband and broadband satellite systems, followed by the issues on the inclusion of the satellites as an important element in future wireless mobile Internet on a global basis for home and business users.

REFERENCES

1. Stallings W, *Data and Computer Communications*, sixth edition, Prentice Hall, Upper Saddle River, N.J., 2000.
2. Comer DE, *Computer Networks and Internets*, second edition, Prentice Hall, Upper Saddle River, N.J., 1999.
3. Halsall F, *Data Communications, Computer Networks and Open Systems*, fourth edition, Addison-Wesley, Reading, Mass., 1996.
4. Leon-Garcia A & Widjaja I, *Communication Networks: Fundamental Concepts & Key Architectures*, McGraw-Hill Higher Education, New York, 2000.
5. Garg VK & Wilkes JE, *Wireless and Personal Communications Systems*, Prentice Hall, Upper Saddle River, N.J., 1996.
6. Jamalipour A, *Low Earth Orbital Satellites for Personal Communication Networks*, Artech House Publishers, Norwood, Mass., 1998.
7. Digital cellular technologies, Special Issue of *IEEE Transactions on Vehicular Technologies*, **40**(2), 1991.
8. Abramson N, The ALOHA system—another alternative for computer communications, *Proceedings 1970 Fall Joint Computer Conference*, 1970, pp. 281–285.
9. Viterbi AJ, *CDMA—Principles of Spread Spectrum Communications*, Addison-Wesley, Reading, Mass., 1995.
10. Gilhousen KS, Jacobs IM, Padovani R, Viterbi AJ, Weaver LA & Wheathley III CE, On the capacity of a cellular CDMA system, *IEEE Transactions on Vehicular Technologies*, **40**(2), 303–312, 1991.
11. Prasad R, *CDMA for Wireless Personal Communications*, Artech House Publishers, Norwood, Mass., 1996.
12. Prasad R & Ojanpera T, An overview of CDMA evolution toward wideband CDMA, *IEEE Communications Surveys*, **1**(1), Fourth Quarter, 1998, http://www.comsoc.org/pubs/surveys.
13. Wilson ND, Ganesh R, Joseph K & Raychaudhuri D, Packet CDMA versus dynamic TDMA for multiple access in an integrated voice/data PCN, *IEEE Journal on Selected Areas in Communications*, **11**(6), 870–884, 1993.
14. Universal Mobile Telecommunications System (UMTS), Forum Web site: http://www.umts-forum.org.
15. The European Telecommunications Standards Institute (ETSI), Web site: http://www.etsi.org.
16. The Third Generation Partnership Project (3GPP), Web site: http://www.3gpp.org.
17. Huber JF, Weiler D & Brand H, UMTS—The mobile multimedia vision for IMT-2000: a focus on standardization, *IEEE Communications Magazine*, **38**(9), 129–136, 2000.
18. Chudhury P, Moher W & Onoe S, The 3GPP proposal for IMT-2000, *IEEE Communications Magazine*, **37**(12), 72–81, 1999.
19. The Third Generation Partnership Project 2 (3GPP2), Web site: http://www.3gpp2.org.
20. Larsson G, Evolving from cdmaOne to third generation systems, *Ericsson Review*, **2**, 58–67, 2000.

21. Mohr W & Konhauser W, Access network evolution beyond third generation mobile communications, *IEEE Communications Magazine*, **38**(12), 122–1133, 2000.

22. Ohmori S, Yamao Y & Nakajima N, The future generations of mobile communications based on broadband access technologies, *IEEE Communications Magazine*, **38**(12), 134–142, 2000.

23. Cai J & Goodman DJ, General packet radio service in GSM, *IEEE Communications Magazine*, **35**(10), 122–131, 1997.

24. Brasche G & Walke B, Concepts, services, and protocols of the new GSM phase 2+ general packet radio service, *IEEE Communications Magazine*, **35**(10), 94–104, 1997.

25. Bettstetter C, Vogel H-J & Eberspacher J, GSM phase 2+ general packet radio service GPRS: architecture, protocols, and air interface, *IEEE Communications Surveys*, Third Quarter, **2**(3) 1999, http://www.comsoc.org/pubs/surveys.

26. Rahnema M, Overview of the GSM system and protocol architecture, *IEEE Communications Magazine*, **31** (4), 92–100, 1993.

27. Haardt M & Mohr W, The complete solution for third-generation wireless communications: two modes on air, one winning strategy, *IEEE Communications Magazine*, **38**(12), 18–24, 2000.

28. Crow BP, Widjaja I, Kim JG & Sakai PT, IEEE 802.11 wireless local area networks, *IEEE Communications Magazine*, **35**(9), 116–126, 1997.

29. IEEE 802.11, Web site: http://www.ieee802.org/11.

30. O'Hara & Petrick, *802.11 Handbook, A Designer's Companion*, IEEE Press, Piscattaway, N.J., 1999.

31. Mobile Wireless Internet Forum (MWIF), Web site: http://www.mwif.org.

32. Umehira M, Nakura M, Umeuchi M, Murayama J, Murai T & Hara H, Wireless and IP integrated system architectures for broadband mobile multimedia services, *Proceedings of IEEE Wireless Communications and Networking Conference (WCNC '99)*, New Orleans, 1999.

33. Macker JP, Park VD & Corson MS, Mobile and wireless Internet services: putting the pieces together, *IEEE Communications Magazine*, June, 148–155, 2001.

34. Oliphant MW, The mobile phone meets the Internet, *IEEE Spectrum*, August, 20–28, 1998.

35. Noerenberg II JW, Bridging wireless protocols, *IEEE Communications Magazine*, November, 90–97, 2001.

36. McCann PJ, Hiller T, An Internet infrastructure for cellular CDMA networks using mobile IP, *IEEE Personal Communications Magazine*, August, 6–12, 2000.

37. Ramjee R, La Porta TF, Thuel S & Varadhan K, IP-based access network architecture for next-generation wireless data networks, *IEEE Personal Communications Magazine*, August, 34–41, 2000.

2

Wireless Cellular Data Networks

In this chapter, we introduce major initiatives to the wireless Internet by summarizing the research and development activities mainly within the framework of the second-generation wireless cellular networks. After a general understanding of the wireless Internet, its characteristics, and requirements provided in the first chapter, this chapter will prepare the reader to start the main issues in wireless Internet, which will be discussed in the following chapters. Network architecture and access technologies of the most popular cellular systems will be introduced in the next two chapters, and therefore in the current chapter the topics have been discussed in a more general format. Since the second-generation cellular initiatives are still far from the ideal structure of wireless Internet protocol (IP) networks, we gave the title *Wireless Cellular Data Networks* to this chapter. By this title we mean that although these systems have provided some sort of data services and Internet capabilities to their mobile users, they cannot be a substitute for a system that offers full Internet service to mobile users. Such an ideal wireless mobile Internet architecture still needs several years for development and in this book we try to illustrate bits and pieces of such an intelligent network.

2.1 INTRODUCTION

In the context of telecommunication technology, one of the most fundamental issues is on how much of the communications channel capacity is given to a single communication session, regardless of whether it is a point-to-point or multipoint communication, in a given communication system and for how long. Sharing the limited capacity in a communication system is a task performed by multiple access schemes, such as time division multiple

The Wireless Mobile Internet: Architectures, Protocols, and Services.   Abbas Jamalipour
© 2003 John Wiley & Sons, Ltd   ISBN: 0-470-84468-X

access (TDMA), frequency division multiple access (FDMA), code division multiple access (CDMA), and so on and is discussed briefly in Chapter 1. Multiple access schemes thus answer the first question. The second question on 'for how long' will be answered by considering whether the allocated channel is dedicated to a communication session for the whole period of that particular session or just when the parties involved in the session are actively using the allocated capacity. This second consideration results in defining different switching techniques in a communication system, traditionally categorized as circuit and packet switching. Whilst this issue has been researched in wired telecommunications networks for many years, a revisit on that will be most beneficial for the wireless networks and especially the wireless Internet. Internet is a packet-switched network and thus delivering its contents would be most efficient if a packet-switched network is in place.

In this section, we will outline some fundamental topics for the wireless data networks, so that the reader attains the basic idea of terminologies used throughout this book. We start this discussion with circuit- and packet-switching techniques, and then define the access and core network concepts in wireless communication systems. Discussions will be kept as abstract as possible to a basic level required for following the topics in this book, and it is suggested that the interested reader consults classic texts in data communications for more details (see References [1–3]).

2.1.1   Circuit switching

Because of restrict delay and delay variation requirements of voice communications, the telephony network has adopted circuit-switched technology right from the beginning. In a circuit-switched system, first a circuit, that is, a dedicated channel in the form of either a time slot or a frequency band is set up between the two ends of the communication link before any information exchange could be performed [1–3]. After the setting-up phase, the allocated channel for this end-to-end communication will be used entirely for that particular communication until either of the end users initiates a circuit termination phase. After completion of this termination phase, the channel may be used for other end-to-end communications. Channel allocations in a circuit-switched network can be managed by a multiplexing scheme such as time division multiplex (TDM) or frequency division multiplex (FDM), respectively, to share the total system capacity in either time or frequency.

Since during the period of communication the circuit or channel is dedicated to the pair of users involved in the communication, delay and delay-variation controls after the setup phase remain minimal on the propagation and transmission time constraints, and thus the circuit-switched system is ideal for real-time applications such as voice conversation. However, even in the case in which no information is exchanged between the two end users, the system capacity allocated to the circuit cannot be given to other users, and thus the capacity would be wasted at those periods.

2.1.2   Packet switching

Packet-switched systems were invented in the early 1970s to remedy the inefficiency in capacity utilization of circuit-switched systems. This was in response to emerging burst data traffic starting to join the traditional voice traffic. Two types of packet-switched systems were initiated: the virtual circuit (VC) and the datagram. In the VC after an initial setup phase, similar to the one used in a circuit-switched system, a path between the source and destination of the communication is found among possible routes (i.e. a combination of network links and nodes). After completion of choosing such a path, which might be selected in accordance to some policy such as minimum link load or cost, all data between the source and the destination will be transported using the selected path, packed in a package called a packet. When the exchange of information has been completed, either of the communications end parties will initiate a termination phase, as in circuit-switched systems. Since in this type of packet switching the route between a source and a destination is selected before any information can be exchanged, the scheme is called a *virtual circuit*. It is virtual because there is no dedicated circuit as in the case of circuit-switched systems between the source and destination, and the packets still need to negotiate with the intermediate nodes each time using the planned route. The delay for transmission of information has thus been increased compared to the circuit-switched systems, but as a reward more users could use the limited channel capacity as they avail of the channel only when they use it and not for the entire period of communications.

Datagram packet-switched systems have come to reduce the total delay by deleting the setup and termination phase of the VC packet-switched systems. Every packet sent from a source node has to find its own path after negotiation with intermediate nodes and routers until it reaches a particular destination. Packets of a same message in a datagram system also could use different routes and thus could reach the destination in a different order than what they have been transmitted. This is another difference between a datagram packet-switched system and the VC packet-switched system, as in the latter all packets of the same message use the same path and reach the destination in the same order as they had at the source. Datagram packet-switched technology is widely used in the Internet.

As a tradition, telephony systems would prefer the circuit-switching system because of its superior performance for delivering real-time traffic such as voice, a system quality that still has no replacement. Packet switching on the other hand was the answer to high-speed data transmission, not taking much care of voice communications. The original packet switching finds even more applications in advanced technologies such as frame relay and asynchronous transfer mode (ATM) for high-speed data transmissions. While typical packet-switched networks provide up to 64-Kbps data rate, frame relay has increased it to a few Mbps and ATM has increased it to a few hundred Mbps. ATM, for example, is a technology that utilizes VC switching. Discussions on frame relay and ATM are outside the scope of this book and readers are suggested to look at these techniques in some classical texts such as References [1–3].

2.1.3 Access network

In a wireless communication system, for example, a cellular wireless network, the network can be divided into two major parts: access network and core network. Access network, or in the context of wireless systems, radio access network defines communications of an end user, named differently in wireless systems as mobile station (MS), mobile terminal (MT), or user equipment (UE), to the first serving entity in the network through radio frequency (RF) channels. The first serving entity is also named differently in wireless systems (as we will see in the following chapters) as base station, access point, Node B, and so on. Radio protocols and radio interfaces are implemented in the access network and usually differentiate the wireless systems one from another.

In older wireless networks, there was an attempt to develop the access network in conjunction with the core network as the system was designed as a whole infrastructure, but in modern technologies and standards, an attempt is being made to keep the core network functions independent from the access network and the technologies utilized at access network. One such example is the Universal Mobile Telecommunications System (UMTS) (to be discussed in Chapter 3) in which access stratum and nonaccess stratum definitions logically separate the two types. The access stratum is the set of protocols and capabilities at core network that are most closely linked to the radio access technology. The nonaccess stratum on the other hand denotes those protocols that are independent of the radio access network.

Multiple access schemes, modulation techniques, source and channel encoding algorithms, wireless channel error detection and correction scheme, and similar issues are considered at the access network. The access network thus has an important role in the end-to-end performance of wireless systems. An appropriate selection of modulation schemes for the considered wireless network, for example, can determine the maximum bit data rate allowable in the wireless system.

2.1.4 Core network

Core network is another component of a wireless system that establishes communications among various sections of the access network. For example, in cellular systems where MSs are communicating with their closest base stations, those base stations communicate with each other and with other network elements such as mobile switching centers (MSC) and database servers through signaling and routing techniques provided by the core network. Packet switching versus circuit switching is an issue that will be discussed in the core network part.

Access network and core network in modern wireless systems communicate with each other through a set of standard interfaces. It is also possible for a given wireless system to modernize the access network entirely and modify the core network slightly, and then to declare it as a new system. As an example, the third-generation wireless system UMTS, as the successor of Global System for Mobile communications (GSM), utilizes a completely new access technology in its access network while using a modified version of an evolved GSM core network.

While radio link control protocols and radio resource managements are handled within the access network, signaling and control, routing, traffic and mobility management, MS database storage, and exchange of user information during handoff from one cell to another are needed to be supported in the core network. Some tasks are handled at

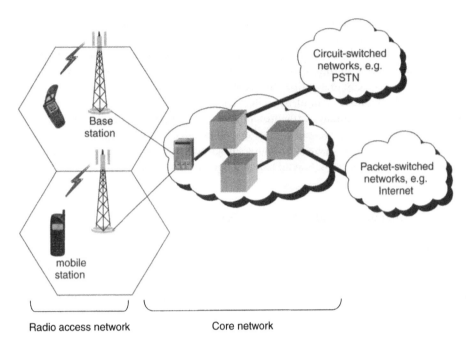

Figure 2.1 Radio access and core network in the context of wireless systems

both networks; for example, when a user moves from one cell to another, link layer protocols should handle the user mobility within the access network while base station-to-base station signaling required in such a handoff needs to be performed within the core network. Authorization of a MS for admission to the wireless system and use of the prescribed services and access to particular information is another example where the task is performed at both radio access network and core network of the considered wireless system.

Throughout this book, whilst we place more emphasis on core network protocols, on many occasions we also look at access technologies, radio access networks and their respective standards. This should not cause any confusion in understanding the main subject of the book on requirements and technologies of the wireless mobile Internet as long as we address the location within the network at which a particular task is being performed. Figure 2.1 tries to illustrate the boundaries of access and core networks in a generic form, although a definite separation is different on a system-by-system basis.

2.2 SECOND-GENERATION CELLULAR DATA SERVICES

Not only was it the public switching telephony networks (PSTN) that preferred circuit switching as their core network technology but also the second-generation cellular systems, designed mainly for voice communication, that preferred to use the same core technology. Therefore, in order to transmit data packets over the mobile network, as a start for the mobile Internet service, other techniques had to be implemented. One simple technique is to encapsulate the data or IP packets and send them over the circuit used for voice communications. In this section, we will look at two of the most successful systems for mobile data services that utilize the cellular networks, Cellular Digital Packet Data (CDPD) and High Speed Circuit-Switched Data (HSCSD). These two systems can be considered as the first initiatives for providing wireless mobile Internet services over cellular networks. They have been developed as value-added services over second-generation systems and still provide services to many subscribers around the world despite the new technologies that utilize packet-switched concepts in their core networks.

2.2.1   Cellular digital packet data

Despite being a relatively old technology, CDPD still has some popularity in providing data services over cellular networks. CDPD network is a peer multiprotocol, connection-less network proposed by the CDPD Forum, a trade association of carriers, equipment suppliers, and application developers [4–8]. CDPD was designed to extend the existing wired data communication networks at the time.

The idea behind CDPD originally was that it is possible to share unused channels in the existing American cellular system called the *Advanced Mobile Phone Systems* (AMPS) [6] to provide a 19.2-Kbps data channel. Specifically, it allows data transmission between mobile and mobile, mobile and fixed, fixed and mobile packet exchange, and fixed and fixed users. Later this concept was utilized in the Personal Communication Services (PCS) cellular systems.

Figure 2.2 gives a general architecture of the CDPD network. CDPD follows the open system interconnection (OSI) model terminology. The mobile node is called a mobile end system (M-ES); the home and foreign agents are called mobile home function (MHF) and mobile serving function (MSF), respectively, and reside in a mobile data intermediate system (MD-IS). A mobile data base station (MDBS) is also defined in the CDPD, which deals with the air link interface and acts as a data link layer relay between the M-ES and the serving MD-IS. Two protocols, the mobile node registration protocol (MNRP) and the mobile node location protocol (MNLP) are responsible for registration of the M-ES with its home MD-IS and the proper routing of packets destined for the M-ES.

Having a similar system structure as that of the Mobile IP in its first versions [9,10] (see Chapter 10 for details on Mobile IP), the mobility functions of CDPD are performed largely in the MD-ISs. Each M-ES is assigned to a fixed home area. Basically, while the home area MD-IS uses the MHF to maintain a database of current serving area for each of its subscribing M-ES, the MSFs, used in all other networks, route packets for all M-ES currently connected to its corresponding serving area. The home area MD-IS encapsulates any M-ES addressed packets and forwards them to MD-IS that the mobile user is currently visiting. The mobility tunnel is based on the connectionless network protocol (CLNP).

The CDPD network communicates with other networks through three interfaces: air link interface, external interface, and interservice-provider interface. The air link interface

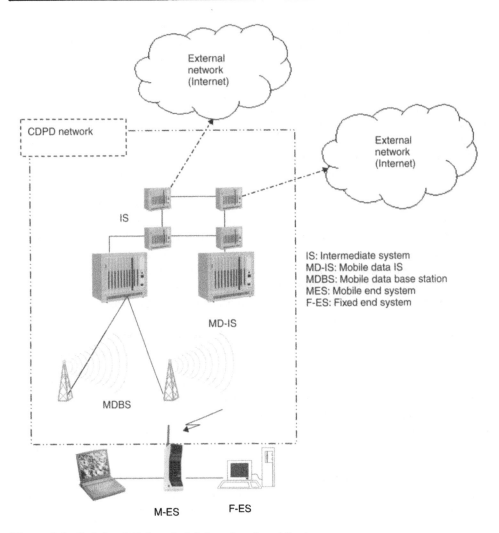

Figure 2.2 Cellular digital packet data network architecture

connects the M-ESs to the network to support mobile data services; therefore, it is the interface between a M-ES and a MDBS. The external interface connects the CDPD service provider to the external networks so that external application service providers can communicate with CDPD subscribers. This interface is between an intermediate system and a fixed-end system. The interservice-provider interface is a CDPD service-provider's interface to cooperating CDPD service-provider networks, so it is the interface between two intermediate systems.

Both CDPD and Mobile IP require mobile hosts to be able to communicate with other systems that do not implement mobility functions. No changes or enhancements are required for systems that do not support mobility to be able to communicate with mobile hosts. In the case of CDPD, there were no external requirements for support of data links other than the CDPD air link. From the beginning, the CDPD architects recognized that mobility for CDPD could be independent of CDPD's air link. To this end, CDPD was designed under a self-imposed requirement for CDPD mobility to be independent of the air link.

CDPD treats the air link as a precious resource and minimizes the number of bytes transferred over the air. Trade-offs made between layering integrity and air-link efficiency in CDPD favor air link efficiency. While Mobile IP was a pure IP solution, CDPD was designed to not only support IP but also to be a multiprotocol mobility solution. Both CDPD and Mobile IP require that mobility be supported without the mobile system needing to change its IP address. This is a departure from traditional wired IP networks.

CDPD assumes that the network is centrally administered, managed, and operated by cooperating cellular service providers. It also assumes a clearly defined network with well-defined boundaries of authority and responsibility. CDPD internetworking is a collection of CDPD service provider networks. On the basis of bilateral agreements, each home MD-IS interoperates with various serving MD-ISs, which may be administered by various CDPD service providers. The infrastructure of the CDPD network is a closed network. This implies that some level of trust, order, and accountability can be expected.

These operational assumptions had a direct impact on many of CDPD's protocol design decisions, particularly in the areas of security, manageability, and scalability. Because the mobility tunnel begins and ends within the CDPD networks, to some extent it does not require the level of security that is necessary between the home agent and the foreign agent in Mobile IP.

Even though securing the network layer of the CDPD network is not required in the CDPD specifications, the CDPD specification team recognized that providing data confidentiality and authentication for the mobility tunnel was important. Network layer security protocol (NLSP), which can be considered to be an adjunct to CLNP, provides comprehensive security services. A complete discussion on the different protocols used in the CDPD network can be found in Reference [6].

One distinct feature that makes CDPD less applicable compared to other protocols is the fact that connectivity can only be maintained if the mobile users remain within the CDPD service providers' networks. Furthermore, in situations in which the mobile subscribers roam in a geographical area that is serviced by a different CDPD provider, internetworking procedures must be available in order to continue the data connectivity.

CDPD with its concept of being on top of a given cellular network infrastructure and using the leftover capacity of that system was considered as a good, short-term solution for data and IP mobility. However, with extensive enhancements in telecommunications and wireless technology as well as exponential increase in wireless data traffic load and mobility requirements this infrastructure-less network was far from a complete and long-term solution to the wireless Internet problem.

2.2.2 High-speed circuit-switched data

HSCSD was an answer in providing data services using the circuit-switched cellular network GSM in its Phase 2+. HSCSD allowed a GSM mobile user to transmit at higher data rates than the usual 9.6 Kbps of GSM (up to eight times) by accessing more than one timeslot per TDMA frame. Later the 2.5G successor of GSM [11], the General Packet Radio Service (GPRS) [12–14] system (to be discussed in Chapter 3), used a different method, that is, using packet-oriented connections on the radio interface and within the core network, to provide high data rates to MSs but using only one channel.

HSCSD utilizes multiple GSM full-rate traffic channels (TCH/F) at the same time for a single connection so that different air-interface data rates could be supported by a common physical link [15–17]. Multiplexing and demultiplexing of user data onto multiple TCHs are handled in the HSCSD at higher layers of the MS and the network. A schematic diagram for the HSCSD architecture is shown in Figure 2.3. As shown in this figure, multiple circuits, for example, TDMA time slots, are allocated at interfaces between the MS and between base transceiver station (BTS) and base station controller (BSC), while a single circuit is utilized between the BSC and the MSC. The architecture of GSM network used in this figure will be discussed in Chapter 3.

A call setup by the MS starts the process of allocation of an HSCSD connection. This connection may support either symmetric transmissions or asymmetric transmissions. In a symmetric transmission, the same number of uplink and downlink transmissions are used, whereas in an asymmetric transmission more timeslots (i.e. TCHs) could be allocated in one direction than in the other. In HSCSD, however, only downlink-biased asymmetry is allowed and uplink timeslots must be a subset of those of the downlink. This means that in the case that the requested data rate by a MS cannot be met by using a symmetric transmission, the air interface should provide asymmetric transmission by giving priority to fulfilling the user's downlink data rate requirements.

The HSCSD user connection can be renegotiated after the setup phase in order to increase or decrease the data rates as well as to change the symmetry or asymmetry configuration of data transmission. Multiple slot allocations to a single HSCSD connection can be either consecutive TDMA time slots or nonconsecutive time slots.

The interesting technological feature used in the HSCSD is that there is no need to touch the configuration of the air interface or access network. The available GSM air interface, for example, could be used to support higher data rates for transmission of burst data

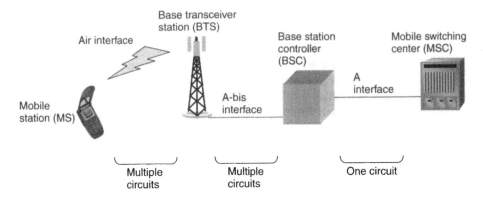

Figure 2.3 High-speed circuit-switched data transmission over GSM network

traffic (such as an Internet session traffic) by allocating more than one TDMA time slot to a single user. In later versions of HSCSD, when the air interface is enhanced by better modulation techniques such as 8-PSK (eight-level phase shift keying) in addition to the GMSK (Gaussian minimum shift keying) modulation of GSM, each single channel could provide higher data rates than 9.6 Kbps, thus allowing smaller number of multislot for an HSCSD connection. This new system is called *Enhanced Circuit-Switched Data* (ECSD). The combination of using two modulation schemes GMSK in poor quality channels and 8-PSK in good-quality channels has resulted in an advanced air interface technique for cellular systems known as EDGE (enhanced data rates for GSM evolution) [18–21].

HSCSD will remain as part of the standards of data communications over circuit-switched cellular network for some time, as is seen by the fact that related technical specifications (TSs) of HSCSD are in place within the third-generation standard bodies. The question, however, remains as to whether transmitting packet-oriented traffic over a circuit-switched network designed for real-time and constant rate traffic is a reasonable way, no matter how the data bit rate is increased in those networks.

2.3 RECENT ADVANCED CELLULAR DATA SERVICES

In the previous section, we introduced two wireless data networks that originated from the second-generation cellular networks. Their original concept was not to touch the physical layer structure of the cellular network while trying to add data and Internet services to mobile users. In this section, we will introduce three more advanced systems that could be considered as the indicators of a real mobile Internet architecture of the future, with quite a good rate of success. Other than the importance of the technological improvement achieved in these systems, their success is also considered as an important factor for future wireless mobile Internet realization.

2.3.1 Wireless application protocol

Though the two wireless data technologies discussed in Section 2.2 were a good start for the inclusion of Internet services in cellular networks, they suffered from a fundamental drawback, that is, being applicable to a single localized second-generation standard. CDPD was implemented over AMPS by utilizing the leftover capacity not used by voice users. HSCSD also was implemented over the GSM-type systems by allowing a single HSCSD connection that uses more than one TDMA channel, resulting in a higher data rate than when only one channel is used. This system dependency that was a common trend among second-generation network architects is no longer acceptable because of the increasing trend in internetworking roaming requests from mobile users. Thus, these creations are going to become obsolete in future generations of wireless networks.

In response to a new trend in having a wireless Internet service network that could work independent of the underlying access technology, a group of wireless industries, including Ericsson, Motorola, Nokia, and Phone.com established a consortium in 1997, named *Wireless Application Protocol (WAP) Forum* [22]. The goal of this forum was to find a universal and open standard to provide wireless users access to the Internet. The protocol first had to be universal so that it would not be limited to a single air interface technology such as GSM or CDMA. It also needed to be open so that third-party application service providers could have access to the WAP network architecture details and could develop their own WAP-compatible services.

WAP technology is basically designed to work with all wireless network technologies, starting with second-generation systems such as GSM, CDMA IS-95 [23–25], and D-AMPS (Digital APMS); short-range connectivity technologies such as Bluetooth [26]; to third-generation systems such as UMTS [27–31] and cdma2000 [32–34]. WAP architecture also claims to be based on existing Internet standards and protocols such as IP and hypertext transfer protocol (HTTP) as well as programming languages such as hypertext markup language (HTML) and XML. Therefore, in summary, WAP should be a protocol that could provide the wireless Internet that is friendly to both the Internet and to cellular networks, resulting in an efficient wireless Internet performance.

One of the distinguishing issues considered in WAP is that the WAP architects understood the limitations of both wireless technologies and mobile devices. Therefore, WAP has been designed to deal with not only the wireless limitations and shortcomings but also the boundaries of mobile device capabilities. Some limitations of a mobile device are limited processing power of microprocessors inside mobile handsets, memory size and battery life of mobile devices, and small and limited display resolution of mobile handset devices. On the other hand, wireless channels suffer from low bandwidth, high latency, low signal-to-noise ratio (SNR) at poor channel conditions, and thus high bit-error rate (BER). Blind spots, where the RF signal is too weak, are unavoidable in wireless networks, and thus higher-layer protocols in the network protocol stack have to compensate their impact by utilizing error recovery and retransmission mechanisms. WAP also has to be designed in such a way that information can be viewed easily when compared to a desktop computer viewer. These days there are many tiny computing devices and cellular phones in the market and despite enormous progress in putting more memory and more powerful and faster microprocessors inside these devices as compared to the previous large-size models, the battery life is still too short. Higher speeds of a microprocessor mean more power consumption and heat generation, and this even more rapidly shortens the mobile device's battery life. A wireless IP has to be designed to reduce the computing processing, thus making the life of mobile devices longer.

The WAP stack is shown in Figure 2.4. The protocol stack is similar to what you can see in a TCP/IP (transmission control protocol/Internet protocol) reference model discussed in all classic texts on data communication networks (e.g. see References [1–3]). At the physical and link layers, standard protocols related to any of the wireless access technologies such as GSM, D-AMPS, CDMA IS-95, third generation (3G), Bluetooth, and DECT (Digital Enhanced Cordless Telecommunication system) can be implemented. The link layer is followed by a wireless datagram protocol, similar to the traditional Internet's IP datagram protocol, with more wireless functions. WAP, as its name suggests, is mostly implemented at high-network layers, and particularly at the application layer on top of the transport layer protocols. The WAP functionality is therefore divided into several

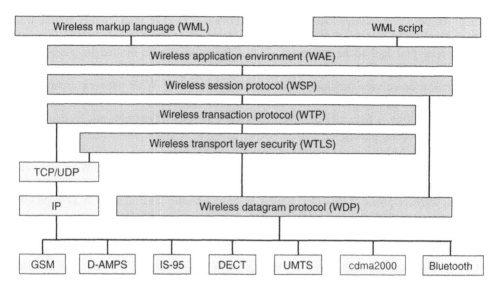

Figure 2.4 Wireless application protocol stack

layers including the wireless transport layer security (WTLS), wireless transaction protocol (WTP), wireless session protocol (WSP), wireless application environment (WAE), wireless markup language (WML), and WML script. Breaking the network stack layers into smaller sublayers makes the WAP protocol stack more similar to the OSI (open systems interconnection), the network reference model of ISO (International Organization for Standardization), than the one usually seen in a TCP/IP network reference model.

Having such a network protocol stack (two-dimensional), WAP assumes that the mobile users may have access to two types of IPs, one designed for a desktop platform (e.g. HTML) and one for a mobile device, such as a cellular phone with WAP capabilities or a palm pilot terminal with a cellular modem for a small-size mobile display (e.g. WML). The Internet contents could also be stored in either an ordinary HTML web server or a WML-capable web server. The WAP-compatible mobile device then needs to have a way to extract the web contents from an HTML server by using appropriate translation protocols provided by WAP.

According to the above requirements for WAP services, a WAP infrastructure can be imagined as shown in Figure 2.5. A WAP-compatible mobile device using any of the prescribed access technologies connects to the wireless cellular network after initiating a WAP session. A WAP proxy server is in the middle of the path between the cellular system backbone network and the Internet. Two cases would be possible: direct access and indirect (translated) access. The first one is the case when the mobile device is looking for Internet content located in a WAP-compatible server, for example, a WML-capable web server. The WAP proxy server connects the mobile user WAP session directly to that WML-capable server. In this case, no translation (between HTML and WML) is necessary as the Internet contents are already in a form that can be viewed by the WAP-compatible mobile device. The second case is when the mobile user is looking for Internet

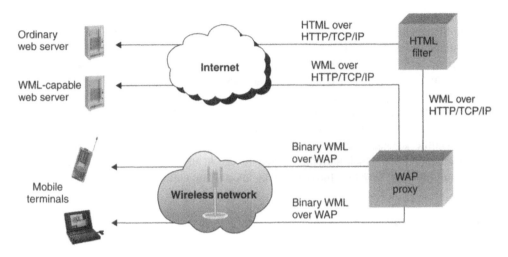

Figure 2.5 WAP infrastructure

content residing in an ordinary server, for example, an HTML web server. In this case, a translation process is required and thus an HTML filter (i.e. another network server) will be required in the path between the WAP proxy and the Internet ordinary HTML server. In the latter case, HTML is running over the HTTP/TCP/IP protocols between the HTML filter and the Internet, whereas in the path between the HTML filter and the WAP proxy server binary, WML is running over HTTP/TCP/IP. In the former case, it was the WML running over HTTP/TCP/IP all the way between the WAP proxy server and the final WML-capable web server. WML-capable servers are increasing in the Internet nowadays.

WAP architecture can be simplified in its programming model, shown in Figure 2.6. The programming model consists of a client, a gateway, and a server. Therefore, it is very similar to the usually used client–server model in computer networks. Assume that a WAP client is looking for content residing in a server named the original server. The WAE user

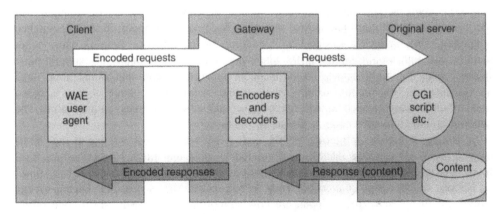

Figure 2.6 WAP programming model

agent, an entity within the client (mobile user) device sends an encoded request via a gateway that includes encoding and decoding algorithms. Whilst WML is used between the client and the gateway, HTML is running between the gateway and the original server. The gateway server forwards the client request to the original server, and if the requested content is available at the original server, a response that piggybacks the contents will be sent back to the gateway server. The gateway server after encoding the contents onto WML sends the contents to the client who had requested that particular content.

WAP is increasingly becoming popular for cellular network users who want to have access to online services such as e-mail, web browsing, mobile banking, Internet shopping, sport event and movie ticket booking, restaurant search, and similar services. It can be considered an important wireless Internet service on existing cellular network infrastructures.

2.3.2 i-mode

i-mode is another important service initiated in recent years by the Japanese cellular network provider, NTT DoCoMo company [35] and introduced in Feb 1999. The service has revolutionized the mobile services and thanks to the great system, features, and business model used in i-mode, the service could get more than 34 million subscribers by July 2002. This figure had begun to increase in 2000 when no third-generation wireless system had been functionally implemented in any part of the world, and therefore, it could exhibit the advanced technologies included in second-generation cellular systems for providing such upgraded mobile Internet service. Most of the features of i-mode can be found in the company's web site, but in this section we briefly highlight the i-mode system architecture in order to help the readers follow our discussions on wireless Internet architectures in this book. The descriptions provided in this section completely reflect the author's understanding of the i-mode service based on publicly available information provided by the respected company on its web site and at international forums.

Similar to WAP, i-mode provides mobile cellular users access to Internet contents such as e-mail, web browsing, mobile banking, Internet shopping, sport event and movie ticket booking, restaurant search, and similar services. The billing scheme used in i-mode is based on payment per volume of data and not the call duration, as for example was the case in other cellular data service providers such as GSM based on circuit-switched telephony. This made the service very attractive for the majority of users who do not want to pay high mobile phone tariffs when they are just occasionally exchanging burst Internet data. For high security requirement in sensitive mobile data applications, such as m-commerce (the mobile version of electronic commerce), i-mode utilizes a leased line circuit between its specialized i-mode server and servers of financial institutions. The network architecture of i-mode is shown in Figure 2.7 [35].

In i-mode, a subset of Internet HTML called iHTML is used. Similar to the WML created for WAP services, iHTML was created to view the Internet contents in a form more appropriate for limited-size and resolution mobile handsets but since it is a subset of HTML, much easier conversion from HTML-to-iHTML is possible. Owing to this simplicity, many web sites in Japan are now supporting the iHTML. An i-mode server or a corporate markup language converter is located between the ordinary HTML server

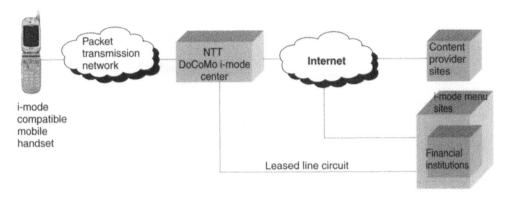

Figure 2.7   i-mode network architecture

and the cellular network providing i-mode service to perform such HTML-to-iHTML conversion in an efficient manner.

i-mode is considered as the first mobile Internet technology that supports packet switching, different from its predecessor circuit-switched cellular data networks, so that it can change the billing scheme based on the volume of data exchanged between the mobile data user and the network. Similar to GPRS (to be discussed in Chapter 3), i-mode is considered the always-on concept for Internet access, and not a dial-up data access. The i-mode network also supports the usual voice communication service. i-mode designers worked in close collaboration for the development of WAP version 2.0 released by the WAP Forum in August 2001, and look forward to more interworking between the two mobile Internet technologies for a global mobile multimedia and Internet service.

The protocol stack used for i-mode is shown in Figure 2.8 [36]. At the UE, the i-mode HTML and HTTP are used at the application layer (optionally) together with a secure socket layer (SSL) protocol [37,38] for the purpose of security of the transaction. For the transport layer, a wireless-profiled TCP based on WAP 2.0 recommendations is implemented. This includes the setting of the initial congestion window size for TCP in accordance with the IETF RFC 2414 [39], congestion window size, MTU (maximum transmission unit) size, and the implementation of selective acknowledgement TCP (SACK-TCP) in accordance with the IETF RFC 2018 [40]. This form of transport protocol implementation is used for higher efficiency of the TCP over the error-prone wireless channel compared to its common types (see Chapter 9 for details on TCP over wireless channel). The WAP 'push' service may be supported too. At the i-mode gateway server a similar protocol stack is used, which because of its role of being between the wireless access segment and wired segment of the network necessarily uses a dual-stack protocol suite.

Before finishing our discussions on i-mode network, it is useful to look at some statistics for subscriber growth for this advanced telecommunication technology. Figure 2.9 shows the number of subscribers for i-mode and compares these figures with voice-oriented (with some data services) cellular networks provided by the same company (based on the data available from Reference [35]). The huge increase in the number of subscribers for i-mode

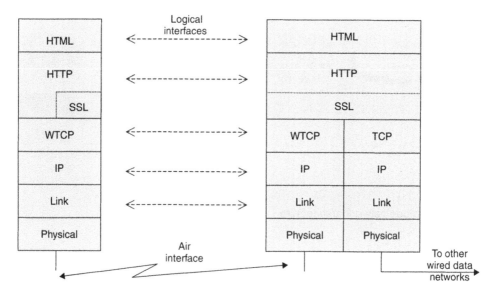

Figure 2.8   The i-mode protocol stack at user terminals and gateway servers

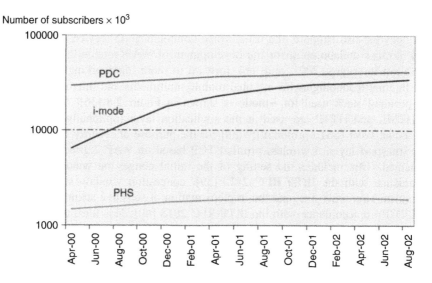

Figure 2.9   Subscriber growth for different cellular networks in Japan

illustrates the fact that this type of mobile Internet services would have a great outlook worldwide as long as they offer sufficient services at reasonable and affordable costs. This figure also restates the worldwide wireless Internet growth prediction previously discussed in Chapter 1. In the same figure, if we look at the subscriber growth for voice-oriented service by the Personal Digital Cellular (PDC) (Japan's cellular mobile system), we may conclude that whilst PDC has its own substantial growth (for example, from 33 million users in the beginning of 2001 to 41 million in July 2002 [35]), it has already exceeded the exponential growth rate and has little space for further increase. PDC provides full wide-area cellular network coverage. Compared to PDC, the pico-cellular mobile system PHS (Personal Handy phone System) that uses a similar concept as its European counterpart, the DECT system, provides low-cost voice and data services (up to 64 Kbps, using two 32-Kbps channels) to its users. PHS users can enjoy wired telephony-like dial-up connections for Internet services at comparable prices. However, the mobility is supported in a very limited geographical area, as the system had been originally designed as a low-cost mobile telephony system for pedestrian and low mobility users, that is, a different concept from wide-area cellular systems such as PDC and GSM. The subscriber growth for this system shown in Figure 2.9 is, however, not very impressive and is opposite to its wide-area counterpart losing the market gradually. As an example, PHS had around 1.8 million users in April 2001, almost 1.9 million in December 2002, and less than 1.9 million in July 2002 [35]. One reason for this lack of interest from users would be the low-range mobility supported in the PHS system, while another reason would be the introduction of more attractive systems such as i-mode. Mobility range is considered an important quality of service (QoS) parameter for future wireless Internet networks, and therefore we will address it in Chapters 5 and 10.

2.3.3 Freedom of multimedia access

Another recent initiative from the Japanese cellular company as the successor of i-mode is the FOMA (Freedom Of Multimedia Access) service [35]. FOMA is known to have initiated 3G multimedia wireless technology in the world, when it was started in November 2001. FOMA is based on wideband CDMA technology considered in third-generation wireless systems, UMTS. Full-motion video image transmission, music, and game distribution as well as other types of data services requiring high-speed and large-capacity wireless media are supported in FOMA in addition to the services already supported by i-mode. A maximum of 384-Kbps data rate is considered on downlinks of FOMA, whereas uplinks support a maximum of 64 Kbps, in line with the asymmetric data transmission concept for future wireless networks, which will be explained later in Chapter 3. The FOMA network is being expanded throughout the country gradually by NTT DoCoMo [35]. A high-level picture of the FOMA architecture is shown in Figure 2.10 [35].

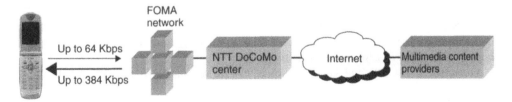

Figure 2.10 FOMA network architecture

An image distribution server will be deployed in FOMA in order to distribute multimedia video contents to mobile users at up to 64-Kbps data rate. The architecture of FOMA is fully based on packet switching technology. Video and audio communications and conferencing will be supported in the new system. Usage of wideband CDMA and spread-spectrum technology provides high quality data and voice transmission at very high bit rates and the usage of Rake receivers in a multipath communications environment [23–25].

The success of FOMA is yet to be experienced because of many factors that affected the telecommunications industry in recent years, which are outside the scope of this book for discussion. In the next chapters, we will continue our discussion on the architecture of 3G systems and we will see technical aspects of the future wireless Internet infrastructure.

2.4 STANDARDIZATION ORGANIZATIONS

The research and development in wireless mobile Internet would be meaningless if we do not look at the standardization activities that were carried out within the related organizations. Throughout this book, as the reader has already experienced, technical specifications and reports from several international standardization bodies will be referenced and therefore it is significantly important for a researcher in the field of wireless Internet to have a basic knowledge about who those standardizing forums are and what their responsibilities are. In this section, we will briefly summarize the most relevant standardization bodies and where a researcher needs to get access to a particular document. In addition to those introduced in this section, the web site of related industries could also always help in getting further technical information. The information provided in this section is based on data available at respective organization web sites, as referenced accordingly, where the reader may further obtain specific information of interest.

2.4.1 International telecommunication union

The International Telecommunication Union (ITU) [41] is an international organization within the United Nations structure that coordinates global telecommunications networks and services by advice and recommendations from the governments and private industries involved in it. ITU is based in Geneva, Switzerland. It is divided into three main sectors: ITU-R, ITU-T, and ITU-D.

ITU-R is the radio communication sector of ITU. It is responsible for the management of the RF spectrum, satellite orbits, finite telecommunication resources increasingly demanded from fixed, mobile, broadcasting, amateur radio, space research, meteorology, global positioning systems, environmental monitoring, and communication services related to the safety of life at sea and in the sky.

According to the ITU, the specific roles of ITU-R within the framework of ITU are:

• Allocation of RF spectrum bands, allotment of radio frequencies, and registration of RF assignments and of any associated orbital position in the geostationary satellite orbit.

- Coordination to avoid harmful interference between radio stations of different countries and improvement of the use of radio frequencies and of the geostationary satellite orbit for radio communication services.

ITU-T is the telecommunication standardization sector of ITU and was created in the new framework of the ITU in 1993, replacing the former International Telegraph and Telephone Consultative Committee (CCITT) whose origins go back to 1865. The mission of ITU-T is to ensure an efficient and on-time production of high-quality standards that cover all fields of telecommunications except radio aspects.

ITU-T standardization activities are carried out by 14 study groups (SG) in which representatives of the ITU-T membership develop recommendations for the various fields of international telecommunications on the basis of areas for study. The ITU-T structure consists of the World Telecommunication Standardization Assembly (WTSA), the Telecommunication Standardization Advisory Group (TSAG), and the ITU Telecommunication Standardization SG. WTSA takes place every four years to define general policy for the sector, establish the SG and approve their work program for each study period of four years, and to appoint the study group chairman and vice chairman.

TSAG reviews priorities, programs, operations, financial matters, and strategies for the sector, follows up on the accomplishment of the work program, restructures and establishes ITU-T SG, provides guidelines to the SG, advises the TSB director, and elaborates A-series recommendations on organization and working procedures. The SG and their working parties study the questions and elaborate the recommendations. SG of ITU-T work on different aspects of telecommunications such as operational aspects, tariff and accounting, telecommunication management, electromagnetic effect and so on.

ITU-D is the telecommunications development sector of the ITU and based on the ITU's constitutions has the following functions: to raise the level of awareness of decision-makers concerning the role of telecommunications in national economic and social development programs and to provide information and advice on possible policy and structural options, promote the development, expansion, and operation of telecommunication networks and services, enhance the growth of telecommunications through cooperation with other relevant organizations, mobilize resources to provide assistance to developing countries in the field of telecommunications, promote and coordinate programs to accelerate the transfer of appropriate technologies to developing countries, encourage participation by industry in telecommunication development activities in these countries, offer advice, carry out or sponsor studies on relevant issue related to the sector, and collaborate with other sectors such as the ITU's General Secretariat and other bodies in its overall coordination work. ITU-D carries out these functions through telecommunication development conferences, their associated development SG, and the Telecommunication Development Bureau (BDT), which is the administrative arm of the ITU-D.

2.4.2 European telecommunications standards institute

European Telecommunications Standards Institute (ETSI) [28] consists of 912 members from 54 countries and is based in Sophia Antipolis, south of France. The member countries are from inside and outside Europe, and members represent administrations, network operators, manufacturers, service providers, research bodies, and users. ETSI's work program is determined by its members, who are also responsible for approving its deliverables. As a result, ETSI's activities are maintained in close alignment with the market needs expressed by its members.

ETSI plays a major role in developing a wide range of standards and other technical documentations as Europe's contribution to worldwide standardization in telecommunications, broadcasting, and information technology. ETSI's prime objective is to support global harmonization by providing a forum in which all the key players can contribute actively. ETSI is officially recognized by the European Commission.

Through the ETSI's website [28], individual researchers could access freely through a broad range of TSs and technical reports (TR) documented for the standards of the telecommunications systems, especially for GSM, GPRS, and UMTS technologies.

2.4.3   Universal mobile telecommunications system forum

UMTS Forum [27] is a forum for researchers and developers of the UMTS technology for updating them on news related to the UMTS, its implementations around the world, and promotion of UMTS-related conferences and activities around the world. Through its website, new 3G services, UMTS-related reports and presentations, and forecasts on 3G licensing are presented to the public. The glossary and acronyms lists provided by the UMTS Forum help new researchers in the field to get an overview of the terminologies used in the UMTS.

2.4.4   Third-generation partnership project

Third-Generation Partnership Project (3GPP) [29] is a collaboration agreement that was established in December 1998 for bringing together a number of telecommunications standards bodies, known as 3GPP Organizational Partners. Currently, these partners include ARIB (Association of Radio Industries and Business, Japan), CWTS (China Wireless Telecommunication Standards Group, China), ETSI, ANSI T1 (T1 Committee of the Telecommunications of the American National Standards Institute), TTA (Telecommunications Technology Association, South Korea), and TTC (Telecommunications Technology Committee, Japan).

The original scope of 3GPP was to produce globally applicable TSs and TRs for a third-generation mobile system based on evolved GSM core networks and the radio access technologies that they support, including the Universal Terrestrial Radio Access (UTRA) both FDD (frequency division duplex) and TDD (time division duplex) modes of operation. This scope was then amended to include the maintenance and development of the GSM TSs and reports including those related to GPRS and EDGE.

Through the 3GPP website [29], it is possible for individuals to find a particular TS or report related to GSM, GPRS, EDGE, and UMTS. 3GPP utilizes a system of parallel 'Releases' to meet the demand for new features in 3G UMTS specifications. Each release has a 'freeze date', which means that no revision is allowed after that date, only corrections can be amended in the TSs and reports numbered in a frozen release. If a new feature is required, then 3GPP will make a new release.

3GPP uses the CCITT method of categorizing specifications. According to that method, each task has three stages:

- Stage 1: Includes service description from a service-user's point of view
- Stage 2: Breaking problem into functional elements
- Stage 3: Implementation of protocols between physical elements

Phases are used to show the progress of specifications. The current 3GPP specifications status is shown in Table 2.1. Release 5 includes the latest complete set of 3GPP specifications, which was frozen in March 2002. All specifications related to Release 5 have a version number such as 5.x.y. New features are currently being incorporated in the 3GPP Release 6, with all specifications being numbered as 6.x.y. The anticipated frozen date for Release 6 currently is June 2003. A list of all specifications in each release can be found in the TR mentioned in the table. Earlier specifications have different terminologies for version numbering and thus special care should be taken.

All 3G and GSM specifications have a four- or five-digit number (e.g. 09.02 or 29.002). The first two digits show the series, while the two extra digits (for 01 to 13 series) or three extra digits (for 21 to 52 series) have special meanings. Series 21 to 35 may apply either to 3G only or to GSM and 3G. Thus, a '0' indicates that it applies to both systems, such as in 29.002 that applies to both 3G and GSM, while a '1' indicates that the specification

Table 2.1 Status of the 3GPP specifications

GSM/EDGE release	3G release	Abbreviated name	Version no.	Freeze date
Phase 2 + Rel 6 (TR 41.104)	Release 6 (TR 21.104)	Rel-6	6.x.y	June 2003
Phase 2 + Rel 5 (TR 41.103)	Release 5 (TR 21.103)	Rel-5	5.x.y	March 2002
Phase 2 + Rel 4 (TR 41.102)	Release 4 (TR 21.102)	Rel-4	4.x.y	March 2001
	Release 2000[a]	R00	4.x.y	
Phase 2 + Rel 2000			9.x.y	
	Release 1999 (TR 21.101)		3.x.y	
		R99		March 2000
Phase 2 + Rel 1999 (TR 01.01)			8.x.y	
Phase 2 + Rel 1998		R98	7.x.y	Early 1999
Phase 2 + Rel 1997		R97	6.x.y	Early 1998
Phase 2 + Rel 1996		R96	5.x.y	Early 1997
Phase 2		PH1	4.x.y	1995
Phase 1		PH2	3.x.y	1992

[a] A temporarily used term that was eventually replaced by the term 'Release 4'.

Table 2.2   3GPP series specifications numbering reference

Subject of specification series	3G GSM R99 and later	GSMonly (Rel-4~)	GSMonly (~Rel-4)
Requirements	21 series	41 series	01 series
Service aspects	22 series	42 series	02 series
Technical realization	23 series	43 series	03 series
Signaling protocols (user equipment to network)	24 series	44 series	04 series
Radio aspects	25 series	45 series	05 series
CODECs	26 series	46 series	06 series
Data	27 series	47 series	07 series
Signaling protocols (RSS-CN)	28 series	48 series	08 series
Signaling protocols (intrafixed-network)	29 series	49 series	09 series
Program management	30 series	50 series	10 series
User identity module (SIM/USIM)	31 series	51 series	11 series
O&M	32 series	52 series	12 series
Access requirements and test specifications		13 series[a]	13 series
Security aspects	33 series	[b]	[b]
Test specifications	34 series	[b]	11 series
Security algorithms	35 series	[b]	[b]

[a]Responsibility of ETSI TC MSG.
[b]Spread throughout several series.

applies only to 3G, such as in 25.101. All other series apply to GSM systems. Each specification also has a title, and a list of those titles can be found in Reference [42]. The series numbering of 3GPP specifications is shown in Table 2.2.

In 3GPP TS 21.103 V1.0.0, available from Reference [29], you can find a complete list of specifications and reports for 3G Release 5. In this TS, you can also find the main working group (WG) responsible for each specification and the current status of the specification.

2.4.5   Third-generation partnership project 2

Third-Generation Partnership Project 2 (3GPP2) [32] is a collaborative third-generation telecommunications standards setting project consisting of North American and Asian interests developing global specifications for ANSI/TIA/EIA-41 cellular Radio telecommunication Intersystem Operations network evolution to 3G, and global specifications for radio transmission technologies (RTTs) supported by ANSI/TIA/EIA-41.

3GPP was an IMT-2000 initiative of ITU, covering high-speed, broadband, Internet protocol-based mobile systems featuring network-to-network interconnection, feature and service transparency, global roaming, and seamless services independent of location. Similar to 3GPP and as a result of its approach for standardization, 3GPP2 as a collaborative project was started in 1998 to work on a 3G standard based on the ANSI-41 system within the given time. 3GPP is an observer to 3GPP2, as TIA is an observer to 3BPP.

Currently, there are five standards development organizations (SDO) collaborating in the project, including ARIB, CWTS, TIA (Telecommunications Industry Association, North America), TTA, and TTC. These are the 3GPP2 organizational partners for the project.

Similar to the 3GPP, 3GPP2 publishes its work results on TSs. There are five technical specification groups (TSG) within the 3GPP2 working on different aspects of telecommunications. These are as follows:

- TSG-A: working on access network interface (*A-Interface*) system
- TSG-C: working on cdma2000
- TSG-N: working on intersystem operation (ANSI-41/WIN)
- TSG-P: working on wireless packet data networking
- TSG-S: working on service and system aspects

In addition, 3GPP2 TSG-S includes an All IP Ad Hoc group. The specifications prepared by 3GPP2 in relation to the development of cdma2000, one part of IMT-2000 3G systems, can be accessed freely by individuals through its web site [32]. These specifications are simply numbered in a list in accordance with the above technical groups of 3GPP. Each 3GPP specification has a number starting with a letter corresponding to the technical group that prepared that report. For example, A.R0003 is a TSG-A specification on cdma2000 spread-spectrum systems and N.S0003 is a TSG-N specification on user identity module. So it is not difficult or complicated to find a particular TS report as in the case of 3GPP standards.

2.4.6 Internet engineering task force

IETF [43] is the standardization body for all Internet-related research activities. It is an open international community of network designers, operators, vendors, and researchers concerned with the evolution of the Internet architecture and the smooth operation of the Internet. The works within the IETF are carried out through its WGs, which are organized by topic into several areas such as routing, transport, security and so on. They have three meetings each year to discuss their activities.

Area directors manage the IETF WG activities, and they are members of the Internet Engineering Steering Group (IESG). The Internet Assigned Numbers Authority (IANA) is the central coordinator for the assignment of unique parameter values for IP. The IANA is chartered by the Internet Society (ISOC) to act as the clearing house to assign and coordinate the use of numerous IP parameters.

In general, there are two types of documents or reports prepared and published by the IETF that are relevant to researchers working on any aspect of Internet: Internet drafts and RFCs. An alphabetical list of IETF current Internet drafts and a numerical order list for all IETF RFCs can be found in Reference [43]. Internet drafts are prepared by individuals or companies by outlining results of a specific research on Internet-related protocols and

IETF gives a release date and expiry date (usually six months after the release date) to each of them to publish the draft on its web site. Individuals can review these drafts and make any comment or correction about them. Since these are not standards, any reference to them should be read as 'work-in-progress' as an Internet draft could be expired without any further promotion.

An RFC is a kind of Internet standard, originated usually from an Internet draft and then promoted, which might be with or without modifications, to a higher level. Each RFC has a status indicator, such as historic, proposed standard, or informational. Each RFC has a four-digit number. The first RFC, RFC 0001, is back to 1969 on host software topic. Documents for all IETF Internet drafts and RFC are available to individuals freely through the IETF web site [43].

Different from telecommunications standards, Internet standards have been developed in an open format as a result of research works performed by individuals and professionals from all parts of the world. This is a unique feature of the Internet compared to other telecommunication networks and systems, and Internet's extensive growth could be considered mainly as this kind of open standardization.

2.4.7   Mobile wireless Internet forum

Mobile Wireless Internet Forum (MWIF) [44] was founded in 2000 as a nonprofit industry consortium to drive acceptance and adoption of a single, open, mobile wireless Internet architecture independent of access technology. Several Internet-related and telecommunications organizations including 3GPP, 3GPP2, and IETF are working with MWIF consortium, and the MWIF members provide studies report and industrial directions for future wireless Internet. Currently, there are 33 principal members, 10 auditing members, and 3 WGs within the MWIF.

The goal of MWIF is to work on a mobile Internet environment with interoperability and operations with all radio and other media access technologies, including legacy wireless and wire-line network, on a common radio access protocol; standard open interfaces among core network components, in a plug-and-play installation and configuration form; true customer mobility across all networks; and, common service and applications development environment.

The MWIF vision is a single IP-based backhaul network, shared equipment between the Internet and Telecommunications communities, and seamless integration of mobile telephony and Internet services and content.

The MWIF web site [44] provides several documents related to the above activities on mobile Internet. Although MWIF is not a standard organization, results of its research activities on harmonization of different 3G systems and air interfaces could be an indication for standard organizations, where many members are also affiliated with the MWIF.

2.5   SUMMARY AND CONCLUSIONS

In this chapter, an outlook on future wireless mobile Internet architecture, the main subject of this book, has been provided by reviewing several examples of initial mobile Internet systems. We called these systems cellular Internet data networks to distinguish them from a complete solution to the mobile Internet. After some fundamental discussions on circuit and packet switching and access network versus core network, we gave examples of CDPD and HSCSD systems, built on second-generation cellular infrastructures. The above two examples mainly target particular cellular systems, which limit the globalization trend in wireless Internet.

The next three advanced examples of WAP, i-mode, and FOMA illustrated a great possibility of providing a wireless mobile Internet on a global basis, independent of access technologies, even with existing cellular infrastructures. We believe that the materials provided in this chapter prepare the reader with a much clearer understanding for following the rest of this book.

To complete our discussion in this chapter, it is also worthwhile to mention the wireless local area network (LAN) involvement in future mobile Internet infrastructure. We will look at the wireless LAN on several occasions throughout this book, including, but not limited to, Chapter 11. Wireless LAN, with its distinguished features of low-cost equipments and high-speed bit-data rates, provides a complementary mobile Internet service to 3G systems in hot spot traffic and indoor environment. They are rapidly increasing as an extension of the wired Ethernet connection of Internet in university campuses, organization buildings, and public locations such as airports, hotels, restaurants, and exhibition centers around the world, and their role in providing short-range broadband Internet services cannot be ignored. The wireless LAN utilizes the RF, mainly from among spread-spectrum techniques, as the transmission media. The increasing popularity in wireless LAN usage would finally promote the cellular-based activities on realization of a global, common access technology, seamless wireless mobile Internet.

REFERENCES

1. Stallings W, *Data and Computer Communications*, 6/e, Prentice Hall, Upper Saddle River, N.J., 2000.
2. Halsall F, *Data Communications, Computer Networks and Open Systems*, 4/e, Addison-Wesley, Reading, Mass., 1996.
3. Leon-Garcia A & Widjaja I, *Communication Networks: Fundamental Concepts & Key Architectures*, McGraw Hill Higher Education, New York, 2000.
4. Quick RR & Balachabdran K, Overview of the cellular digital packet data (CDPD) system, *Proceedings of Personal, Indoor, and Mobile Radio Communications (PIMRC '93)*, Yokohama, Japan, 1993, pp. 338–343.
5. CDPD Industry Coordinator, *Cellular Digital Packet Data Specification*, Release 1.0, Kirkland, Washington, 1994.
6. Garg VK & Wilkes JE, *Wireless and Personal Communications Systems*, Prentice Hall, Upper Saddle River, N.J., 1996.
7. Jedrzycki C & Leung V, Channel selection strategy for channel hopping in CDPD systems, *Proceedings of IEEE Vehicular Technology Conference (VTC '96)*, 1996, pp. 761–765.

8. Sushko M, Reverse channel performance for CDPD packet data traffic, *Proceedings of IEEE Vehicular Technology Conference (VTC '96)*, 1996, pp. 766–770.

9. Perkins C, IP Mobility Support Version 2, IETF Internet draft (work in progress), draft-ietf-mobileip-v2-00.txt, November 1997.

10. Perkins C, Mobile IP, *IEEE Communications Magazine*, **35**(5), 84–99, 1997.

11. Rahnema M, Overview of the GSM system and protocol architecture, *IEEE Communications Magazine*, **31**(4), 92–100, 1993.

12. Cai J & Goodman DJ, General packet radio service in GSM, *IEEE Communications Magazine*, **35**(10), 122–131, 1997.

13. Brasche G & Walke B, Concepts, services, and protocols of the new GSM phase 2+ general packet radio service, *IEEE Communications Magazine*, **35**(8), 94–104, 1997.

14. Bettstetter C, Vogel H-J & Eberspacher J, GSM phase 2+ general packet radio service GPRS: Architecture, protocols, and air interface, *IEEE Communications Surveys*, Third Quarter, 1999, http://www.comsoc.org/pubs/surveys.

15. ETSI TS 101 038 V5.0.1, Digital Cellular Telecommunications System (Phase 2+) (GSM); High Speed Circuit Switched Data (HSCSD); Stage 2, April 1997.

16. ETSI TS 123 034 V5.0.0, Digital Cellular Communications System (Phase 2+); Universal Mobile Telecommunications System (UMTS); High Speed Circuit Switched Data (HSCSD); Stage 2, 3GPP TS 23.034 Version 5.0.0, Release 5, June 2002.

17. Steele R, Lee C-C & Gould P, *GSM, cdmaOne and 3G Systems*, John Wiley & Sons, Chichester, West Sussex, England, 2001.

18. Furuskar A, Naslund J & Olofsson H, EDGE—enhanced data rates for GSM and TDMA/136 evolution, *Ericsson Review*, **1**, 1999.

19. Schramm P, et al., Radio interface performance of EDGE, a proposal for enhanced data rates in existing digital cellular systems, *Proceedings of IEEE Vehicular Technology Conference, (VTC '98)*, Ottawa, Canada, May 1998, pp. 1064–1068.

20. Furuskar A, Frodigh M, Olofsson H & Skold J, System performance of EDGE, a proposal for enhanced data rates in existing digital cellular systems, *Proceedings of IEEE Vehicular Technology Conference, (VTC '98)*, Ottawa, Canada, May 1998, pp. 1284–1289.

21. Hamiti S, Hakaste M, Moisio M, Nefedov N, Nikula E & Vilpponen H, EDGE circuit switched data—an enhancement of GSM data services, *Proceedings of IEEE Wireless Communications and Networking Conference (WCNC '99)*, New Orleans, 1999.

22. The Wireless Applications (WAP), Forum Web site: http://www.wapforum.com.

23. Viterbi AJ, *CDMA Principles of Spread Spectrum Communications*, Addison-Wesley, Reading, Mass., 1995.

24. Gilhousen KS, Jacobs IM, Padovani R, Viterbi AJ, Weaver LA & Wheathley III CE, On the capacity of a cellular CDMA system, *IEEE Transactions on Vehicular Technology*, **40**(2), 303–312, 1991.

25. Prasad R, *CDMA for Wireless Personal Communications*, Artech House, Norwood, Mass., 1996.

26. Bray J & Sturman CF, *BLUETOOTH: Connect Without Cables*, Prentice Hall PTR, Upper Saddle River, N.J., 2001.

27. Universal Mobile Telecommunications System (UMTS), Forum Web site: http://www.umts-forum.org.
28. The European Telecommunications Standards Institute (ETSI), Web site: http://www.etsi.org.
29. The Third Generation Partnership Project (3GPP), Web site: http://www.3gpp.org.
30. Huber J et al., UMTS—The mobile multimedia vision for IMT-2000: a focus on standardization, *IEEE Communications Magazine*, **38**(19), 129–136, 2000.
31. Chudhury P, Moher W, and Onoe S, The 3GPP proposal for IMT-2000, *IEEE Communications Magazine*, **37**(12), 72–81, 1999.
32. The Third Generation Partnership Project 2 (3GPP2), Web site: http://www.3gpp2.org.
33. Larsson G, Evolving from cdmaOne to third generation systems, *Ericsson Review*, **2**, 58–67, 2000.
34. Prasad R & Ojanpera T, An overview of CDMA evolution toward wideband CDMA, *IEEE Communications Surveys*, **1**(1), Fourth Quarter, 1998, http://www.comsoc.org/pubs/surveys,
35. NTT DoCoMo, Web site: http://www.nttdocomo.com.
36. NTT DoCoMo, Inc., i-mode service guideline, Version 1.0.1, November 2001.
37. The SSL Protocol Version 2.0, available at http://www.netscape.com/eng/security/SSL_2.html.
38. The SSL Protocol Version 3.0, available at http://www.netscape.com/eng/ssl3/draft302.txt.
39. Allman M, Floyd S & Partridge C, *Increasing TCP's Initial Window*, IETF RFC 2414, September 1998.
40. Mathis M, Mahdavi J, Floyd S & Romanow A, *TCP Selective Acknowledgement Options*, IETF RFC 2018, October 1996.
41. The International Telecommunication Union (ITU), Web site: http://www.itu.int.
42. www.3gpp.org/ftp/Information/Databases/Spec_Status/3GPP-Status.zip.
43. The Internet Engineering Task Force, Web site: http://www.ietf.org.
44. Mobile Wireless Internet Forum (MWIF), Web site: http://www.mwif.org.

3

Cellular Mobile Networks

In this chapter we will describe network architecture of the third-generation (3G) system, UMTS (Universal Mobile Telecommunications System). UMTS is the successor of the second-generation (2G) cellular network Global System for Mobile communications (GSM), which has been very successful in getting the largest share in the worldwide cellular telephony market. As an intermediate system enabling the most evolutionary developments toward the UMTS system, General Packet Radio Service (GPRS) is considered as an important development. GPRS is the packet service designed on top of the GSM network in order to provide data services at higher rates than GSM to mobile users. Despite the slow growth in the number of subscribers of this 2.5G system worldwide, it is very important to understand the architecture of GPRS system, because of many commonalities with the UMTS core network. Another important 3G cellular technology, cdma2000, will not be discussed until the next chapter for two reasons. The first reason is that the UMTS will cover the majority of user population and geographical regions worldwide, thus making it more important in our discussions in this book. The second reason is that despite different system and architectural concepts for these two 3G technologies, there are some basic similarities between the UMTS and the cdma2000 that make it possible for the reader to follow one system after understanding the other.

In recent years, many literatures have been written on the subject of the GSM system, explaining its access and core network as well as its capabilities and comparison with other 2G systems, such as personal digital cellular (PDC) and cdmaOne. Therefore, in this book we are not going to explain the GSM system in detail and assume that the reader has sufficient knowledge about this system. However, for the sake of consistency in our discussions on GPRS and UMTS systems, we will review some characteristics of the GSM network in the first section.

The first section is followed by the packet-switched cellular system GPRS and its enhanced version that has been migrated to the 3G system UMTS. Our discussion here is

The Wireless Mobile Internet: Architectures, Protocols, and Services.   Abbas Jamalipour
© 2003 John Wiley & Sons, Ltd   ISBN: 0-470-84468-X

mainly network-oriented, but some important characteristics of the relevant transmission systems will be addressed too.

3.1 GLOBAL SYSTEM FOR MOBILE COMMUNICATIONS

The GSM is a European initiative for creating a new cellular radio interface to replace the analog cellular mobile telephony already in place in the early 1980s. In 1982, the Conference of European Post and Telecommunications (CEPT) administration set up the Group Special Mobile to derive the specification of a common European cellular mobile system. The new digital cellular technology has been designed to operate in the 900-MHz band and coexist with the analog system. The major motives for the new system were to provide a high speech quality telephony system (compared to its predecessor analog systems), a high-capacity cellular system to cover the increasing population of mobile users in Europe, and an affordable low-cost (both operator's and user's) mobile system. There are many journal papers and books in the literature describing the GSM system (e.g. see References [1,2]), but the main characteristics of the system can be found through the standard drafts available from the ETSI (European Telecommunications Standards Institute) web site [3]. Some of the most important features of the GSM system are included in References [4–10]. A short description on how to use the standard drafts has been provided in this chapter.

GSM is an open system interconnection (OSI) network reference model compatible system. This enables users to use a number of OSI Layer 7 applications, such as X400 service, as well as the ISDN (Integrated Service Digital Network) supplementary services, such as calling line identification (CLI). Both synchronous and asynchronous data will be provided in increments between 300 and 9600 bps. Telephony services as well as emergency call, messaging, fax, and data services up to 9.6 Kbps are available through the GSM system.

The important issue of the selection of a spectrally efficient multiple access scheme for the GSM system was a big debate within the European research community in the mid-1980s. Many GSM prototype systems have been prepared by the industry in different European countries. Eventually, in accordance to the available very large scale integrated (VLSI) technology at the time and consideration of wideband versus narrowband systems and choices of TDMA (Time Division Multiple Access), FDMA (Frequency Division Multiple Access), and CDMA (Code Division Multiple Access), a narrowband TDMA has been agreed upon for the new cellular system. Initially, eight channels per carrier were supported in the GSM system with an eventual increase to 16 channels per carrier. A nice historic discussion on the creation of the GSM system can be found in Chapter 2 of Reference [2].

As a usual method in illustrating the work progress in the specifications of the telecommunications networks, which came from the International Telegraph and Telephone Consultative Committee (CCITT), the GSM standardization also divided into phases. The first phase of specifications of the GSM system had been frozen in 1990. This included the most commonly used services of the system such as call forwarding and call barring. The rest of the service specifications such as supplementary services as well as other performance improvement and fault repairs have been left to phase 2. Supplementary services of the GSM include number identification, call waiting, call hold, advice of charge, group multiparty service, closed user group, and so on. Phase 2 was completed in 1994 and then phase 2+ became the framework for further developments in the GSM system. A good example of the phase 2+ is the GPRS that we will describe in the next section. GPRS is usually referred to as a 2.5G system. Since early 1990s, the GSM system has started its increasing deployment in Europe and in other parts of the world.

The original GSM system was using the 900-MHz band and was therefore called GSM900. Later, for the purpose of inclusion of requirements of the emerging personal communications networks (PCN) in the GSM system, a new operating band at 1800 MHz was introduced and accordingly called DCS1800 (Digital Cellular System). Although the two operating systems of the GSM first used different documentation sets, after 1993, phase 2 of the specifications has included both the GSM900 and the DCS1800 in common documents. The North American GSM counterparts used the 1900-MHz band and introduced the PCS1900 (Personal Communications Systems). This GSM-type system has been one of the cellular systems in North America and has been added to the IS-136 D-AMPS (Digital Advanced Mobile Phone System) and IS-95 CDMA systems, both operated at the 1900-MHz band.

3.1.1 GSM architecture

A basic architecture for the 2G wireless systems is shown in Figure 3.1. The wireless system is connected to the wired telephony network, that is, the public-switching telephony network (PSTN), through mobile switching centers (MSC). Each MSC supports several base station subsystems (BSS). Each BSS includes a base station controller (BSC) that supports several base transceiver stations (BTS). The mobile stations (MSs), consisting of

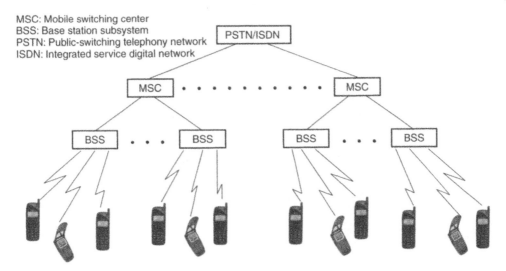

MSC: Mobile switching center
BSS: Base station subsystem
PSTN: Public-switching telephony network
ISDN: Integrated service digital network

Figure 3.1 Basic architecture of the second-generation cellular mobile systems

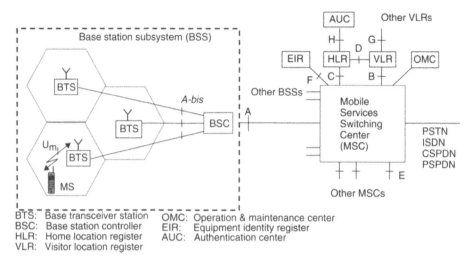

BTS: Base transceiver station   OMC: Operation & maintenance center
BSC: Base station controller   EIR: Equipment identity register
HLR: Home location register   AUC: Authentication center
VLR: Visitor location register

Figure 3.2 Basic architecture of the GSM system

the mobile terminal (MT) and the terminal equipment (TE), are connected to the cellular mobile system through a BTS with an air interface defined by the GSM standard.

The interfaces between the above GSM components are defined in the standard. The basic architecture of the GSM system is shown in Figure 3.2. One of the distinguishing features of the GSM system is the inclusion of a subscriber identity module (SIM), a removable smart card that includes all the subscriber's network and personal information. A user can easily remove this card from his mobile terminal and insert it in any other GSM-compatible phone to receive the same type of services from the subscribed network. A kind of device mobility is thus illustrated by such a feature considered in the GSM system.

Three different types of MSs are considered in the GSM system:

- Vehicle mounted units
- Portable units
- Handheld units

MSs are classified in accordance to the power into five classes as shown in Table 3.1. Base stations are also classified in a similar way to the MSs with 8 classes in 3-dB steps from 2.5 to 320 W.

Table 3.1 Mobile station power classes in the GSM system

Mobile station class	Power (watt)
1	20
2	8
3	5
4	2
5	0.8

3.1.2 GSM bandwidth allocation

In the GSM900 system, frequency bands of 890 to 915 MHz with 25-MHz and 935 to 960 MHz with the same 25-MHz channels are used, respectively, for the uplink and the downlink. A 200-kHz carrier spacing has been chosen. Excluding the two 100-kHz edges of the band, this gives 124 possible carriers for the uplink and the downlink. The use of carriers 1 and 124 are optional for operators. Figure 3.3 illustrates the channel allocation in the GSM900 system.

The multiple access scheme used in the GSM is a combination of FDMA and TDMA. That is, the total available band is divided into 124 200-KHz bands (FDMA) and each group of 8 users transmits through a 200-KHz band sharing the transmission time (TDMA).

3.1.3 GSM control and data channels

Two types of channels are considered: traffic channels (TCH) and control channels (CCH). The TCHs are intended to carry encoded speech or user data, whereas the CCHs are intended to carry signaling and synchronization data between the base station and the MS. TCHs are subsequently divided into full-rate traffic channels (TCH/F) at a net bit rate of 22.8 Kbps and half-rate traffic channels (TCH/H) at a net bit rate of 11.4 Kbps. Speech channels are defined for both full-rate and half-rate TCHs. The latter is for the future systems. Data channels support a variety of data rates (300 bps to 9.6 Kbps) on both half-rate and full-rate TCHs. The 9.6-Kbps data rate is only defined for the full-rate applications. Figure 3.4 shows the full-rate and half-rate slot allocation in the GSM system.

Figure 3.3 Channel bandwidth allocations in the GSM900 system

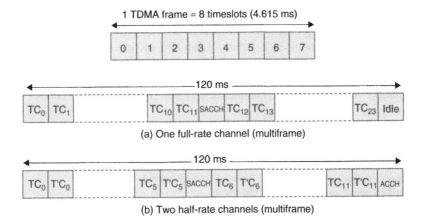

Figure 3.4 Full-rate and half-rate channels in the GSM system

CCHs could be of one of the following types:

- Broadcasting CCHs (for downlink only)
  — Frequency correction—FCCH
  — Synchronization—SCH
  — Broadcast—BCCH
- Common control channels (CCCHs)
  — Access grant—AGCH (downlink)
  — Paging—PCH (downlink)
  — Random access—RACH (uplink)
- Dedicated control channels (DCCHs)
  — Standalone dedicated—SDCCH
  — Slow associated—SACCH
    Fast associated—FACCH

Figure 3.5 shows different CCHs in a multiframe case for the GSM system. Broadcast control channels (BCCH) broadcast to all mobiles general information regarding their own cell as well as the neighboring (up to 16) cells, for example, the information used for cell selection and for describing the current CCH structure. Frequency correction channels (FCCH) are used for mobiles for the frequency correction. Synchronization channels (SCH) are used for frame synchronization of the mobiles and identification of the base station.

CCCHs are used in both downlinks and uplinks. Access grant channels (AGCH) are used on downlinks for assignment of a dedicated channel (DCH) after a successful random access. Paging channels (PCH), again on downlinks, are used for paging to mobiles. Random access channels (RACH), on uplinks, as their names suggest, are used for random access attempts by the mobiles.

DCCHs are used on both downlinks and uplinks. Standalone dedicated control channels (SDCCH) are the major signaling channels used for location updation, registration, point-to-point SMS (short message service), and handover preparation. Eight SDCCH are sent through one physical channel each having a bit rate of approximately 782 bps. Slow associated control channels (SACCH) are always associated with TCH, SDCCH, or FACH (forward access channel) and carry timing advance and power control measurement results and information. The bit rate per channel is 391 bps. Fast associated control channels

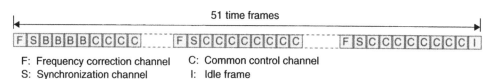

51 time frames

F: Frequency correction channel   C: Common control channel
S: Synchronization channel   I: Idle frame
B: Broadcast control channel

Figure 3.5 A control channel multiframe in the GSM system

(FACCH) carry the same signaling data as the SDCCH. They are used in the case when a very fast exchange of information is needed, for example, in the case of a handover. It accesses the physical resource by stealing frames from the TCH. The bit rate of this channel is 9.2 Kbps.

Different combinations of the control and TCHs would be possible. The four most common combinations are:

1. Full rate TCH combination: TCH/FS + FACCH + SACCH

2. Broadcast channel combination: BCCH + CCCH

3. Dedicated channel combination: SDCCH/8 + SACCH/C8

4. Combined channel combination: BCCH + CCCH + SDCCH/4 + SACCH/C4.

In a low-capacity cell configuration, one radio frequency (RF) carrier represents eight physical channels. One physical channel (time slot 0) is configured as BCCH + CCCH + SDCCH/4 + SACCH/C4 and seven physical channels (time slots $1, \ldots, 7$) are configured as TCH/F + FACCH + SACCH. In high-capacity cell configuration, five RF carriers represent 40 physical channels. One physical channel (time slot 0) is configured as BCCH + CCCH, two physical channels (time slots 2, 4) are configured as CCCH, two physical channels (time slots $0, \ldots, 7$) are configured as SDCCH/8 + SACCH/C8, and the remaining 35 physical channels are configured as TCH/F + FACCH + SACCH.

3.1.4   GSM system features

GSM uses an adaptive time alignment. The base station initially calculates the timing advance of the MSs on the basis of the received access burst on the RACH. The required timing advance for each MS is calculated in terms of the number of bit periods and sent to the MS as a 6-bit number. Timing advances from 0 to 63 bit periods can therefore be accommodated, giving a maximum base station–mobile station separation of 35 Km.

RF power control is used in the GSM mobile station and base station to reduce the transmit power to the minimum required to achieve the minimum quality objective and hence reduce the level of cochannel interference. The MS will be capable of varying its transmit power from its maximum output down to 20 mW in steps of nominally 2 dB. The base station calculates the RF power level to be used by the MS and sends a 4-bit number instruction to the corresponding mobile station.

The handover between cells in the GSM system uses the following procedure. A GSM mobile is only active, that is, either transmitting or receiving, in two or eight time slots in one frame. The MS scans transmissions from the surrounding base stations in the spare time slots. It then reports the measured results, together with those for the serving base station, back to the fixed network via the base station, where the handover decision is made. The procedure involved in a handover between base stations in the GSM system is outlined in Figure 3.6.

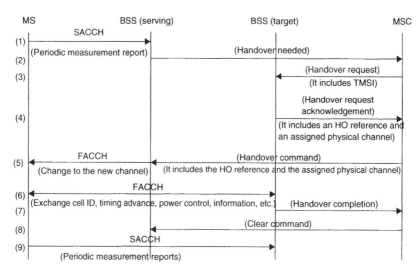

Figure 3.6 The handover procedure in the GSM system

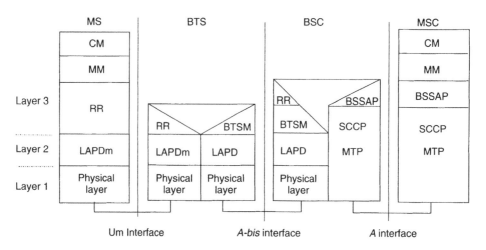

Figure 3.7 The GSM network architecture

3.1.5 GSM network architecture

The GSM network architecture is shown in Figure 3.7. Layer 3 functions are divided into three categories. Radio resource (RR) management function is related to the establishment of physical connections for the purpose of transmitting call-related signaling information. Mobility management (MM) functions are related to the location registration, paging, attachment/detachment, handover, dynamic channel allocation, and management. Connection management (CM) are functions related to call control (CC), SMS, and service handling.

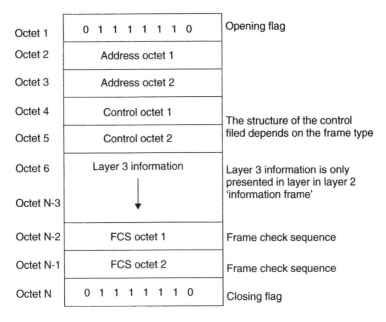

Octet 1	0 1 1 1 1 1 1 0	Opening flag
Octet 2	Address octet 1	
Octet 3	Address octet 2	
Octet 4	Control octet 1	The structure of the control
Octet 5	Control octet 2	filed depends on the frame type
Octet 6	Layer 3 information	Layer 3 information is only
Octet N-3	↓	presented in layer in layer 2 'information frame'
Octet N-2	FCS octet 1	Frame check sequence
Octet N-1	FCS octet 2	Frame check sequence
Octet N	0 1 1 1 1 1 1 0	Closing flag

Figure 3.8 The LAPD frame structure

The data link layer (Layer 2) over the radio link is based on a modified LAPD (Link Access Protocol for the D channel) referred to as LAPDm. On the *A-bis* interface, the Layer 2 protocol is based on the LAPD from ISDN. The LAPD frame structure is shown in Figure 3.8.

A-bis interface

CM and MM messages are not interpreted by the BSC or the BTS. They are transferred over the *A-bis* interface as transparent messages and over the *A* interface using the direct transfer application part (DTAP). RR messages are mapped to the BSS application part (BSSAP) in the BSC. In the BTS, most of them are handled as transparent by the BTS (e.g. random access, start ciphering, paging). BTS management (BTSM) is used to transfer all OAM (operating and maintenance)-related information to the BTS.

A interface

The message transfer part (MTP) and the SCCP (signaling connection control part) are used to support the transfer of signaling messages between the MSC and the BSS. The SCCP is used to provide a referencing mechanism to identify a particular transaction relating to, for instance, a particular call. The SCCP can also be used to enhance message routing, operation, and maintenance information. The MTP provides a mechanism for reliable transfer of signaling messages. A subset of MTP is used between the BSS and the MSC. The BSSAP provides the channel switching and aerial functions, and performs the RR management and the interworking functions between the data link protocols used on the radio and the BSS-MSC side for transporting signaling-related messages.

3.1.6 DCS1800 and PCS1900

DCS1800 was developed under the auspices of ETSI as a European standard for PCN. This role was given to a technical team by the GSM working group. DCS1800 is based on the GSM technology but configured around a hand-portable terminal with lower power mobile terminal and smaller cell size. Choosing a GSM approach overcomes the development problems but increases the investment cost. Because the cell sizes in DCS1800 are small, handset power can be reduced, improving the handset battery life and reducing size.

DCS1800 system is not only a simple voice telephony but it also provides all add-on services provided by GSM such as short messages services. The network is the same as for GSM. Equipment developed for a GSM system can be used for DCS1800 with very little modification. The RF ends are the main differences. The lower power requirements mean that high power amplifiers are not needed.

DCS1800 differs from GSM in two major ways. First, it enjoys a higher capacity. It provides a maximum of 374 radio channels compared to 124 for the GSM900. Second, it requires lower transmitter power. DCS1800 is designed to support hand-portable terminals with a transmit power not exceeding 1 W.

The allocated frequency band of 1710 to 1880 MHz in DCS1800 provides 75-MHz duplex bands with a 20-MHz spacing. The BTS links to the BSC may use 38-GHz radio to avoid laying costly underground cable links. DCS1800 cell size is less than 1-km radius for the city centers and around 6 km for the country.

DCS1800 MSs are in power class 1 or 2 with 1 or 0.25 W powers, respectively. DCS1800 base stations are divided into four categories of 1 to 4, with a power of 20 to 40, 10 to 20, 5 to 10, and 2.5 to 5 W, respectively.

PCS1900 system is based on the GSM technology reconfigured for the North American market. Its main difference from DCS1800 is its use of an enhanced full rate (EFR) speech codec. The speech codec is based on the code excited linear predictive (CELP) coding technique optimized for PCS1900 full-rate TCHs. The codec operates at 13 Kbps and offers the best quality available for cellular and PCS use today. It also offers good performance with nonspeech signals such as music.

3.2 GENERAL PACKET RADIO SERVICE

The increase in usage of Internet applications in the daily life of people and the success in service development and popularity of the 2G wireless cellular system, particularly in the second half of 1990s, together have raised this question of why the Internet access should be restricted to fixed access points inside buildings. People started using their portable laptop computers and palm pilot handheld computers to access their electronic information such as e-mail by dialing up to their Internet service providers when they were away from home or office. The age of nomadic computing has started, which means that people now could move around and when they find a telephone line can connect their computer using a dial-up connection and take the advantage of the Internet services.

Indeed, this was a great change in human life but as a natural fact, it has not stopped at that point. Soon cellular phone companies together with their partners started developing cellular phone modems so that people could dial up their Internet service providers not only through a fixed telephone line but also through their cellular handset phones. With this method, the nomadic computing has been changing to some kind of mobile computing, that is, the users could continue their connection session to the Internet while they were moving in a wide area, thanks to the reliable coverage and handoff capabilities of the advanced cellular systems.

The above method was practical, but nonetheless suffers from many problems. Almost all these problems are the result of the fact that all 2G cellular systems including the GSM system have been designed and optimized for voice communications, leaving very limited data transfer capabilities in their systems. In the core network of the 2G cellular systems, the old (but voice-friendly) circuit-switching technique has been dominantly implemented.

Circuit-switched networks provide a very ideal quality of service to low-bit-rate real-time applications that require a constant bit rate and those that are delay-sensitive, such as voice telephony. However, the same technique fails to provide efficient bandwidth utilization in the network. In particular, for the wireless network with very limited available bandwidth and capacity, dedicating the circuits to individual users for the whole period of conversation is too far from being efficient. The circuit-switching technique could not support the burst of data traffic and thus it would be a waste of resources to use it in a mobile computing environment.

The nature of the circuit-switching network implies that the user has to pay on the basis of the time of connection and not the amount of data traffic transmitted during the connection. Therefore, the practical use of the cellular radio interface to connect to the Internet comes together with a high cost for the users, which in many cases is simply unaffordable.

On the other hand, having a circuit-switched network as the core transport network implies a very unfriendly environment for transmitting the TCP/IP (transmission control protocol/Internet protocol) packets. A packet-switched network would be the only way of transporting data packets both from the cost and the efficiency points of view. The advanced GSM system, for example, could handle data traffic at a rate up to 9.6 Kbps, which is far below the current rates in wired networks, and thus is simply too low and unacceptable for the majority of the Internet users.

Although some of the cost-related problems for mobile computing over cellular networks could be solved by better management and billing strategies and a higher data rate is achievable through, for example, circuit-switched data (CSD) and high-speed circuit-switch data (HSCSD) [11] (see Chapter 2), the ultimate solution could never be found within the circuit-switching technology. A new core network built on a packet-switching technology would be the only answer. Nevertheless, an improvement in radio access technology is also necessary in order to achieve higher data rate, which is the subject of, for example, EDGE (Enhanced Data rates for GSM Evolution) [12–16]. (In some literature, the 'G' in EDGE refers to 'Global' since the evolutionary radio access can be utilized in non-GSM systems too.)

3.2.1 GPRS architecture

GPRS [17–22] is one of the initiatives in the GSM phase 2+ series but it is rather usually called a 2.5G cellular system owing to major changes included in the system compared to the GSM system. GPRS, as a network with a packet-switched core architecture, came to resolve the packet data transmission problems raised in the GSM system and that are listed above. In summary, GPRS is an evolution of the GSM that uses a time frame structure similar to the GSM, an FDMA-/TDMA-based packet-switched radio technology with 200-kHz channels (see Figure 3.9), and an evolved packet-switched core network. Similar to GSM, GPRS has been defined by the ETSI, but unlike GSM, it targets data applications such as web and e-mail services. The system allows for higher data rates and bandwidth, such as 144 to 384 Kbps. Different packet protocols such as X.25 and IP are supported in the GPRS system.

The packet-switched core network considered in the GPRS permits the offering of IP-based services efficiently. The GPRS network architecture is shown in Figure 3.10. Figure 3.11 shows the same network configuration as Figure 3.10 after highlighting the existing network entities in a circuit-switched cellular system. A close look at these two figures will show the effort taken in making the cellular architecture of the GSM system into a more data-friendly architecture.

3.2.2 GPRS new routers

The main entities added in the GPRS system are the two routers (gateways) called a *serving GPRS supporting node* (SGSN) and a *gateway GPRS supporting node* (GGSN).

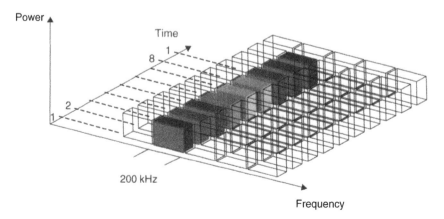

Figure 3.9 Physical channels in the GPRS system

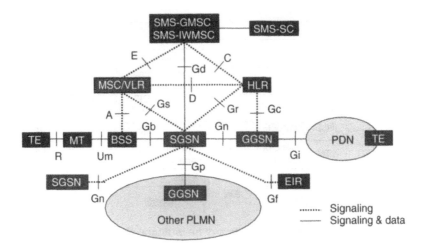

Figure 3.10 GPRS network architecture

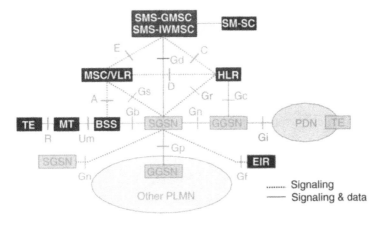

Figure 3.11 The network entities of the current circuit-switched system

BSSs are connected to SGSNs and therefore the SGSN can be considered as an access router to the GPRS core network. On the other hand, GGSN is a gateway router interfacing the GPRS core network to other packet data networks (PDN) and to the global Internet. GGSN maintains routing information used to tunnel IP datagrams to the correct SGSN. The GPRS protocol is also designed to be data-friendly for sufficient support of the bursty data traffic over the cellular network. The GPRS data transmission and signaling paths are shown in Figures 3.12 and 3.13, respectively.

The functions listed for the GGSN (see Figure 3.14) are as follows:

- Message screening
- Billing data collection

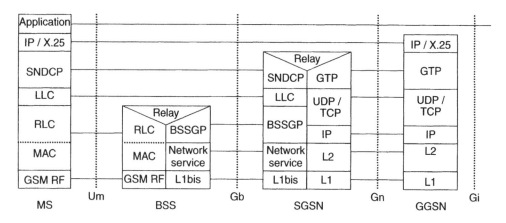

Figure 3.12 GPRS data transmission path and the protocol stack

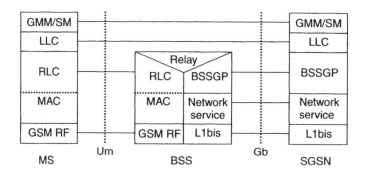

Figure 3.13 The GPRS signaling path

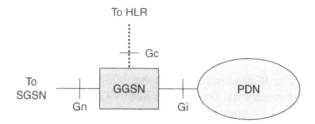

Figure 3.14 The gateway GPRS supporting node

- Relaying and routing
- Address translation and mapping
- Encapsulation and tunneling (GPRS tunneling protocol, GTP)
- Mobility management

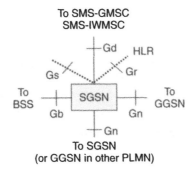

Figure 3.15   The serving GPRS supporting node

The functions for SGSN (see Figure 3.15) are as follows:

- Authentication and admission control
- Billing data collection
- Relay, routing, address translation, and mapping
- Encapsulation and tunneling
- Domain name server
- Mobility management
- Ciphering (logical link control (LLC) layer)
- Logical link management (LLC layer)
- Compression (subnetwork-dependent convergence protocol (SNDCP) layer).

3.2.3   GPRS signaling

Most of the interfaces in the core network of the GPRS system, that is, C, D, E, Gc, Gf, Gr, and Gs Interfaces, use the signaling system number 7 (SS7), the signaling that has been developed for advanced wired packet networks such as ISDN. Figure 3.16 shows the layered protocol of SS7 used in the GPRS interface signaling. In particular, SCCP provides global network connectivity. This is illustrated in Figure 3.17.

GPRS has many similarities at the physical layer with the GSM system, which makes it possible to use both at the same air interface. The difference between GSM and GPRS comes in their core network and logical channel arrangements. The discussion on GPRS logical channels is outside the scope of this book. To highlight some similarities between the GSM and the GPRS physical layers, we can see in both systems

- an FDMA/TDMA multiple access scheme,
- each physical channel with 200-kHz band,
- division of each channel into eight time slots.

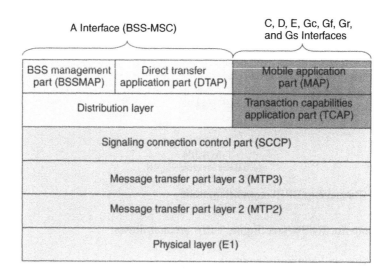

Figure 3.16   SS7 signaling in the GPRS system

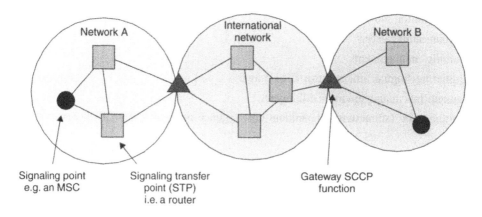

Figure 3.17   Global network accessibility using the SS7 signaling

TCHs in GPRS system similar to the GSM system are in a multiframe structure, but instead of 26, in GPRS the length is twice longer, that is, 52.

3.2.4   GPRS mobility management

The GPRS mobility management (GMM) procedures at the MS and at the SGSN are shown in Figure 3.18. Also Figure 3.19 shows the details of states involved in the GPRS mobility management in the MS. Similar states could be seen in the SGSN, and therefore we leave this to the reader.

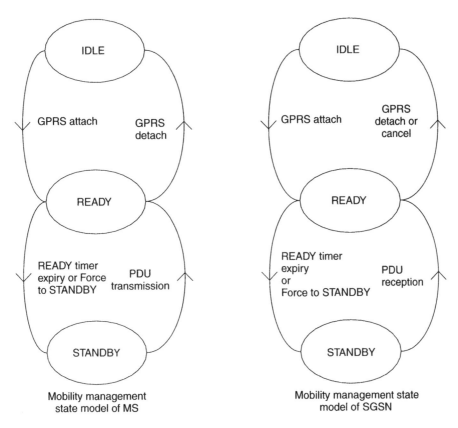

Figure 3.18   GPRS mobility management

As an example of the procedures involved in the GPRS mobility management, Figure 3.20 shows the time line for a normal attach procedure for a MS in the GPRS system.

3.3   ENHANCED GENERAL PACKET RADIO SERVICE

There are a few interpretations about which network is named *enhanced general packet radio service* (EGPRS) and what its differences are with the GPRS that was discussed in the previous section. Without getting involved in those definitions and naming, what we mean here from the EGPRS is a kind of stepped evolution starting from the GSM system into the GPRS and toward the 3G UMTS system. This makes the discussions easier and also makes it possible to see the fundamental issues behind the network design rather than naming.

We see the EGPRS as an evolved version of the GPRS, which continues to use the GPRS core network. A new air interface, EDGE, however, is introduced in order to support

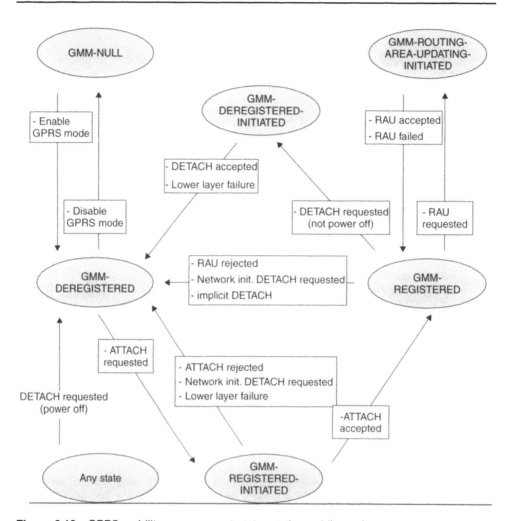

Figure 3.19 GPRS mobility management states at the mobile station

higher data rates by use of a higher-level modulation 8-PSK in addition to the traditional Gaussian minimum shift keying (GMSK) modulation scheme. By this approach, a data rate of up to 384 Kbps and a spectrum efficiency of 0.5 bps/Hz/base-station is achieved.

EGPRS, similar to the GPRS, overlays on the existing cellular systems. The EGPRS air interface supports registration, authentication, paging, and handoff (now called *cell reselection*), and channel access. For the MM a combination of link layer and a newly defined higher-layer technique is used. EGPRS follows a two-phase development process. These two phases are distinguished in accordance with the traffic types to be supported by the network and their relevant core network architecture.

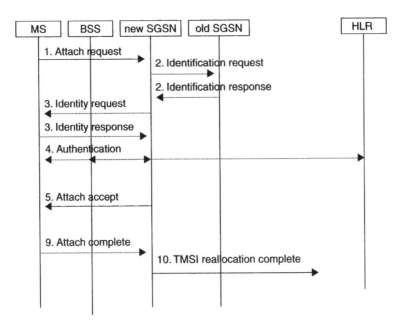

Figure 3.20 A normal attach procedure in the GPRS mobility management

3.3.1 EGPRS phase 1

EGPRS will follow two major phases in its development. In the first phase, which is similar to the GPRS, two different paths for different types of traffic will be used. The circuit-switched path consists of the BSS, the MSC, and the public-switched telephony network. This path is used to carry voice traffic similar to the current cellular networks. Such a voice-based path is required during the transition period, firstly to reuse the current cellular infrastructure and secondly to provide the required quality of service to circuit-switched traffic such as voice.

The second path is a packet-switched one to carry the data traffic related to nonvoice applications and in particular to the Internet-based services. This path consists of the BSS and the two routers introduced within the GPRS network, that is, the SGSN and the GGSN. The first phase architecture of the EGPRS, discussed above, is illustrated in Figure 3.21. This architecture as mentioned earlier is the most straightforward architecture, because it reuses the current GSM infrastructure that is vastly deployed in many countries for the low-bit-rate voice communications and then additional infrastructure for transporting the Internet data traffic is implemented, so that data traffic can be transported more efficiently and at higher speed between the end mobile user and the network. As shown in the figure, the BSS now has a new task of deciding to route a packet to the voice network (i.e. to the MSC) or to the packet network (i.e. to the SGSN) depending on the nature of traffic.

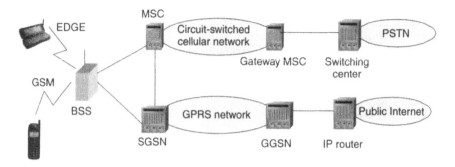

Figure 3.21   Architecture of the first phase of the EGPRS

Different air interfaces between the mobile terminal and the base station may be used in this architecture.

3.3.2   EGPRS phase 2

Apparently, having two different paths, one for transmission of voice traffic and the other for transporting nonvoice data traffic, is not an efficient approach. In addition to the fact that in such a system two subnetworks are working simultaneously where many of the elements are in common, more network management and billing would be required. Moreover, it is desired that the circuit-switched-type networks be eliminated completely from the architecture of the future mobile systems. Any circuit-switched friendly traffic such as real-time voice or video then has to be transported using packet-switched technology and in particular the IP. Network utilization, network integration, and reduced operational cost will be protected in such a one-path architecture.

Figure 3.22, as a result of the above requirements, shows the second phase of the EGPRS architecture. Nevertheless, in order to achieve consistency in such an advanced

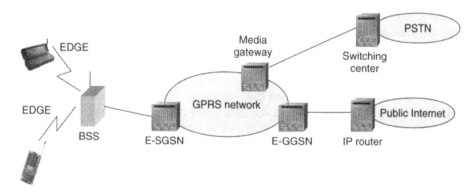

Figure 3.22   Architecture of the second phase of the EGPRS

network, further enhancement in the air interface and network entities, such as the SGSN and the GGSN router, are required. For this purpose these two routers are renamed E-SGSN and E-GGSN in Figure 3.22.

3.4 UNIVERSAL MOBILE TELECOMMUNICATION SYSTEM

Despite many advanced features included in the 3G UMTS, after introducing its predecessor networks, GSM, GPRS, and EGPRS, it is very straightforward to understand the main concepts of this new system. Again our discussion on UMTS is limited to the knowledge the reader needs to have for the purpose of this book, as the complete system description for the UMTS requires a book itself. Fortunately, in recent years many tutorial papers and books have been published in this area and many relevant information can be simply gathered from the public domain web site. (The readers who are interested in a complete survey on UMTS and other 3G systems are referred to References [23–36].) Frequency spectrum allocation for the UMTS is shown in Figure 3.23. Different UMTS modes of operation (described later in this section) as well as the satellite part of the UMTS, referred to as satellite UMTS (S-UMTS), the GSM1800, and the digital enhanced cordless telecommunications (DECT) frequency allocations are also shown in the same figure for comparison.

Cellular networks have followed an interesting pattern throughout their evolution since the first-generation analog systems until the most recent 3G systems. In one way, this was the multiple access technology that differentiated the different cellular systems around the world. Examples are the 2G systems in Europe, North America, and Japan using either TDMA or narrowband CDMA. This trend is not of our interest in this book. Another

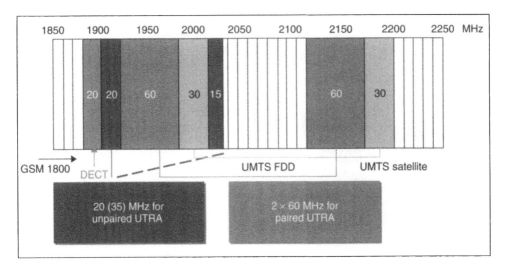

Figure 3.23 Spectrum allocations to wireless networks

visible trend in the way of evolution of these systems, which is of our interest, is the target traffic type that these systems were designed to transport. Second-generation systems were mainly designed to transport voice traffic, and thus circuit-switching technology was used. 2.5G systems such as GPRS have changed this target traffic into the packet-based traffic such as short message and e-mail. The 3G systems target the IP traffic as the main portion in future communication systems. It is expected that this IP-based technology development will continue even for the cellular systems beyond 3G. Figure 3.24 explains the evolution path within the cellular mobile technologies. The figure also suggests some features of the wireless communication systems after the 3G, as being provided with more mobility and roaming capability and flexibility, higher data rates and more services within a smaller number of standards.

Figure 3.25 outlines another change of direction during the evolution of cellular networks, so that CDMA-type systems became more dominant in the new-generation systems, but in accordance with wider bands, which is a necessity for higher data rates.

3.4.1 Evolution at all logical layers

The improved features considered in the UMTS could not be realized without enhancements in all logical layers of the system. Figure 3.26 illustrates the four logical layers involved during the evolution of the GSM system into the UMTS. These layers are radio access network, core network, terminal, and the application [36].

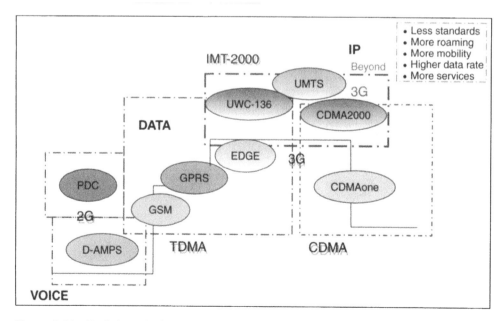

Figure 3.24 Evolution of cellular mobile standards

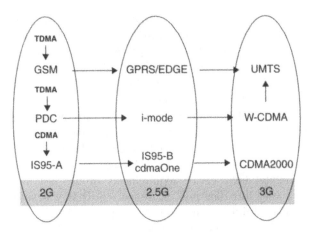

Figure 3.25 Merging paths between the cellular technologies

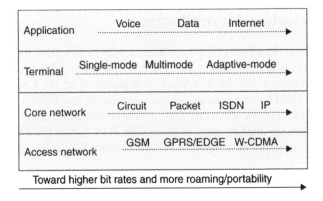

Figure 3.26 Evolution technologies in wireless cellular systems

Providing higher data rates to mobile users could not be possible without enhancement in radio access technologies. For this purpose, the radio access technology has been improved from the original GSM systems, created in the GSM phase 1, to the GPRS and the EDGE and finally through the UMTS system.

The core network requires even more enhancement during this evolution, in order to accommodate more complex mobility and security management protocols. The circuit-switched technology used in the GSM system also had to be upgraded into packet-switched technologies, such as ISDN, broadband ISDN (B-ISDN), asynchronous transfer mode (ATM), and eventually IP.

The cellular networks started their service through single mode terminals. For example, one could have a cellular phone subscribed to the GSM900 only. During the progress in the cellular systems, multimode terminals have been implemented, allowing users (either manually or automatically) to choose to connect to one of two or more available networks.

The available networks could be GSM900 and GSM1800, or GSM and ANSI-136, or IS-95 and Advanced Mobile Phone Systems (AMPS), or during the transition period between 2G and 3G, a dual-mode terminal of GSM and UMTS. Eventually this will be changed into an adaptive type of terminal based on software radio technology, for example, which is capable of using new source coding technologies for reduced multimedia data rate generated by or for the cellular user terminal.

The deriving parts for all these system enhancements are the applications. New Internet and multimedia applications such as video conferencing, image messaging, and m-commerce are asking for higher data rates and more reliable and secure transmission networks. The applications are also being developed to accommodate more user satisfaction.

The change in mobile data service requirements in the last decade is shown in Figure 3.27. While a very low data rate of around 9.6 Kbps was sufficient for the first SMS users, over a period of time, applications that require higher data rates and bandwidth are coming up, asking for more enhanced systems, such as UMTS and beyond in mobile communications [27].

3.4.2   UMTS network architecture

The UMTS network architecture is shown in Figure 3.28 [23]. In this figure, it is assumed that the UMTS system is cooperating at the same time with a 2G system GSM, which is a reasonable assumption for the first years of deployment of the UMTS. The wireless access part in the UMTS configuration is very similar to the GSM system with some changes in the naming of the elements and of course the more complex and advanced algorithms and protocols implemented in them. The BTS in the UMTS system is called a *Node B* and BSC uses the new name of Radio Network Controller (RNC). The access

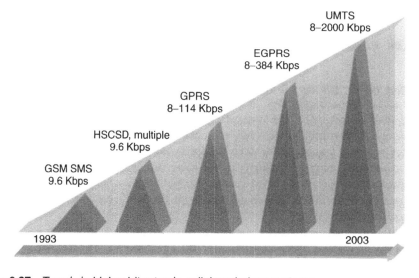

Figure 3.27   Trends in higher bit rates in cellular wireless systems

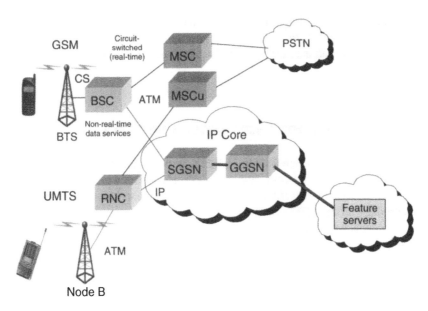

Figure 3.28 The UMTS network architecture

network of the UMTS follows the air interface defined by ETSI and will be reviewed shortly. The core network is recognized by the SGSN and the GGSN routers, that is, the two main components of the GPRS system. Connection of the UMTS user terminal to the public telephony network is provided via an UMTS-type MSC, shown as MSCu in the figure. System specifications of the UMTS can be found in References [23–25] and some tutorials and system analysis can be found in References [33,34] as well as many other literatures referenced at the end of this chapter.

After this short overview of the UMTS system architecture, let us have a closer look at it. The UMTS is the 3G evolution of the GSM (2G) and GPRS (2.5G) cellular systems. Three distinct parts can be recognized in this system:

- The *serving network domain*, commonly referred to as the core network (CN)
- The *access network domain*, commonly referred to as the UMTS Terrestrial Radio Access Network (UTRAN)
- User equipment (UE)

At the core network, UMTS mainly reuses the GSM/GPRS network elements. The MSC (MSCu) performs transcoding (e.g. voice coding) and bridges the cellular network to the public-switched telephone network. Serving GPRS service node (SGSN) and the gateway GPRS service node (GGSN) provide packet (e.g. Internet) services.

Access network domain or UTRAN manages specifications of the access technology of the UMTS, that is, the wideband CDMA (W-CDMA). The RNC provides data link layer services and the *Node B* supplies the physical (radio) channel access. Many *Node*

Bs, say 300, may subtend a single RNC in the UMTS. UTRAN consists of multiple radio network subsystems (RNS). We will discuss the role of RNS later.

User terminal is the end user UMTS cellular phone and provides data and voice services to the system users.

3.4.3   UMTS core and radio access network

Figure 3.29 provides an overview of the UMTS network architecture showing the relationship between the core network and the radio access networks [23]. One important thing that can be seen in this figure is the independency of the core network and the access technology in the UMTS architecture. The two parts are designed independently and they are connected to each other through a set of standard interfaces. This kind of network design should remind the reader of the OSI or the TCP/IP model, in which only the logical layers and the interfaces connecting these layers are defined by the standard, and the contents and the design of what would be inside these layers (i.e. layer protocols) have been left to the developers.

The UMTS core network consists of two domains: the circuit-switched service domain and the packet-switched service domain. These two domains are responsible for providing appropriate services to the circuit-switched traffic such as voice and the packet-switched traffic such as web and other IP-related applications, respectively. Two types of interfaces, Iu-CS and Iu-PS, connect the circuit-switched service domain and the packet-switched service domain to the UTRAN, respectively.

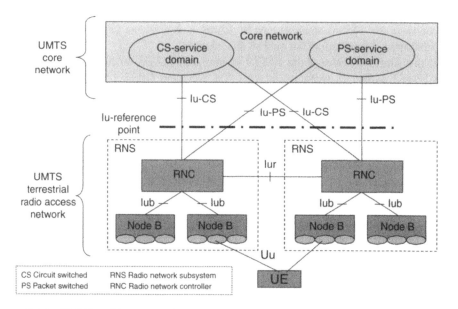

Figure 3.29   UMTS architecture reference model

UTRAN consists of several RNSs. Core network–independent procedures run between RNSs. This again emphasizes the layered architecture design considered in the UMTS. RNSs are communicating with each other through the interface Iur.

Each RNS consists of an RNC and several base stations, *Node Bs*. The interfaces between the RNC and the *Node Bs* are Iub.

Each *Node B* is responsible for connecting many end user terminals, UEs, to the UTRAN through the Uu interfaces. W-CDMA is used to provide multiple access shares to the users at the physical layer. The modular and layered design considered in the UMTS can be highlighted as a distinguishing characteristic with the previous systems.

3.4.4 UMTS modes of operation

ETSI special mobile group (SMG) defines two different modes of operation for the UMTS radio access, namely, the Universal Terrestrial Radio Access (UTRA):

- Frequency division duplex (FDD)—called UTRA FDD
- Time division duplex (TDD)—called UTRA TDD

The above two modes are illustrated in Figure 3.30. UTRA FDD uses different carrier frequencies for uplinks and downlinks [27]. A minimum of two 5-MHz spectrum are allocated to the UTRA FDD. For the UTRA TDD, same carrier frequency is used at uplink and downlink, which are multiplexed in time. 5-MHz minimum spectrum is allocated to the UTRA TDD. Both frequency bands are in the 2-GHz region (see Figure 3.23). Despite having two different modes of operation, some harmonization is available between the two, for example, both use some basic system parameters such as carrier spacing, chip rate, and frame length. Dual-mode FDD/TDD terminals and GSM inter-networking are also considered in the UMTS.

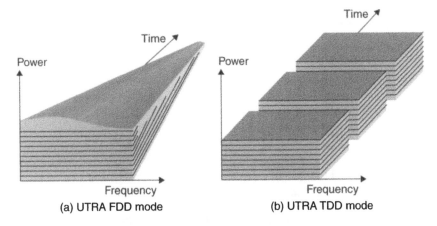

(a) UTRA FDD mode   (b) UTRA TDD mode

Figure 3.30 UMTS radio access FDD and TDD modes of operation

As seen in the description of Figure 3.30, UTRA FDD mode is purely a CDMA-based system, differentiating user signals in accordance with their powers and codes. On the other hand, the UTRA TDD is a kind of TDMA plus CDMA system, differentiating user signals with their powers and codes and also their time slot allocations. As mentioned, UTRA TDD is used for unpaired bands in uplinks and downlinks. The scheme is sometimes referred to as a time-division CDMA (TD-CDMA) system.

From a technical point of view (as opposed to a political one), there are important reasons for having the two modes of operation in the UMTS. The UMTS network has to provide service to a variety of multimedia applications. Multimedia applications in nature show both circuit-switched and packet-switched characteristics. Examples of multimedia applications are voice, audio/video, image, data, Internet access, and so on. These applications require different quality of services and the UMTS has to provide those diverse qualities. FDD and TDD together can define different capacity allocations for those traffics in different situations, but neither of them alone can provide the flexibility required here.

Most data applications show very asymmetric characteristics these days [27]. An example is the web service of the Internet. When you want to check a web page, a short message through the hypertext transfer protocol (HTTP) protocol is sent to the server, and then a large amount of information including the web page text, background image, pictures included in the web page, and so on will be downloaded from the server to the end user. It is found that on an average the ratio amount of traffic load on uplink to the one on downlink is 1 to 10 in a web service. This type of asymmetry is becoming very usual as more and more data services become available. The situation is far different from the voice communications in which the traffic loads on both directions are almost equal. Figure 3.31 illustrates the changes in the proportional amount of traffic load on downlink and uplink of the telecommunications systems over the past few years and the expectation of the future years. As it can be seen from this figure, soon the downlink traffic load will become the major part of the total traffic.

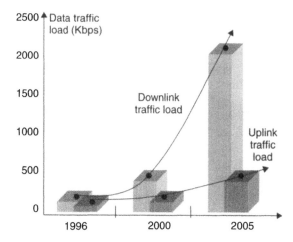

Figure 3.31 Asymmetry in downlink and in uplink traffic loads of the future communication networks

TDD is the only method that can flexibly share the system capacity to uplinks and downlinks. Since in TDD both directions use the same frequency spectrum, it is possible to allocate different ratio of TDD time slots to uplinks and downlinks in accordance to the service requirements at a particular time. This flexibility is not available in an FDD system, as a fixed amount of total system capacity is devoted to the uplink and the rest to the downlink. No change can be done after that in such a capacity allocation in an FDD system. In the future systems that require transportation of both symmetric and asymmetric traffics, having both FDD and TDD schemes in hand would be beneficial. In the next chapter, we further discuss the existence of the two modes of operation in the UMTS.

3.4.5 UMTS network protocol

The UMTS radio interface protocol architecture is shown in Figure 3.32. The architecture consists of a control plane for signaling and user plane for data information transportation [24]. The main functionality layers are as follows:

- Physical layer (PHY)
  — defines physical layer issues such as modulation and coding
- Medium access control layer (MAC)
  — provides DCHs and/or schedule bursts over shared channels
- Radio link control layer (RLC)
  — responsible for data delivery, fragmentation and reassembly, error checking, acknowledged and unacknowledged modes
- Broadcast/multicast control layer (BMC)
- Packet data convergence protocol layer (PDCP)
  — for IP header compression and serving radio network controller (SRNS) (serving RNC) relocations
- Radio resource control layer (RRC)

In the following, we will list services provided by each layer and the physical and logical channels at the physical layer and MAC layer, respectively.

3.4.5.1 Physical layer

The physical layer services are

- provision of the physical channels for transport of data;
- error detection, FEC (forward error correction) coding and decoding, interleaving and deinterleaving;
- modulation and demodulation, spreading and despreading;

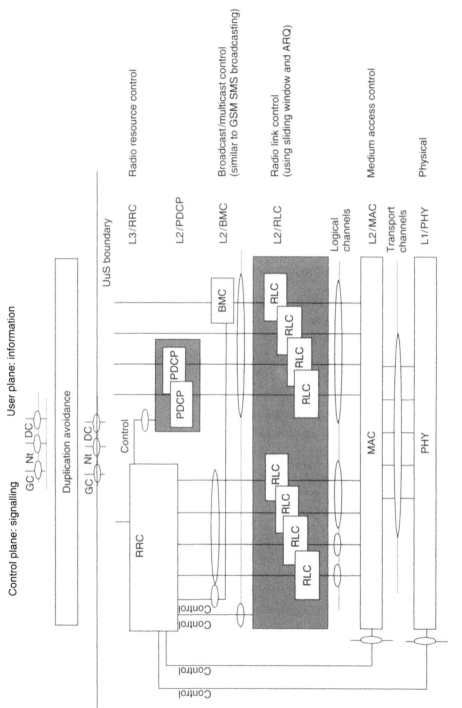

Figure 3.32 UMTS radio interface protocol architecture

- power control;
- RF processing.

Physical channels could be of one of the following types:

- *Random access channel (RACH)*
  - — Contention based, uplink
  - — Initial access to network
  - — Non-real-time uplink data transfer
- *Common packet channel (CPCH)*
  - — Contention based, uplink
  - — Non-real-time uplink data transfer
- *Forward access channel (FACH)*
  - — Common downlink channel
  - — Small data transfer
- *Downlink shared channel (DSCH)*
  - — Downlink channel *shared* by several UEs
  - — Data transfer
- *Broadcast channel (BCH)*
  - — Downlink
  - — Broadcast of system information
- *Paging channel (PCH)*
  - — Downlink
  - — Broadcasting of pages
- *Dedicated channel (DCH)*
  - — Uplink and downlink
  - — Traffic and signaling

3.4.5.2 Medium access control layer

The MAC layer services provide

- a set of logical channels for data and signaling transfer,
- mapping between logical and physical channels
  - — MAC may select between multiple possible physical channels,
- selection of transport format
  - — mapping of source data rate onto transport data rate,
- dynamic scheduling of access to common or shared channels.

The logical channels provided by the MAC layer are as follows:

- *Control Channels* (*CCH*)
  — Broadcast control channel (BCCH)
    - system broadcast information
  — Paging control channel (PCCH)
    - used to page a UE to which no DCCH exists
  — Dedicated control channel (DCCH)
    - established during an RRC connection procedure
    - point-to-point, bidirectional, dedicated
  — Common control channel (CCCH)
    - used to establish an RRC connection
    - bidirectional
  — Shared control channel (SHCCH)
  — ODMA dedicated control channel (ODCCH)
  — ODMA common control channel (OCCCH)
- *Traffic Channels* (*TCH*)
  — Dedicated traffic channel (DTCH)
    - dedicated to traffic for one UE
    - may be multiple DTCH per UE
  — ODMA dedicated traffic channel (ODTCH)
  — Common traffic channel (CTCH)

Mapping of the logical channels defined at the MAC layer to the physical channels used at the physical layer in UMTS is shown in Figure 3.33.

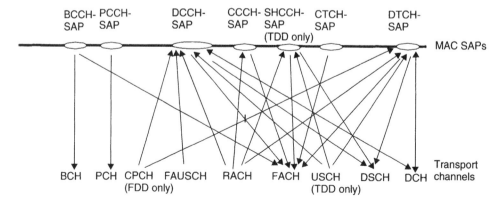

Figure 3.33 Logical to physical channel mapping in UMTS radio access network

3.4.5.3 Radio link control layer

The RLC layer services are as follows:

- Segmentation (fragmentation) and reassembly
- Concatenation and padding
- Transfer of user data
  - — Acknowledged mode
  - — Unacknowledged mode
  - — Transparent mode
- In-sequence delivery
- Flow control
- Duplicate detection
- Ciphering

The link layer characteristics of UMTS are error-control schemes such as Layer 2 ARQ (automatic repeat request) and FEC. A selective repeat and sliding window ARQ is used in the radio link layer (RLC) of UMTS W-CDMA. The maximum number of retransmissions for the RLC is a configurable parameter specified by the RR controller during the RLC connection initialization. The inclusion of ARQ and FEC in the radio link layer of UMTS provides a packet service with a small probability of undetected errors. Moreover, delivery of upper-layer traffic is performed with a low probability of loss. However, ARQ introduces high latency and delay jitter for IP flows, which as we will see in Chapter 9, will affect the transport layer protocol performance during transmission of IP and multimedia traffic.

3.4.5.4 Packet data convergence protocol layer

The PDCP layer services are

- TCP/IP, user datagram protocol (UDP)/IP header compression (RFC 2507),
- support for SRNS loss-less relocation
  - — sequence numbering of service data units
  - — buffering of unacknowledged data.

3.4.5.5 Radio resource control layer

The RR control layer services are

- broadcast of information provided by NAS (i.e. core network),
- broadcast of information related to the access stratum,

- establishment, maintenance, and release of RRC connection between UE and UTRAN,
- establishment, maintenance, and release of radio bearers,
- assignment and/or release of RRs (e.g. CDMA codes),
- mobility (e.g. handover, SRNC relocation),
- control of quality of service,
- setting of power control target,
- control of cell broadcast service.

3.4.6 UMTS open service architecture

UMTS provides wideband access to its subscribed users, which necessarily means higher data rates toward mobile multimedia application requirements. The convergence in mobile to fixed Internet access is one of the targets of the UMTS. This means a more uniform way to offer cross-domain (i.e. fixed to mobile and vice versa) service to the users. Service portability across heterogeneous networks and terminals should be supported by the UMTS. The problem is that services and applications are changing everyday and new applications (with new requirements) are coming to the network day after day.

All these improvements ask for a flexible service architecture for the UMTS [32]. Enhancing the creativity and flexibility in the network for new services could be realized by standardizing the blocks that make up services and not services themselves. This ignites the idea of open service architecture (OSA) for the UMTS. Also, being open provides simpler access of the third-party service providers to the UMTS service architecture. Internet as a network that has been developed on an open architecture basis is a good example of a successful network becoming global.

In order to provide the access of UMTS service architecture to the third-party service providers and further modifications in services, UMTS uses OSA. This OSA enhances the portability of the telecommunications services between networks and terminals and is explained in the UMTS Release 5, TS 22.127 [24].

Virtual Home Environment (VHE) is a system concept for personalized service portability across networks boundaries and between terminals, as a result of the OSA consideration in the UMTS. VHE is considered by Third-Generation Partnership Project (3GPP) and is explained in UMTS Release 5 TS 22.121 [24]. It simply specifies the use of services available at the user's home network even after roaming into another network. For example, if the user's home network provides Wireless Application Protocol (WAP) and the user is moved into a visiting network where the WAP is not available, then the VHE converts the WAP message into an SMS. That is, the user still receives some sort of service in the visiting network. Having something is always better than having nothing and thus the SMS service in the above example gives the user that something instead of the complete WAP service. The concept of VHE is shown in Figure 3.34 [32].

3.4.6.1 VHE elements

As shown in Figure 3.34, VHE looks at a layered architecture, so that services could be developed independently of their underlying network. The service layer includes different application servers. Each application within the service layer is developed inside a box, so that the contents of each box is not an important issue for the network designer, as long as the interfaces in and from the box are in accordance with those defined in the standard. Therefore, the third-party developers could develop new applications and they can still be used within the UMTS network. So we emphasize here that similar to the seven-layer OSI or the five-layer TCP/IP network reference models, in the new architecture of the UMTS it is not the detailed architecture that is standardized but it is the boxes and interfaces that are standardized.

The standardized OSA interfaces connect the service layer entities to the network layer. The network layer consists of several service capability servers (SCS). These are the servers that provide functionality used to construct services, such as MSC. Each SCS is composed of a service capability feature (SCF). SCFs are classes of the OSA interface. SCSs are network elements, whereas SCFs are merely additional software layers of interface classes on top of SCSs. Examples of SCFs are call control, location and positioning, and notifications. Several common SCSs are shown in Figure 3.34 and will be addressed later.

Each SCS is connected through an appropriate interface protocol to the transport network of the cellular network.

3.4.6.2 VHE SCS specifications

Figure 3.34 shows five typical SCSs, which are explained in detail in Reference [32]:

- *Call control* (CC) server: the MSC to support circuit-switched telephony using the 24.08 CC protocol (Release R99).
- *Home location register* (HLR) server: the database for location and subscriber information using an enhanced GSM-MAP (mobile application part).
- *Mobile execution environment* (MExE) server: used for value-added services through the WAP.
- *SIM application toolkit* (SAT) server: designed to offer additional capabilities to communications protocol between the UMTS-enhanced SIM and the mobile terminal.
- *Customized application for mobile networks–enhanced logic* (CAMEL) server: it extends the scope of IN (intelligent network) service provisioning to the mobile environment and is also used to exchange the mobile-specific service information between the CAMEL and the service switching point (SSP) and the service control point (SCP).

Additional SCSs are coming into the architecture as the network design progresses.

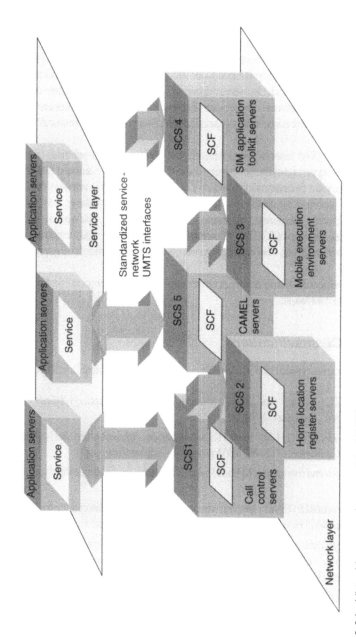

Figure 3.34 Virtual home environment for UMTS

3.5 SUMMARY AND CONCLUSIONS

In this chapter, we have provided a concise but comprehensive overview on the most popular cellular systems and their evolution path from the 2G to the 3G. GSM and its packet-switched successor, the GPRS, has been outlined. The enhanced features of the GPRS system are included in the EGPRS, which has found its migration path to the UMTS.

The discussions provided in this chapter reveal the fact that it is very essential for the future mobile systems to develop in accordance with the requirements of the new multimedia applications and their severe traffic and bandwidth requirements. In the next chapter, we will describe the requirements of the future generations of mobile communications and propose a layered architecture that could become a reference model for network architecture design in those systems. A primary form of such an architecture has been included in the UMTS. We discussed the OSA design and the concept of VHE in the UMTS. These concepts, in spite of having great benefits for the 3G service providers, will need further improvement in future.

Owing to the exponential increase in the usage of mobile communications, UMTS and other enhanced packet cellular networks need to increase the core network capacity by a factor of 10^6 in 10 years. Such a huge capacity increase would not be possible without the introduction of advanced technology in the new systems. Some of these technologies are

- plesiochronous digital hierarchy (PDH),
- synchronous digital hierarchy (SDH),
- wavelength division multiplexing (WDM),
- dense WDM (DWDM).

Discussion of the above technologies are outside the scope of this book, but we need to raise the issue that major improvement in core network technology has to be done in order to cope with the future traffic loads in the cellular networks. At this stage, the IP technology is considered as the most promising candidate that can achieve such an improvement. Therefore, introduction of IP in all segments of the cellular networks becomes a typical research theme. Whether IP can be the right choice or another technology can be created to replace it in future is an issue for which there is no resolution at this time.

REFERENCES

1. Redl SM, Weber MK & Oliphant MW, *An Introduction to GSM*, Artech House, Norwood, Mass., 1995.
2. Steele R, Lee C-C & Gould P, *GSM, cdmaOne and 3G Systems*, John Wiley & Sons, Chichester, West Sussex, England, 2001.

3. Institute of European Telecommunications Standards, Web site: http://www.etsi.org.

4. Rahnema M, Overview of the GSM system and protocol architecture, *IEEE Communications Magazine*, **31**(4), 92–100, 1993.

5. GSM 02.17 (ETS 300 509), European Digital Cellular Telecommunications System (Phase 2); Subscribers Identity Modules (SIM) Functional Characteristics.

6. GSM 05.04 (ETS 300 576), European Digital Cellular Telecommunications System (Phase 2); Modulation.

7. GSM 05.05 (ETS 300 577), European Digital Cellular Telecommunications System (Phase 2); Radio Transmission and Reception.

8. GSM 05.02 (ETS 300 574), European Digital Cellular Telecommunications System (Phase 2); Multiplexing and Multiple Access on the Radio Path.

9. GSM 05.03 (ETS 300 575), European Digital Cellular Telecommunications System (Phase 2); Channel Coding.

10. GSM 05.08 (ETS 300 578), European Digital Cellular Telecommunications System (Phase 2); Radio Subsystem Link Control.

11. ETSI TS 101 038 Version 5.0.1 (1997-04), Digital Cellular Telecommunications Systems (Phase 2+); High Speed Circuit Switched Data (HSCSD)-Stage 2 (GSM 03.34).

12. Furuskar A, Mazur S, Miller F & Olofsson H, EDGE: enhanced data rates for GSM and TDMA/136 evolution, *IEEE Personal Communications Magazine*, **6**(3), 56–66, 1999.

13. Furuskar A, Naslund J & Olofsson H, EDGE—enhanced data rates for GSM and TDMA/136 evolution, *Ericsson Review*, **1**, 1999.

14. Schramm P et al., Radio interface performance of EDGE, a proposal for enhanced data rates in existing digital cellular systems, *Proceedings of IEEE Vehicular Technology Conference, (VTC '98)*, Ottawa, Canada, May 1998, pp. 1064–1068.

15. Furuskar A, Frodigh M, Olofsson H & Skold J, System performance of EDGE, a proposal for enhanced data rates in existing digital cellular systems, *Proceedings of IEEE Vehicular Technology Conference, (VTC '98)*, Ottawa, Canada, May 1998, pp. 1284–1289.

16. Hamiti S, Hakaste M, Moisio M, Nefedov N, Nikula E & Vilpponen H, EDGE circuit switched data—an enhancement of GSM data services, *Proceedings of IEEE Wireless Communications and Networking Conference (WCNC '99)*, New Orleans, 1999.

17. ETSI TS 03.64 Version 5.1.0 (1997–2011), Digital Cellular Telecommunications Systems (Phase 2+); General Packet Radio Service (GPRS); Overall Description of the GPRS Radio Interface; Stage 2 (GSM 03.64, Version 5.1.0).

18. ETSI TS 03.60, Digital Cellular Telecommunications Systems (Phase 2+); General Packet Radio Service (GPRS); Service Description; Stage 2 (GSM 03.60, Version 7.1.1), 1998.

19. Cai J & Goodman D, General packet radio service in GSM, *IEEE Communications Magazine*, **35**(10), 122–131, 1997.

20. Brasche G & Walke B, Concepts, services, and protocols of the new GSM phase 2+ general packet radio service, *IEEE Communications Magazine*, **35**(8), 94–104, 1997.

21. Hoff S, Meyer M & Schieder A, A performance evaluation of Internet access via the general packet radio service of GSM, *Proceedings of the IEEE Vehicular Technology Conference '98*, 1998, pp. 1760–1764.

22. Bettstetter C, Vogel H-J & Eberspacher J, GSM phase 2+ general packet radio service GPRS: architecture, protocols, and air interface, *IEEE Communications Surveys*, Third Quarter, 1999, **2**(3), http://www.comsoc.org/pubs/surveys.

23. The European Telecommunications Standards Institute (ETSI), Web site: http://www.etsi.org.

24. Universal Mobile Telecommunications System (UMTS), Forum Web site: http://www.umts-forum.org.

25. The Third Generation Partnership Project, Web site: http://www.3gpp.org.

26. Holma H & Toskala A, *WCDMA for UMTS, Radio Access for Third Generation Mobile Communications*, John Wiley & Sons, Chichester, West Sussex, England, 2001.

27. Haardt M & Mohr W, The complete solution for third-generation wireless communications: two modes on air, one winning strategy, *IEEE Personal Communications Magazine*, December, 18–24, 2000.

28. Jamalipour A & Tekinay S (Eds), Guest Editors, Feature Topic of the *IEEE Communications Magazine on Next Generation Wireless Networks and Navigation Systems*, February, 2002.

29. Noerenberg II JW, Bridging wireless protocols, *IEEE Communications Magazine*, **39**(11), 90–97, 2001.

30. Patel G & Dennett S, The 3GPP and 3GPP2 movements toward and all-IP mobile network, *IEEE Personal Communications Magazine*, **7**(4), 62–64, 2000.

31. Adachi F & Sawahashi M, Challenges in realizing the multimedia mobile communications era: IMT-2000 and beyond, *Personal, Indoor and Mobile Radio Communications Conference (PIMRC '99)*, Osaka, Japan, 1999.

32. Bos L & Leroy S, Toward an all-IP UMTS system architecture, *IEEE Network*, **15**(1), 36–45, 2001.

33. Prasad R, Mohr W & Konhauser W, *Third Generation Mobile Communications Systems*, Artech House, Norwood, Mass., 2000.

34. Huber J, Weiler D & Brand H, UMTS—the mobile multimedia vision for IMT-2000: a focus on standardization, *IEEE Communications Magazine*, **38**(9), 129–136, 2000.

35. Chaudhury P, Moher W & Onoe S, The 3GPP proposal for IMT-2000, *IEEE Communications Magazine*, December, 72–81, 1999.

36. Mohr W & Konhauser W, Access network evolution beyond third generation mobile communications, *IEEE Communications Magazine*, **38**(12), 122–133, 2000.

4

Mobile Networks
of the Future

In this chapter, we complete our discussion on third-generation (3G) wireless system that
we had started in Chapter 3 by introducing the Universal Mobile Telecommunications
System (UMTS) family. IMT-2000 (International Mobile Telecommunications) standards
will be introduced and details on cdma2000 will be provided. We will see how these
systems would provide a harmonized solution to the wireless mobile Internet of the
future. Completing this discussion brings us to the question of what would be the next
after third-generation networks. We try to answer this question by investigating different
proposals from industry and academia. A functional layered architecture for the future
mobile Internet will be proposed and discussed finally in this chapter, which will pave
the way for the detailed discussions in the second part of this book.

4.1 IMT-2000

In the preceding chapter, we have described the European-based 3G system UMTS [1–5]
as an evolved cellular wireless system from the Global System for Mobile communications (GSM) [6] and its packet-switched predecessor system, General Packet Radio
Service (GPRS) [7–9]. The two modes of operation for the access technology in UMTS
were outlined as time division duplex (TDD) and frequency division duplex (FDD). The
International Mobile Telecommunications as the standard body within the International
Telecommunication Union (ITU) [10], however, has introduced more technologies for
the 3G wireless systems [11–13]. All these technologies come under the umbrella of the
IMT-2000 family, as shown in Figure 4.1. The '2000' in IMT-2000 has been interpreted

The Wireless Mobile Internet: Architectures, Protocols, and Services.   Abbas Jamalipour
© 2003 John Wiley & Sons, Ltd   ISBN: 0-470-84468-X

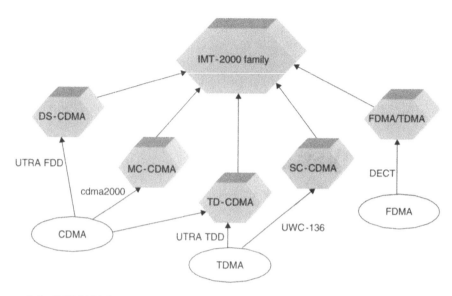

Figure 4.1   IMT-2000 family radio access technologies

in three different ways during the standard developments: As systems that are working at 2000 MHz bands; as systems that could provide data-bit-rate of 2000 Mbps; and finally as systems that are going to be completed by around the year 2000. It is now clear that the third interpretation is no longer valid.

One reason for describing the UMTS in particular in Chapter 3 was that UMTS will include the majority of population and geographical regions worldwide, but another reason was the basic similarities between UMTS and, for example, the cdma2000 [14], another 3G technology evolved from the North American second-generation (2G) system based on IS-95 [15–17] air interface used in cdmaOne cellular network [18,19]. Despite different system and architectural concepts of these two 3G technologies, the reader would find it straightforward to follow one system after understanding the other. As an example, the enhanced modulation schemes used first in the Enhanced Data rates for GSM Evolution (EDGE) [20–23] for GSM-based 2.5G systems could also be used in other cellular networks. As another example, in Figure 4.2 we have illustrated the cdma2000 architecture that is to be compared with the UMTS architecture shown in Figure 3.28 of Chapter 3. A very rough comparison between the two figures shows that both systems, though using different names for their access parts, provide similar connections to the public-switching telephony network and to the packet data networks such as Internet. The main difference would be in the core network elements used in each system. In a more detailed comparison, however, more differences would be discovered, as we will discuss shortly in this section.

4.1.1   IMT-2000 standards family

Let us go back to our discussion on Figure 4.1. According to this figure, the IMT-2000 standard family consists of five major technologies. The European UMTS covers two

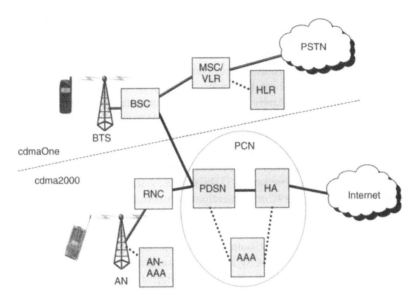

Figure 4.2 Network architecture for the cdma2000

of those standards, namely, the UTRA (Universal Terrestrial Radio Access) FDD and the UTRA TDD. UTRA FDD, as discussed in Chapter 3, is a wideband code division multiple access (CDMA) system designed to operate in paired frequency spectrum, that is, one band for uplink and one for downlink each occupy a minimum of 5 MHz (up to 60 MHz each) of the frequency spectrum in the 2-GHz band (see Figure 3.23 of Chapter 3 for details). Differentiation between uplink and downlink signals is provided by the FDD techniques, thus getting the title of UTRA FDD. Normal concepts of a direct-sequence spread spectrum CDMA (DS-CDMA) scheme are applied to the UMTS FDD.

Another mode of UMTS is called *UTRA TDD* in which only one frequency band is used for both uplink and downlink. Differentiation between the signals on uplink and downlink is provided by their separation in the time domain, that is, by allocating different time slots to uplink and downlink signal transmissions. UTRA TDD is basically used as a hybrid multiple access scheme by using both time and code to separate signals from each other. Therefore, this UMTS radio interface is also named as *time-division CDMA* (TD-CDMA)

European Telecommunications Standards Institute (ETSI) has also initiated the third member of the IMT-2000 family on the basis of its Digital European Cordless Telecommunications (DECT). This technology has originally been developed by ETSI for digital cordless telephony applications to be used in household cordless phones. DECT uses TDD and a hybrid combination of frequency division multiple access (FDMA) and time division multiple access (TDMA) as the multiple access schemes.

The North American cellular network was historically dominated by the CDMA as it was in personal communication systems known as IS-95 and later as cdmaOne. The CDMA was the main technology accepted for the 3G systems and thus cdmaOne could be evolved into a 3G system for North America. Especially, parts of the allocated 3G spectrum was already licensed to 2G operators and satellite systems in North America, and this could be another reason for having a 3G system in that region being evolved from the 2G cdmaOne system rather than being a completely new system. The voice-centric cdmaOne cellular system thus is needed to evolve so that it can accommodate data traffic at a bit rate of several times of that could be supported by the cdmaOne system. Therefore, cdma2000 as the 3G evolution of cdmaOne is recognized by the ITU as the fourth member of IMT-2000 family. cdma2000 has considered a multicarrier CDMA, different from DS-CDMA in UTRA FDD and TD-CDMA in UTRA TDD.

Because of the same reason of the unavailability of the 3G spectrum, already allocated to the 2G CDMA system in North America, it has been decided that an upgrade of the 2G TDMA system in North America, IS-136, is also necessary, and thus, the fifth member of IMT-2000 standard family became a TDMA-type system, called *UWC-136* from the names of the Universe Wireless Communications consortium and the 2G IS-136 standard. This new member of IMT-2000 has many similarities with the enhancements performed on the GSM system by the EDGE, in which particularly the data rate transmission per radio time slot has been increased compared to the original Gaussian minimum shift keying (GMSK) modulation scheme by additional usage of an 8-level phase shift keying (8-PSK) modulation. In UWC-136 the fact that at a high signal-to-noise ratio it is possible to increase the data rate without increasing the bit error rate is used. That is, by making the cells smaller, it is possible to get a higher signal-to-noise ratio and thus increase the data rates without high bit error.

In addition to the above standards, a synchronous TD-CDMA, called *TD-SCDMA*, for TDD applications of mobility and wireless local loops (WLL) can be considered as another 3G standard. The physical layer specification of the TD-SCDMA, however, is different from UTRA TDD. For example, UTRA TDD uses a 3.84-Mchips per second chip rate, whereas in TD-SCDMA the chip rate is 1.28 Mchips per second. This new access technology has been developed in conjunction with China's wireless telecommunications systems.

The works on completing the standardization of 3G systems are now followed by Third Generation Partnership Project (3GPP) and Third Generation Partnership Project 2 (3GPP2), as discussed in Chapter 2. Now other organizations also try to add new initiatives to the 3G standards in the form of harmonization and the mobile Internet.

4.1.2 cdma2000

The cdma2000 is North America's main 3G cellular wireless technology. It is an evolution from its predecessor CDMA-based system, cdmaOne, in which the IS-95 [15–17] air interface and the ANSI-41 [24] core network for signaling between base stations and base station controllers were used. The cdmaOne system is used for voice and low bit rate data communications. A later version of air interface standard IS-95B has been developed to increase the data rate of the cdmaOne system up to 64 Kbps. The system is used in several countries in Asia, particularly in South Korea, in addition to North America, and continually gains popularity specifically owing to lower power emission compared to the GSM system. Most services available in the GSM system in addition to voice such as short message service, short e-mail, call waiting, call holding, and call conferencing are also supported by the cdmaOne system. One reason for this could be the similarity between the core network of the two 2G cellular systems.

cdma2000 will be very similar to cdmaOne in its first stages, so that in the 1X version, it will be backward compatible with cdmaOne. However, it will provide twice the voice capacity as of its predecessor and data rates of up to 144 Kbps using the same frequency spectrum and a single carrier with a bandwidth of 1.25 MHz. It will support the always-on data transmission, as in GPRS. The second version of cdma2000, cdma2000 3X, will be the actual 3G standard that provides data rates of up to 2 Mbps using multicarrier CDMA technology. In the early stage, similar to the approach taken by UMTS, the cdmaOne will provide voice services and communications to the public-switched telephony network and the cdma2000 network will handle the data services and the communications with the packet data networks and the global Internet.

The cdma2000 architecture is shown in Figure 4.2, when it is cooperating with its predecessor network cdmaOne. Comparing this figure with Figure 3.28 (UMTS architecture), we can see that the cdma2000 packet core network (PCN) uses a packet data serving node (PDSN) in place of serving GPRS supporting node (SGSN) used in the UMTS core network. Different from UMTS in which the mobility management was handled by home location register (HLR) and was using signaling system number 7 (SS7), in the cdma2000 an extended version of Mobile IP is utilized for the purpose of mobility management. Thus, entities such as home agent (HA) and authentication, authorization, and accounting (AAA) familiar in the Mobile IP networks are seen in the cdma2000 network architecture. Mobile IP will be discussed in Chapter 10. As seen in the figure, in the case of cdmaOne the mobility management is handled by a similar method as in the GSM, that is, by utilizing HLR and VLR (visiting location register).

The foreign agent of the Mobile IP protocol, however, is not seen in Figure 4.2. The reason is that the PDSN acts as the Mobile IP foreign agent for providing the care-of address to cdma2000 mobiles and for decapsulating IP packets tunneled from the HA. As will be seen in Chapter 11, the link from the PDSN to mobile users is provided by a point-to-point protocol (PPP) modified for the Mobile IP usage.

Radio network consists of access nodes (AN) and mobile terminals connecting each other through the cdma2000 air interface. Each AN is connected to a packet control function (PCF) unit. AN and PCF in the cdma2000 are the equivalent network entities, respectively, to *Node B* and radio network controller (RNC) in the UMTS, explained in Chapter 3. Each AN may provide tasks related to user authentication, authorization, air interface accounting, and thus an AN-AAA is attached to the AN in Figure 4.2. More detailed discussions on these functions will be provided in Chapter 11.

cdma2000 will utilize the radio link protocol (RLP) type 3 [25] in its traffic channels to support CDMA data services. Having an octet stream transport service without being aware of the higher layer framing is the characteristic of the RLP type 3. RLP can significantly reduce the CDMA traffic channel's error rate. RLP utilizes negative acknowledgements (NACK) and a finite selective repeat protocol for its flow control. The fundamental concept of NACK and the selective repeat protocols can be found in almost all traditional data communications networks textbooks. The receiver uses NACK packets to recover any missing frame. Depending on the channel speed, in each physical layer of cdma2000 one or more RLP frames can be sent.

Before ending this section, we need to make two important conclusions after describing the cdma2000 architecture. The first conclusion is that now the reader should have a better understanding of our initial statement in this section. That is, by having a very rough comparison between the UMTS and cdma2000 system architecture, despite the usage of different radio access interface and network entities, both systems provide similar connections to the public-switching telephony network and to the packet data networks such as the Internet. Therefore, understanding of one system would be sufficient for the purpose of the content of this book.

The second conclusion is that during the explanation of cdma2000 core network functionality in this section, we have repeated many terms usually used in IP networks and not in cellular networks. This could be an indication of a more IP-friendly core network architecture utilized in the cdma2000 system than what we can see in the UMTS. Although both the 3G systems are developed as a result of increasing Internet applications and services and both promise to offer efficient and high-speed packet data and Internet services to mobile users, the cdma2000 would perform its Internet tasks more efficiently than the UMTS. We will discuss this issue in more detail in this chapter when reviewing the wireless Internet architectures.

For readers who are interested in IP data transport and signaling in cdma2000 and the role of Mobile IP in providing these core network functions and mobility management, Chapter 11 gives a detailed discussion. Chapter 10 also provides detailed description of the Mobile IP protocol.

4.1.3   IMT-2000 standards harmonization

The initial work on 3G systems was based on the idea of having a single air interface standard in all parts of the world so that there would be no complicated roaming issues as in the case of the 2G cellular system. This idea has changed soon after consideration of different requirements, services, and existing technologies deployed in different regions. The result was finally several standards as discussed in the previous section.

Other than having a different air interface used in GSM, CDMA, and IS-136 TDMA systems, the 3G systems were going to evolve from two different network standards, the GSM-MAP (mobile application part) and ANSI-41 [24]. These latter protocols are working at the core network of the cellular systems and thus could be independently evolved. This independent design approach has been decided by the ITU in the 3G systems. The ITU however specifies the protocols to be used between the core networks in the form of standardization of network-to-network interfaces (NNI) [24]. With this method it is possible that the users of two different networks roam from one network to another. Such an independent evolution at air interface and network levels for the 3G is illustrated in Figure 4.3.

The standard ITU air interface standards will be connected to either the evolved GSM-MAP network or the evolved ANSI-41 network. The air interfaces use different frequencies and physical layer specifications and even with the NNI consideration, it would be difficult for a user to roam using a handset designed for one system in hardware to another air interface network. The work on the development of software-defined

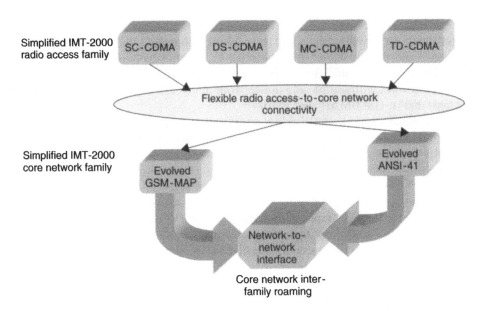

Simplified IMT-2000 radio access family

SC-CDMA   DS-CDMA   MC-CDMA   TD-CDMA

Flexible radio access-to-core network connectivity

Simplified IMT-2000 core network family

Evolved GSM-MAP

Evolved ANSI-41

Network-to-network interface

Core network inter-family roaming

Figure 4.3   Core network communications between different air interfaces

radio, which would allow the use of a unique handset hardware design even after roaming to another air interface, is going on [26,27]. An example of these activities for the UMTS terminals has been given in Section 3.4. It is notable that despite the long history of software-defined radio research, there is no final clue on whether this will solve the problem of internetwork roaming or not. The change of handset functionality by using different software implementations instead of hardware designs for cellular handsets is logically reasonable and promising but its practical feasibility would be another thing that requires further investigations.

In accordance to the above discussions on air interface standards and core network architecture diversity in third-generation systems, and the fact that the demand for the mobile users roaming into different networks used in different regions is increasing rapidly, some researchers have been looking at other methods for harmonizing the 3G standards. The ultimate goal would be to simplify the global user roaming, to provide connectivity to the evolved GSM-MAP and ANSI-41 core networks, and eventually to connect UTRA to an all-IP core network (to be discussed later).

In Reference [28] a comprehensive discussion on the harmonization of the 3G systems is provided. According to the discussion given in that paper, the third-generation harmonization will benefit the three groups involved in the new technology:

- Cellular network operators
- Cellular network and handset manufactures
- 3G cellular users

From a cellular network point of view, 3G harmonization minimizes the investment risk required during the development of the new cellular technology. It also provides compatibility and a smoother evolution from the existing 2G infrastructures, vastly deployed in almost all parts of the world. Any newly designed 3G core network, for example, and an all-IP core network, will also be able to interwork more easily with the 2G core network evolutions, that is, GSM-MAP and ANSI-41.

From a cellular network and handset manufacturer point of view, harmonization in diverse third-generation standards could reduce the research and development cost and efforts, which means a reduced final cost for the network services and handsets that will be passed to cellular users. This reduced cost will have a major role in the marketing of the 3G services, which has currently slowed down the telecommunications industry worldwide.

From a third-generation cellular user point of view, always the final service received from the network provider is the most important factor. The user looks at the quality of service (QoS) received from the network measured by the call dropping rate, the call blocking rate, the voice or data reception quality, and the service cost. A harmonized third-generation system will provide simpler roaming between regions, countries, and cellular systems, which are favorite aspects seen by the end users of any cellular system. Harmonization also reduces the retailer device cost and the provider service cost paid by the user.

All in all, it is clear that having a unique global cellular system that can provide the service requirements and telecommunications authorities regulations in all regions of the world is the ideal for third-generation systems and beyond. However, when such a unique standard is not feasible, either because of different local regulations in telecommunications or because of geographic and existing telecommunications infrastructure, harmonization would be an appropriate alternative.

4.2   BEYOND THIRD-GENERATION SYSTEMS

In Section 4.1 we have discussed different standards in the third-generation mobile networks and how they have been developed more or less as a kind of evolution from their respective predecessor networks. In the last part of that section the harmonization requirement for diverse 3G mobile systems has also been addressed. Since the 3G could not support the original idea of having a unique standard for all the regions of the world that simplifies the travelers' roaming between countries or internetwork roaming between heterogeneous networks, harmonizing the developed 3G systems would be considered as the first alternative solution.

Another solution to the shortcomings of the third-generation systems is of course to go for another generation development. Historically, each generation of the mobile communications requires around 10 years to be completed and if we assume this time as the completion year for the 3G systems (as it has started in a few countries), then initial system designs and proposal for the next-generation wireless networks, say the fourth generation, need to be started now.

The issue is, however, not as simple as it looks and the telecommunication industry does not have the same view in developing a new system as it was in the early 1990s when the work on 3G started. The 3G with all accompanied advanced technologies is struggling to gain a proper position within the mobile network in many countries and the situation would be similar for quite some time.

Despite the poor situation, recently researchers have started to look at what it would be after 3G. There is a fundamental difference of opinion about fourth-generation (4G) system—whether it would be a completely new system as for the 3G system or it would be a combination of existing networks. Even if we assume that the 4G will be a brand new system, we should think again when we see that its predecessor 3G systems despite being new will need to work in conjunction with second-generation networks for many years. This is firstly because of the vast deployment and investment in 2G cellular infrastructures all around the world and secondly because of the satisfactory services of the 2G systems both from a user's and from the service providers' point of view. 3G systems will provide additional services and Internet services that could not target all mobile users. Many 2G systems have already provided Internet and data service through Wireless Application Protocol (WAP), for example, to their users and thus the additional services to be provided by 3G would not be very much sensible to users.

4.2.1   4G mobile: Interconnecting networks

Having said that the situation for working on a next generation of mobile system is not as ready as it was when 3G was developed, researchers have already started proposing their ideas on what would be next. In recent years many technical papers and even a whole special issue of a magazine have been devoted to the work on this topic (see, for example, References [29–34]).

We cannot specifically state what 4G would be, but it is possible, on the basis of current observation on the telecommunication technology, to say what it would look like and what requirements are to be accommodated in such an advanced system.

In accordance with the experience from the 3G development in which first a single standard was targeted and eventually several standards had finalized it, the first thing that we can say is that it is very unrealistic to think that there will be a new single system to be named 4G. There are quite a few systems for modern communications and mobile environment that have outstanding features in their respective platforms. Wireless local area network (LAN), for example, provides a relatively high bit rate with cheap equipments for the wireless Internet needs. The wireless LAN technology both at the hardware and the software layers is improving over the years and as a result higher data rates of up to 54 Mbps are no longer a dream for mobile Internet users. The significant thing is that the price of this broadband data network is reasonable and a minimal infrastructure is needed.

The wired Internet is also enhancing and better Internet switches and routers with advanced routing technologies make it possible to go above the 100 Mbps into Giga-bit networks.

The voice-oriented second-generation cellular systems such as cdmaOne and GSM are increasing their services and the GPRS provides additional packet-switched data delivery on top of these enhanced features.

Third-generation cellular systems ultimately increase the network capacity for the voice and the bit rate for data applications and multimedia and Internet applications are becoming easily accessible over the mobile network.

Digital telephony and asynchronous digital subscriber line (ADSL) are following their own technology improvement and provide better services and more capabilities both for voice and for data traffics. On a global basis, new satellite systems provide direct audio and video broadcasting (DAB/DVB) and support the Internet services at broadband range to home and to office users (see Chapter 13).

Modern short-range connectivity networks such as Bluetooth and infrared networking have achieved outstanding performance again at reasonably low prices. Also, picocellular systems such as the Japanese PHS (personal handy phone system) and the European cordless digital system DECT offer good voice and data delivery to their respective mobile users.

Having all these modern and enhanced telecommunication technologies, it is reasonable to consider the next-generation mobile network as a platform to cover all these technologies and to utilize all their advantages so that the shortcomings of individual technologies could be complemented by other systems. Such a view is illustrated roughly in Figure 4.4.

We call this the 4G mobile network, rather than a wireless network. Mobility is not the same as wireless. Mobility means that the user can move around and use network services with seamless handoff between heterogeneous networks. Sometimes a mobile user could be physically fixed in one location and thus the user connection to the Internet through cables does not change his mobile nature.

This view is different from the one approached by the second- and the third-generation wireless cellular network designers. The wireless will become a part of the mobile network but not necessarily cover it all.

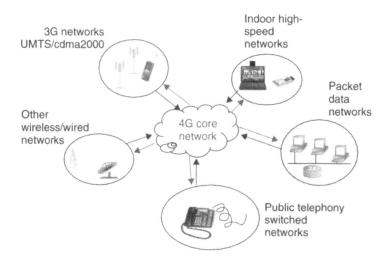

Figure 4.4   A view of the 4G mobile network

4.2.2 All-IP networks

Recently, there is a great interest in making the 3G networks and its immediate improvements, say 3G+, an all-IP network. This means that, owing to the great success of IP networks, it is desirable to expand the IP features not only in the core network but also right through the access network of the future wireless networks. Many literatures describe how such an all-IP network is achievable and we refer the reader interested in this topic to References [35–39]. Some people even name such full utilization of the IP features in 3G systems as the fourth generation.

Since, as we will see in Section 4.3, the future generation of mobile networks are application-driven, based dominantly on Internet and mobile Internet applications and services, an efficient support of these Internet-based services would not be possible without a core network totally based on IP. The GSM evolution toward an IP overlay to support GPRS and EDGE was therefore insufficient, as a circuit-switched architecture design still is behind the whole structure. Similarly, the access network needs to be changed into IP so that an end-to-end service could be efficiently provided by the mobile network.

The cdma2000 as discussed in the previous section has a better approach in this all-IP solution. The technologies constructing the cdma2000 such as its enhanced Mobile IP have an IP-friendly nature that can accommodate IP functions. In some research studies such as the European Union work in BRAIN project, an IP2W (IP to wireless) interface is developed that allows converging of the link layer and the IP layer, for example, an IP over the link layer Ethernet [40]. How the access network can accommodate IP functions and features is still an unsolved question though.

4.2.3 A modular approach toward 4G mobile

Following the discussion provided previously in this section, now we want to find a modular and logical approach toward a 4G mobile architecture. Nonetheless, we are not claiming that we will provide the final answer to the 4G structure, as still there is a long way to go until that time.

We have already mentioned that the fourth generation mobile network will potentially be a combined network of networks, which utilizes the advantages of all existing modern telecommunication technologies and will provide a common access platform to join those networks. Such a platform is shown in Figure 4.5. In this figure, the major telecommunication partners, such as 2G, 3G, wireless LAN, wired Internet, ADSL, and the telephony network, are included.

The networks shown in the figure are connected via a common media access network that supports the protocol translations required for internetworking of the heterogeneous networks. This could be achieved by the so-called interworking units (IWU) currently used, for example, in connecting a 2G system such as GSM to a 3G system such as UMTS. All the parts of this network will merge their connectivity functions through an IP-based core network. Through signaling and connectivity utilized in this core network, different networks can complement the services provided by other networks. A short

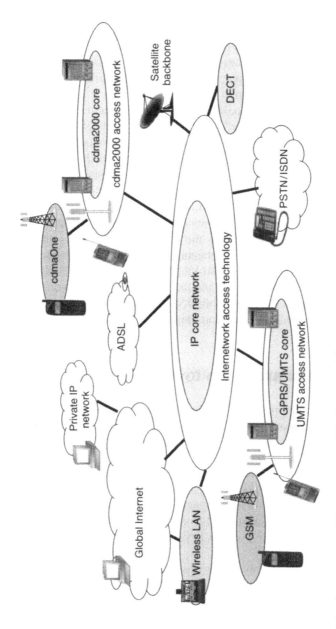

Figure 4.5 A network architectural view of the future mobile networks

version of this implementation is considered in 3G systems so that the hot spot traffics can be supported not by the cellular networks but by the wireless LAN inside buildings and campuses; so the proposed architecture in Figure 4.5 is not imaginary but is realistic. Note that satellite networks are also included in this figure so that global data communications between terrestrial networks and among users could be achieved too.

In order to achieve such internetworking principles in future mobile networks, both horizontal service handover among the systems of the same kind and vertical service handover among the systems of different type (as well as different generation) would be necessary. (A similar approach is discussed in Reference [12].) Different-generation cellular networks, for example, GSM/GPRS versus UMTS, can complement advantageous voice and data delivery of each other through a vertical service handover, whereas same-generation cellular systems, for example, cdmaOne and GSM, could cover regional roaming issues on a horizontal service handover basis. Figure 4.6 provides a close illustration of this handover services among heterogeneous networks.

Through such collaboration among networks of the same type or same generation and also among networks of different type or different generation, it will be possible to achieve a complete set of mobile Internet services in the future. Therefore, it will be possible to develop a new generation of mobile systems without a huge investment and a long research period being used, for example, in the case of third-generation systems. Different geographical coverage area offered by each network will complement the services so that a complete coverage could be possible. The satellites will provide global internetworking facilities among terrestrial cellular systems, and low-range systems such as wireless LAN and DECT will provide hot spot and indoor coverage to the wide-range cellular networks. Telephony network and ADSL provide further wired coverage to the Internet users and again complement the Internet services to less mobile users and to the broadband internetworking trunks connecting the core of the mobile systems.

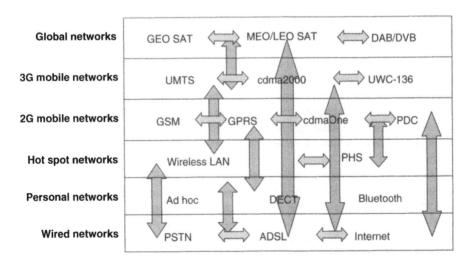

Figure 4.6 Two-dimensional internetworking in the future mobile network

4.2.4   Mobile wireless Internet forum

After the above discussion on the features of different standards in IMT-2000 family as well as how a new 4G network could be designed using the available modern telecommunications technology, it is worthwhile to introduce another activity sponsored by some related telecommunication industry toward a wireless Internet.

Mobile Wireless Internet Forum (MWIF) [41] was founded in the year 2000 as a nonprofit industry consortium to drive acceptance and adoption of a single, open, mobile wireless Internet architecture independent of access technology. Several Internet-related and telecommunications companies are the members of the MWIF consortium and they provide reports on studies and industrial directions for the future wireless Internet.

Very related to MWIF is the Operator Harmonization Group (OHG) founded in 1999 as an informal steering group of wireless operator companies dedicated to promoting 3G harmonization (see Section 4.1.3). OHG provides advice in harmonization areas to the appropriate standardization bodies and to other industry organizations. Its mission claims that OHG advices will improve the development of the wireless technologies so that they will be more efficient for both the industry and the consumers than their current status.

In order to achieve the goal of a single and access-technology-independent wireless Internet architecture, MWIF first summarizes and then compares the network architecture of the UMTS (3GPP) with that of cdma2000 (3GPP2) and tries to put the elements of the network architecture of each system into four layers of application, service, control, and transport. By recognizing the gaps still available in the two 3G network architectures, MWIF tries to propose its own architecture built on the fundamentals taken from the two standards, but incorporating some modifications to fill the gaps of the previous two architectures.

In accordance to the MWIF reports available from its web site [41], a summary of gaps between the two 3G systems is provided in this section. MWIF mentions the legacy network support and the mobility support as the areas with the largest gaps between 3GPP and 3GPP2 architectures. Since the two systems have been developed on the basis of different 2G systems using completely different signaling and database mechanisms, specific and complex internetworking protocols would be needed to support legacy networks. Also, it is said that the mobility support in the 3GPP architecture has to be improved by alternative techniques such as the Mobile IP protocol.

MWIF mentions several other gaps between the 3GPP and 3GPP2 architectures as significant. These include a common mechanism for geographic location across the networks and the lack of a more formalized AAA infrastructure in 3GPP architecture. Also, QoS mechanisms and control flow in an access-independent manner is stated as an area with a workable gap.

In a recent technical report, MWIF proposes its OpenRAN architecture as a radio access network (RAN) architecture characterized by being open, flexible, distributed, and scalable [42]. Open means that the proposed architecture defines standardized interfaces in major parts of the previous (3G) architectures where they were closed and proprietary. This will assist the network to be developed easier and faster as it happened for the global Internet as an open architecture. Accepting the available technologies toward development of the proposed architecture provides flexibility to the MWIF OpenRAN. By breaking the network elements of the previous architectures into functional entities, the proposed architecture becomes distributed. Design of the core network independent of the access network will be provided by defining standard interfaces between the core and the access networks. The technical report [42] provides a comprehensive discussion on functional entities in the MWIF OpenRAN architecture and how this architecture can be interfaced to the 3GPP and 3GPP2 architectures.

In another technical report [43], MWIF provides recommendations on how IP networks and protocols can be applied as the transport technology for the RANs in 3G mobile systems. The 3G RAN architectures or the radio control protocols will not be changed as the IP is only considered as a transport option over the RAN internal interfaces. Technical assessment on the viability of IP transport in the RAN, applicable IP protocols, 3G RAN traffic models, and some simulation results carried out by different companies for IP protocol delay and other performance measures are provided in this report. The report concludes that IP in the RAN is a viable option when considering delay and bandwidth efficiency factors.

In Reference [44] MWIF proposes a layered functional architecture to serve as the basis for the development of the forum's network reference model. Without detailing the layered architecture, which the reader can find in Reference [44], here we summarize the main parts of the architecture. The architecture consists of four logical layers, namely, application, service, control, and transport. These layers are communicated to each other through application programming interfaces (API). Also, some functional elements such as operations, administration, management, and provisioning (OAM&P) as well as security span several layers. The MWIF layered functional architecture is shown in Figure 4.7.

In the application layer, services provided to end users by the third parties, who do not own the service layer and are not under the direct administrative control of the network operator, are included. Service layer provides service control to the end users and other requirements for the effective operation of the control and the transport layers. Policy server, directory services, and name servers are included in functional elements of the service layer. The control layer consists of functionality necessary for the control of the IP transport such as authentication, accounting, mobility management, resource management, and address management. The transport layer provides the IP bearer and signaling transport from the user to the core network. It includes both access network–specific functional elements and access-independent core network elements. The core network functional elements in the transport layer are the network gateways and their controllers. Media gateways, inter/intranet gateways, and signaling gateways are included in network gateways. Media gateway is connected to the public-switching telephony networks (PSTN) or an external circuit-switched network, inter/intranet gateway is connected to an external IP network, and signaling gateways are connected to legacy 2G networks and other signaling networks. OAM&P consists of all necessary functions for provisioning, maintenance, operation, and administration of a network and is responsible for ensuring proper operation of network transport, control, and service infrastructure. It performs configuration management, fault management, performance management, billing management, and security management.

In summary, the MWIF architecture adopts existing or evolving IPs defined by Internet Engineering Task Force (IETF) to extend wireless support services, interoperate with other

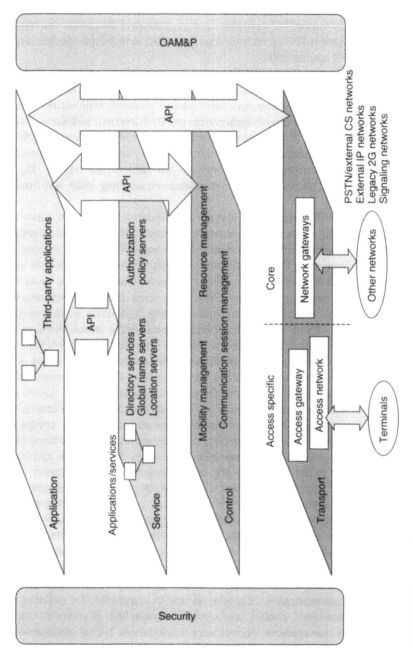

Figure 4.7 MWIF layered functional network architecture

next-generation fixed or mobile networks, and interoperate with media gateways such as the legacy networks and the telephony networks [45]. The MWIF approach is thus very similar to the all-IP architecture. It is also a similar concept to what we have discussed in the previous parts of this section and thus emphasizes on industry activities toward our outlined future mobile networks beyond the 3G.

MWIF considers some guidelines to achieve this goal. Firstly, it tries to extend the Internet technology across the IP layer in access networks and core networks for both transport and control. Secondly, it tries to change relevant specifications and protocols of 3GPP, 3GPP2, and IETF to meet the MWIF requirements. This includes extension of IP-based signaling and transport beyond the core network into the RAN while respecting the need for spectrum efficiency in the RAN. Support for connectivity from an IP-based mobile subscriber to any other hosts, subscribers, and web sites on the Internet shall be considered. Network address translation (NAT) is not considered as a fundamental part of the MWIF architecture, but the IP version 6 (IPv6) should be supported extensively in the MWIF architecture together with the inclusion of compatibility with IP version 4 (IPv4) networks and devices in the MWIF architecture. In Section 4.4 we will propose our own layered network architecture for future wireless mobile Internet and the reader can compare the industry-initiated harmonized architecture considered by MWIF with the one we propose.

4.3 FUTURE MOBILE INTERNET APPLICATIONS

User applications were the driving wheels for the exponential increase in the popularity of the Internet. As discussed in Chapter 1, the Internet network development progress was very slow in the beginning when there was only remote machine access and simple file transfers of file transfer protocol (FTP) type and e-mail. It was the World Wide Web (WWW) application that accelerated the use of Internet to an uncontrollable level by this time and it is still growing even faster than it was in the past.

Although remote access and file transfer applications were interesting capabilities given to the small number of Internet users in the early 1990s, they have been incorporated in future applications written under more user-friendly operating systems (OS) such as Microsoft Windows platform, so that more users, even unspecialized people, could use them in their daily life. The invention of the hypertext markup language (HTML) and the respective application protocol, hypertext transfer protocol (HTTP), as well as the availability of modern, simpler-to-use web browsers such as Netscape and Microsoft Internet Explorer has speeded up the full usage of the global Internet and the development of network architecture elements such as LAN technologies, routers, and Internet switches. These are the facts we cannot ignore during the development of the wired Internet. Still after almost one decade there are new applications for multimedia data transmission over the Internet, Internet telephony, Internet videoconferencing, and many others that come to the market and attract more subscribers for the Internet service providers. Electronic commerce and Internet online shopping are the newest types of applications that are becoming popular.

If we accept the above facts, we could say that the Internet is an application-driven technology and business. This is irrespective of the access network technology, that is, whether it is a twisted pair telephone line that provides a low 33-Kbps speed to the dial-up users, an ADSL that provides a dedicated high-speed Internet access of around 1 Mbps, a hybrid cable modem system that provides a shared high-speed Internet access up to 1 Mbps, a LAN Ethernet connection of 10 or 100 Mbps, or any other access technology. The role of speed will become important as a secondary factor for users, who use the Internet applications very frequently.

Therefore, if the wired Internet was an application-driven technology, we cannot ignore the similar fact for the wireless mobile Internet. The wireless mobile Internet will follow the same pattern as that for the development of the wired Internet, maybe with a more accelerated speed as a result of more applications and more opportunities available now compared to the time the wired Internet was being developed.

The mobile Internet applications consist of not only those applications that have a mobile nature but also the traditional wired Internet applications. This makes another accelerating factor in the wireless mobile Internet compared with its predecessor, the wired Internet. Mobile audio- and videoconferencing and navigation services are, for example, included in the wireless mobile Internet list of applications, which is already flooded with numerous applications that have migrated from the wired Internet network.

In conclusion, the wireless mobile Internet has to be independent of its underlying access technology and the core network supporting it has to be sufficiently flexible and scalable. We will discuss in the next section on how such an independency from the underlying access technology could be achieved in future mobile networks. But before that we need to explore the mobile applications a little further.

Figure 4.8 tries to illustrate and categorize the most predictable applications for the future wireless mobile Internet networks. The list is by no means complete and no one

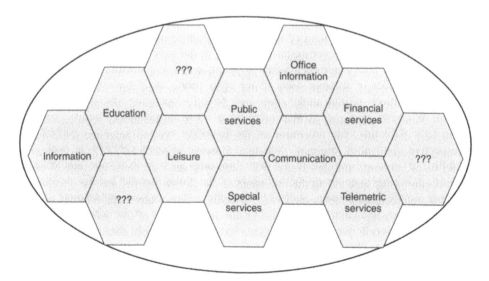

Figure 4.8 Application examples in the future mobile networks

can claim to provide a complete list as the applications are invented everyday and added to the list. Some have major inventory ideas, whereas some give minor modifications to previously available applications. Thus we put some question marks on the cells of the applications list shown in Figure 4.8. In the following, we briefly list and explain current examples of these applications with the prediction of their usage either in the wireless Internet or in the wired Internet.

- *Information*: Internet surfing, intelligent information searching and filtering agent, online media, online translation service, local information such as hotel, hospital, doctors, and weather forecast, booking and reservation, and news are the examples of applications currently used intensively within the wired Internet. These services are required to be supported more or less by the future mobile Internet. Usual reliable data transfer is sufficient for these applications, but faster data delivery speed would be desirable.

- *Education*: Virtual school, online laboratories, online library, online training, and remote consultation are some of the educational examples in the usage of the Internet. Depending on the amount of data and the desired format of receiving the information (e.g. to be easily readable on the screen monitor), some of these could be mainly limited to the wired Internet. In smaller data deliveries, mobile Internet would be also used.

- *Leisure*: Virtual bookstore, music on demand, games on demand, video clips, virtual sightseeing, entertainment and theme park information, and lottery services are the examples of this Internet application category. Although they can be used in both wired and wireless Internet networks, they are potentially favorite mobile applications.

- *Public services*: Public elections and voting, public information, help, broadcast services, and online yellow and white page services are potentially attractive in both wired and wireless Internet networks.

- *Special services*: Security services, hot line, and telemedicine are some examples of this category and are potential traffic generators of the mobile Internet networks.

- *Office information*: Virtual working groups, mobile office, teleworking, schedule, and data book synchronization are mostly desirable for mobile users rather than the users of the wired Internet.

- *Communications*: Video telephony, videoconferencing, speech and lecturing, e-mail, service announcements, short message services, and electronic postcards are examples that might be used in both wired and wireless networks. However, in case a reliable and cost-effective mobile Internet service is available, users would prefer it than using the wired Internet.

- *Financial services*: Online banking, universal credit card services, home shopping, and stock quotes and trading are applications popular for both wired and wireless Internet but again could be more desirable if used in a mobile environment.

- *Telemetric services*: Location-based tracking services such as GPS (global positioning system), navigation assistance, travel information, fleet management, and remote diagnostics are some of the telemetric services that are to be provided to the mobile users and therefore they are most suitable in a wireless mobile Internet.

4.3.1 Common Internet applications

Some of the applications (as mentioned above) would be common for both wired and wireless mobile Internet. However, mobile access would provide more availability and thus popularity to these common Internet applications. These applications will have significant impact on the development of the mobile Internet toward a more practical network architecture as the users can feel any difference between the usages of these applications in the two environments. For example, if an application requires a fast bit rate or another quality metric such as reliability, then the wireless mobile Internet should compete with its wired counterpart. The topic for the next chapter is QoS.

4.3.2 Mobile only applications

Although some applications can be used in both wired and wireless Internet networks, they have a mobile feature nature. The user of these applications would have less chance to compare the performance of the mobile Internet with the wired counterpart. However, still the user will require a certain level of quality from the services provided by the mobile network associated with these applications. As a result, the wireless mobile Internet has to accommodate these service qualities during the course of development until a satisfactory service becomes available.

4.4 LAYERED ARCHITECTURE FOR THE FUTURE MOBILE INTERNET

In the previous sections of this chapter, we have looked at the future mobile data networks architecture using different methodologies. First, we had another look at the IMT-2000 standards family and tried to find out the conceptual differentiating features among these standards. We also discussed the cdma2000 network architecture and its advanced features in providing a platform for the future wireless mobile Internet. Harmonization of the 3G systems has been addressed to emphasize the need for simpler and more flexible user roaming among heterogeneous networks.

Later, characteristics of the networks beyond 3G have been introduced and the activities within the MWIF for harmonizing the 3G systems and also providing a unique platform for the mobile Internet have been outlined. The future mobile networks have been later named as being application-driven.

In this section, we try to move away from the industry directions and pave the path for our discussions on specific technical issues toward realization of wireless mobile Internet to be given in Part 2 of this book. A generic picture of wireless Internet thus will be given followed by a practical and functional layered architecture of the future wireless mobile Internet.

4.4.1 Approaching the mobile Internet

The mobile Internet architecture can be simplified into the two major segments: the core network and the access network, as shown in Figure 4.9. The access network provides all radio or wireline access communications between the mobile terminal and the rest of the network, starting from an access point or an AN. The core network includes network entities responsible for routing the packets within the local network and also between the local access network and other packet data networks including the global Internet. Signaling between these network entities are also included in the core network task list. As mentioned in the previous section, in an ideal case, it would be most desirable to have both segments implemented using IP technologies.

In recent years many researchers have devoted their work on how such a mobile Internet could be implemented, either through the use of advanced features offered by the third-generation systems or by utilizing new techniques as well as improvement in the existing techniques such as Mobile IP (see, for example, References [46–52]). Some literatures such as References [48–50] try to approach the mobile Internet by introducing core and access networks of the 3G systems and utilizing their features. Some others such as References [51,52] try to treat the mobile Internet using routing algorithms such as Mobile IP and other initiatives. These latter works have tried to solve the issue by finding the answer within the network layer and in particular by enhanced internetworking routing techniques.

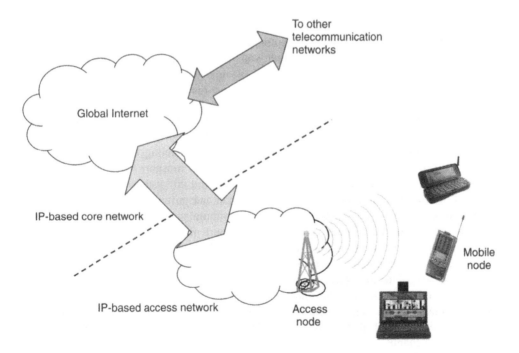

Figure 4.9 The mobile Internet

In a broader sense, the wireless mobile Internet issue needs to be addressed as an end-to-end problem, as many user applications require reliability in packet delivery as well as flow control, congestion control, and sufficient bandwidth allocation on an end-to-end semantic. Therefore, albeit the network layer has an outstanding role in achieving such an end-to-end service provision, there are other parts within the protocol stack that need sufficient attention.

Transport layer, because of its important position in transporting the data packets in networks, for example, is one of those parts that need special attention. Application layer protocols also need enhancements in order to achieve a reliable wireless Internet. Enhancements in link layer and physical layer protocols will reduce the dependency of the end-to-end Internet data delivery to the transport layer functionality by providing wiredlike performance of the wireless channel, but this would be a long way to come. Therefore, we need to address all layer protocols to achieve our wireless Internet goal, which is the subject of this section in summary and the six chapters included in Part 2 in detail.

4.4.2 Layered architecture

The future networks will have two pushing parameters. The first one is the traffic generated from different user applications, as discussed in Section 4.3, and the second one is the enabling access technologies, introduced in Section 4.1 and Chapter 3, for example. The transmission of data traffic over the telecommunications networks has already taken over the voice traffic volume in several countries and is going to be a common case for all networks around the world. This is a direct result of the popularity of Internet-based applications in recent years and the exponential trend in increasing the usage of the Internet. The voice communications, which was the dominant part of traffic until the last decade, will soon become an option and will occupy just a small fraction of the entire global telecommunications traffic volume. Thus, in order to transport the data-dominant telecommunications traffic, a data-friendly protocol such as IP would be required.

In such a network, voice or other continuous-rate traffics must be transported first by using encapsulation and tunneling techniques and ultimately by using enhanced analog-to-digital encoding algorithms. The GPRS approach in tunneling IP packets within the cellular packet structure and voice-over-IP techniques to transport voice traffic over the Internet are examples of the former approach. Therefore, all system parameters must be designed in order to efficiently transmit discrete data and provide QoS to these data-type traffics. Appropriate quality in voice traffic transportation (such as limited delay and delay variation) then must be provided under data transport platform, which could sometime put strict restrictions on the whole network design. Figure 4.10 illustrates this trend in future mobile telecommunication networks in a summarized format.

Enabling access technologies, such as wireless cellular and wireless LAN, also are required optimization for discrete data transmission rather than the traditional trends in voice-oriented systems. Sophisticated smart antenna design as well as source and channel coding algorithms will all be required for data transmission efficiency, and bandwidth utilization and channel capacity are described for bit transmissions. Figure 4.11 illustrates this part of the layered network architecture of the future mobile networks.

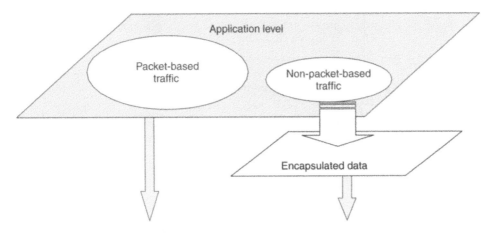

Figure 4.10 Application level in the architecture of the future mobile networks

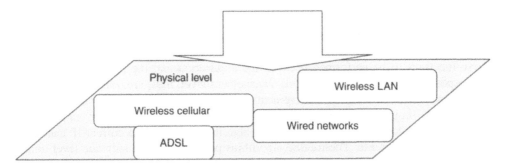

Figure 4.11 Physical level in the architecture of the future mobile networks

A full incorporation between existing modern access technologies in wired and wireless networks is necessary to achieve the reliable end-to-end data transportation in these future networks. Same-generation and different-generation wireless networks will work together in a horizontal and vertical cooperation, as discussed in Section 4.2.3, in order to complement the services of each other. For hot spot traffic handling and indoor broadband services, wireless LAN and wired networks such as LANs and ADSL will assist the wireless cellular systems to achieve their goal in providing a complete service. Not shown in the figure, the satellite networks will also be there to provide internetworking among heterogeneous networks as well as to individual mobile users where terrestrial networks are absent through direct broadcasting and direct user-satellite communications.

The internetworking among these different access technologies, while provided by some core network elements such as interworking function servers, needs to be handled at the network level. Therefore, between the two levels shown in Figures 4.10 and 4.11, that is, application and access levels, this is the network layer that needs to manage all the features that are to be provided to the applications under circumstances, restrictions, and limitations of the physical layer. We call this layer the network management level, shown

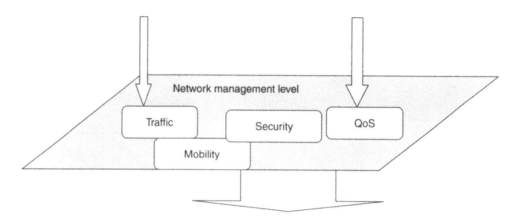

Figure 4.12   Network management level in the architecture of the future mobile networks

in Figure 4.12, and emphasize the fact that it has a vital role in the realization of future mobile networks.

The tasks to be performed by the network management level are endless, but we can say that this architectural level is responsible for all management tasks and cooperative functions to be performed between the application and the physical levels. The most important elements of the network management level, thus, are traffic management, mobility management, security management, and QoS management. The volume of the data traffic to be transported through the core network is increasing very rapidly and thus the question here is whether the routing algorithms used in the current IP can cope with such a huge increase. The routing algorithms performed at the software level in the routers could produce unacceptably long latency in the future networks, and removing the fast asynchronous transfer mode (ATM) switches and giving all responsibilities to the IP routers can intensify this latency. However, with the new traffic management techniques (e.g. queue scheduling, admission control, distributed multiqueue systems) deployed at IP routers, it is possible to increase the processing speed of the datagrams at the router and decrease the latency in the network.

The functional architecture shown in Figure 4.13 will have essential burden on the network management level but requires minimum dependency on the limitations and restrictions imposed by the physical access level. The architecture is also scalable to the new applications that will come into the mobile Internet services, as it does not specify the service itself but the traffic generated by that application. The former provides independency in architectural design—an important factor for the future mobile Internet networks.

Research on mobility and security management within the fixed and mobile IP platform have been started many years ago but still needs more achievements in order to be used in the core network. The route optimization and hierarchical mobile agent techniques, to be discussed in Chapter 10, are the examples of these activities but many other similar or revolutionary approaches are needed for achieving this goal.

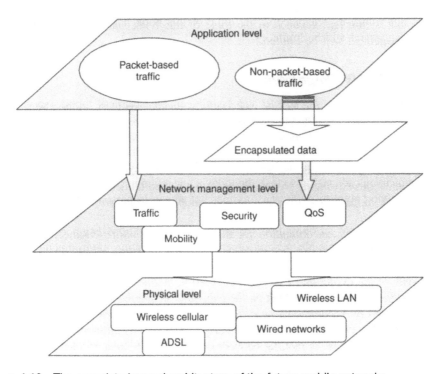

Figure 4.13 The complete layered architecture of the future mobile networks

If appropriate traffic and mobility management techniques are developed and employed in the system, then we can consider the possibility of having perceived QoS in heterogeneous mobile IP networks. The traffic management techniques will provide the assurance of the availability of capacity (e.g. by means of reservation protocols such as resource reservation protocol, RSVP) after roaming a user terminal from a network to another (or from one cell to another cell in a cellular network). The QoS metrics will, however, remain as flexible parameters when the roaming from indoor to outdoor environment and wired to wireless access are considered in future mobile networks.

4.4.3 Network management level

In the previous section, we have named mobility, traffic, and QoS managements as the fundamental functional elements inside the network management level of the future mobile networks. These topics will be covered in the following four chapters because of their vital importance to the realization of the future wireless mobile Internet, and more generally to all telecommunications networks. Security management though shown at the network management level in Figure 4.13 should be considered at all levels in the layered architecture. Accordingly, security management will be discussed in several parts of this book but within its relevance to the topic of this book and thus the discussion on security management will be limited.

4.4.3.1 Mobility management

Mobility management is the key to successfully enable seamless mobile services. Its process can be largely divided into three steps, namely, location management, routing management, and handoff management. As a very rough overview, we will be looking at the problem of finding the moving mobile node's location and delivering data packets, destined for it, along the best route. With technology in the twenty-first century telecommunications advancing so fast, the today's telecommunication challenge no longer provides satisfying point-to-point transmissions but person-to-person and person-to-device communications.

This in turn brought an obligation for the telecommunications engineers and service providers to supply a reliable person-to-person communicating environment, in which frequent user mobility is not an exception but a criterion that needs to be incorporated into the path of the evolution of the next-generation mobile communication systems.

Mobility implies adaptability, that is, the capability of maintaining any established network connections by accommodating different system characteristics when a mobile user roams within and between networks. Particularly, it refers to the initiation of a handoff process, not only when a user is moving between cells (as in a cellular wireless environment) but also when a user is roaming from one communication network to another.

It is widely agreed that to allow seamless user mobility, several considerations are necessary to ensure smooth transitions between different wireless technologies. Ultimately, it is essential to develop a mobility managing mechanism that can accommodate the many deficient service offerings encountered when a user roams in various systems. For example, the capability of tolerating the dramatic change in data bit rate when a subscriber migrates from a university campus network, which supports only local-area mobility, to a cellular mobile data environment, in which the provision of wide-area mobility becomes necessary.

The term *mobility management* has been conventionally understood as simply routing packets from the source to their intended destinations, and hence, the cascaded procedures of location, routing, and handoff management as it was previously defined in the literature. However, such an assumption becomes somehow inadequate as more and more irresolvable issues gradually become apparent.

To be able to critically identify the actions necessary to promote seamless user roaming, the criteria being imposed on the network should be considered. Some of these concerns include an appropriate registration into a service directory, a fast connection setup, and also the internetworking capabilities between various technologies.

4.4.3.2 Traffic management

Burst traffic and stringent QoS constraints characterize data transmission. This gives rise to traffic management issues in order to obtain high network utilization and QoS guarantee to the data stream.

The explosive growth of the Internet over the past few years combined with the ever-increasing demand for mobility offer many opportunities and challenges to the research community. Among these challenges is the area of traffic management. Given its complexity, traffic management in wireless data networks has not received much attention. At present, the work related to traffic management is one of the several unfilled gaps in the areas related to wireless mobile Internet.

Traffic management is the set of policies and mechanisms used to control traffic in a network in order to obtain high network utilization, avoid network congestion, and provide acceptable service quality. It spans multiple issues from scheduling, shaping, and flow control to bandwidth allocation and admission control and congestion control. We will discuss the traffic issues in a mobile environment in Chapters 6 and 7.

4.4.3.3 *Quality of service management*

QoS is an important issue that should be discussed in conjunction with the environment that we are working on and is always limited within a range. In general, in a layered network model, QoS is an appropriate performance level of the service that a layer is capable of delivering to a higher layer. Here, performance refers to such underlying network characteristics as bandwidth, delay, delay variance, and error rate. For example, transmission control protocol (TCP) as a transport protocol guarantees an error-free delivery of data packets but makes no guarantees with respect to bandwidth and delay. In a cellular telephony network in which voice communication has a higher priority than data communications, QoS must guarantee mainly delay and delay variance requirements. Thus, it is completely meaningless to discuss the QoS without specifying the environment in which we want these requirements to be guaranteed. The QoS in each environment can be also defined by the applications that are supported in that environment. When a cellular system with the major application of real-time voice communication is considered, then delay and delay variance become the main metric of QoS. However, when a mobile computing environment with the dominant application of non-real-time data file transfer is discussed, error-free transmission of data packets would be the main QoS metric. On the basis of new applications, there are always possibilities to define new QoS metrics.

The management of the system resources becomes more complicated as we move from simple voice or data services in the network into multiservice networks. Moreover, because of certain limitations in portable computers, such as restriction of battery life, screen size, and connection cost, management of delivering the required QoS in a mobile environment becomes even more complicated.

Besides the complexity of QoS management for multimedia applications compared to simple voice or data services, the mobility in a mobile computing environment produces new complexities and difficulties in providing the required QoS to end users. Moreover, as the required data rate, amount of traffic, and amount of data varies significantly in a multiservice network compared with a single-service one, we need to have much more sophisticated expectation calculations to define the QoS requirement both for real-time and non-real-time traffics in a mobile computing environment.

4.5 SUMMARY AND CONCLUSIONS

Discussion on fundamental architecture and issues in next-generation mobile networks toward the wireless mobile Internet was the main topic of this chapter. The standards family of the IMT-2000 has been explained and after discussing the cdma2000 access and core network architecture, a comparative study with the UMTS was provided. The cdma2000 network has been detailed in order to recognize its IP-friendly architectural features so that we can get to know the future wireless mobile Internet. Future mobile Internet applications have been briefed so that we could conclude that the future mobile networks and on top of them the wireless mobile Internet are applications- and services-driven.

A functional layered architecture for the future wireless mobile Internet has been proposed as the conclusion to this chapter so that we can start our detailed discussions on particular topics of interest in the next six chapters in Part 2.

The main part of this layered architecture has been considered to be the network management level that supports the traffic generated by the user applications given the boundary limitations of different access technologies available to the telecommunication systems. The proposed layered architecture could be the only way for facilitating research and development toward handling the increasing data traffic and accommodating the new application services in future mobile networks. IP connectivity however requires more enhancements in mobility management, traffic arrangement, and QoS management areas in order to completely take over the position of previous fast packet switching networks such as ATM. The layered architecture provides simpler treatment for the necessity of making the mobile core network independent from the underlying access technology than those provided in the third-generation systems such as UMTS and cdma2000. It also provides a framework for works on utilizing all available access technologies such that they can complement the service shortcomings of each other and also provide simpler, more flexible mobile user internetworking roaming. The layered architecture also provides a solution to the scalability problem in future Internet networks. All these issues are vital and need some solutions before a reliable and practical wireless mobile network could be realized on a geographically global basis. In the following parts of this book, we will explore these issues in more detail so as to cover these network requirements.

REFERENCES

1. The Universal Mobile Telecommunications System (UMTS), Forum Web site: http://www.umts-forum.org.
2. The European Telecommunications Standards Institute (ETSI), Web site: http://www.etsi.org.
3. The Third Generation Partnership Project (3GPP), Web site: http://www.3gpp.org.
4. Huber JF, Weiler D & Brand H, UMTS—The mobile multimedia vision for IMT-2000: a focus on standardization, *IEEE Communications Magazine*, **38**(9), 129–136, 2000.

5. Chaudhury P, Moher W & Onoe S, The 3GPP proposal for IMT-2000, *IEEE Communications Magazine*, **37**(12), 72–81, 1999.
6. Rahnema M, Overview of the GSM system and protocol architecture, *IEEE Communications Magazine*, **31**(4), 92–100, 1993.
7. Cai J & Goodman DJ, General packet radio service in GSM, *IEEE Communications Magazine*, **35**(10), 122–131, 1997.
8. Brasche G & Walke B, Concepts, services, and protocols of the new GSM phase 2+ general packet radio service, *IEEE Communications Magazine*, **35**(8), 94–104, 1997.
9. Bettstetter C, Vogel H-J & Eberspacher J, GSM phase 2+ general packet radio service GPRS: architecture, protocols, and air interface, *IEEE Communications Surveys*, **2**(3), Third Quarter, 1999, http://www.comsoc.org/pubs/surveys.
10. The International Telecommunication Union (ITU), Web site: http://www.itu.int (see also http://www.itu.int/imt for IMT-2000).
11. Harrison F & Holley K, The development of mobile is critically dependent on standards, *BT Technology Journal*, **19**(1), 32–37, 2001.
12. Haardt M & Mohr W, The complete solution for third-generation wireless communications: two modes on air, one winning strategy, *IEEE Personal Communications Magazine*, December, 18–24, 2000.
13. Prasad R, Mohr W & Konhauser W (Ed.), *Third Generation Mobile Communications Systems*, Artech House, Norwood, Mass., 2000.
14. The Third Generation Partnership Project 2 (3GPP2), Web site: http://www.3gpp2.org.
15. Viterbi AJ, *CDMA Principles of Spread Spectrum Communications*, Addison-Wesley, Reading, Mass., 1995.
16. Gilhousen KS, Jacobs IM, Padovani R, Viterbi AJ, Weaver LA & Wheathley III CE, On the capacity of a cellular CDMA system, *IEEE Transactions on Vehicular Technology*, **40**(2), 303–312, 1991.
17. Prasad R, *CDMA for Wireless Personal Communications*, Artech House, Norwood, Mass., 1996.
18. Larsson G, Evolving from cdmaOne to third generation systems, *Ericsson Review*, **2**, 58–67, 2000.
19. Prasad R & Ojanpera T, An overview of CDMA evolution toward wideband CDMA, *IEEE Communications Surveys*, **1**(1), Fourth Quarter, 1998, http://www.comsoc.org/pubs/surveys.
20. Furuskar A, Naslund J & Olofsson H, EDGE—enhanced data rates for GSM and TDMA/136 evolution, *Ericsson Review*, **1**(1), 1999.
21. Schramm P et al., Radio interface performance of EDGE, a proposal for enhanced data rates in existing digital cellular systems, *Proceedings of IEEE Vehicular Technology Conference, (VTC '98)*, Ottawa, Canada, May 1998, pp. 1064–1068.
22. Furuskar A, Frodigh M, Olofsson H & Skold J, System performance of EDGE, a proposal for enhanced data rates in existing digital cellular systems, *Proceedings of IEEE Vehicular Technology Conference, (VTC '98)*, Ottawa, Canada, May 1998, pp. 1284–1289.
23. Hamiti S, Hakaste M, Moisio M, Nefedov N, Nikula E & Vilpponen H, EDGE circuit switched data—an enhancement of GSM data services, *Proceedings of IEEE*

Wireless Communications and Networking Conference (WCNC '99), New Orleans, 1999.

24. Bi Q, Zysman GI & Menkes H, Wireless mobile communications at the start of the 21st century, *IEEE Communications Magazine*, January, 110–116, 2001.

25. TIA/EIA/IS-707-A-2.10, Data Service Options for Spread Spectrum Systems: Radio Link protocol Type 3, January 2000.

26. Mitola J, The software radio architecture, *IEEE Communications Magazine*, May, 26–38, 1995.

27. Winters JH, Signal acquisition and tracking with adaptive arrays in the digital mobile radio system IS-54 with flat fading, *IEEE Transactions on Vehicular Technology*, **42**(4), 377–384, 1993.

28. Zeng M, Annamali A & Bhargava V, Harmonization of global third-generation mobile systems, *IEEE Communications Magazine*, **38**(12), 94–104, 2000.

29. Bria A, Gessler F, Queseth O, Stridh R, Unbehaun M, Wu J, Zender J & Flament M, 4th generation wireless infrastructures: scenarios and research challenges, *IEEE Personal Communications Magazine*, **8**(6), 25–31, 2001.

30. Arroyo-Fernandez B et al. (Eds), Guest Editors, Life after third-generation mobile communications, *IEEE Communications Magazine*, Feature Topic Issue, **39**(8), 2001.

31. Jamalipour A & Tekinay S, Guest Editors, Fourth generation wireless networks and interconnecting standards, *IEEE Personal Communications Magazine*, Special Issue, **8**(5), 2001.

32. Jamalipour A & Tekinay S, Guest Editors, Next generation wireless networks and navigation systems, *IEEE Communications Magazine*, Feature Topic Issue, **40**(2), 2002.

33. Ohmori S, Yamao Y & Nakajima N, The future generations of mobile communications based on broadband access technologies, *IEEE Communications Magazine*, **38**(12), 134–142, 2000.

34. Mohr W & Konhauser W, Access network evolution beyond third generation mobile communications, *IEEE Communications Magazine*, **38**(12), 122–133, 2000.

35. Patel G & Dennett S, The 3GPP and 3GPP2 movements toward and all-IP mobile network, *IEEE Personal Communications Magazine*, **38**(8), 62–64, 2000.

36. Adachi F & Sawahashi M, Challenges in realizing the multimedia mobile communications era: IMT-2000 and beyond, *Personal, Indoor and Mobile Radio Communications Conference (PIMRC '99)*, Osaka, Japan, 1999.

37. Bos L & Leroy S, Toward an all-IP UMTS system architecture, *IEEE Network*, **15**(1), 36–45, 2001.

38. Ramjee R, La Porta TF, Salgarelli L, Thuel S, Varadhan K & Li L, IP-based access network infrastructure for next-generation wireless data networks, *IEEE Personal Communications Magazine*, **7**(4), 34–42, 2000.

39. Wisely D, Eardley P & Burness L, *IP for 3G, Networking Technologies for Mobile Communications*, John Wiley & Sons, Chichester, West Sussex, England, 2002.

40. The European Union BRAIN Project, Web site: http://www.ist-brain.org.

41. Mobile Wireless Internet Forum (MWIF), Web site: http://www.mwif.org.

42. Mobile Wireless Internet Forum, *OpenRAN Architecture in 3rd Generation Mobile Systems*, Technical Report MTR-007, Release Version 1.0.0, September 2001.

43. Mobile Wireless Internet Forum, *IP in the RAN as a Transport Option in 3rd Generation Mobile Systems*, Technical Report MTR-006, Release Version 2.0.0, June 2001.

44. Mobile Wireless Internet Forum, *Layered functional architecture*, Technical Report MTR-003, Release Version 1.0, August 2000.

45. Mobile Wireless Internet Forum, *Architecture requirements*, Technical Report MTR-002, Release 1.7, February 2001.

46. Umehira M, Nakura M, Umeuchi M, Murayama J, Murai T & Hara H, Wireless and IP integrated system architectures for broadband mobile multimedia services, *Proceedings of IEEE Wireless Communications and Networking Conference (WCNC '99)*, New Orleans, 1999.

47. Noerenberg II JW, Bridging wireless protocols, *IEEE Communications Magazine*, **39**(11), 90–97, 2001.

48. Oliphant MW, The mobile phone meets the Internet, *IEEE Spectrum*, August, 20–28, 1998.

49. McCann PJ & Hiller T, An Internet infrastructure for cellular CDMA networks using Mobile IP, *IEEE Personal Communications Magazine*, **7**(4), 6–12, 2000.

50. Ramjee R, La Porta TF, Thuel S & Varadhan K, IP-based access network architecture for next-generation wireless data networks, *IEEE Personal Communications Magazine*, **7**(4), 34–41, 2000.

51. Macker JP, Park VD & Corson MS, Mobile and wireless Internet services: putting the pieces together, *IEEE Communications Magazine*, **39**(6), 148–155, 2001.

52. Das S, Misra A, Agrawal P & Das S, TeleMIP: Telecommunications-enhanced Mobile IP architecture for fast intradomain mobility, *IEEE Personal Communications Magazine*, **7**(4), 50–58, 2000.

Part II
Fundamental Topics in Wireless IP

Chapter 5   QUALITY OF SERVICE IN A MOBILE ENVIRONMENT

In this chapter, the term *quality of service* (QoS) will be defined clearly in order to know exactly what the problem is and how it is possible to establish a network with guaranteed quality of its services. The discussions on QoS will be more general than being only used for wireless Internet, but the discussion is concluded with the usage and deployment of QoS in the wireless Internet.

Chapter 6   TRAFFIC MODELING FOR WIRELESS IP

In this chapter, appropriate traffic models for future data networks and the wireless IP will be introduced. Several characteristics of the traffic in data networks will be addressed and the major available models will be formulated. The discussion provided in this chapter will be sufficient for any researcher who is looking for fundamental understanding and knowledge to start working on the important topic of traffic modeling in wired and wireless data networks.

Chapter 7   TRAFFIC MANAGEMENT FOR WIRELESS IP

In case a precise traffic modeling is difficult to achieve in a communication network, traffic-management techniques would be the only choice to maintain quality in that network. Traffic management includes many different techniques from admission control to scheduling algorithms, buffering management, and many more and could by itself be the topic of a single book. In this chapter, several aspects of traffic management will be discussed in order to see its benefits in a wireless IP network. Admission control techniques, and specifically a measurement-based admission control, will be the main focus of this chapter.

Chapter 8 MOBILITY IN CELLULAR NETWORKS

This chapter will provide a complete overview of the mobility models used in cellular wireless systems and the location management techniques as the two main parts of mobility management required in mobile networks. In a wireless network, the users are assumed basically to be mobile, which means that they will change their network point of attachment frequently, irrespective of whether they are idle or active in terms of exchanging data with the network and other network users. Therefore, understanding the user mobility models and location management techniques becomes profoundly important.

Chapter 9 TRANSPORT PROTOCOLS FOR WIRELESS IP

Transmission control protocol (TCP) is the *de facto* transport protocol for today's global Internet. It performs at an acceptable efficiency over traditional wired networks in which packet losses are usually caused by network congestion. However, in networks with wireless links in addition to wired segments, this assumption would be insufficient, as the high wireless bit error rate could become the dominant cause of packet loss, thus making TCP perform suboptimally under these new conditions. In this chapter, the suitability of TCP for wireless IP will be discussed and several techniques that could improve the situation will be explained.

Chapter 10 INTERNET PROTOCOL FOR WIRELESS IP

Network layer has a distinguished role in the realization of future wireless IP networks. The network layer functionality could determine the efficiency of the wireless system and its performance in terms of quality-of-service parameters. The main part of the network layer is the network protocol. In today's Internet, it is the Internet protocol that functions as the network protocol. Therefore, for the study of future wireless Internet networks, an in-depth understanding of Internet protocol and recognition of its merits and drawbacks is of vital importance. This understanding will assist researchers in the field to find solutions for improving the Internet protocol toward its position within the future wireless IP networks. This chapter will provide such an understanding by reviewing the current version of the Internet protocol, its next-generation version and also the initiatives toward migrating the Internet into the mobile environment.

5

Quality of Service in a Mobile Environment

Quality of Service (QoS) is a terminology that has been around for quite some time and maybe it is one of the most common words that have been used by the people in the field of telecommunications in the past few years. The popularity of this usage, however, could not provide a clear definition of this important term and in many situations leads to misunderstanding and confusion. When the meaning of the term is not clear, then it would be difficult to provide its capabilities in a system, namely, a QoS network, as the expectations from different people would be different.

In this chapter, we try to define the QoS very clearly so that we know for sure what the problem is and how we can establish a network with guaranteed quality in its services. Our discussion on QoS will be more general than QoS being only used for wireless Internet, that is, the subject of this book, but we will try to limit the discussion to the usage and deployment of QoS in wireless Internet. After defining the QoS term and its requirements, we will establish a framework for a QoS network and exercise the Internet protocol (IP) and wireless cellular initiations for the QoS. Finally, we will run through wireless data networks and wireless Internet to see the prospects of QoS in these emerging networks.

5.1 DEFINING THE QUALITY OF SERVICE

QoS can be defined as a set of specific requirements for a particular service provided by a network to users. These requirements, however, are usually described by using some quantitative figures. So instead of asking for a good network service, the user is asked to specifically request other sorts of measures such as connection speed or delay, which can

The Wireless Mobile Internet: Architectures, Protocols, and Services.   Abbas Jamalipour
© 2003 John Wiley & Sons, Ltd   ISBN: 0-470-84468-X

be described by a numerical value, for example, 56 Kbps or 300 ms, respectively, for the speed and delay. Having a quality term such as good or bad described by a quantitative metric simplifies the process of allocation of that quality to a particular service by the provider and also prevents any possible ambiguity during the user request and service fulfillment process.

Changing quality into a measurable quantity is a good step toward clearing the meaning of the term but still there are other things that have to be done. The ambiguity in QoS definition can be pointed out in many directions by posing some of the following questions:

- What types of qualities can be attributed to a particular service?
- Which entity in the network is responsible for providing a particular service?
- Who is the accounting entity in the network that authorizes a user to receive a particular service?
- Is the requested service a network service or an end-user terminal service?
- Who judges the need for a particular service, the user or the network?
- What is the source of the service requirements: user, network, or technology?
- Is it possible to fulfill a service quality at a particular time and location?
- What should be done if the requested service is not available at a particular time or location?

The above questions and many similar ones simply illustrate that there cannot be a definite definition for the QoS and any attempt to find a single answer would be a waste of time. In recent years, many companies have started to raise the issue that the next-generation telecommunications networks, including Internet users, can receive a guaranteed QoS. However, the topic is too broad and no one can explain what the guaranteed QoS would be. Everyone knows that if a network can provide a full commitment on its services at all times, then it would be the ideal network, but the issue is what type of services we are considering, are they fixed for all users or different on a user base. We will explain this issue in this section by separating user-based, network-based and technology-based requirements of the QoS. The reader may also refer to some survey papers on QoS for further reading [1–4].

5.1.1 User-level QoS requirements

At the user level, requirements of QoS are mainly those that can be seen by the user. This means that many system-level QoS architectures are essentially transparent to the user or that because they are not directly related to the end-user service, they are ignored by the user. For example, if you are using a cellular phone for your daily voice communications, your ultimate purpose and requirement from your service is to have a reliable phone conversation and a reasonably acceptable level of voice quality. If you move from the service area of one base station to another one, the cellular network needs to perform a complicated procedure of location updating and handoff between cells in order to maintain the continuity of your call and service. For the user, all these procedures are transparent and ignored, unless a call drop or sensible change in quality of communication happens during the handoff.

The above example raises an important parameter in defining the QoS at the user level. This is the user application. In the above example, a voice application has been used and on the basis of that application, the user expectations of communications continuity and voice quality are considered as the perceived QoS metrics. We can generalize this example to any type of network including cellular, Internet, wireless LAN, and so on. So we conclude that from the user point of view the user application has a determining role in defining the QoS requirement.

In general, the user-level QoS requirements can be categorized into three:

- Criticality
- Cost
- Security

Criticality is defined in accordance with the perceived QoS based on data transmission and application type. To make this clear, let us consider an example of multimedia transmission of a video clip over the Internet with voice. A user may consider several factors in order to illustrate either satisfaction or a problem with such a communication system. These are:

- Video rate
- Video smoothness
- Picture detail
- Picture color accuracy
- Audio quality
- Video/audio synchronization

The topic of multimedia QoS is discussed in many literatures (e.g. see References [5–9]). These factors are self-explaining and are usual in the case of videoviewing on the Internet. But the important thing that is not very visible and that we want to conclude from this example is that not all users use the same set of factors to determine the quality of such a video transmission. One might be interested in smooth playback of the video at an acceptable rate without paying much attention to the audio quality or even the picture color quality or picture detail. Therefore, it is not the case that even for the same application we put the same set of QoS requirements for all users. Users can choose the application and there are a limited number of QoS requirements associated with each application (such as the set we listed for the video transmission example). However, among all these requirements there will be a subset that makes the user QoS profile to be satisfied by the network service provider.

The second category in the user QoS requirements is the cost. This is one of the most indicative parameters for users when considering the quality. Cost is the money value of the service fees that the service provider charges a user. When a user wants to include this as a QoS metric, two different types of cost can be considered: per-use cost or per-unit cost. In a data-communication session, it is important for a user to see if the user is charged either on the basis of the period of communications, that is, the usage time of the service (e.g. measured in seconds), or according to the amount of data (e.g. measured in bits) transmitted in the uplink and the downlink from and to the user. Charging on the basis of the amount of data has become very interesting for many users recently, thanks to the increase in Internet and data applications compared to traditional voice and other constant rate and real-time applications. This can be considered an important factor in the success of i-mode for wireless Internet.

The third category for QoS requirement is security. This can be further divided into several types, such as

- Confidentiality
- Integrity
- Digital signature capability
- Authentication

Confidentiality refers to the service in which a particular user's information can be accessed only by appropriate and recognized users. If the user is worried that the information is not to be corrupted during the course of transmission, then the integrity becomes the desired security QoS metric. Digital signature provides an example of methods by which a user can make sure of the identity of the sender of a particular package of information. So if you are among those people who do not open a mail when there is no sender address on it, then for an electronic mail session, you will need this type of digital signature too. They also provide a safe method of making sensitive financial transactions. Verification of a user's identity and the right to access a particular service and information is provided through a process called *authentication*.

As we can see, for the second and third categories of the QoS requirement, there still is a general set (maybe expandable from what we listed here) and the user has the freedom to choose and customize his own subset. The chosen subset will then be forwarded to the service provider and if both parties agree, then the user QoS profile will be prepared.

5.1.2 Technology and network QoS requirements

On the basis of the technology and the network architecture, we can find more indicative figures to illustrate the QoS provided to users. Although many of these indications can be seen by users, they are more or less related to the technology behind the service and thus a user will find limited flexibility in changing the profile after subscription to the service.

We may categorize these requirements mainly into three types:

- Bandwidth
- Timeliness
- Reliability

Bandwidth illustrates the speed or data rate available to a user application. Very loosely speaking, we can say that the more the bandwidth available in the system, the higher the data rate that can be provided to each user application. The statement above is loose in the sense that it does not include other determining parameters that could affect the actual data rate given to a particular application at a specific period of time. For example, when you compare a 100-Base-T with a 10-Base-T LAN, with nominal data rates of 100 Mbps and 10 Mbps, respectively, each with N hosts attached, you may say that the 100-Base-T LAN is faster than the 10-Base-T LAN. However, this comparison does not consider the loading of the two LANs. If, for example, the 100-Base-T network is fully loaded and the 10-Base-T network is very lightly loaded, then each of these N hosts in the latter network can receive a faster connection speed than the users in the former network, because the LAN system is a bandwidth-shared system. For the sake of discussion in this section, we will use this loose relationship between bandwidth and speed. In Chapter 7 that deals with traffic management in wireless IP networks, more discussion will be provided.

To make the definition of bandwidth more precise, we need to distinguish between three different rates, including the system-level data rate, the application-level data rate, and the transaction data rate.

System-level data rate shows the actual data rate at the physical transmission media at uplink (from user terminal to the network) and downlink (from the network to user terminal) directions. This rate relates to static network characteristics such as the type of media used for connecting the user terminal to the network, network technology, and network topology as well as network dynamic characteristics such as current traffic loading, current network capacity, and also the service agreement between the user and the subscribed network. The system-level data rate could have a nominal value that can be within a range agreed to between the user and the network. The system-level data rate could also be further limited by interactions between protocols at the higher layers of the network stack such as transmission control protocol (TCP) and IP.

Application-level data rate could have a completely different value from the system-level data rate. Application protocols designed for high-bandwidth applications such as multimedia usually use different compression algorithms in order to reduce the amount of data exchanged between the application and transport protocols and eventually passed to the physical layer. Usually, the more the application data is compressed, the less the bandwidth that is required to transmit the data, but at the same time this means reducing the quality of the received information. So, there is always a trade-off between how much bandwidth you may use and the quality of information you receive at the other side of the network connection.

The transaction rate illustrates something completely different from either of the above two rates. If you assume a transaction as one single task to be done in the transmission of certain information, the transaction rate simply shows the rate at which the predefined tasks can be performed by the user, successfully supported by the attached network.

Depending on the nature of applications run by the user, one or some of these bandwidth indicators can be used to illustrate the QoS provided by the network. A user might use different indicators, something that is more sensible for human beings such as delay time, to quantify the bandwidth service provided by the network.

The second category of network- and technology-based QoS is timeliness. Timeliness can be sensed through delay time, response time, and delay variation, as well as similar indicators. Delay can be defined as the time spent by a user from the instance the user requests some information from the network until the instance that the information is completely downloaded to the user terminal. Note that this is not the only way in defining the delay. According to the user or network requirement, you might find another definition more appropriate and useful. However, the definition given here is the most straightforward way for quantifying the QoS in a data network similar to the Internet. Such a delay definition covers all type of delays that could happen within the network, including the user terminal processing time and transmission delay, link propagation delay, queuing delay at the input ports of the intermediate routers, backbone network delays (including link delays and router processing delay), and also the processing delay at the destination host, which has the requested information.

By not using the very loose relationship that exists between the bandwidth (at system level) and delay, we can say that with a higher bandwidth you may experience a smaller delay in most situations. But you need to be very careful here. This relationship always exists but in some occasions it is affected severely by other network parameters so that the concluded result shows an opposite relationship. Since our delay definition includes the processing delay at the destination, for example, it could be the case that even with a high-speed link and network a user experiences long delay when the destination host is too busy or the requested information is accessed by many other users. That is, the traffic load at the destination network or host, as well as loading of the backbone network (partly or entirely), could result in a long delay even with high bandwidth locally.

Response time can be considered as part of the delay definition given earlier or in some occasions as a single indicator of the quality. It simply tries to illustrate how fast the network as a whole is in providing the requested information to a user.

Delay variation is the third timeliness indicator that we have specified. In the usual situation, the previous two timeliness indicators, delay and response time, could be sufficient to illustrate the service timeliness quality. However, for some applications, such as real-time multimedia, it is not the delay but the delay variation that affects the quality. If the network as a whole imposes a long but fixed delay at all times during the period that the application is running (e.g. a videoconferencing), it is possible to compensate the effects of delay by simple methods such as buffering and delayed replay. However, if the delay variation shows very diverse values from time to time, it would be very difficult for the application protocol to adjust to a good method of compensation. Therefore, the delay variation would be necessary in some situations that include increasing usage in future networks.

The third category we have named for the network- and technology-based QoS is reliability. Reliability in a networked system could be quantified by measuring the time or the frequency. The time could show the average time for a failure to happen, the average time the system needs to recover from the failure, or the mean time between failures that happen in the network. It is also possible to count the rate at which system failure, data loss, or data corruption happens in the network.

The reliability measure could be more important for the network than the individual users for quantifying the network QoS. It would be very important for the network to avoid long failure times or very frequent failures or corrupts, as this will affect all users, whereas for individuals who use the network services from time to time, delay and bandwidth metrics will be more visible.

5.1.3   Correlation between the QoS indicators

Until now, we have discussed different QoS requirements and tried to quantify them through numerical measures, so that it could be possible for a user to specify precisely what his expectations are from the attached network in terms of QoS, and also for the network to advertise for its users what type of services can be offered to them. The indicators defined in the previous two subsections are all important and they can define the service quality individually or together according to the application and the users' needs. According to the discussion provided there, however, it should be clear by now that having all those indicators as the QoS metrics for all users is neither feasible nor necessary. On the basis of the user requirements or the application requirements at a particular time, there will only be a subset of those QoS indicators that need to be provided by the network to a user. Therefore, the ambiguity of the QoS should have become clear such that the QoS must be defined on a case-by-case basis and not as a general rule that can cover all requirements.

In addition, we need to note that it is difficult to provide a guideline that can cover the QoS in all situations. We can see a very diverse relationship between the QoS indicators observed in different systems. To illustrate this fact, we use an example from the wireless that is relevant to our topic in this book. We assume that data transmission (as opposed to voice communications) is our required service for the purpose of this example.

For the wireless, we can add another QoS indicator, namely, the mobility range. Mobility range in our definition can have two different meanings. The first one is how big is the geographical area in which a user can move around and can still receive the service from the attached network. Again, similar to the previous indicators defined in previous subsections, this is not something that is independent of the user's application or that can solely determine the QoS for a particular network. For example, if you need a wireless service within the borders of a room, then having a one-mile coverage would not be an advantage in choosing the system to be used. The coverage, however, would be very important for a cellular mobile network in which users want to move very widely.

Mobility range can also be defined as the size of the area covered by a single base station or an access point (AP), for example, the size of a cell in a cellular mobile network. We will now see the relationship between the mobility range (mainly defined as the former one) and other important QoS metrics. Bandwidth (as a network-related QoS requirement) and cost (as an important user-based QoS requirement) are considered here in conjunction with the user mobility range.

Table 5.1 summarizes several known wireless networks and lists their usual coverage (i.e. the mobility range offered to the respective users of each system) and the bandwidth they offer. On top of the list in the table is the cheapest wireless connectivity technology, the infrared. Infrared ports can provide a very reliable and cost-effective short connectivity (in the range of a few inches to a few feet) between computers, handheld terminals, cellular phones, and peripheral devices such as printers and scanners. Without any kind of infrastructure, these devices can make a computer network or a point-to-point connection at a speed of up to 4 Mbps or more. The second listed system is the wireless LAN, defined in IEEE 802.11 standards. With low-cost APs and access cards, the wireless LAN can provide a very high-speed computer network (such as a LAN or an ad hoc network). Starting with its first version, which provided 2-Mbps data rate, the successive versions of

Table 5.1 Mobility coverage and capacity of different wireless networks

Wireless network	Coverage	Data rate
Infrared	Room	19.2 kbps–4 Mbps
IEEE 802.11	100–500 m around each AP	2–11 Mbps
GSM	Cellular network	9.6 kbps
CDPD (for AMPS[a], IS-95, IS-136)	Cellular network	19.2 kbps
DECT, PHS	Cellular network	32 kbps
GPRS (for GSM)	Cellular network	155 kbps
UMTS/IMT-2000[b]	Cellular network	384 kbps–2 Mbps
Iridium LEO[c] satellite	Global	2.4 kbps
Broadband satellites	Global/regional	2 Mbps

[a]AMPS Advanced Mobile Phone Systems
[b]IMT-2000 International Mobile Telecommunications
[c]LEO low earth orbit

the wireless LAN IEEE 802.11b and IEEE 802.11a can achieve a maximum of 11 Mbps and 54 Mbps speed, respectively. The cost of the system, although very low, is still higher than the infrared but on the other hand it can provide larger mobility range up to a few hundred meters.

In the cellular world, second-generation systems, such as Global System for Mobile communications (GSM), Cellular Digital Packet Data (CDPD), Digital Enhanced Cordless Telecommunication (DECT), Personal Handyphone System (PHS), and the packet-switched 2.5 generation system General Packet Radio Service (GPRS), the successor of the GSM, and finally the third-generation (3G) wireless cellular systems such as Universal Mobile Telecommunications System (UMTS) and cdma2000 offer very large mobility range up to a few miles in radius around a single base station with further coverage expansion through their cellular topology and handoffs between cells. Because of the complexity and infrastructure involved in all these cellular networks (more or less), data service cost is much higher than the first two wireless data systems, the wireless LAN and infrared. However, when we look at the range of data rate they offer to their users, they are tens or hundreds of times below a wireless LAN system.

The last two systems listed in the table are still wireless but utilize the satellites as their base stations. In these systems, even higher initial and running costs are involved compared to cellular terrestrial systems and thus we can see much more expensive service cost to data users. Again, the data rate is too low to be considered as a major breakthrough for today's communications even when considering their global mobility coverage.

The wireless data networks listed in the table and their three QoS metrics show no direct relation. For example, we cannot say that if a user pays more, he can achieve higher mobility range and data rate. For some systems among those listed, it is possible to upgrade the mobility range by paying more (for example, from a wireless LAN to GPRS) but you cannot expect to achieve a higher data rate at the same time. On the contrary, you may get a very low-speed service, too slow to be useful for your particular application that was running in the original network.

This simple example illustrates that although all QoS are important, there must be a limit on the number of these metrics that can be provided to a user simultaneously. The current example might show the present-day technologies and one might say that this limitation is because of the current limitation in technology. However, we can find other examples for which there is no such technological limitation, but it is simply not possible to provide all things under one umbrella of QoS at the same time.

The QoS provisioning and guarantee is all about the trade-off between the many sides of the QoS requirements. Providing all these requirements to users at the same time is not only impossible but also unnecessary and inappropriate for any network. References [10–13] provide further readings on QoS in distributed systems.

5.2 QUALITY-OF-SERVICE GUARANTEE IN IP NETWORKS

In this section, we try to formulate some general ideas on how QoS can be guaranteed in IP networks. The section performs this task by providing simple and very basic examples, but the results are applicable to all kinds of data networks, including our targeted wireless IP network.

The current global Internet service is based on the so-called best-effort service [14,15]. This service does not guarantee any thing other than delivering the IP packets within the network. That is, once a packet is generated and left to the Internet for delivery to a destination host, the network does not guarantee any specified delivery time (delay), the speed at which the packet will be forwarded (data rate and throughput), the available bandwidth for delivering the packet, or even that the packet does not get lost during this delivery. The network only guarantees that it will do its best to deliver the user information with all the resources it has, but if the packet is lost or corrupted, the respective entities should try to retransmit the lost packet and recover it. The IP providing this type of service is said to be unreliable. This unreliable protocol, however, can be overlaid on top of any link layer (e.g. Ethernet or asynchronous transfer mode (ATM)) and that is one of the advantages of the IP. The reliability to the network delivery must be then provided by other layer protocols such as TCP at the transport layer, and therefore it becomes possible to use the Internet.

Internet Engineering Task Force (IETF) [16], the main body in standardization of the Internet, and the Internet research community are working on new proposals to provide better services and some type of QoS support in IP networks. This may start first by services called better than best-effort, with the QoS eventually guaranteed in the future. In such services, IP as the network protocol will have to guarantee some QoS metrics such as delay, average, minimum, or peak throughput, bandwidth, or loss probability for delivering Internet datagrams.

Before going to detailed discussions on these activities, in this section we will see how we can basically establish a QoS network and what our restrictions and requirements are for such a service. We will outline four fundamental principles in providing QoS in data and IP networks. These four principles are common in any data communications network.

5.2.1 Packet classification

Assume a simple example in which a single application is running at two source hosts A and B, respectively, directly connected to a single router R_1. The first one is a delay and bandwidth sensitive application, such as a real-time voice over IP application that requires around 1-Mbps bandwidth and short delays. The second one is a delay and bandwidth insensitive application such as FTP (File Transfer Protocol) that can tolerate the data rate and delay requirements reasonably. Hosts A and B are connected directly to the router R_1 that is connected to a second router R_2. A limited capacity link of 1.5 Mbps connects the two routers R_1 and R_2. All packets have to be routed through this connecting link to the other parts of the network.

The voice over IP application needs its typical bandwidth and delay requirements in order to have sensible communications. On the other hand, the FTP application can take longer time for delivery of packets so that no restrictive delay or bandwidth requirements are assumed here for this application. This simple example also illustrates different QoS requirements for different applications, as outlined in the previous section.

In an ideal situation, a network manager wants to provide 1 Mbps out of the available 1.5 Mbps to the voice application and the leftover capacity of 0.5 Mbps to the FTP application. One way to do this is to classify and mark different packets (voice packets versus FTP packets) at the input port of the router R_1 so that the router can share the total capacity proportionally to the two hosts. By providing such a share policy, we will be able to provide the QoS to the two hosts connected to our example network. Therefore, the first principle in providing the QoS is that we need to differentiate between different types of packets generated from individual applications.

The currently used version of the IP, IP version 4 (IPv4), has a field in its header called *type of service* (TOS) and the next-generation IP, or IP version 6 (IPv6), also includes a Traffic Class (TC) field within its header. (See Chapter 10 for detailed discussions on IPv4 and IPv6 protocols.) The TOS or TC field in the IP header can, for example, be used for this type of classification or for marking the packets generated from different applications. When the router has the appropriate information on distinguishing between different traffic classes and is equipped with a new discrimination policy according to the packet classes, it will be possible to provide different services to different classes of packets (applications). The current IP, however, rarely uses the TOS field as all packets are handled equally so that we have just a best-effort service. This is a service that allows every user to grab the bandwidth as much as possible without any control or priority consideration.

5.2.2 Packet isolation

The classification of the packets is a very good start in providing QoS in IP networks. But what happens if the applications misbehave and use more network resources than what they really need. For example, if the host A uses more than 1 Mbps for its voice application, it may improve its service slightly but on the other hand it will destroy the host B FTP application performance. So there should be some entity within the network to monitor the behavior of applications and their use of the network resources. Therefore, our second principle here will be that in addition to packet classification, we need to monitor and control that no one uses more resources than what they have been allocated.

The most directly connected router to the hosts (in this example router R_1) can perform this monitoring role. By this method, we will make sure that the task of control and monitoring is distributed within the network and it is assigned to the most appropriate entity in the network. It also provides other benefits usually known for distributed systems (as opposed to central control) such as reliability and minimal exchange of control messaging.

5.2.3 Efficient resource management

One way to provide monitoring that no application uses network resources excessively is to partition these resources. In our example, the bandwidth is the main resource and we can partition it into two parts of 1 Mbps and 0.5 Mbps allocated to host A and host B, respectively. This can be easily done by maintaining two different queues at the input port of router R_1, which can be easily implemented by the software. Note that when we say allocating resources to a user, it does not mean that this allocation is permanent. The allocations can be managed and reconfigured dynamically, for example, only for the duration of the respective application.

One problem that could be raised here is what happens if host A's voice application does not use its allocated resources for some time. This means that although we have tried to discriminate the two applications to provide a good QoS, we may waste the precious network resources. So we come to our third principle that although we need to differentiate individual application's packets and monitor their limit on usage of the available resources in order to provide QoS in our network, we still need to make sure that our resources are not wasted at any time. Therefore, the resource management will be an important issue in any QoS network and we need to use the network resources as efficiently as possible. Management of the queues maintained at the routers could be thought of as part of the overall resource management in the system.

5.2.4 Traffic load control

Our three principles so far are very important and can provide a good service quality in our network. They are also very general and can be used in any network. But we have not included one important factor in our discussions. The fact is that our network resources are limited. In our above example, we had 1.5-Mbps capacity and thus we could share it between two applications, at 1 Mbps and 0.5 Mbps, so that we could provide a good QoS to both the applications. But this is not always the case. Especially, when your network has many users, sharing the available capacity will not be an easy task. For instance, consider our simple example when hosts A and B are both running voice applications and both need 1-Mbps capacity in order to comply with their QoS requirements. Using the simple calculation of 'one plus one equals two', we can see that it is not feasible to share the available 1.5 Mbps between the two hosts and still claim that we provide the QoS as desired by the users.

In such a situation, we can simply forget the QoS and give each user half the available capacity. But if we want to provide QoS, then we need to do something else. That is, we need to allocate to one of the hosts the required 1 Mbps and ask the second one to wait until the required bandwidth is available. The issue of who gets the capacity first and who gets it next is another issue. We may allocate the capacity on a first-in-first-served basis, or on a user subscription priority basis, or any other policy.

Thus, the fourth principle in providing the QoS in a data network is that we need to have Call Admission Control (CAC) in our network (e.g. implemented at routers) in order to handle the situations in which requests for allocation of the network capacity, such as bandwidth, are more than available resources. CAC thus will be a major foundation in any QoS network. The issue of admission control has been widely addressed in many networks for many years (e.g. see References [17–27]) and still there is a lot of work to be done. We will discuss the issue of traffic management, which includes CAC, in more detail in Chapter 7.

5.2.5 Summary

Let us summarize all the principles for providing QoS in a network that we have outlined in this section. As a basic understanding, we should now know that QoS is a term that has to be associated with a particular application run by a user at a given time. The QoS requirements for each application thus might be different from those that are necessary for another application. Therefore, a user needs to have a QoS profile listing appropriate requirements associated with particular applications enabled in the user terminal.

Considering the limited available network resources such as bandwidth, therefore, if we want to provide QoS to a particular user application sharing these resources with other users and applications, we first need to find a way to classify the nature of packets generated by the users. We can mark the packets and show this marking by using some methods such as the field within the IP datagram header to the control entities such as routers.

We then need to monitor the usage of network resources by the users, both to make sure that no one takes more resources than what is assigned to them and also to make sure that these resources are used efficiently.

Finally, we need to make sure that we do not commit some QoS that is more than what we have in hand. So a second control called *traffic control* or CAC is necessary. The admission control policy makes sure that we will accept a new user with some predefined QoS metrics only when we can support these requirements on the basis of the available network resources.

The QoS principles outlined in this section can be considered as the fundamentals of the QoS provisioning in any data packet network. We will use them throughout this book and try to evaluate the QoS provisioning approaches taken by the research communities in different networks to see if they are promising permanent solutions or they are just short-term answers with no future.

5.3 INTERNET SOLUTIONS TO QUALITY-OF-SERVICE PROVISIONING

IETF [16] has started working on QoS in IP networks in the mid-1990s. Two different approaches have been introduced: Integrated Services (IntServ) in 1994 [28] and Differentiated Services (DiffServ) in 1998 [29–32]. Since these services are discussed in many traditional data networks and IP literatures, here we will just review their characteristics in brief for the sake of keeping consistency in our discussions. Readers who are interested in more details of these two services are referred to the references provided at the end of this chapter.

5.3.1 Integrated services

This service has been introduced in IP networks in order to provide guaranteed and controlled services in addition to the already available best-effort service. IntServ is an extension to the Internet architecture to support both non real-time and real-time applications over IP. Each traffic flow in this service can be classified under one of the three service classes:

- Guaranteed-service class
- Controlled-load service class
- Best-effort service

Guaranteed-service class provides for delay-bound service agreements such as voice and other real-time applications, which require severe delay constraints. Controlled-load service class on the other hand provides for a form of statistical delay service agreement, for example, with a nominal mean delay. Finally, best-effort services have been included to match the current IP service mainly for interactive burst traffic (e.g. web), interactive bulk traffic (e.g. FTP), and background or asynchronous traffic (e.g. e-mail).

Guaranteed and controlled-load services are based on quantitative service requirements and require signaling and admission control in network nodes (similar to what we discussed in the previous section). Usually, for these type of services a resource reservation protocol (RSVP) is used [33,34]. RSVP is a signaling protocol used to reserve resources in the routers, in a hop-by-hop basis, considering the applications requirements (e.g. throughput guarantees, end-to-end delay bounds) for a given IP flow.

The main advantages of the IntServ are that it provides service classes that closely match different application requirements; it leaves the existing best-effort service almost unchanged, so that no change will be necessary to the existing applications and they can continue to enjoy the current IP service, and finally, it leaves the forwarding mechanism in the network unchanged, so that nonupgraded networks can still receive data from an IntServ network, without any problem.

On the negative side, the architecture of IntServ requires that for an end-to-end service guarantee, all intermediate nodes need to support the service agreement for a given

Internet flow. Therefore, if in a network somewhere in the middle between the source and destination the service guarantee is not available, then the whole issue of end-to-end guarantee will be lost. In addition, subdivision of the best-effort service may cause problems in commercial networks.

The IntServ and RSVP proposals have failed to become an actual end-to-end QoS solution, mostly because of the scaling problems in large networks and because of the need to implement RSVP in all the network elements from the source to the destination. Because of these scalability problems and other disadvantages discussed above, IntServ will probably never be deployed beyond access networks.

5.3.2 Differentiated services

DiffServ came to remedy the disadvantages of IntServ in providing QoS in IP networks. DiffServ aims at providing simple, scalable, and flexible service differentiation using a hierarchical model. That is, the resource management now divides into two domains:

- Interdomain resource management
- Intradomain resource management

DiffServ also allows the network provider to differentiate different traffic streams, using different per-hop-behaviors (PHB) when forwarding the IP packets of each stream. The advantage of such a scheme is its scalability, since many IP flows can be aggregated in the same traffic stream or behavior aggregate (BA). The PHB applies to an aggregate and is characterized by a DiffServ code point (DSCP) marked in the header of each IP packet. In IPv4 header the TOS field and in IPv6 header the TC field can be used for this purpose, which in DiffServ terms are renamed as DS field, shown in Figure 5.1. PHBs are implemented on IP routers through the management of network resources, namely, of classifiers, markers, meters, queues, droppers, and schedulers. These network resources are managed and allocated to traffic streams according to the provisioning policies of the network provider.

At the local network (now named *local DS domain*), three types of routers can be distinguished: access routers, interior DS routers, and border DS routers. These are shown in Figure 5.2. Access routers are the routers close to the end-user hosts. Several access routers are connected to an interior router. So the interior routers are at the second level far from the end hosts. At the highest level of the local DS domain, all interior routers are connected to a border DS router that connects the local DS domain to the outside world

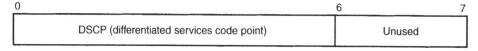

Figure 5.1   DS field in the IP header for the purpose of DiffServ

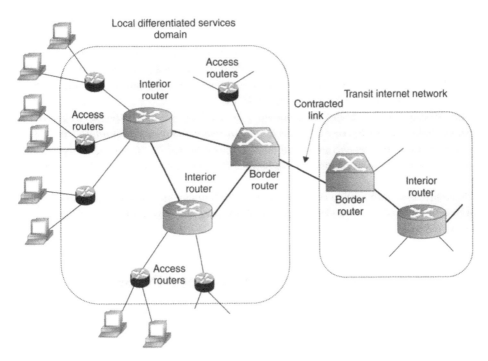

Figure 5.2 Differentiated services network architecture and the three types of DS routers

or the service provider network. The link between the border DS router and the service provider network will be contracted at the DS aggregate rate.

At the interdomain resource management, unidirectional service levels are agreed at each boundary point between a customer and a provider for traffic entering the provider network. At the intradomain resource management on the other hand, the provider is solely responsible for configuration and provisioning of resources within its domain. Therefore, different from IntServ in which all control and resource management have been performed on an end-to-end basis, in DiffServ the local network has to share the resources allocated by the outside network (or service provider) to its users. Scalability, simplicity, and flexibility of DiffServ compared with IntServ come from this hierarchical management.

DiffServ does not impose either the number of traffic classes or their characteristics on a service provider. The provider builds its offered services with a combination of traffic classes, traffic conditioning, and billing.

So, in DiffServ architecture a service-level agreement (SLA) is provided to govern the traffic handling between a local network and the service provider network [35]. After that, it will be the local network that provides the required services to its end users. Per-flow state is also avoided in DiffServ within the network since individual flows are aggregated in classes and will be supported by the local network resource management using the available resources provided on the basis of the SLA.

In summary, in DiffServ the entire customer's local network requirements for QoS are aggregated and then an SLA will be made with the network service provider. The SLA could be static, that is, negotiated and agreed on a long-term basis (e.g. monthly) or could be dynamic, which changes more frequently. The local network is then responsible for providing DiffServ to end users within the network. This is usually done by marking packets with specific flags shown in the TOS field of the IPv4 or the TC field of the IPv6. For DiffServ purpose, these fields are now renamed DS field and it will supersede the existing definition of IPv4 TOS and the IPv6 TC field.

The provisioning of a DiffServ network is the key for the network to exhibit the expected behavior. Moreover, admission control mechanisms are required at the edge of DiffServ domain in order to avoid network congestion and to prevent QoS degradation. And when this situation occurs, the dynamic reprovisioning of the DiffServ network is required.

Typically, this technology is intended for deployment at the core network, although end-to-end DiffServ is conceivable when the end-to-end chain fully relies on IP Diff-Serv networks.

5.3.3   Comparison between IntServ and DiffServ

DiffServ comes with some advantages and disadvantages. On the positive side, DiffServ provides the kind of discrimination based on payment for service. Traffic classes are accessible without additional signaling as a traffic class is a predefined aggregate of traffics. Network management will be simpler in DiffServ compared to IntServ, since classification of the traffic needs to be performed at the end systems.

On the other side, DiffServ tries to keep the operating mode of the network simple by pushing as much complexity as possible onto the network provisioning and configuration. DiffServ also does not make the provision of several services with different qualities within the same network easier.

So in summary, IntServ requires flow-specific state for each flow at the routers. State information will be increased in accordance with the number of flows. This will need huge storage space and processing power at the routers and makes routers much more complex.

DiffServ on the other hand is simpler and more scalable compared to IntServ. The reason for the scalability of DiffServ is that the per-flow service is now replaced with per-aggregate service. The complex processing is also now moved from the core of the network to the edge.

5.3.4   IntServ over DiffServ

Recently, it has been proposed to apply the IntServ end-to-end model across a network containing one or more DiffServ regions [31]. Such a proposal fully endorses the use of RSVP as an end-to-end solution to provide QoS in the context of IntServ. Compared to a pure IntServ solution, this approach has some advantages because it removes the per-flow processing from the core routers. However, the per-flow processing remains essential at both the edge and border routers.

5.4 CELLULAR NETWORK SOLUTIONS TO QUALITY-OF-SERVICE PROVISIONING

In this section, we will check the status of QoS establishment in two cellular technologies that are considered as the gateway technologies to the future wide-area wireless Internet. We will see the QoS examples for the 2.5G GPRS and the 3G UMTS systems. This discussion has a twofold purpose. On one side, we would like to see what the cellular researchers think about establishing the service quality to Internet applications that they offer in their systems. On the other side, which is more important than the former, we want to see how the cellular QoS provisioning approach is close (or far) from its Internet counterpart. Future wireless Internet will be based on both technologies, cellular and Internet, and it is very reasonable to think that we need harmony in any improvement attempt toward the wireless Internet from the two major technologies. Without such harmony and cooperation, it would be difficult to think of any reliable wireless Internet system in the near future.

5.4.1 GPRS quality-of-service support

GPRS is the packet version of its well-treated predecessor second-generation cellular system GSM. GPRS is intended to provide a data friendly core and access network that can accommodate data services, mainly Internet types, to the users of cellular networks. GPRS was a result of increasing demand in Internet applications for mobile users and thus it can be considered as the first initiative in wide-area wireless Internet. The advanced features of the GSM network and the new network architecture of the GPRS made it possible that the core network of the 3G system UMTS follows almost a similar concept as its two predecessors.

There is, however, an important fact that we need to note here for GPRS and UMTS. The fact is that both systems are mainly developed by cellular engineers mostly from the International Telecommunication Union (ITU) community with little cooperation from either the Internet community or the IETF.

Implementation of Internet applications, such as e-mail and web browsing, and the increasing demand in providing service quality in telecommunication networks have resulted in consideration of QoS in the new cellular systems.

GPRS defines the QoS requirements for each subscribed user in a QoS profile, which is defined and maintained at the GPRS network Home Location Register (HLR). Serving GPRS Support Node (SGSN) is responsible for fulfilling the user QoS profile at all times, including periods when the user is located outside his home network. (See Chapter 3 for more details of the GPRS network architecture.)

Every subscriber to the GPRS network is allocated a QoS profile that consists of a number of the following QoS indicators:

• Traffic precedence class: defines the priority of service within the network
   — High, normal, or low priority

- Delay class: defines how much delay can be tolerated for a given service
  — Four classes
- Reliability class: defines how much reliability (e.g. corruption, loss) can be tolerated for a given service
  — Five classes
- Peak throughput class: defines the maximum rate allocated for the delivery of a given service to a user
  — 8, 16, 32, 64, 128, 256, 512, 1024, or 2048 Kbps
- Mean throughput class: defines the average data rate at which the service will be available to the user
  — 19 classes from best effort to 111 Kbps

The QoS profile of each subscribed user consists of one of the classes defined above and must be maintained by the network in all possible situations. These definitions are in line with our general QoS requirements defined in the first section of this chapter. The question now, however, is whether they are in line with the QoS activities from the Internet community, if the GPRS wants to share the wireless Internet efficiently. We will discuss this issue shortly.

5.4.2   UMTS quality-of-service support

The 3G system UMTS while using a similar core network architecture as the GPRS and following similar concepts for the QoS provisioning, adds specific classifications for the traffic loads, so that the handling of a given service can be considered in conjunction with particular QoS for that particular TC.

UMTS defines four traffic classes:

- Conversational traffic class
- Streaming traffic class
- Interactive traffic class
- Background traffic class

Conversational traffic class refers to the traffic generated mostly from real-time applications that usually require a constant bit rate (CBR) during the course of communications. Typical examples are voice and videoconferencing, and some network games. Those applications require preserved time relation between the information entities of the stream, and they follow a stringent and low delay pattern. A bit error rate (BER) of less than 10^{-3} is necessary for these applications.

Streaming traffic class usually requires a preserved time relation between the information entities of the stream. The increasing applications of streaming multimedia, including streaming audio and video over the Internet, are the main drivers for inclusion of this traffic class in UMTS. Typically, a BER of less than 10^{-5} is necessary for these applications.

Interactive traffic class refers to the traffic generated from applications such as web browsing and Internet games. Request response pattern and preserved data integrity are essential characteristics of these applications as, for example, it would be very unattractive or impractical to play an Internet game when the response time from different players are inconsistent or too long or are in an unordered fashion. A BER of less than 10^{-8} is typically necessary for these applications for reliable data transfer, whereas the delay constraints are not as severe as in the case of conversational traffics.

Background traffic class are those that come from delay insensitive applications such as e-mail or FTP downloads. For this traffic class, the destination is not expecting the data within a certain period of time but the data integrity and reliable data transfer are very important. Therefore, a BER of less than 10^{-8} should be given to these traffics.

The UMTS traffic classification approach shows a very Internet-oriented mechanism so that the cellular focus of voice communications has been included only partly in the system.

5.5 QUALITY-OF-SERVICE ESTABLISHMENT IN MOBILE NETWORKS

We have outlined the QoS considerations in GPRS and UMTS systems in the previous section. When you look at these considerations and compare them with the QoS considerations within the Internet community in the form of IntServ and DiffServ, discussed in Section 5.3, we can see very little harmonization between the approaches taken by the two major parts of the future wireless Internet. The Internet approach follows the instructions from computer experts within the IETF, whereas the cellular experts work on their own within the ITU. The two technologies however, target the same thing, that is, providing QoS in future networks that support the Internet access to users regardless of their geographical location.

QoS must be seen as an end-to-end process. Assume, for example, that you want to establish a videoconferencing over the Internet using the UMTS as the access network for your communications. At the two very end points of this communication process we have the end user terminals, for example, a cellular phone at one end and a desktop computer connected to the wired Internet at the other end. The access technology here is thus composed of several systems: the local bearer service providing the service to the cellular phone user, the UMTS bearer service, and the external bearer service providing service to the desktop user. This configuration is illustrated in Figure 5.3.

Without the support of the required QoS indicators (e.g. delay and bandwidth in our current videoconferencing example) by all segments of the network from end to end, we cannot claim that we have a QoS support. UMTS has its own share in providing the QoS but the end-point bearer services also need to support similar QoS indicators in order to complete the end-to-end process. Although it is possible to provide the QoS with different ways of support by the individual segments in the network, it will be much more efficient and reliable to provide QoS with close interrelation between the individual segments.

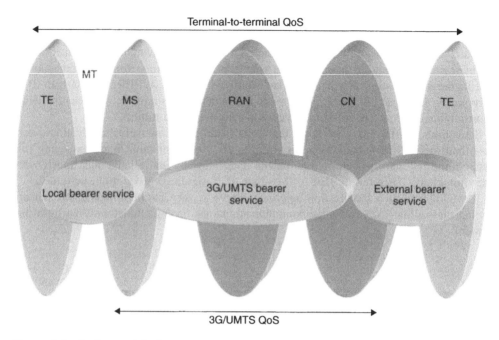

Figure 5.3 End-to-end QoS realization in cellular networks

The discussions given in the previous sections show that, unfortunately, at this time we do not see a close relationship between the Internet and cellular approaches on providing QoS. They have aimed at improving the QoS by their own approaches without paying much attention to the other. Providing end-to-end QoS with such a configuration would be a very difficult task, if not impossible, and therefore it will be a long time before we can see an end-to-end QoS support for the wireless Internet. Harmonization between the two approaches in a way that the service of one technology can cooperate and complement the service of the other remains the main issue toward QoS establishment for future networks.

The simple example above also illustrates that any promise from one system provider in supporting the QoS to its users has no basis as long as the QoS is not supported by all the system providers that complete the end-to-end line. The QoS definitions provided in this chapter should by now have cleared the differences between an end-to-end QoS system and a system with partial QoS support. The latter cannot be considered as QoS support at all.

5.6 SUMMARY AND CONCLUSIONS

In this chapter, we have developed a fundamental understanding of the QoS in telecommunication networks. After defining the meaning of quality, we have concluded that the QoS could not be set as a series of parameters to be used for all networks and all applications.

The QoS should be determined as a subset of required parameters for each network and each application. Therefore, the QoS is application- and network-oriented.

Further, we have developed a set of principles for providing QoS in a communication network, irrespective of the type of the network being mobile or fixed, data or voice. These principles are the requirement of packet classifications, packet isolation, efficient bandwidth utilization, and admission control. These principles can be implemented in any communication network that seeks QoS guarantee.

We have overviewed the Internet and cellular network initiatives for the QoS provisioning. The Internet main directions are the IntServ and DiffServ, with more promising views of the latter, in the context of being practical and feasible. Reservation protocols are named as the means for providing this Internet QoS so that the current best-effort service can be evolved into a guaranteed service.

For cellular networks, the QoS provisioning is discussed in different ways in the literature. There is little in common between the cellular QoS initiatives and the Internet approaches. Examples of GPRS and UMTS are given for the cellular part.

It is concluded that the diverse approach taken for providing the QoS in the Internet and in the cellular mobile communication systems could cause major problems in future wireless IP networks. The wireless IP needs both technologies as its foundation and taking different approaches on the same issue in the network would never provide an efficient resolution. Moreover, this will make the end-to-end QoS guarantee very difficult and costly, and without an end-to-end QoS solution, we cannot claim any victory in achieving QoS.

We will address QoS on many occasions in the following chapters in this book. Chapters on traffic management (Chapter 7) and mobility in cellular network (Chapter 8) are closely related to this important issue but other chapters will also go through the QoS provisioning in relation to the subjects in perspective (e.g. ad hoc networks in Chapter 12 and satellites in Chapter 13). Therefore, it is simply not possible to limit discussions on QoS to what has been provided in this chapter, and neither will the researchers in the field stop doing research on this subject, and, therefore, the research on QoS will have a long way to go.

REFERENCES

1. Chalmers D & Sloman M, A survey of quality of service in mobile computing environments, *IEEE Communications Surveys*, Second Quarter, 2(2), 2–10, 1999.
2. Guerin R & Peris V, Quality-of-service in packet networks: basic mechanisms and directions, *Computer Networks* 31, 169–189, 1999.
3. Aurrecoechea C, Campbell AT & Hauw L, A survey of QoS architectures, *ACM Multimedia System Journal*, Special Issue on QoS Architecture, May, 1998.
4. Knoche H & de Meer H, Quantitative QoS-mapping: a unifying approach, *Proceedings of 5th IFIP International Workshop on QoS*, 1997.
5. Hutchison D, Mauthe A & Yeadon N, Quality of service architecture: monitoring and control of multimedia communications, *Electronics and Communications Engineering Journal*, 9 (3), 100–106, 1997.

6. Das SK, Sen S K, Agrawal P & Basu K, Modeling QoS degradation in multimedia wireless networks, *Proc. IEEE Int. Conference on Personal Wireless Communications (ICPWC)*, Mumbai, India, December 1997.

7. Das SK & Sen SK, Quality-of-service degradation strategies in multimedia wireless networks, *Proc. IEEE 48th Vehicular Technology Conference (VTC '98)*, Ottawa, Canada, May 1998, pp. 1884–1888.

8. Nahrstedt K & Steinmetz R, Resource management in networked multimedia systems, *IEEE Computer*, **28**(5), 1995.

9. Campbell A & Coulson G, A QoS adaptive multimedia transport system: design, implementation and experiences, *Media Distributed Systems Engineering*, Vol. 4, 1997, pp. 48–58.

10. Hutchison D et al., In Sloman M (Ed.), *QoS Management in Distributed Systems in Network and Distributed Systems Management*, Addison-Wesley, Reading, Mass., 1994, pp. 273–302.

11. G Bochmann, and A Hafid, Some principles for quality of service management, *Distributed Systems Engineering*, Vol. 4, IOP Publishing, 1997, pp. 16–27.

12. Das SK, Jayaram R & Sen SK, An optimistic quality-of-service provisioning scheme for cellular networks, *Proc. IEEE Int. Conference on Distributed Computing Systems (ICDCS)*, Baltimore, Md., May 1997, pp. 536–542.

13. Blair G & Stefani J-B, *Open Distributed Processing and Multimedia*, Addison-Wesley, Reading, Mass., 1997.

14. Xiao X & Ni LM, Internet QoS: a big picture, *IEEE Network*, March/April, 8–18, 1999.

15. Fry M et al., QoS management in a world wide web environment which supports continuous media, *Distributed Systems Engineering*, Vol. 4, 1997, pp. 38–47.

16. Internet Engineering Task Force, Web site: http://www.ietf.org.

17. Knightly EW & Shroff NB, Admission control for statistical QoS: theory and practice, *IEEE Network*, March/April, 20–29, 1999.

18. Kim J & Jamalipour A, Measurement-based admission control for wireless IP networks, *2002 International Symposium on Performance Evaluation of Computer and Telecommunication Systems SPECTS 2002*, San Diego, Calif., 14–19 July 2002, pp. 587–591.

19. Grossglauser M & Tse D, A framework for robust measurement-based admission control, *Proc. ACM SIGCOMM '97*, Cannes, France, September 1997.

20. Gibbens R, Kelly F & Key P, A decision-theoretic approach to call admission control in ATM networks, *IEEE Journal on Selected Areas in Communications*, **13**(6), 1101–1113, 1995.

21. Jamin S, Shenker S, Danzig P, Comparison of measurement-based admission control algorithm for controlled-load service, *Proceeding of IEEE ICCS 1997*, Kobe, Japan, April 1997, pp. 973–980.

22. Jamin S et al., A measurement-based admission control algorithm for integrated service packet networks, *IEEE/ACM Transactions on Networking*, December 1996.

23. Cheng L, QoS-based on both call admission and cell scheduling, *Computer Networks and ISDN Systems* **29**, 555–567, 1997.

24. Knightly E & Shroff N, Admission control for statistical QoS: theory and practice, *IEEE Network*, March/April, 20–29, 1999.

25. Misic J, Chanson S & Lai F, Admission control for wireless multimedia networks with hard call level quality of service bounds, *Elsevier Computer Networks*, **31**, 125–140, 1999.

26. Peha J, Sched0.uling and admission control for integrated services networks: the priority token bank, *Elsevier Computer Networks*, **31**, 2559–2576, 1999.

27. Ayyagari D & Ephremides A, Admission control with priorities: approaches for multirate wireless systems, *Mobile Networks and Applications*, **4**, 209–218, 1999.

28. Braden R, Clark D & Shenker S, *Integrated Services in the Internet Architecture: An Overview*, RFC 1633, June 1994.

29. IETF DiffServ Working Group Charter, RFCs and Internet Drafts: http://www.ietf.org/html.charters/diffserv-charter.htm.

30. Blake S, Black D, Carlson M, Davies E, Wang Z & Weirs W, *An Architecture for Differentiated Services*, RFC 2475, December 1998.

31. Bernet Y, Ford P, Yavather R & Baker F, *A Framework for Integrated Services Operation Over DiffServ Networks*, RFC 2998, November 2000.

32. Nickols K, Jacobson V & Zhang L, *A Two-Bit Differentiated Services Architecture for the Internet*, RFC 2638, July 1999.

33. Braden R, Zhang L, Berson S, Herzog S & Jamin S, *Resource Reservation Protocol (RSVP) - Version 1-Functional Specification*, RFC 2205, September 1997.

34. Zhang L et al., RSVP: a new resource reservation protocol, *IEEE Network*, **7**(5), 1993.

35. *Service Level Specification Semantics and Parameters*, IETF Internet Draft (work in progress), February 2002, http://search.ietf.org/internet-drafts/draft-tequila-sls-02.txt.

6

Traffic Modeling for Wireless IP

Traffic modeling becomes increasingly important in future quality of service (QoS) wireless IP (Internet protocol) networks. It is indeed vitally important for any communication network to perform efficiently and to utilize the network resources more appropriately. The topic has been researched for many years in voice-based telephony networks but after the invention of the packet-switched networks and increasing the data applications over the Internet, it was not followed up accordingly. In continuation of our discussion in the previous chapter on QoS, we need to either design a perfect network by employing appropriate data traffic models or we need to rely on traffic management techniques, in order to provide QoS in data networks.

In this chapter, we look at the first approach, that is, to find appropriate traffic models for the future data networks and the wireless IP. In the next chapter, we will look at the traffic management techniques for wireless IP networks. We will describe several different characteristics of traffic in data networks and formulize the major models available. The discussion provided in this chapter will be sufficient for any researcher who is looking for a fundamental understanding and knowledge to start working on the important topic of traffic modeling in wired and wireless data networks.

6.1 INTRODUCTION

Telecommunication networks are evolving and they include more nonvoice traffic generated from Internet applications and other digital data sources. In a voice-centric network like most of the current telephony networks, the traditional traffic models, listed in

The Wireless Mobile Internet: Architectures, Protocols, and Services.   Abbas Jamalipour
© 2003 John Wiley & Sons, Ltd   ISBN: 0-470-84468-X

Table 6.1 Traditional traffic models for voice-centric networks

Probability distribution	Usage
Poisson	Packet and connection arrival
Exponential	Packet interarrival

Table 6.1, could be sufficient to evaluate the network performance, such as queuing performance and congestion control as well as the designing process.

In addition, the well-known Erlang formulas have provided universal solutions to network problems for both wireline and wireless circuit-switched networks. Reference [1] is a classic reference for traffic modeling in cellular networks.

6.1.1   Emerging trend of the next-generation mobile traffic

Today, Global System for Mobile communications (GSM) is the most widely used second-generation digital cellular system. Although the current GSM is optimized for voice communications, the next-generation cellular mobile, that is, the third-generation mobile, will accommodate voice, data, and multimedia technology with a vast range of applications as illustrated in Figure 6.1. The main focus of the next-generation mobile will be anywhere-anytime communications for both voice and other types of data transmission.

Internet and multimedia traffic can be characterized by frequent transitions between active and inactive states, often called *ON/OFF patterns*. The ON period represents the file-downloading time and the OFF period is the user-reading time. If the present circuit-switched technique is used, the bandwidth of the dedicated circuit is wasted during the OFF period. However, the packet-switched technology allows higher data transmission rates and uses the bandwidth only within the ON period [2]. For the emerging future

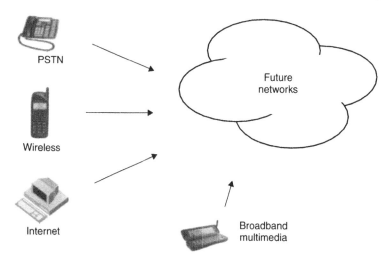

Figure 6.1   Emerging trends in the third-generation mobile traffic

network traffic, the current circuit-switched technique and the Erlang formulas are no longer appropriate to use [3,4].

6.1.2 Importance of traffic modeling

Although traffic modeling can be a time-consuming and resource-intensive process, it is the basic tool for performance evaluation and resource provisioning [4–10]. Figure 6.2 shows how traffic models are used as the input for analytical and simulation studies of telecommunication networks [4].

Traffic models have a lot of important roles in planning and managing new and existing networks. Let us name a few of their important roles.

- They support efficient network-dimensioning procedures and traffic management functions.
- They assist in characterizing and modeling traffic behavior that is used for accessing QoS.
- They help estimate the resource utilization in a network environment.

6.1.3 Traffic modeling criteria

A good traffic model should be able to characterize the network dynamics with an acceptable level of accuracy. By doing so, it has to be [11]

1. *General* enough to provide a good approximation to the field data. It means that the proposed model should rely on a few parameters that can readily and reliably be estimated from measured observation.
2. *Simple* enough to obtain analytically tractable results for performance evaluation. It means that the proposed model should be simple in terms of
   - mathematical analysis,
   - programming,
   - computing (i.e. fast simulation and numerical analysis).

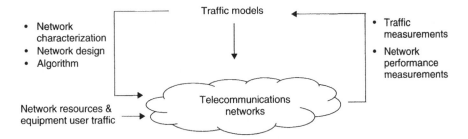

Figure 6.2 The role of traffic modeling in telecommunication networks

Table 6.2   Three important traffic characteristics in traffic modeling

Traffic characteristics	Description
Queuing performance	Buffer size and parameters
Marginal distribution	Statistical multiplexing and source traffic control
Autocorrelation	Prediction of queuing behavior

From an analytical point of view, a good traffic model should be able to capture three of the most important traffic characteristics of the measured data, that is, queuing performance, marginal distribution, and autocorrelation. These are described in Table 6.2.

The suitability of a traffic model is primarily determined by its ability to predict the queuing performance. More refined models predict a better marginal distribution and auto-correlation of the modeled traffic but usually at the cost of increase in model complexity.

6.2   POISSON AND MARKOV MODELS

Because of their theoretical simplicity, the Poisson and Markov Modulated Poisson Process (MMPP) are used extensively for packet-switched data networks. Although the self-similar nature of today's data traffic was noticed for some time, many practitioners ignored this phenomenon because of

1. inadequate physical explanation for the observed self-similar nature of measured traffic from today's packet networks,
2. lack of studies on its impact on the network, and protocol design and performance analysis.

Since the traditional traffic models are inadequate to capture today's network charac-teristics, the packet-switched data traffic models have been developed on the basis of measurements from actual data networks. However, their availability in wireless network modeling is still to be proven [12].

6.2.1   Limitation of the Poisson and Markov traffic models

When the traditional traffic modeling such as Poisson or MMPP is used in the framework of the ON/OFF pattern, the ON or OFF periods display either exponential or geometric distribution, that is, finite variance distribution. The traffic displays memory-less property, meaning that its correlation is of short-range-dependence (SRD). The aggregate traffic behaves like white noise and fails to capture any of the three most important traffic characteristics described in Table 6.2.

Recent traffic analyses on network traffic such as local area network (LAN) and wide area network (WAN) and application traffic such as World Wide Web (WWW) and vari-able bit rate (VBR) video traffic have revealed the prevalence of a long-range dependence

(LRD) on packet-switched networks [5–7,9,11,13–18]. This means that there is a high correlation of traffic over many timescales. Although the significance of traffic correlation on queuing performance was recognized, most of the studies were concentrated on SRD [5]. Table 6.3 shows some of the fundamental differences between traditional voice traffic and today's and emerging high-speed data traffic.

Apart from the differences described in Table 6.3, the next-generation mobile networks will offer many different applications and each application will have different QoS requirements. For example, in circuit-switched wireless networks, the network performance will be measured in terms of (1) continuous coverage and (2) high reliability of handovers. The failure of one of these two conditions results in dropped calls or inadequate QoS. However, in packet-switched networks, the nature of service is discontinuous and there is no strict restriction on delay requirements. Instead, packet error rates and loss rates are more important parameters to consider. Therefore, the network performance criteria have to be changed as well. So far, most of the work on self-similar traffic is concentrated on its impact on queuing performance [5,15,19–22]. However, its impact on admission and congestion control is rather neglected. Therefore, a close examination of these impacts on end-to-end QoS requirements of voice, data, and multimedia applications will be the focus of the next chapter on traffic management.

6.2.2   The need for new traffic models

Emerging high-speed network traffic displays new characteristics. Traditional traffic models fail to capture these characteristics and lead to an overly optimistic estimation of performance. The unexpected poor performance of asynchronous transfer mode (ATM) switches in the field may indicate that traditional traffic models are inappropriate for use in data-centric networks. With today's phenomenal increase in data traffic, it is essential

Table 6.3   Comparison between traditional and emerging network traffic

	Traditional traffic	Emerging network traffic
ON/OFF traffic distribution	*Exponential* or *geometric* distribution (i.e. finite variance distribution)	Heavy-tailed *distribution* (i.e. infinite variance distribution)
Burstiness	Multiplexing traffic streams tend to produce '*smoothed out*' aggregate traffic with reduced burstiness	Aggregate self-similar traffic streams can actually *intensify* burstiness
Aggregate traffic	Gaussian	LRD
Queuing performance	Queue length decreases *exponentially* with increase in buffer size	Buffer gain is *linear* so that queue length decreases linearly
Admission control	Extensive studies are done	Subject of future studies
Congestion control	Extensive studies are done	Subject of future studies

to understand the characteristics of data traffic in order to utilize the network resources and to optimize the network performance.

In theory, the traffic should become more and more like the Gaussian processes in the future [5,23]. The prevalent effect of a single application will be less significant in terms of aggregate traffic. However, at the moment the network traffic is not anywhere close to the Gaussian model. Over the past 20 years, numerous attempts were made to find an Erlang-like formula for the traditional telephony for broadband (i.e. multimedia) traffic [23]. However, so far, there is no such model that fits the role. Presently, the level of aggregation is not sufficient enough for the bad behavior of one traffic stream to dominate the overall network traffic characteristics. The need for good traffic models are more acute than ever.

6.3 CHARACTERISTICS OF THE EMERGING TRAFFICS

It is reasonable to assume that (1) session arrival is Poisson with an arrival rate of λ sessions per second and (2) the duration of each session is exponentially distributed. However, the packet-arrival patterns within the session depend on the application. Recent analysis on traffic measurements on packet-data networks such as LAN and WAN, show heavy-tailed, self-similar, fractal, and LRD characteristics. In this section, we have defined the terms that are frequently used to describe today's traffic and the emerging networks traffic.

6.3.1 Heavy-tailed

A distribution is heavy-tailed if the asymptotic shape of the distribution follows a power-law so that

$$P[X > x] \cong x^{-\alpha} \quad \text{as } x \longrightarrow \infty, 0 < \alpha < 2 \tag{6.1}$$

The parameter α describes the heaviness of the tail distribution so that as α gets smaller the distribution becomes more heavy-tailed. Figure 6.3 shows the effect of α in the heavy-tailed distribution. The asymptotic (i.e. tail) shape of the distribution is hyperbolic and converges slower than the exponential distribution. It appears to have a thicker tail distribution, and is therefore called a *fat-tailed* or *heavy-tailed distribution*. The heavy-tailed nature of the distribution comes from the fact that the larger portion of the probability mass may be present in the tail of the distribution. It differs from exponential, geometric, and Poisson distributions so that

- If $\alpha \leq 2$, the distribution has an infinite variance,
- If $\alpha \leq 1$, the distribution has an infinite mean.

Most commonly used examples of the heavy-tailed distributions are the Pareto and Weibull distribution.

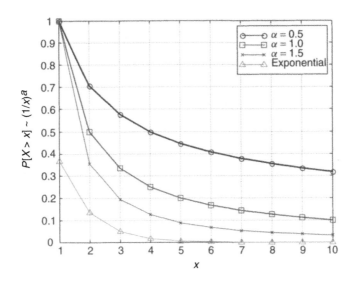

Figure 6.3   The effect of α in a heavy-tailed distribution

6.3.1.1 Pareto distribution

It is the simplest heavy-tailed distribution. Its distribution is hyperbolic over its entire range. Mathematically, the cumulative distribution function of the Pareto distribution, $F_p(x)$, is

$$F_p(x) = 1 - \left(\frac{k}{x}\right)^\alpha \tag{6.2}$$

where k is the minimum value of x and α is the heaviness of the tail distribution. Figure 6.4 shows the effect of k in the Pareto distribution. k is simply the scaling factor and does not affect the tail distribution. The effect of α is shown in Figure 6.3.

6.3.1.2 Weibull distribution

The cumulative distribution function of the Weibull distribution, $F_w(x)$, is

$$F_w(x) = 1 - e^{-(x/a)^b} \tag{6.3}$$

Both parameters a and b affect the tail distribution. However, the heavy-tailed nature of the Weibull distribution is more sensitive to the value of b. Figure 6.5 shows the effect of a and b in the Weibull distribution.

Usually, a heavy-tailed distribution describes traffic processes such as packet inter-arrival times and burst length. If traffic is heavy-tailed, it is highly correlated. It means that the arrival rate is higher than the service rate. In the context of traffic modeling, it is often used to describe the burst individual source traffic distributions.

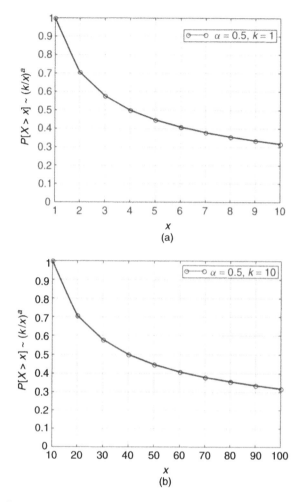

Figure 6.4   The effect of k in the Pareto distribution with (a) $k = 1$; and (b) $k = 10$

6.3.2   Self-similar

It is a scaling behavior of the finite dimensional distributions of a continuous- or discrete-time process. Traffic is *self-similar* if the aggregate traffic

- exhibits time correlation over a wide range of timescales, and
- can be characterized by a single parameter called *Hurst parameter* (H).

6.3.2.1 Self-similarity indicator

The Hurst parameter, H, is the measure of the degree of self-similarity of the aggregate traffic stream. As $H \to 1$, the degree of self-similarity increases. The Hurst parameter

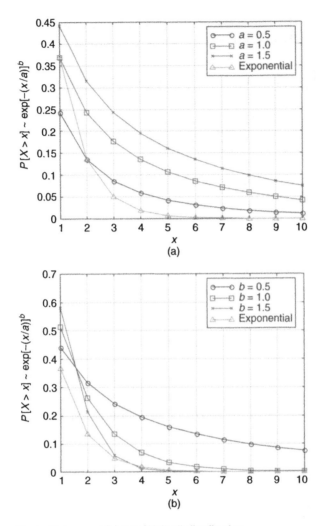

Figure 6.5 The effect of (a) *a*; and (b) *b* in Weibull distribution

can be measured in various ways. However, three of the most common methods are as follows:

1. *Variance versus Time*: If traffic is self-similar, then its slope $-\beta < -1$. For some historical reason, the relationship between the slope, $-\beta$, and H is

$$H = 1 - \frac{\beta}{2} \tag{6.4}$$

Therefore, H can be calculated by obtaining the slope of variance versus time graph.

2. *R/S plot*: Let $\{Y_k\}_{k=1}^n$ be an empirical time series with sample mean $\overline{Y}(n)$ and sample variance $S^2(n)$. The rescaled adjusted range, R/S statistic, is given by $R(n)/S(n)$ with

$$R(n) = \max\left\{\sum_{i=1}^{k}(Y_i - \overline{Y}(n)) : 1 \le k \le n\right\} - \min\left\{\sum_{i=1}^{k}(Y_i - \overline{Y}(n)) : 1 \le k \le n\right\}$$

(6.5)

$$E\left[\frac{R(n)}{S(n)}\right] \cong n^H, \qquad \text{for large } n$$

(6.6)

Normally, the H value of a self-similar process is $0.5 < H \le 1$ whereas that of the SRD process is $H \approx 0.5$.

3. *Whittle Estimator*: It provides the confidence interval but it requires some form of underlying stochastic process, which is a drawback. The most commonly used forms are

- fractional Gaussian noise (FGN) with $0.5 < H < 1$,
- fractional ARIMA (p, d, q) with $0 < d < 1/2$ (to be discussed shortly).

6.3.2.2 Description of self-similarity

- *Exactly self-similar (H = 1)*: A distribution appears indistinguishable from one another but distinctively different from pure noise.
- *Asymptotically self-similar (0.5 < H < 1.0)*: A distribution converges to a time series with nondegenerate autocorrelation structure.
- *Second-order self-similar*: For stationary sequences, whose aggregate processes possess the same nondegenerate autocorrelation functions as the original process.

This characteristic is often explained in terms of the high variability of individual connections that contributes to the aggregated traffic. Self-similarity is often used to describe individual application traffic.

6.3.3 Fractal

A fractal process is characterized by significant long bursts. These bursts are caused by downloading large files such as video files, long periods of high levels of VBR video, or intensive bursts of database activities. It is another term to describe the self-similarity of traffic. Current WAN traffic is often described as multifractal. Multifractal traffic can be considered as an extension of self-similar traffic, by considering properties higher than second-order characteristics so that it can capture more irregularities in the distribution.

6.3.4 Long-range-dependence

A process with LRD has an autocorrelation function, $r(k)$, of:

$$r(k) \approx k^{-\beta} \quad \text{as } k \longrightarrow \infty \quad \text{where } 0 < \beta < 1, \text{ and } \Sigma\, r(k) \longrightarrow \infty \qquad (6.7)$$

In other words, the autocorrelation function (1) decays hyperbolically and (2) is non-summable. For the conventional short-range dependence (SRD) process, an autocorrelation function decays exponentially. It is often used to describe the tail-end behavior of the autocorrelation function of a stationary time series. In traffic modeling, LRD is often used to describe the aggregate traffic such as WAN, whereas self-similarity is usually used in the context of LAN or individual application traffic.

Table 6.4 summarizes some typical traffic types and associated traffic distributions and models.

6.3.5 Suitability of self-similar and long-range dependence

After studying the terms that describe current and future network traffic characteristics, the next appropriate question would be "why does the traffic display these characteristics?" In References [9, 14, 24], it is pointed out that the heavy-tailed nature of ON and OFF periods has more to do with basic properties of information storage and processing. It is not a result of the network protocols or user preference. Therefore, changes in protocol processing and document display cannot remove the self-similarity of the web traffic. Also, it is shown that both the user's thinking or reading times and the file-size distributions are strongly heavy-tailed. In addition, Internet provides explicit support for multimedia formats; the file distribution is strongly heavy-tailed. Figure 6.6 shows the effect of multimedia files such as image and audio files on the file distribution. The values of α are taken from Reference [14].

Often, self-similarity in today's network traffic is explained in terms of application traffic. The burst data traffic and VBR real-time applications such as compressed video

Table 6.4 Traffic distributions and frequently used traffic models

Traffic types	Traffic distribution	Frequently used traffic models
Individual source traffic	Heavy-tailed ON/OFF distribution	• Pareto • Weibull
Individual application traffic or LAN	Self-similar	• FGN • FARIMA
Aggregate traffic	LRD Multifractal	• Fractional Brownian motion (FBm) model • M/G/∞ • M/Pareto

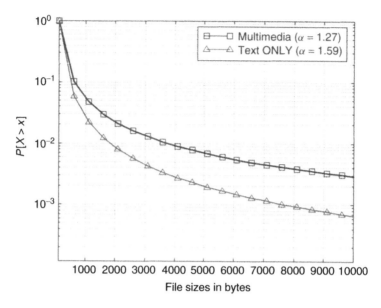

Figure 6.6 The effect of multimedia files on file distributions

and audio display (1) a certain degree of correlation between arrivals and (2) slow LRD in time. As a result, the aggregate traffic is self-similar. Or, it could be the high variety of individual connections (i.e. infinite variance) that contributes to the aggregate traffic.

Overall, the factors, apart from application traffic itself, that contribute to the self-similar nature and the LRD behavior of the emerging network traffic are

- user behavior—user-reading time and user-induced delay,
- file-size distribution,
- set of files available in the server.

Table 6.5 summarizes different traffic distributions and their associated applications.

Table 6.5 Traffic distributions and suitable applications

Traffic distribution	Description
Poisson	Session arrival process
Exponential	Session duration
Heavy-tailed	Suitable for burst individual source traffic with ON/OFF patterns
• Pareto	File-transfer time distribution, user-reading (thinking) time, user-induced delay
• Weibull	Machine-processing time, file downloading time

6.4 SELF-SIMILAR AND LRD TRAFFIC MODELS

As a conclusion, on the basis of the previous section, it appears that self-similar and LRD models are the most suitable models for future data networks, including the wireless IP. In this section, we explore these models further.

6.4.1 Traditional traffic models

Because of the long history of traditional telephony networks, there are plenty of traffic models available for voice-centric network traffic. The network traffic characteristics have been identified and extensive studies have already been completed to optimize the network resources.

6.4.1.1 Poisson

It is the oldest and one of the most elegant traffic models. The Poisson model is suitable for traffic applications that physically comprise a large number of independent traffic streams. Mathematically, the Poisson process is expressed as

$$P(n) = \frac{(\lambda t)^n}{n!} e^{-\lambda t} \tag{6.8}$$

where λ is the arrival rate per session and n is the number of individual traffic streams. The interarrival times $\{A_n\}$ are exponentially distributed with

$$P\{A_n \leq t\} = 1 - e^{-\lambda t} \tag{6.9}$$

The Poisson model has some elegant analytical properties:

- The superposition of the independent Poisson process is a new Poisson process.
- It is a memory-less process.

However, the model fails to capture the autocorrelation of traffic as it vanishes identically for all nonzero lags. It is expected that burst data traffic will dominate the future network traffic. In that case, it is essential to capture the autocorrelated nature of the traffic for predicting the performance. In high-speed data networks, the Poisson process is no longer appropriate and has lost its merits.

6.4.1.2 Markov

Unlike the Poisson model, the Markov model introduces some dependency into the random sequence $\{A_n\}$; therefore, it capture the traffic 'burstiness'. The process $\{A_n\}$ is defined in terms of a Markov transition matrix $P = [p_{ij}]$. The Markov property introduces dependency into inter-arrival separation, batch sizes, and successive workloads.

However, any traffic modeling requires a multistate Markov and each state adds several free parameters. In practice, it is time consuming to estimate these parameters.

6.4.1.3 Markov modulated

It introduces an explicit notion of state into the description of a traffic stream. Let $M = \{M(t)\}_{t=0}^{\infty}$ be a continuous-time Markov process with state space $\{1, 2, \ldots, m\}$. Assuming M is in state k, the probability law for traffic arrivals is completely determined by k and this holds for every $1 \leq k \leq m$. When M undergoes a transition to state j, then a new probability law for arrivals takes effect for the duration of state j, and so on. The most commonly used form of the Markov modulated process is the MMPP.

MMPP combines the simplicity of the modulating Markov process with that of the modulated Poisson process. It is particularly suitable for use in a single traffic source with a variable rate, by quantifying the rate into a finite number of rates so that each rate gives rise to a state in some Markov-modulating process. For example, a simple two-state MMPP model has been widely used to model voice traffic sources.

6.4.2 Current and future models

6.4.2.1 Fluid traffic model

In this model, traffic is considered as volume and is characterized by a flow rate. It is suitable to model the traffic where the individual traffic unit is insignificant, for example, individual cells in broadband ISDN (B-ISDN) ATM networks. Here, larger traffic units provide a simpler and better analysis of the network performance as well as saving, simulation, and computing resources. Fluid models are suitable for modeling burst traffic with ON/OFF patterns. For analytical tractability, the following assumptions are made:

- The ON-state traffic arrives deterministically at a constant rate λ.
- Traffic is switched off during the OFF state.
- The ON and OFF periods are exponentially distributed and mutually independent.

6.4.2.2 Self-similar models

Here, we describe three commonly used models for the self-similar process.

- *Fractional ARIMA (FARIMA)*: For LRD modeling, FARIMA is one of the most commonly used models for the self-similar process. The main advantage of this model is that it can model both LRD and SRD processes simultaneously. In addition, FARIMA provides quick simulation. It is particularly useful to simulate the queuing performance of SRD and LRD traffic simultaneously. By changing the parameters that affect the degree of SRD and LRD, we can identify the parameters that are more or less sensitive to SRD or LRD.

- *Fractional Gaussian Noise (FGN)*: Together with the FARIMA, FGN is another most frequently used stochastic model for self-similar traffic modeling. It is suitable for burst data and multimedia application traffic modeling with a prevalence of LRD. It provides a good estimation of queuing performance for aggregate traffic.

- *Transform-Expand-Sample (TES)*: This is able to capture both the marginal distributions and the autocorrelations of the measured traffic. A good transform expand sample (TES) model should satisfy the following three requirements simultaneously:

  1. The histogram of measured traffic matches the model's marginal distribution.

  2. The model's autocorrelations should match the measured traffic up to a reasonable lag.

  3. Good correspondence exists between the sample paths of the simulated and the measured data.

6.4.2.3 Long-range-dependence (LRD) models

Here, we describe three commonly used models for the LRD process.

- *Fractional Brownian Motion (FBm)*: It is a Gaussian process with a mean zero and stationary increments. Let us define B_H as an FBm and its covariance function as:

$$B_H(s)B_H(t) = (1/2)\{s^{2H} + t^{2H} - |s - t|^{2H}\} \tag{6.10}$$

Its increments

$$Gj = B_H(j) - B_H(j - 1) \quad j = 1, 2, \ldots \tag{6.11}$$

are called fractional Gaussian noise and

$$G_H(j)G_H(j + k) \approx H(2H - 1)k^{2H-2} \text{ as } k \longrightarrow \infty \tag{6.12}$$

The power-law decay of the covariance characterizes long-range-dependence. As H becomes larger, the decay becomes slower.

- *M/G/∞*: The M/G/∞ model is chosen to generate self-similar arrivals. The advantage of this model is that it introduces multifractal behavior at small/medium timescales without affecting the asymptotic self-similarity. It is considered to be more conservative than FBm as it predicts a stricter queuing performance.

- *M/Pareto*: The M/Pareto model is a particular type of the general M/G/∞ model. It is simple and particularly useful to estimate the queuing performance of a variety of realistic multimedia traffic streams. Another benefit of using M/Pareto is that the superposition of multiple independent M/Pareto processes is an M/Pareto process with a combined Poisson rate, λ. With an appropriate choice of λ, the M/Pareto process provides an accurate prediction of the queuing performance. Some of drawbacks are (1) there is no systematic way of calculating the appropriate value of λ and (2) it is difficult to estimate the Hurst parameter, H, from a finite data set.

Table 6.6 summarizes characteristics of different traffic models.

Table 6.6 Traditional, current, and future traffic models

Traffic model	Applications	Mathematical complexity	Computing complexity	Advantages	Disadvantages
Poisson	• Voice • Large number of independent traffic streams	Low	Low	• Oldest and commonly used model • Superposition of Poisson process is a new Poisson process • Memory-less process	• Fails to capture autocorrelation • Optimistic estimation of queuing performance for burst traffic
Markov	N/A	High	High	• Capable of capturing correlation of traffic (i.e. nonzero autocorrelations)	• Inflexible • Complexity overshadows accuracy
MMPP	• A single traffic source with variable rates	Low	Low	• Simple and flexible • Possible to capture some degree of correlation of traffic	• Inadequate autocorrelation • Unsuitable for LRD traffic
Fluid	• ATM traffic • Bursty traffic	Medium	Low	• Simple • Fast simulation • Suitable to model bursty traffic with ON/OFF patterns	• Unsuitable for variable rate traffic
Fractional ARIMA	• Voice • Bursty data and multimedia traffic	Low	Medium—high	• Flexible • Suitable for self-similar traffic with SRD and LRD	• High computing complexity
TES	• Broadband traffic streams • Nonstationary traffic	Medium	Low	• Fast simulation • Suitable to capture both marginal and autocorrelation functions of the traffic	• Requires high programming complexity

Gaussian	• Aggregated network traffic	• Low	• Low	• Simple • Good representation of network traffic as more traffic is aggregated together	• Overly optimistic estimation of network performance if the aggregation level is low
FBm (continuous-time)	• Real-audio • Real-video • Aggregated network traffic	• Low	• Medium—high	• Flexible • No need to select a sampling interval • Simplest Gaussian model to capture today's network traffic	• Unsuitable for small timescales simulation • Optimistic estimation of queuing performance
Fractional Gaussian noise (Discrete-time)	• Burst data & multimedia application traffic	• Medium	• Medium	• Flexible • Good estimation of queuing performance for aggregated traffic	• Unsuitable for self-similar traffic with both SRD and LRD
Hyper-Erlang	• User mobility • Self-similar traffic	• Low	• Low	• Simple and general • Provides a good user mobility model in wireless and mobile networks	• Unsuitable in traffic management context
M/Pareto	• Broadband traffic streams (Ethernet, IP)	• Low	• Low—medium	• Simple • Suitable for current network traffic where traffic is not Gaussian enough • Good estimation of queuing performance	• Inadequate marginal distribution or autocorrelation function • No simple formula to determine the appropriate value for λ or H
M/G/∞	• Aggregated network traffic	• Medium	• Medium	• Introduce multifractal behavior at small/medium timescales • Good estimation of queuing performance	—

6.4.3 Traffic models for the Internet applications

In Reference [18], four types of traffic profiles have been proposed, on the basis of the most frequently used wireless applications, e-mail, WWW, file transfer protocol (FTP), and telemetry traffic. Table 6.7 summarizes data traffic models and their respective numerical parameters. We will discuss the first three traffic types in this section. For the readers who are interested in other literature on the Internet data traffic model, Reference [24] and the references given therein provide some mathematical representations.

6.4.3.1 E-mail traffic

E-mail traffic models are summarized in Table 6.8. The message is downloaded from the mail server to the mobile terminal during the ON period. The length of the ON period depends on the message size and the instantaneous throughput available to the user. The OFF period is the reading time taken by the user.

The OFF period distribution of the e-mail is Pareto. The minimum OFF period (i.e. k_e) is the minimum time required by a user to read an e-mail message. From the given parameters, the e-mail OFF time distributions are illustrated in Figure 6.7 for $k_e = 30$ s and 60 s. Comparing the OFF time distributions of $k_e = 30$ s and $k_e = 60$ s, it is reasonable to assume that $k_e = 30$ s, since most users will finish reading an e-mail message in 2 to 3 min, provided there is no attachment.

6.4.3.2 WWW traffic

Typical WWW traffic models are summarized in Table 6.9. For the WWW traffic, the ON and OFF patterns are still clear but we have also started observing active and inactive OFF patterns (see Figure 6.8). As in e-mail, the file is transferred on the downlink during the ON period and its period depends on the file size, α, and the available downlink bandwidth.

The ON period distribution is based on the file size. Here, k_w is the minimum file size in bytes during the ON period. However, the Inactive OFF period distribution is based on the user reading time; therefore, k'_w is the minimum time required by the user to read a web page.

Active OFF time

By definition, active OFF represents the time needed to process transmitted files such as interpret, format, and display a document component. Generally, if the OFF time is less than 1 s, it is assumed to be the machine-processing and display time for data items that are retrieved as part of a multipart document. However, some embedded components require more than 30 s to interpret, format, and display. As a rule, if the OFF time is greater than 30 s, it is considered as user-initiated delay (i.e. reading time). Therefore, the minimum value of k'_w for the inactive OFF-time distribution should be at least 30 s (i.e. $k'_w = 30$ s). Figure 6.9 shows the active OFF time distribution based on the parameters given in

Table 6.7 Wireless packet data traffic models and parameters [18]

Application	Period	Distribution	Formula	Parameters
E-mail	Packet arrival	Poisson	$P(m_e = n) = \dfrac{(P_e \lambda_e T_e)^n}{n!} e^{-P_e \lambda_e T_e}$	
	ON	Weibull	$F_e(x_e) = \begin{cases} 1 - e^{-e^{k_1} \cdot x_e^{c_1}} \\ 1 - e^{-e^{k_2} \cdot x_e^{c_2}} \end{cases}$	$C_1 = 1.2 - 3.2(m = 2.04)$, $C_2 = 0.31 - 0.46(m = 0.37)$ $k_1 = 14.0 - 21.0(m = 17.64)$, $k_2 = 2.8 - 3.4$
	OFF	Pareto	$\Gamma_e(t_e) = 1 - \left(\dfrac{k_e}{t_e}\right)^{\alpha_e}$	$k_e = 30 - 60$ s, $\alpha_e = 0.5 - 1.5$
WWW	ON	Pareto	$f_w(x_w) = 1 - \left(\dfrac{k_w}{x_w}\right)^{\alpha_w}$	$k_w = 1000$ bytes, $\alpha_w = 1.1 - 1.5$
	Active OFF	Weibull	$\Gamma_w(t_w) = 1 - e^{-\left(\frac{t_w}{a}\right)^b}$	$a = 0.328$, $b = 1.46$
	Inactive OFF	Pareto	$\Gamma'_w(t'_w) = 1 - \left(\dfrac{k'_w}{t'_w}\right)^{\alpha'_w}$	$k'_w = 1$ sec, $a'_w = 1.5$
FTP	ON	Pareto	$F_f(t_f) = 1 - \left(\dfrac{k_f}{t_f}\right)^{\alpha_f}$	$0.9 \leq \alpha_f \leq 1.1$ (by Crovella [14])
	OFF	Weibull	$\Gamma_f(t_f) = 1 - e^{-\left(\frac{t_f}{b}\right)^a}$	

Table 6.8 E-mail traffic models

E-mail	Traffic models
ON period	Weibull distribution
OFF period	Pareto distribution

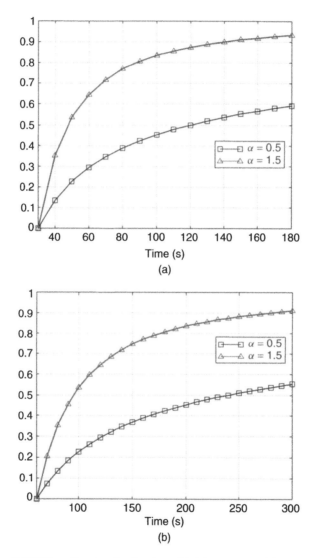

Figure 6.7 E-mail OFF time Pareto distribution with (a) $k_e = 30$ s; (b) $k_e = 60$ s

Table 6.9 WWW traffic models

WWW	Traffic models
ON	Pareto distribution
Active OFF	Weibull distribution
Inactive OFF	Pareto distribution

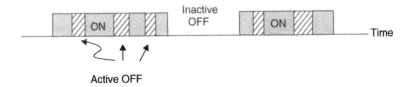

Figure 6.8 Active and inactive OFF patterns in WWW traffic

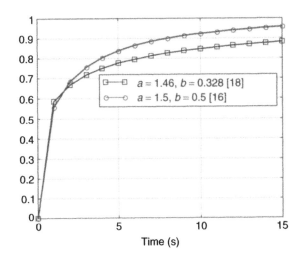

Figure 6.9 WWW active OFF period with different parameters

References [16,18]. The active OFF-time distribution provided by Reference [16] is more heavy-tailed. If the web page is text-intensive, the parameters provided by Reference [18] are more suitable. However, today, there is a lot of image, audio, and even video files in the web page; therefore, the parameters provided by Reference [16] seem more appropriate to use.

Inactive OFF time

The inactive OFF time is the user reading time. According to References [14,18], the ON period is more heavy-tailed (i.e. smaller α) than the OFF period. However, in Reference [16], it is the inactive OFF time that contributes more to the heavy-tailed behavior. Assuming that the minimum reading time of a web page (i.e. k'_w) is 30 s, the parameters given in References [13,17] provide a reasonable inactive OFF-time distribution. Reference [16] has also assumed that $k'_w = 30$ s and the OFF-time distribution assumed there is more appropriate for the text-intensive web pages, where it takes more time for a user to finish reading. However, $k'_w = 1$ s is too short a time and provides an inappropriate OFF-time distribution. This is shown in Figure 6.10. For the sake of comparison, Figure 6.11 also illustrates the WWW ON period file size distribution for different k_w.

Web file size

In Reference [14], it is interesting to notice that the web file system prefers documents in the 256–512 byte range, while with the UNIX file system the file sizes are more commonly in the 1000–4000 byte range. Also, UNIX files show heavier tail distribution

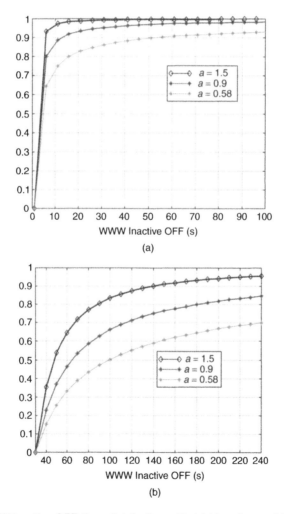

Figure 6.10 WWW inactive OFF-time distribution with (a) $k'_w = 1$ s; and (b) $k'_w = 30$ s

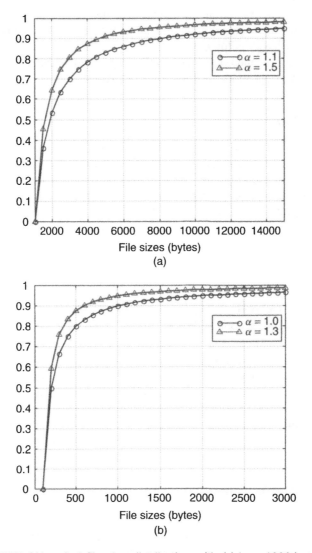

Figure 6.11 WWW ON period file size distribution with (a) $k_w = 1000$ bytes; and (b) $k_w = 100$ bytes

Table 6.10 File types and their sizes in bytes

File sizes (bytes)	File types
<1000	Text
1000–30 000	Image
30 000–300 0000	Audio
300 000	Video

(i.e. smaller α) than web files despite the emphasis on multimedia in the web. The web file systems are currently more biased toward small files than UNIX systems. Some typical Internet file sizes are listed in Table 6.10.

Table 6.11 provides a comparison between the traffic models and numerical parameters proposed for WWW applications in References [14,16,18].

6.4.3.3 FTP traffic

The behavior of the FTP sessions is similar to e-mail but with larger file sizes and longer ON periods. A summary of appropriate FTP traffic models is given in Table 6.12.

In case of an FTP session, the OFF periods may be shorter than the ON periods. The OFF-periods distribution rather depends on the user-induced delay such as user think time and typing speed. As pointed out in Table 6.5, the Weibull distribution is more appropriate to describe the machine-processing, interpret, and display times. Therefore, the Pareto distribution will provide a better fit for the OFF-period distribution.

6.5 SHORT-RANGE AND LONG-RANGE DEPENDENCE MODELS

Recent studies on high-speed traffic such as Ethernet packets show not only LRD but also strong short-range dependence (SRD) as well. As the network gets larger and carries traffic from more independent sources, future traffic will be more and more Gaussian-like. However, the current network traffic is not anywhere near Gaussian. Therefore, in order to capture the current and emerging network traffic characteristics, it is necessary that the traffic models are able to represent both LRD and SRD simultaneously.

6.5.1 Self-similar traffic models

Both FGN and Fractional ARIMA (FARIMA) are the most commonly used stochastic self-similar traffic models. However, FARIMA is the preferred model as it can be used to model both SRD and LRD simultaneously. In addition, although there is no extensive work done in TES modeling, it can also be used to model both SRD and LRD and promises to give the three important traffic characteristics described previously in Table 6.2. On the basis of these conclusions, the most preferable self-similar traffic models are FARIMA, TES, and FGN in that order. Table 6.13 illustrates this conclusion.

6.5.2 Long-range-dependence traffic models

Although it is hard to determine the sufficient aggregation level where short-range dependence (SRD) effects can be ignored, if the traffic is aggregated enough, SRD would be

Table 6.11   Comparison of the WWW traffic models and corresponding parameters

Application	Period	Reference [17]	Reference [15]	Reference [13]
WWW	ON	Pareto $f_w(x_w) = 1 - \left(\dfrac{k_w}{x_w}\right)^{\alpha_w}$ x_w: WWW file size k_w: minimum file size $\alpha_w = 1.1 - 1.5$ $k_w = 1000$ bytes or larger	Weibull $\Gamma_{w_{ON}}(t_{w_{ON}}) = 1 - e^{-\left(\frac{t_{w_{on}}}{\theta}\right)^k}$ $\theta : e^{4.4} - e^{4.6}$ $k : 0.91 - 0.77$	Pareto $f_w(x_w) = 1 - \left(\dfrac{k_w}{x_w}\right)^{\alpha_w}$ x_w: WWW file size k_w: minimum file size $\alpha_w = 1.0 - 1.3$ $k_w = 100$ bytes or larger
	Active OFF	Weibull $\Gamma_w(t_w) = 1 - e^{-\left(\frac{t_w}{a}\right)^b}$ $a = 0.328,\ b = 1.46$	Weibull $\Gamma_w(t_w) = 1 - e^{-\left(\frac{t_w}{a}\right)^b}$ $a = 1.5,\ b = 0.5$	Weibull
	Inactive OFF	Pareto $\Gamma'_w(t'_w) = 1 - \left(\dfrac{k'_w}{t'_w}\right)^{\alpha'_w}$ $k'_w = 1,\ \alpha'_w = 1.5$	Pareto $\Gamma'_w(t'_w) = 1 - \left(\dfrac{k'_w}{t'_w}\right)^{\alpha'_w}$ $k'_w = 30,\ \alpha'_w = 0.9 - 0.58$	Pareto $\Gamma'_w(t'_w) = 1 - \left(\dfrac{k'_w}{t'_w}\right)^{\alpha'_w}$ $k'_w = 30,\ \alpha'_w = 1.5$

Table 6.12   FTP traffic models

FTP	Traffic model
ON period	Pareto distribution
OFF period	Weibull distribution

Table 6.13   Self-similar traffic modeling preferences

Preference	Traffic models	Traffic types	Applications
1	FARIMA	Self-similar traffic with both SRD and LRD	• Ethernet traffic modeling • LAN • Cooperate network
2	TES	Self-similar traffic with both SRD and LRD	• LAN • Cooperate network traffic modeling
3	FGN	Self-similar traffic with LRD only	• WAN

Table 6.14   Traffic models for LRD modeling

Preference	Traffic models	Traffic types	Applications
1	M/Pareto	• LRD	• Multimedia traffic • Broadband traffic in general
2	M/G/∞	• Multifractal LRD traffic	• WAN

averaged out. We only need to consider the LRD properties. On the basis of the mathematical and computational complexity, the M/Pareto and M/G/∞ models are appropriate for LRD modeling, as shown in Table 6.14.

A traffic model should match most of the measured traffic characteristics. However, a model is a tool for decision-making. Its quality depends on the quality of the decisions it leads to rather than on its closeness to physical reality [12].

6.6   SUMMARY AND CONCLUSIONS

In this chapter, we have examined the most suitable traffic models for the communication networks, with an emphasis on current and future data networks and wireless IP networks. The future networks will have the Internet applications as their primary sources of traffic and, similar to the requirement of an appropriate model in the traditional telephony networks, we will need to come up with respective traffic models for the future wireless data network, in order to design them more appropriately.

Modeling of data traffic loads, however, is not an easy task and not comparable with the voice-centric telephony networks. There are many different multimedia traffics coming from current and future applications, and having a single model to illustrate the characteristics of all these traffic would be a complex research task in the years to come.

Considering the exponential increase in the traffic load of the data networks and the necessity of designing these systems by using precise traffic models, there are not many available models. This could be because of the complexity involved in finding these models or the lack of feeling the requirement for such a traffic model at this time. Soon, the wireless data technology will find the need to investigate more on this important issue, the fundamentals of which we have described in this chapter. The materials presented here can provide the required knowledge for the traffic engineering as well as for researchers in the field.

When a good traffic model is not available during the design process of a communication network or when applying an available traffic model, it makes the network design too complicated, and we need to search for other alternatives. Traffic management techniques are considered as appropriate partial replacements to precise traffic modeling, and we thus discuss this topic in the following chapter.

REFERENCES

1. Hong D & Rappaport SS, Traffic model and performance analysis for cellular mobile radio telephone systems with prioritized and nonprioritized handoff procedures, *IEEE Transactions on Vehicular Technology*, **VT-35**(3), 1986.
2. Ho J Zhu Y & Madhavapeddy S, Throughput and buffer analysis for GSM general packet radio services, *Proceedings of IEEE WCNC '99*, New Orleans, September 1999.
3. Wirth P, Teletraffic implications of database architectures in mobile and personal communications, *IEEE Communications Magazine*, **33**(6), 54–59, 1995.
4. Wirth P, The role of teletraffic modeling in the new paradigm, *IEEE Communications Magazine*, **35**(8), 86–92, 1997.
5. Addie R, Zukerman M & Neame T, Broadband traffic modeling: simple solutions to hard problems, *IEEE Communications Magazine*, **36**(8), 88–95, 1998.
6. Dahlberg TA & Jung J, Teletraffic modeling for mobile communications, *Proceedings of IEEE ICC '98*, Atlanta, Ga., June 1998.
7. Fiorini P, On modeling concurrent heavy-tailed network traffic sources and its impact upon QoS, *Proceedings of IEEE ICC '99*, Vancouver, Canada, June 1999.
8. Lam D, Cox D & Widom J, Teletraffic modeling for personal communications services, *IEEE Communications Magazine*, **35**(2), 79–87, 1997.
9. Lazar A, Programming telecommunication networks, *IEEE Network*, **11**(5), 8–18, 1997.
10. Sahinoglu Z & Tekinay S, On multimedia networks: self-similar traffic and network performance, *IEEE Communications Magazine*, **37**(1), 48–52, 1999.
11. Fang Y, Hyper-Erlang distributions and traffic modeling in wireless and mobile networks, *Proceedings of IEEE WCNC '99*, New Orleans, September 1999.

12. Pirhonen R, Rautava T & Penttinen J, TDMA convergence for packet data services, *IEEE Personal Communications Magazine*, **6**(3), 68–73, 1999.

13. Chan MC & Woo T, Next-generation wireless data services: architecture and experience, *IEEE Personal Communications Magazine*, **6**(1), 20–30, 1999.

14. Crovella M & Bestavros A, Self-similarity in world wide web traffic: evidence and possible causes, *IEEE/ACM Transactions on Networking*, **5**(6), 835–846, 1997.

15. Desaulniers-Soucy N & Iuoras A, Traffic modeling with universal multifractals, *Proceedings of IEEE Globecom '99*, Rio de Janerio, Brazil, December 1999, pp. 1058–1065.

16. Deng S, Empirical model for WWW document arrivals at access link, *Proceedings of IEEE ICC '96*, Dallas, Tex., June 1996, pp. 1797–1802.

17. Frost V & Melamed B, Traffic modeling for telecommunications networks, *IEEE Communications Magazine*, **32**(3), 70–81, 1994.

18. Ho J & Zhu Y, *Wireless Packet Data Traffic Profile*, Nortel Networks, February 1999, Draft version 0.1.1.

19. Grossglauser M & Bolot J, On the relevance of long-range dependence in network traffic, *IEEE/ACM Transactions on Networking*, **7**(5), 629–640, 1999.

20. Kant K, On aggregated traffic generation with multifractal properties, *Proceedings of IEEE Globecom '99*, Rio de Janerio, Brazil, December 1999, pp. 1179–1186.

21. Li J-S, Wolisz A & Popescu-Zeletin R, Fast simulation of self-similar traffic, *Proceedings of IEEE ICC '98*, Atlanta, Ga., June 1998.

22. Shu Y, Jin Z, Zhang L & Wang L, Traffic prediction using FARIMA models, *Proceedings of IEEE ICC '99*, Vancouver, Canada, June 1999.

23. Neame TD, Addie RG & Zukerman M, Modeling superposition of many sources generating self similar traffic, *Proceedings of IEEE Globecom '99*, Rio de Janerio, Brazil, December 1999, pp. 1048–1052.

24. You C & Chandra K, Time series models for Internet data traffic, *Proceeding of the IEEE LCN* 1999, pp. 164–171.

7

Traffic Management for Wireless IP

In case precise traffic modeling is difficult to achieve in a given communication network, traffic management techniques would be the only choice in order to maintain quality in that network. Traffic management includes many different techniques from admission control to scheduling algorithms, buffer management, and many more and it could be the subject of a single book. In this chapter we describe several aspects of traffic management to see the benefits of proper traffic management implemented in a wireless Internet protocol (IP) network. Admission control techniques and specifically measurement-based admission control (MBAC) will be our main focus in this chapter. The chapter also covers some practical issues such as parameter design and simulation techniques, which are important in all research topics in the field.

7.1 INTRODUCTION

Traffic management is a set of policies and mechanisms that allow a network to efficiently satisfy a diverse range of service requests. Admission control, scheduling, buffer management, and flow control can all be considered as forms of traffic management. The main issue in traffic management is how to balance the tension between *diversity* and *efficiency*; both are necessary for providing quality of service (QoS) [1–8]. In order to achieve this main objective, any traffic management scheme has to be efficient enough to prevent and recover from network congestion [9–12]. In the following, a summary of these techniques with an emphasis on wireless networks is presented.

Bandwidth allocation: Most of the earlier research into bandwidth allocation concentrated on the problem of optimizing frequency reuse in the cellular system's air interface.

The Wireless Mobile Internet: Architectures, Protocols, and Services.   Abbas Jamalipour
© 2003 John Wiley & Sons, Ltd   ISBN: 0-470-84468-X

However, since the introduction of data communication over cellular networks, the focus has been shifted onto the issues of bandwidth sharing and dynamic bandwidth allocation. Considering the varying data rate services that are demanded by mobile users, the amount of bandwidth used at any one time may be different. Given the limited amount of system bandwidth, all the proposed mobile data solutions would be needed to implement channel allocation algorithms that attempt to optimize bandwidth usage. In wireless Internet, the transport layer protocol header compression, for example, could be one method to optimize bandwidth usage and decrease packet loss. Further work on an efficient bandwidth allocation scheme will require knowledge about all layers of the network protocol stack.

Admission control: Admission control is an evaluation a network makes before accepting a proposed new connection. It is the process of deciding what channel to allocate to a new call. We will discuss admission control techniques in detail in this chapter.

Flow control: One important issue in a network is the flow control. The purpose of flow control mechanisms is to solve the incompatibility of the speed of transmission from a fast sender to a slow receiver. With a connectionless network, no flow control is applied to packets inside the network. It is left to the transport layer protocol within each end system to perform flow control on an end-to-end basis. Transmission control protocol (TCP) provides a means for the receiver to govern the amount of data sent by the sender. Changing the congestion window size and retransmission strategy in TCP determines how fast data can flow through the TCP connection, and also helps to control and avoid congestion. The minimum amount of time that is required for the transmission of a TCP segment plus the time required for reception of its corresponding acknowledgement is called the round-trip time (RTT). The TCP window determines the maximum number of packets that can be transmitted within a round-trip time. A bigger window offered by the receiver will result in higher throughput.

Traffic shaping and rate control: A network can be managed much more efficiently if the traffic entering the network is smooth. For transmitting data over a wireless link, the burst stream can be shaped to smooth out the stream. This may, however, incur additional delay. Shapers always use a buffer. Little has been published in the area of rate control in wireless IP networks. Most research has focused on the rate control of signaling traffic.

Congestion control: The challenge of congestion control is to develop algorithms at the system and/or network levels that allow a reasonable level of throughput to be maintained even in the face of massive surges of traffic. The congestion control problems associated with pure datagram networks are difficult, but effective solutions do exist. The existing approaches for congestion control in packet-switching networks cover a broad range of techniques, including window (buffer) flow control, source quench, slow start, schedule-based control, and so on. Implementing similar congestion handling techniques for use in wireless IP networks will be most important for successful network operation.

Scheduling: The basic function of the scheduler is to arbitrate between packets that are ready for transmission on the link. There are a number of scheduling algorithms available for use in mobile data networks such as the round-robin scheduling mechanism for resource assignment on the base station side in a cellular data network, and weighted fair queuing (WFQ) or the multilevel feedback queue-based approach. Also, a policy-based scheduling is a priority-based scheduling scheme in which a packet from a non-real-time queue is never scheduled until the real-time queue is empty.

Figure 7.1 shows the general network architecture of wireless networks based on the open system interconnection (OSI) reference model. Figure 7.2 shows the main functions carried out at the network and data link layers. The most distinct difference between these two layers is that in the case of the network layer, traffic management is focused on an *aggregate* basis, whereas in the data link layer, it is focused on an *individual* basis. For example, admission control is implemented at the network layer and it is on a *call* basis, whereas access control is implemented in the data link layer and it is on a *packet* basis. Although both admission and access controls try to achieve similar goals such as high utilization, their objectives and performance measurements are different.

One of the main issues in traffic management is how efficiently a congestion event in the network is handled. Congestion is a state in which the network performance degrades because of the saturation of network resources such as communication bandwidth, processor cycles, and memory buffers. As a result, a network will experience long delays,

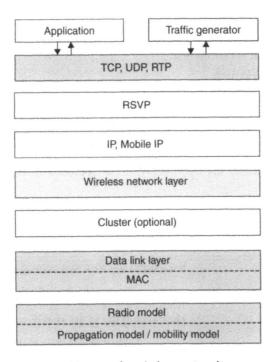

Figure 7.1   General network architecture for wireless networks

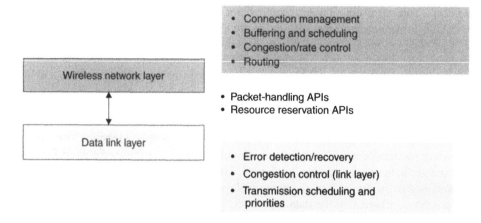

Figure 7.2   Main functions of the network and data link layers

waste of system resources, or even network collapse. Network congestion has been well recognized as a resource-sharing problem. Congestion control is about preventing, avoiding, and recovering from network congestion. A certain measurement or mechanism is needed to prevent the network from operating in a congested region for any significant period of time. This is one of the main objectives of *traffic management*.

In a broad sense, there are two approaches to deal with network congestion [11]. They are

- avoidance/prevention approach, and
- detection/recovery approach.

Table 7.1 describes the pros and cons of each approach for congestion control. Traffic management schemes such as admission control and scheduling are used in systems where the avoidance/prevention approach is the preferred option to manage network congestion problems. On the other hand, flow control and other feedback traffic management schemes are used in systems where the detection/recovery approach is sufficient to control the network congestion.

Table 7.1   Two basic approaches in congestion control

Congestion control	Pros and cons
Avoidance/prevention	√ Reasonable approach in a network based on virtual connections or circuits
	× Tends to waste resources on average
Detection/recovery	√ More appropriate in the TCP/IP world where there are no explicit connections at the IP level
	× Waste resources during the transient periods

As networks become larger and heterogeneous with higher speeds and integrated traffic loads, the congestion problem becomes more important and difficult to handle. *Congestion is a dynamic problem and it is not trivial to solve.*

According to the discussions in Chapter 6, we have observed that recent network traffic displays long-range dependence (LRD) or self-similar characteristics. This trend is due to the increase in data traffic. In recent studies [13–16], it is pointed out that in the presence of LRD, it takes longer to recover from congestion, once it occurs. Also, a small increase in traffic causes drastic degradation in QoS. Considering that most wireless IP network traffic will be of the data type, which has LRD properties, network congestion problems should be dealt with an *avoidance/prevention* approach. On the other hand, in case network congestion is unavoidable, its damage is minimal and easily recovered by employing *detection/recovery*-based traffic management schemes. With that point in mind, we have focused our attention on congestion *avoidance/prevention*-based traffic management schemes. As a fundamental congestion-avoidance type of traffic management, in this chapter we consider the admission control in wireless IP networks.

In Section 7.2, we have divided admission control schemes into two groups: (1) parameter-based schemes and (2) measurement-based schemes, with brief descriptions of each scheme. The section also explains the major difference between these two schemes and summarizes the advantages and disadvantages of both schemes.

In Section 7.3, wireless IP networks are discussed. The discussion is focused on network configurations and the unique characteristics of the wireless access channels and its traffic in wireless IP networks. It also discusses why an admission control is required in wireless IP networks. In addition, it explains why we have focused on measurement-based approach.

In Section 7.4, MBAC is described in detail, including network loading estimation algorithms and measurement parameters. In addition, it also shows possible sources of errors and weaknesses of the MBAC that might adversely affect its performance.

In Section 7.5, the network reference model for the discussions in this chapter is provided followed by implementation issues of the MBAC. We have also described how admission criteria were implemented on new and handoff traffics.

In Section 7.6, we have shown some preliminary simulation results to justify the parameter value selections. We have also verified our simulation system by comparing the average service waiting time with the analytical system using an M/G/1 queuing model.

In Section 7.7, two of the most common admission criteria are examined, namely (1) reservation and (2) priority, on the basis of MBAC. It is assumed that the system has a single service class with *tolerant-and-adaptive* real-time applications. Here, we have examined two aspects: (1) the effect of admission control and (2) the effect of traffic characteristics on the system performance. Simulation results are shown and the analysis is drawn from the simulation. A conclusion on the issue of traffic management and the schemes discussed in the chapter are provided in Section 7.8.

7.2 ADMISSION CONTROL

Admission control limits the number of flows to be admitted into the network such that each individual flow obtains the desired QoS [17–22]. The network task is to evaluate

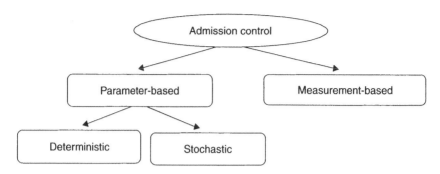

Figure 7.3 Admission control schemes

the impact of admitting the new flow beforehand to prevent possible QoS deteriorations of the existing flows due to the admission of the new flow. By definition, admission control is a policy by which the admission of traffic to the network is controlled by the imposition of a policy constraint. In general, admission control schemes can be separated into two categories: parameter-based and measurement-based schemes. This is shown in Figure 7.3.

7.2.1 Parameter-based admission control

Parameter-based admission control (PBAC) schemes use *a priori* traffic specifications to determine the parameters of either deterministic or stochastic models. Here, the basic admission question is,

> *Does granting a new service request cause the worst-case behavior of the network to violate any delay bound?*

A deterministic model is a peak-rate and worst-case basis approach, whereas a stochastic model is based on effective bandwidth. That is, deterministic models specify the worst-case behavior of traffic on a single timescale, whereas stochastic models are based on effective bandwidth and therefore they are more suitable to achieve good statistical multiplexing gain. The parameter-based approach provides guaranteed QoS but often yields low network utilization.

7.2.1.1 Deterministic admission control

Deterministic admission controls could be either peak-rate or worst-case basis. The peak rate reserves the bandwidth at a connection's peak rate. The worst case, on the other hand, characterizes the source by an *average* rate and the burst size. It uses WFQ or a rate-controlled discipline to reserve the bandwidth at the average rate.

7.2.1.2 Stochastic admission control

Stochastic admission control uses the *equivalent bandwidth* concept. Usually, *a priori* traffic characterization is based on either a fluid flow approximation or a stationary approximation.

Fluid flow approximation is suitable if the impact of the individual source characteristic is critical, whereas the stationary approximation is appropriate when the effect of statistical multiplexing is significant. A call is admitted if the sum of equivalent bandwidth at a link is less than the link capacity.

7.2.1.3 Drawbacks of the parameter-based schemes

Although this approach can provide a guaranteed service, it suffers two major drawbacks as detailed below:

- It is difficult for the user to tightly characterize its traffic in advance. As a result, the traffic specification is quite loose.
- There exists a trade-off between the ability of the policy and the statistical multiplexing gain.

7.2.2 Measurement-based admission control

MBAC is an attractive mechanism to concurrently offer QoS to users without requiring *a priori* traffic specification and online policing [17]. It relies on the measurement of the actual traffic load and the QoS performance in making admission control decisions.

- *Existing flows*: MBAC relies on the measurement of the actual traffic load in making admission decisions.
- *New incoming flow*: uses the *a priori* source characterization and admission policies imposed by the network.

It is suitable for renegotiated traffic such as real-time applications. A call is admitted if the sum of peak and average is less than the capacity.

7.2.2.1 Advantages of MBAC

MBAC offers several benefits compared to the parameter-based schemes such as:

- *Simpler user specified traffic descriptor*: Given the diversity of the Internet traffic, it will be increasingly difficult to tightly and accurately characterize the traffic in advance (see Chapter 6 for details). Therefore, it is important to rely on the admission control procedures that make as few assumptions as possible in traffic characterization. In fact, for most real-time traffic, peak-rate characterization would be sufficient.

- *Adaptability*: An overly conservative traffic specification does not result in large waste of resources for the entire session. After a measurement-time window period, resource allocation will be recomputed on the basis of the measured values. However, because of unpredictable variations in individual flows, the measurement-based approach must be very conservative.

- *Better estimate of aggregate behavior*: When the traffic from different flows is multiplexed, the QoS experienced depends on their aggregate behavior. Also, it is easier to predict the aggregate traffic behavior rather than the behavior of an individual flow.

7.2.2.2 Drawbacks of the MBAC

The fundamental objective of any admission control scheme is to achieve higher network utilization while providing satisfactory QoS requirements. In order to achieve this goal, network engineers need refined traffic models to extract the full statistical multiplexing gain. However, it can cause an unacceptable burden on network clients to accurately characterize their traffic in advance. Alternatively, either renegotiation of services or measurement-based services can be employed. However, renegotiation needs signaling overhead and measurement-based services bear a risk of predicting future resource requirements based on past measurements. The latter scheme would not always result in a correct decision.

- *Possible inaccuracy of measurements*: It is assumed that a dominant fraction of Internet traffic will continue to use the best-effort service and it will not use explicit reservation [21]. Therefore, it is possible that the measured values could be unrepresentatively low for a period of time and then return to the normal and therefore, higher level. This can lead to admitting more flows than the system can cope with, thereby causing congestion.

- *Unsuitable for guaranteed service*: Although MBAC is very conservative, it is possible that the measured parameter values of the past time intervals may not be a good predictor for the future. This is particularly true in the presence of long-range dependence. Therefore, MBAC is more suitable for *more* relaxed service commitments.

- *Invalid if delay variation is too large*: As the system reaches full utilization ($\rho \rightarrow 1$), large delay variation is common. MBAC is bound to fail if the delay variation is too large. Therefore, it is necessary to set the utilization target.

- *Unsuitable for a link with a low level of aggregation*: In case of low level of aggregation, it is best to use a *peak-rate*-based admission control. The benefit of MBAC is more substantial for links with a higher level of aggregation.

Nevertheless, it is predicted in References [17,20,21] that MBAC will play a key role in achieving high network utilization in wireless networks. Table 7.2 summarizes the advantages and disadvantages of both PBAC and MBAC schemes.

Table 7.2 Advantages and disadvantages of the admission control schemes

Admission control	Pros	Cons
Peak-rate admission control	• Simple • Zero delay and loss • Suitable for small number of sources	• Wasting bandwidth
Worst-case admission control	• More bandwidth-efficient than peak-rate admission control • Provide guaranteed QoS • Easy to police traffic	• Not suitable for low-delay bound traffic • Implementation complexity • Low statistical multiplexing gain
Admission control with statistical guarantees	• Good statistical gain • Trade-off is a small loss probability for a large decrease in bandwidth reservation • Delay bound is available	• Assumes *uncorrelated* sources • Mathematical complexity • Hard to police traffic • Waste of resource if overestimated
Measurement-based admission control	• Higher network utilization for real-time traffic that are tolerant of QoS deterioration • Shift the task of traffic specification from the user to the network • Relieving the network of the burden of policing	• Hard to determine suitable measurement period • Hard to determine how influential past behavior is in terms of the future.

7.2.3 Quality of service parameters

QoS parameters can be measured at four different levels, such as packet level, connection level, call level, and network level [23–28].

Table 7.3 shows possible QoS parameters that can be used at each level. Since admission control is implemented in the network layer, our QoS is focused on call-level parameters. Especially, new call blocking and handoff call-dropping probabilities are the two most important parameters to consider in wireless access networks.

7.3 WIRELESS IP NETWORKS

Wireless IP networks consist of two basic components, the wireless access network and the IP backbone network. Figure 7.4 illustrates these two components. We briefly discuss the two components in this section.

Table 7.3 QoS parameters associated with each level

Level	QoS parameters
Packet-level	• Packet-loss probability • Packet delay • Packet delay variation
Connection-level	• New connection blocking probability • Handoff dropping probability • Renegotiation failure probability
Call level	• New call blocking probability • Handoff call dropping probability • Forced call termination probability • QoS violation rate • Call degradation probability
Network level	• Link utilization • Probability of encountering congestion

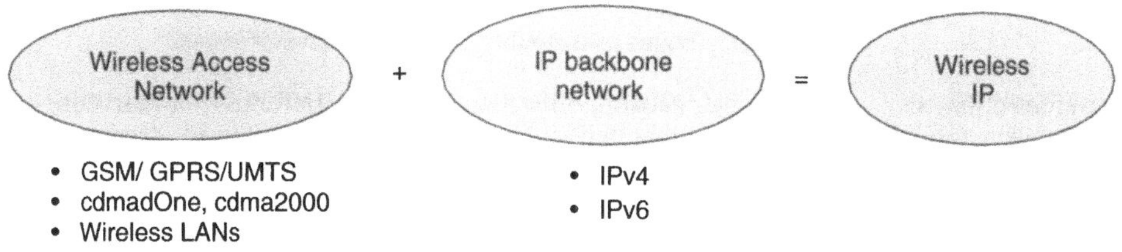

Wireless Access Network + IP backbone network = Wireless IP

- GSM/ GPRS/UMTS
- cdmadOne, cdma2000
- Wireless LANs

- IPv4
- IPv6

Figure 7.4 A simple representation of wireless IP networks

7.3.1 Wireless access networks

The wireless access network can either be the existing cellular networks or the wireless local area networks (LANs). The current trend in wireless access networks is to use as much of the resources as possible from cellular mobile networks because it can

- provide instant wide geographical coverage area,
- allow the use of existing administrative system for billing and maintenance, and
- provide a reliable and cost-effective service in the eyes of most potential customers.

In this chapter, however, for the sake of simplicity and consistency we have considered the wireless LAN based on the IEEE 802.11 standards [29,30]. The discussions provided in this chapter, however, are also applicable to the general situation.

7.3.2 Wireless LAN — The IEEE 802.11 standard

In this section, we provide a brief description of the wireless LAN, based on IEEE 802.11, to provide the necessary knowledge for following the discussions. A detailed

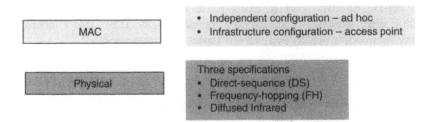

Figure 7.5 The wireless LAN — IEEE 802.11 standard

description is outside the scope of this book and the reader may refer to the numerous literatures available in this field. Chapter 12 also provides additional information about the wireless LAN.

7.3.2.1 Basic structure of the wireless LAN

The basics of the IEEE 802.11 standard are shown in Figure 7.5. The standard provides the specifications of the link and physical layers for providing wireless data transfer over the wireless link.

7.3.2.2 Wireless LAN configurations

The wireless LAN standard can provide the means to establish a wireless data network (specifically for LAN applications) either for an infrastructure-based (client/server) system or an ad hoc network.

Client/server networks

The client/server network in a wireless LAN is shown in Figure 7.6. It uses an access point that controls the allocation of transmit time for all stations and allows the mobile stations to roam from one cell to another cell. The network has an infrastructure in place and will be connected to the wired network. In that sense, the wireless LAN can be considered as an extension of the current LAN structure into the wireless world.

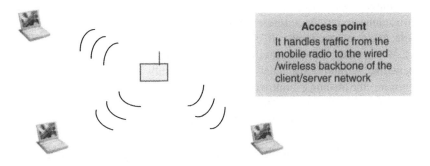

Figure 7.6 The client/server configuration in a wireless LAN

For the purpose of analysis and discussion in this chapter, we have considered a wireless LAN with a direct-sequence code division multiple access (DS-CDMA) scheme and a client/server network in which each server handles 18 access points.

Ad hoc networks

Ad hoc networks refer to simple networks in which wireless data communications are established between multiple stations in a given coverage area without the use of an access point or a server. The ad hoc networks are usually set up for a temporary network communication purpose without significant infrastructure supporting the network. An example of an ad hoc network is a network established among the portable computers of people in a meeting, in order to exchange information, presentation slides, and similar files. Therefore, in principle there is no server or client and all users are at the same network control level and no particular system administration is in place.

A good text on mobile ad hoc networks can be found in Reference [31]. For the purpose of this book, we assume that the reader has a fundamental knowledge on ad hoc networks. An advanced review on ad hoc networking is given in Chapter 12.

7.3.3   Unique characteristics of a wireless LAN

7.3.3.1 Physical channel characteristics

Wireless channels are prone to burst and to location-dependent errors. Also, contention for the wireless channel is location-dependent. As a result, wireless channel resources are highly *dynamic*.

7.3.3.2 User mobility

In a wireless LAN environment, a computer may be connected to the network without frequent moves (e.g. when the wireless LAN provides network connection to a desktop personal computer) or with some kind of mobility (e.g. when a palmtop or a laptop computer is connected to the wireless LAN). We call these two types of users as stationary and mobile users, respectively. In both cases, we should note that user mobility in a wireless LAN is much more limited compared with the mobility of a user on a cellular mobile network. A mobile user may move from a lightly loaded cell to a heavily loaded cell. Therefore, the resource contracts that are made in one cell may not be valid when the user moves to another cell. The two types of users in a wireless LAN network can therefore affect the resource management in different ways:

- *Stationary users*: Maximizing the resource allocation along the current path of a flow.
- *Mobile users*: Minimizing the variation in resource allocation across handoffs.

7.3.3.3 Diverse QoS requirements

Current cellular mobile systems are developed for voice applications and therefore their traffic characteristics and QoS requirements are rather uniform. However, wireless LANs are designed for specified data services and therefore they require very diverse QoS requirements. The most promising applications in wireless LANs are multimedia applications. Usually, multimedia traffic can be classified into two classes:

- Real time (voice and video), and
- Non-real time (data).

Real-time applications need strong bandwidth and delay requirements and some sort of reservation to support a *better-than-best-effort* service. On the other hand, the service commitment for non-real-time applications is more relaxed. However, they also have their own minimum bandwidth requirements. Therefore, in the presence of real-time multimedia applications, an admission control has to be adaptive to network conditions.

7.3.3.4 IETF suggestions on real-time applications

Current IP networks operate with a single service class in mind, that is, the *best-effort* service. It is designed for data traffic applications. It does not provide for delay or loss bounds and therefore it is impossible to provide QoS guarantees for real-time traffic in which the delay and loss bounds are required. Today, more and more IP applications contain multimedia traffic and a single service class in current IP networks is not sufficient to satisfy the diverse QoS requirements requested by multimedia traffic. The Internet Engineering Task Force (IETF) has recognized this problem and suggested service class models based on reservation and priority [23,26,27]. Table 7.4 describes the service classes defined by the IETF. A more detailed discussion on this issue can be found in Chapter 5.

7.3.4 Admission control in wireless IP networks

Ubiquitous information accessing and processing is a strong requirement in modern society. This requirement has motivated the development of wireless communications

Table 7.4 Internet service classes defined by the IETF

Internet QoSmechanisms	Service class
Integrated services (IntServ)	• Guaranteed • Controlled load • Best-effort
Differentiated services (DiffServ)	• Premium • Assured/Olympic (gold, silver, bronze) • Best-effort

infrastructure with different technologies. Currently, two of the most dominant wireless networking technologies are cellular systems and wireless LANs. Cellular systems were originally developed for voice applications, therefore their traffic characteristics and QoS requirements are rather uniform. However, wireless LANs were designed mainly for specified data services and require diverse QoS requirements.

Wireless networking environments that support real-time applications have characteristics of a shared unbuffered environment in which the management of transmission resources is most critical because of its scarcity. In order to deliver a target QoS, admission control and resource management (i.e. buffer and bandwidth management) are employed. Here we will focus on the admission control, and especially the measurement-based approach.

Traditional real-time services provide *absolute* bounds on delay delivery of every packet, and therefore it provides a *guaranteed* service. However, contrary to popular belief, some real-time applications are more flexible and can adapt to current network conditions, such as delay variations and packet losses. Table 7.5 describes possible classifications of real-time traffic in IP networks.

The main difference between the guaranteed and better-than-best-effort services is that in case of a guaranteed service, it uses precomputed worst-case delay bound, whereas the better-than-best-effort services use measured performance of the network in computing the delay bounds.

If a guaranteed or better-than-best-effort service is based on the service commitment, in accordance to the service model, the real-time applications can be categorized as intolerant-and-rigid and tolerant-and-adaptive.

Intolerant-and-rigid applications require a guaranteed service, whereas tolerant-and-adaptive applications can also be supported by a better-than-best-effort service. Tolerant-and-adaptive applications assume that the network service in the near future will be similar to that delivered in the recent past. Any violations of this assumption in the direction of increased delay or loss will result in brief degradation of the application's performance. Adaptive applications typically ignore *a priori* bounds on delay and adapt to the current delivered service.

It is predicted that most real-time applications in future will be playback applications [21,23]. This indicates that future research direction also needs to focus on predictive or less relaxed service commitment. In addition, in Reference [21], it is pointed out that guaranteed and controlled-load service would be proposed as standards in IP networks.

Table 7.5 Real-time traffic classification

QoS requirement	Real-time traffic classification
Service commitment	• Guaranteed • Predictive, controlled delay, controlled load
Delay or loss	• Tolerant • Intolerant
Adaptability to network condition	• Rigid • Adaptive

7.4 MEASUREMENT-BASED ADMISSION CONTROL

MBAC schemes consist of two logically distinctive parts, the estimator and the criteria. The estimator is the measurement mechanism, that is, it estimates the current network load. Criteria are determined by the choice of algorithm and decide whether to admit or reject a new traffic flow.

- *Criteria*: admission criteria are determined by the choice of algorithm
- *Estimator*: the measurement mechanism to find the traffic-load level in the network.

  Basically, there are two tasks in an MBAC:

1. Estimating the network load by measurement, and
2. Determining whether to accept or reject new traffic.

7.4.1 Network-load estimation

There are a few algorithms that are available for estimating the network traffic load [17–21]. In the parameter-based approach, the simplest algorithm is the *simple sum*. The *measured-sum* algorithm in MBAC has adapted the simple sum in measurement-based environments. In this section, we will first describe the simple sum. This will be followed by other estimation algorithms including the measured sum, the acceptance region, and the equivalent bandwidth.

7.4.1.1 Simple sum

In parameter-based schemes, a simple sum is the most commonly used algorithm to estimate the network load. With the simple-sum algorithm, the admission decision is simply based on checking if the sum of new and existing flows exceed the link capacity such that

$$v + r^\alpha < \mu \tag{7.1}$$

where v is the sum of existing flows, r^α is a new flow, and μ is the link capacity.

Because of its simplicity, it is most widely implemented by switch and router vendors together with the WFQ scheduling discipline [20].

7.4.1.2 Measured sum

Measured sum is an adaptation of a simple-sum algorithm in a measurement-based environment. With the measured sum, the admission criteria is

$$\hat{v} + r^\alpha < \upsilon\mu \tag{7.2}$$

In this algorithm, the existing network load, $\hat{v}$, is obtained through measurement and the admission criteria are constrained by a user-defined *utilization target*, υ. MBAC fails if the delay variation is exceedingly large, which will occur at very high utilization. Therefore, in order to obtain an optimum performance, it is important to set a reasonable value for the utilization target. For future wireless IP networks, admission control schemes should make minimum assumptions and be simple to implement. In this context, the measured sum will be the most promising algorithm to be used in measurement-based schemes.

7.4.1.3 Acceptance region

The admission criteria for this algorithm are to ensure that measured instantaneous load plus the peak rate of a new flow is below the acceptance region. For a flow described by a token bucket filter (r, b), its peak rate is derived from the token bucket parameters using the equation:

$$\hat{p} = r + b/U \tag{7.3}$$

$$\hat{v} + \hat{p} < \text{ acceptance region} \tag{7.4}$$

where U is a user-defined average period. If a flow is rejected, the admission control algorithm does not admit another flow until the existing one leaves the network. This algorithm is based on maximizing the reward of utilization against the penalty of packet loss.

7.4.1.4 Equivalent bandwidth

The equivalent bandwidth of a set of flows is defined as the bandwidth $C(\varepsilon)$ such that the stationary bandwidth requirement of the set of flows exceeds this value with the probability being the highest value of ε. Similar to the acceptance region approach, if a flow is denied admission, no other flow of similar type will be admitted until the existing one departs. Table 7.6 summarizes how to estimate the existing traffic load using the equivalent bandwidth.

Because of its simplicity, the simple sum is the most commonly used mechanism to estimate the existing network load in parameter-based approaches. For the MBAC, however, the measured-sum algorithm, that is, the adaptation of the simple sum algorithm, is more appropriate and therefore will be used in this chapter.

7.4.2   Measurement parameters

MBAC estimates the current network loads, $\hat{v}$, by using three measurement parameters: sampling period, measurement-window size, and average arrival rate estimation. We will describe these parameters in the following sections.

Table 7.6 Estimation of network load of the existing traffic based on the equivalent bandwidth

Traffic distribution	Description
Gaussian distribution	*Assumptions* Instantaneous aggregate arrival rate S_T having a normal (Gaussian) distribution $$\hat{C}_N(\mu_S, \sigma^2, \varepsilon) = \mu_S + \alpha\sigma, \text{ and } \alpha = \sqrt{2\ln\frac{1}{\varepsilon} + \ln\frac{1}{2\pi}}$$ *Problems* • Since it has assumed a Gaussian distribution for the class arrival rate, this approach is not suitable for small or moderate size classes as it underestimates the actual equivalent capacity.
Hoeffding bound	*Assumptions* • Arrival rates for the different flows are independent • For δ sufficiently large, $X_{i,T}$ and $X_{i,T+\delta}$ are not correlated The equivalent capacity $\hat{C}_H$ based on the peak-rate policing is $$\hat{C}_H(\mu_S, \{p_i\}_{1\leq i\leq n}, \varepsilon) = \mu_S + \sqrt{\frac{\ln\left(\frac{1}{\varepsilon}\right)\sum_{i=1}^{n}(p_i)^2}{2}}$$ Admission decision is based on checking if a new flow α is requested then $$\hat{C}_H + \mathrm{p}^\alpha \leq \mu$$

7.4.2.1 Sampling period, s

The sampling period, s, controls the sensitivity of the rate measurement. If s is small, it is more sensitive to burst, whereas for a larger s, traffic appears smoother. In References [20,22], s is recommended to be greater than a 500-packet-transmission time for wired Ethernet networks. However, here we consider wireless LAN based on code division multiple access (CDMA) and its link capacity is much smaller than the wired Ethernet. Therefore, we will use a smaller sampling period for wireless LAN.

7.4.2.2 Measurement window size, T

During the period T, the network traffic load will be measured x times in every sampling period, that is, $s = T/x$. At the end of each period T, the network estimates the current network loading of the existing traffic. Out of the $x-$ measured values, it chooses the largest value as the current network load. This value is used for the next period T, and will be updated again.

Usually, the ratio between the measurement-window size, T, and the sampling period, s, is $T/s \geq 10$. In Section 7.6, we have presented some preliminary simulation results on suitable choices for the MBAC parameters. On the basis of these results we infer that $T/s = 10$ is good enough for the wireless LAN based on DS-CDMA.

7.4.2.3 Average arrival rate estimation

MBAC gambles on the fact that network behavior in the near future will be similar to that observed in the recent past. However, in the presence of long-range dependency, the measured average arrival rate over some time interval may not be a good predictor for the average arrival rate for a future time interval. In order to minimize measurement error, the average arrival rate can be calculated using an exponential weighted moving average with a weight w. A small value of w provides a smoother average by keeping a longer history. As w becomes large, its averaging process becomes more adaptive to the network load changes.

7.4.3 Possible sources of error

The possible sources of error in an MBAC algorithm are the errors in the estimation of parameters used in the algorithm and an unfair admission decision. In this section, we describe these sources of error for our MBAC scheme.

7.4.3.1 Parameter estimation error

From the traffic measurements, we can obtain mean and variance of the traffic flow and the estimated capacity of the link. There are plenty of possibilities that measured values could be either underestimated or overestimated. In MBAC, underestimation of the traffic flow is more problematic than overestimation since it can cause congestion. Therefore, MBAC tends to be very conservative. Table 7.7 shows the impact of parameter values, such as sampling period and measurement-window sizes on the accuracy of measurement.

7.4.3.2 Unfair admission decision

The effect of flow dynamics is briefly mentioned in Reference [22]. It points out that almost all admission control algorithms are based on a violation prevention paradigm.

Table 7.7 The impact of parameter values on the accuracy of traffic measurement

Parameter	Impacts on inaccuracy of measurements
s: Sampling period (sensitivity of the rate measurement)	**Small**: More sensitive to burst **Large**: Traffic appears smoother
T: Measurement-window size	**Small**: More adaptive **Large**: Greater stability
w: Exponential-weighted moving average weight	**Small:** Smoother average by keeping a longer history **Large:** Averaging process becomes more adaptive to load changes

Admission decision is based on the fact that the service commitment will be violated as a result of a new admission. Under this paradigm, there could be two distinct problems for heterogeneous flows and heterogeneous sources.

Heterogeneous flows

When flows with different characteristics, such as different service requirements, different holding times, or different path lengths, compete for admission into a network, multihop flows face an increased chance of being denied service in the network. As a consequence, it also affects the link utilization since it will not consume the reserved bandwidth for the flows.

It is an important point to note in wireless IP networks. Assume that the wireless IP networks support only two classes of service:

- Better than best-effort service, and
- Best-effort service.

Assuming that the traffic consists of new and handoff users at any instant, call dwell times or call holding times for new and handoff traffic will be different. Also, like multihop flows, handoff traffics requires special treatment to avoid an increasing chance of service denial. This special treatment can be reservation, priority, or other admission criteria that can reduce the service denial rate on handoff traffics.

Heterogeneous sources

When sources have different characteristics, sources that request a smaller rate can prevent those requesting larger rates from getting into the network. Also, delay of the lower priority class is affected by both the rate and the bucket size of the higher priority flows, and the admission algorithm is more likely to reject flows with larger bucket sizes and higher priority than those with smaller bucket size or lower priority.

7.4.4 Suitability of MBAC in wireless IP networks

In Reference [21], there are six assumptions to justify the usage of MBAC schemes. We summarize these assumptions in this section.

1. In the near future, some of the Internet traffic needs explicit admission control procedures to provide an adequate service.
2. Most real-time traffic has adaptive playback times, which means that they tolerate occasional packet drops and varying delays. However, it is worthwhile to point out that an MBAC is not an option if the delay variation (jitter) is too large.
3. The controlled-load or the better-than-best-effort service will meet the needs of most real-time applications that use an explicit admission control. However, not all real-time applications will be adaptive or tolerant. In that case, a guaranteed service is

Table 7.8 Real-time traffic classifications and objectives defined by IETF

Service category	Objectives
Predictive	• For applications that require an upper bound on end-to-end delay • Priority queuing discipline
Controlled delay	• Applications can dynamically change the level of packet delay they request from the network. This service is designed for applications that need some control on delay, but no need for specified delay bound.
Controlled load	• Admission control goal: Adequate bandwidth and packet processing resources are available to handle the requested level of traffic.

required. In an attempt to classify real-time applications, IETF has suggested four service categories:

- Guaranteed
- Predictive
- Controlled delay
- Controlled load

Of the above four classes, the guaranteed and controlled load classes are to become the proposed standards. The distinction between predictive, controlled-load, and controlled-delay service is described in Table 7.8.

4. The MBAC scheme is the most beneficial to use if the traffic is hard to tightly and accurately be characterized in advance. Given the diversity of Internet traffic, tightly characterizing the source traffic is not plausible. For most real-time traffic, peak-rate characterization is the tightest appropriate characterization.

5. MBAC is recommended if there is more chance of utilizing the link capacity by employing it.

6. Most Internet traffic will still be over the best-effort service.

The above six assumptions are valid in all wireless IP networks in terms of traffic characteristics and network applications.

7.5 IMPLEMENTATION OF MEASUREMENT-BASED ADMISSION CONTROL

In this section, we outline the implementation issues of MBAC in our wireless IP network example.

7.5.1 Network reference model

The network reference model can be drawn in two perspectives:

- Physical layout
- Logical layout

Figures 7.7 and 7.8 show the physical and logical layouts of wireless IP networks using the wireless LAN as the access networks, respectively.

7.5.2 Wireless IP networks characteristics

We have considered the two most unique characteristics of wireless IP networks, that is, their limited available bandwidth and the effect of user mobility.

- *Limited bandwidth*: It is well known that the bandwidth available in wireless access networks is limited. Furthermore, wireless channels are prone to bursty and location-dependent errors. This causes further reduction in the effective available bandwidth. This is the biggest limitation imposed on wireless access networks.
- *User mobility*: In wired networks, the task of admission control is to admit or reject a new traffic request depending on the probability of QoS violation. However, in wireless networks, we also need to consider the handoff traffics, that is, the continuing traffic coming from neighboring cells due to user mobility. As forced call termination due to handoff failure can have significant negative effects on the user's perspective on network reliability, extra care is needed in handling handoff calls.

With the user mobility in mind, we have considered the following three scenarios:

1. A system with a small number of mobile users,
2. A system with an equal number of stationary and mobile users, and
3. A system with a large number of mobile users.

7.5.3 Simulation descriptions

In wireless access networks, resource management decisions are made as a result of updating or changing resource allocations. Table 7.9 describes events that are associated with resource management decisions in a wireless environment. These events are closely related to admission decisions. Two of the QoS parameters that are most relevant in wireless networks are the new call blocking probability and the handoff dropping probability. Accordingly, the effectiveness of admission control schemes is measured in terms of these two parameters.

7.5.3.1 The simulation framework

For the purpose of our discussion in this chapter, we have used a simulation framework as outlined in Table 7.10.

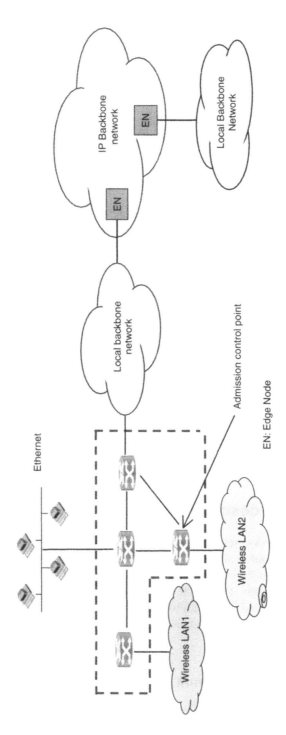

Figure 7.7 The physical layout of the wireless IP networks

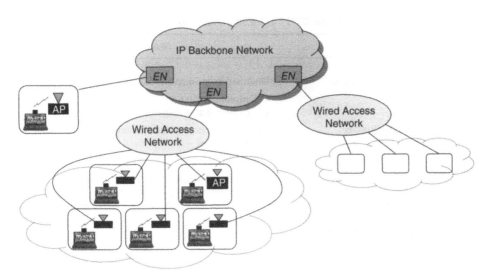

Figure 7.8 The logical layout of the wireless IP networks

Table 7.9 Resource management events and the associated QoS parameters in a cellular environment

Event	Main QoSparameters involved in the event
Call setup	• New call blocking probability
Unexpected handoff into a cell	• Handoff call dropping probability
Call termination	• Updating the resource allocation
Advance resource setup	• Handoff call dropping probability
Advance resource teardown	• Updating the resource allocation
Resource increase	• Renegotiation failure probability
Resource decrease	• Renegotiation failure probability

Table 7.10 Description of the simulation framework

Component	Assumption
Service class	• Best-effort • Better-than-best-effort
Service model	Tolerant-and-adaptive real-time application
Service environment	Wireless LAN based on DS-CDMA
Traffic management	MBAC (with measured sum)

In order to implement the measured-sum MBAC in a wireless LAN, we need to know the user-defined utilization target, the measured load of existing traffic, and the resource requested by the new flow. In addition, we need to consider the traffic models, call arrival models, and call dwell time models in order to make appropriate simulation environments for the wireless IP networks. For traffic models, we have chosen Pareto ON/OFF distribution. Table 7.11 lists simulation assumptions.

Table 7.11 Simulation assumptions

Parameter	Assumptions
User-defined utilization target	1
Measured load of existing traffic	Obtained from measurements
	• Sampling period (s)
	• Measurement-window size (T)
Rate requested by the flow α	Constant rate is assumed for both new and handoff traffics users
Call arrival model	Poisson distribution
Traffic model	
	Pareto ON/OFF distribution
Call dwell time model	Negative exponential distribution

7.5.3.2 Admission criteria

Previously we have mentioned that handoff traffics should be handled more carefully since they have direct effects on the network reliability perceived by network users. In order to reduce the handoff call dropping probability, reservation or priority schemes could be used as the admission criteria. Providing that most real-time applications in future wireless IP networks would be delay tolerant, we have encountered the delay tolerance nature of the IP traffic. In this chapter, we have considered two of the most common admission criteria, that is, reservation and priority.

7.5.3.3 MBAC procedure

The MBAC procedure can be summarized by the four main procedures involved in the algorithm:

1. Measuring the current network load,
2. Evaluating the available capacity for new and handoff traffics,
3. Applying the admission criteria, if available, and
4. Making the admission decision.

Depending on the admission criteria considered in the algorithm, the third procedure would be different. This is shown in the flowcharts given in Figure 7.9.

7.6 TRAFFIC MANAGEMENT PARAMETERS

For the simulation given in this chapter, a C^{++} program has been developed. The choice of this programming method, as apposed to the use of other available simulation packages, has been justified by some preliminary numerical comparison between the results obtained from our analytical method and the simulation. These methodology comparisons are, however, outside the scope of this book.

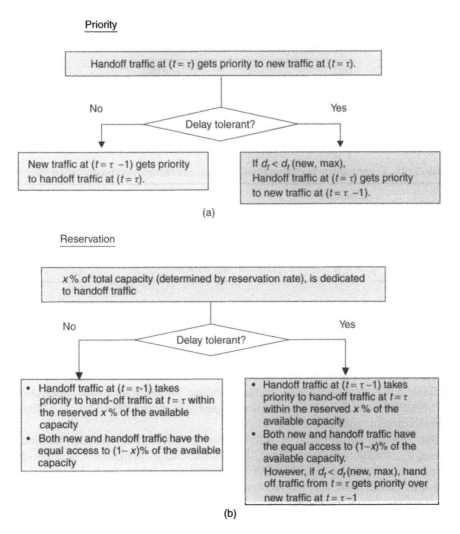

Figure 7.9 Admission criteria consideration in MBAC (a) priority and (b) reservation

7.6.1   Choice of the parameters

In this section, we will describe the numerical value selection for the parameters used in the MBAC procedure. The process of this selection could be considered as a guideline for similar research works based on a different network technology.

7.6.1.1 Pareto shape, α

For World Wide Web (WWW) traffic, ON time and inactive OFF time distributions are Pareto (see Chapter 6). In case of ON time distributions, the Pareto shape factor α has

Table 7.12 File types and their typical size

File types	Web file sizes (bytes)
Text	< 1000
Image	1000–30,000
Audio	30,000–300,000
Video	300,000

Table 7.13 A comparison between the Pareto shape factor and the minimum file size

Time	Literature A	Literature B	Current simulation
ON	$\alpha = 1.1 \sim 1.5$	$\alpha = 1.0 - 1.3$	$\alpha = 1.2$
	$k_w \geq 1\,000$ bytes	$k_w \geq 100$ bytes	$k_w = 125$ bytes
OFF	$\alpha = 1.5$	$\alpha = 1.5$	$\alpha = 1.2$
	$k'_w = 1$ s	$k'_w = 30$ s	$k'_w = 3$ s

values from 1.1 to 1.5 (i.e. $\alpha = 1.1 \sim 1.5$). For the minimum packet size, k_w, we have chosen the value in accordance with the information given in Table 7.12 and assumed $k_w = 125$ bytes.

In this chapter, we focus on real-time services such as audio and video applications. From Table 7.12, we assumed that average file size of audio and video applications is around 100,000 bytes. Considering the link capacity of our wireless LAN is 1 Mbps, the average ON time is assumed to be 1 s.

For the OFF time distribution, in different literatures it is recommended the minimum OFF time, k'_w, should be between 1 and 30 s. For the sake of comparison, we have chosen the minimum OFF time as 3 s. The OFF time in previous literatures is interpreted as the reading time. Here, however, we are considering real-time applications, so it would be most appropriate to interpret this time as the data processing time. Therefore, the choice of 3 s as our average OFF time would be reasonable. These parameters from previous literature and from our simulation, are compared in Table 7.13.

7.6.1.2 Sampling period s

In the literature, it is recommended to choose a sampling period, s, of at least 500 packet-transmission time. However, this is mostly suitable for wired networks. For wireless access networks, the available link capacity is a lot smaller than for wired networks. In addition, this value fluctuates. Therefore, instead of $s \geq 500$ packet-transmission time, we choose the sampling period s to be around 10 packet-transmission time. In Figure 7.10, we have compared the accuracy of measurements between $s = 0.1$, 0.01, and 0.001 s. We found that $s = 0.1$ s could provide a reasonable estimation for network load measurement and thus it justifies our original selection of the sampling period.

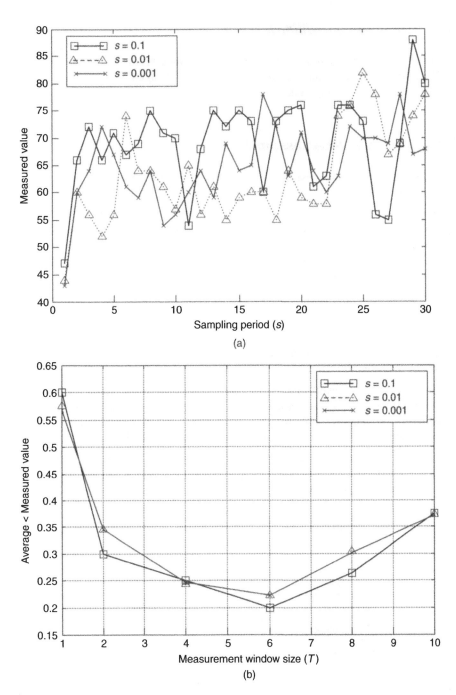

Figure 7.10   Accuracy of the measurement with different sampling periods: (a) the measured values at each sampling period and (b) the average measured value with different sampling periods

7.6.1.3 Measurement-window size, T

The ratio between the sampling period s and the measurement-window size T in an MBAC should be greater than or equal to 10. In this chapter, we choose T/S equal to 10 for our wireless LAN example.

7.6.1.4 Other simulation assumptions

In the simulations, we have also made the following assumptions:

- Throughout the simulation, we have assumed a wireless LAN with DS-CDMA. Each subnet has 18 access points and each access point handles up to 11 users simultaneously. Therefore, the allowable maximum number of users at any instant is 198. The link capacity is assumed to be 64 kbps. This capacity is well below the actual one in a wireless LAN network.

- At any given time, the traffic consists of two parts, the newly generated traffic within the subnet and the handoff traffics from other subnets.

- Considering that the ON time is for data transfer and downloading information and the OFF time is for data processing and reading time, we have assumed that the ON time is shorter than the OFF time.

- Considering the call dwell time is the time a call stays in the subnet before it moves to another subnet, we have assumed that the newly generated call dwell time is longer than that of the handoff calls. It means that a newly generated call tends to stay in the subnet in which it was generated longer than the handoff calls.

- We have assumed that the data is transmitted in the form of packets. Each packet has a fixed size assumed to be 125 bytes. It is also assumed that during the ON time, every user generates at least one packet.

The simulation parameters and the corresponding values used here are shown in Table 7.14.

Table 7.14 Simulation parameters and values

Parameters	Values
Pareto shape factor (α)	1.2
Average ON time (s)	1.0
Average OFF time (s)	3.0
Average call dwell time (s)	• New traffic: 5.0
	• Handoff traffics: 2.5
Sampling period (s)	0.1
Measurement-window size (s)	1.0
Minimum file size (Kb)	1

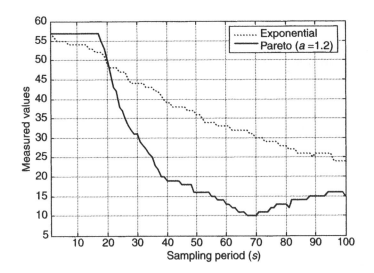

Figure 7.11 Comparison between exponential and Pareto distributions

7.6.1.5 Justification of measurement-based approach

Figure 7.11 shows why a measurement-based approach is more suitable in the presence of LRD. For exponential distribution, the network load is increased or decreased gradually. However, for Pareto distribution, it shows sharp increases or decreases in network load.

7.6.2 Verification of the simulation

In order to verify our simulation system, we carried out a service waiting time analysis with an M/G/1 queuing model and compared it with our simulation results.

In order to investigate the effect of placing a priority scheme on the handoff users on the service waiting time, we carried out some calculations using the M/G/1 queuing model.

Suppose the traffic arrival rate of handoff calls is λ_H and for newly generated calls it is λ_N. At any instant, we assume that the traffic consists of two components, new and handoff traffics. Let us define p as the ratio of handoff traffics to the total traffic (i.e. new plus handoff traffics) such that $p = \lambda_H/(\lambda_N + \lambda_H)$. Therefore, p is the proportion of handoff traffics, whereas $(1 - p)$ is that of the new traffic. Let the exponential service rate or the session holding time of the new calls be μ_N and that of handoff calls be μ_H. This is shown in Figure 7.12.

The service distribution function is described as

$$f_\tau(x) = p\mu_H e^{-\mu_H x} + (1 - p)\mu_N e^{-\mu_N x} \qquad (7.5)$$

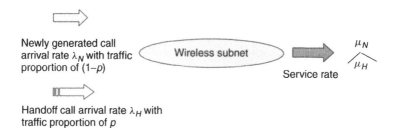

Figure 7.12 A simple description of the simulation traffic flow

The average waiting time for a call arrival in the subnet is

$$E[W] = \frac{\lambda E[\tau^2]}{2(1 - \lambda E[\tau])}$$ (7.6)

where λ is the total arrival rate and $E[\tau]$ and $E[\tau]^2$ are

$$E[\tau] = \frac{p}{\mu_H} + \frac{1-p}{\mu_N} \quad \text{and} \quad E[\tau^2] = 2\left(\frac{p}{\mu_H^2} + \frac{1-p}{\mu_N^2}\right)$$ (7.7)

The general waiting time in an M/G/1 queue is

$$E[R] = \frac{\lambda E[\tau^2]}{2} = \frac{\lambda}{2}\left(\frac{p}{\mu_H^2} + \frac{1-p}{\mu_N^2}\right)$$ (7.8)

Without the priority admission criteria, the average service waiting time in an M/G/1 queue will be

$$E[W] = \frac{E[R]}{1 - \rho}$$ (7.9)

where

$$\rho = \lambda\left(\frac{p}{\mu_H} + \frac{1-p}{\mu_N}\right)$$ (7.10)

For priority systems, the average waiting time for a k-priority system with λ_i as the total arrival rate of the ith priority subset is

$$E[W_k] = \frac{\sum\limits_{i}^{k} \lambda_i \, E[\tau^2]}{2(1 - \rho_1 - \cdots - \rho_{k-1})(1 - \rho_1 - \cdots - \rho_k)}$$ (7.11)

Since the traffic consists of new and handoff users, by placing the priority admission criteria on handoff traffics, the average waiting time for new and handoff users would be

Average waiting time for handoff users: $E[W_1] = \dfrac{E[R]}{(1 - \rho_1)}$ (7.12)

Average waiting time for newly generated users: $E[W_2] = \dfrac{E[R]}{(1 - \rho_1)(1 - \rho_1 - \rho_2)}$ (7.13)

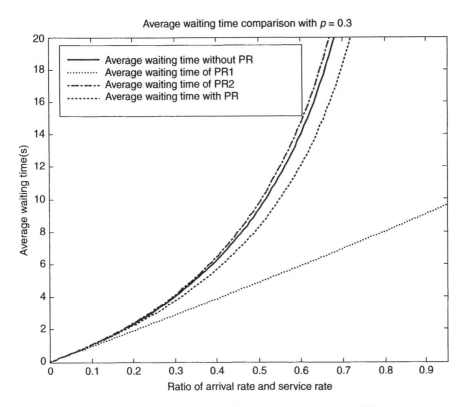

Figure 7.13 Average waiting time of an M/G/1 queuing system ($p = 0.3$)

where

$$\rho_1 = \frac{p\lambda}{\mu_H} \quad \text{and} \quad \rho_2 = \frac{(1-p)\lambda}{\mu_N} \tag{7.14}$$

The average service waiting time for both users would be

$$E[W] = pE[W_1] + (1-p)E[W_2] \tag{7.15}$$

Figure 7.13 shows the expected average service waiting time for $p = 0.3$. It shows the average service waiting time for a system without priority and for a system with priority given to the handoff users, and a system with priority admission criteria.

7.7 COMPARISON BETWEEN PRIORITY AND RESERVATION SCHEMES

In this section, we will compare the performance of priority and reservation schemes in wireless IP networks, and we will see which scheme is more beneficial in traffic management.

7.7.1 Without reservation or priority

Before we investigate the effect of admission control in wireless IP networks, especially in wireless access networks, we start with a simple system without any admission criteria. New and handoff traffics is served on a first-come-first-served (FCFS) basis. They are admitted or rejected in the network according to the network loading of the existing traffic. Throughout the simulation, we have investigated three scenarios.

- A system with a small number of mobile users ($p = 0.3$),
- A system with the same numbers of mobile and nonmobile users ($p = 0.5$), and
- A system with a large number of mobile users ($p = 0.9$).

As defined earlier, p is the ratio of handoff traffics to the total traffic (i.e. new plus handoff traffics) and $(1 - p)$ is that of the newly generated traffic.

In addition, most of the real-time applications in wireless IP networks are delay tolerant and adaptive to network conditions. With that point in mind, we have examined two cases, (1) applications without delay tolerance and (2) applications with delay tolerance.

7.7.1.1 Without delay tolerance

At any instant, the traffic consists of two components, the newly generated traffic and the handoff traffics. The traffic proportion of handoff users is expressed in p and that of the newly generated users is expressed in $(1 - p)$. Therefore, if $p > 0.5$, there are more mobile users than the newly generated users. Without any reservation or priority, as the newly generated traffic increases [i.e. $(1 - p) > 0.5$], lower values of the new call blocking probability can be obtained. The same applies to the handoff users. As the traffic proportion of the handoff users increases, its call failure rate also drops. However, in both cases, it is interesting to note that both call failure rates reach a saturation level at 0.5. Overall, the majority users dominate the system performance and the minority users receive less favorable treatment. This is shown in Figure 7.14a and b, respectively for the new and handoff traffics.

7.7.1.2 Introduction of delay tolerance

Suppose that the traffic is delay tolerant so that it can be placed in the queue and can wait for its service for a certain period of time. Here ($n = x$, $h = y$) means that the newly generated traffic can be placed in the queue and waits up to x s and the handoff traffics can wait up to y s before it is served. If the waiting time, d_t, is greater than x or y s, the call fails. Here, two cases are considered:

1. Only new users are delay tolerant, and
2. Both new and handoff users are delay tolerant.

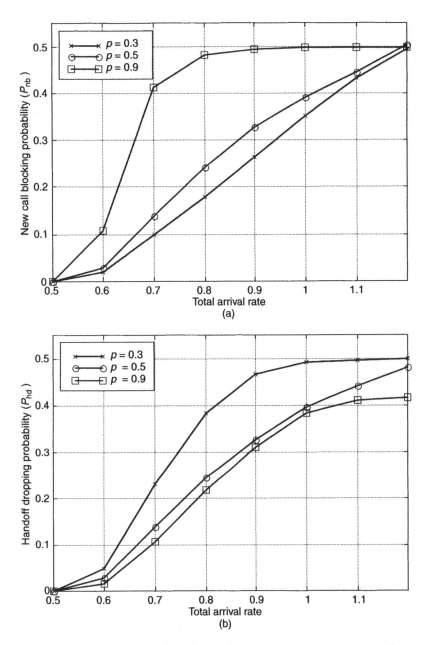

Figure 7.14   (a) New and (b) handoff traffics performance with various values of p

A. Delay tolerant new traffic

If the newly generated traffic is delay tolerant or delay insensitive, there is a significant improvement in the new call blocking probability. In addition, if the handoff traffics is dominant (i.e. $\lambda_h > \lambda_n$), then substantial improvement can be achieved for the new traffic. For $p = 0.9$, the new call blocking probability drops to zero. This is true even in congestion. Further improvement in new traffic performance can be achieved if new traffic has a greater delay tolerance (i.e. $d_t > 1$). The performance of the new traffic is shown in Figures 7.15a and 7.16a for $p = 0.3$ and $p = 0.9$, respectively. From this point on, we call the system with $p = 0.3$ as the *less mobile system* and the one with $p = 0.9$ as the *highly mobile system*.

If the new traffic is delay tolerant, it has profound negative effects on the handoff traffics performance. Its negative effect is more apparent in less mobile systems (i.e. $\lambda_n > \lambda_h$). However, no matter what the new traffic portion is, its negative effect on handoff traffics performance is most dominant when $d_t = 1$. Further increase in the delay tolerance in the new traffic has small to negligible effects on handoff traffics performance.

Overall, if the system is highly mobile (i.e. $\lambda_h \gg \lambda_n$), the introduction of delay tolerance on new users is most beneficial to keep the new call blocking probabilities down to zero. However, if the system is less mobile (i.e. $\lambda_h \ll \lambda_n$), an increase in delay tolerance has greater adverse effects on the handoff traffics. In both cases, profound positive or negative effects of delay tolerance were most dominant when $d_t = 1$. Further increase in delay tolerance has very small to negligible effects on handoff traffics performance. This is shown in Figures 7.15b and 7.16b.

B. Delay tolerance in both new and handoff traffic

From Figures 7.15 and 7.16, it is shown that the introduction of delay tolerance on newly generated traffic causes a drastic degradation of handoff traffics performance. In this section, we will investigate the case where both new and handoff users are delay tolerant. The relevant results are shown in Figures 7.17 and 7.18. We have compared the following four cases:

Case 1   Without delay tolerance (i.e. $n = 0, h = 0$)

Case 2   Only the new traffic is delay tolerant (i.e. $n = 1, h = 0$)

Case 3   Both the new and handoff traffics have the same degree of delay tolerance (i.e. $n = 1, h = 1$)

Case 4   Both the new and handoff traffics are delay tolerant but the new traffic has a greater degree of delay tolerance (i.e. $n = 5, h = 1$).

New call blocking probability: Compared with Case 1, both the new and handoff traffics outperform in Cases 3 and 4, regardless of the new traffic proportion. For highly mobile systems ($p = 0.9$), the new call blocking probability drops more than 0.26 at $t_a = 0.7$, provided both the new and the handoff users are delay tolerant (i.e. $n = 1, h = 1$). This is shown in Figure 7.18a.

Assuming that the new traffic has a greater delay tolerance, substantial improvement in the performance can be achieved for the new traffic. This benefit is more significant if there are more mobile users in the system (i.e. $p > 0.5$). When $p = 0.9$, the new call blocking probability reduces to 0.02, even at full capacity (i.e. $t_a = 1$, where t_a is the normalized total arrival rate).

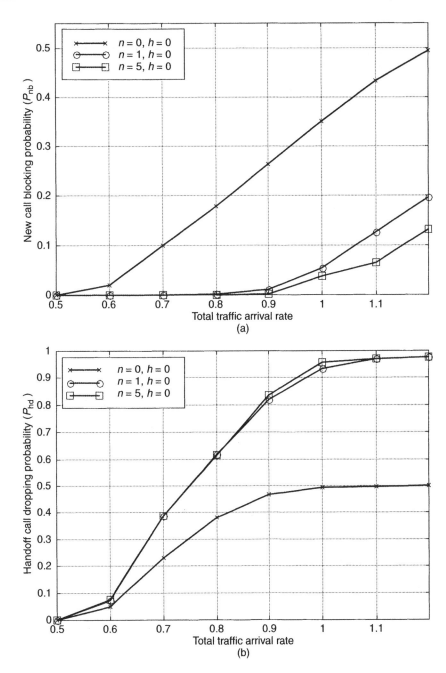

Figure 7.15 (a) New call blocking and (b) handoff call dropping probabilities after introduction of delay tolerance in newly generated traffic ($\lambda_h < \lambda_n$)

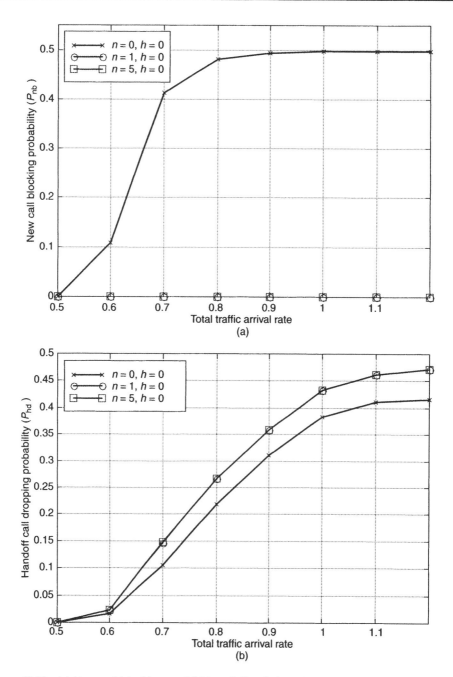

Figure 7.16 (a) New call blocking and (b) handoff call dropping probabilities after introduction of delay tolerance in newly generated traffic ($\lambda_h > \lambda_n$)

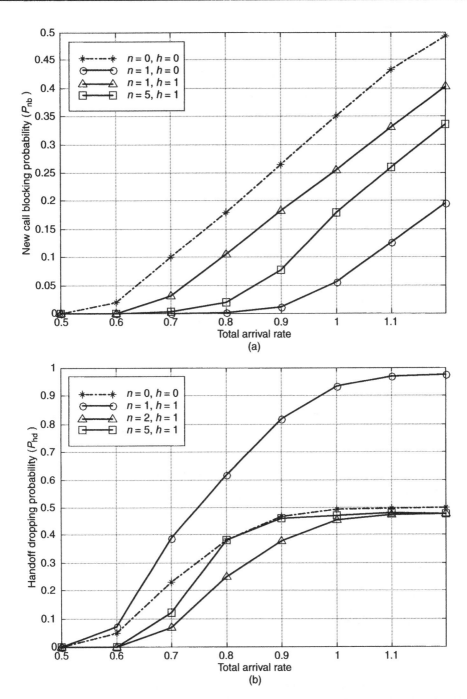

Figure 7.17   The effect of delay tolerance in new and handoff traffics ($\lambda_h < \lambda_n$): (a) new call blocking probability and (b) handoff call dropping probability

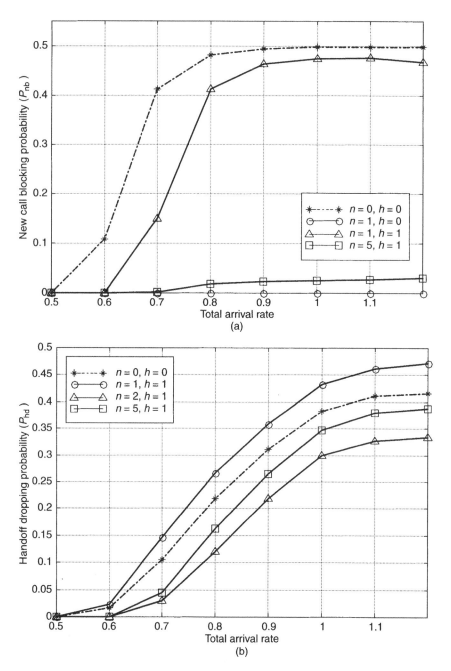

Figure 7.18 The effect of delay tolerance in new and handoff traffics ($\lambda_h > \lambda_n$): (a) new call blocking probability and (b) handoff call dropping probability

Whether the system is less or highly mobile, the delay tolerance nature of the new traffic is most appreciated at $t_a = 0.7$. A greater delay tolerance in the new traffic has greater positive effects on the new traffic performance when the system is highly mobile (i.e. $p = 0.9$). The reader may compare these results with the case of a less mobile system, shown in Figure 7.17a.

Handoff call dropping probability: Like the newly generated users, if both new and handoff traffics are delay tolerant, the overall handoff traffics performance is improved. However, the delay tolerant nature of the handoff users is more appreciated for highly mobile systems. This is shown in Figures 7.17b and 7.18b. Assuming the newly generated traffic has a greater delay tolerance [i.e. Case 4 where $(n = 5, h = 1)$], its negative effect is more dominant for less mobile systems. However, it is worthwhile to note that even in Case 4, the handoff traffics performance is still better than in Case 1. In the case of highly mobile systems, the handoff call dropping probability gradually increases with an increase in delay tolerance of the new traffic. However, in both cases, the handoff traffics performance is superior to that in Case 1.

Therefore, if the system is highly mobile (i.e. $\lambda_h \gg \lambda_n$), the delay-tolerant nature of the handoff traffics is more desirable to achieve an improved performance. If the new traffic shows a greater delay tolerance as compared to the handoff traffics, it's negative impact on the handoff traffics becomes more apparent in less mobile systems, especially at $t_a = 0.8$.

7.7.1.3 Effect of greedy users

From Figure 7.14, it is shown that the majority users determine the system performance and the minority users receive less favorable treatment. In this section, we have investigated the negative impacts of greedy users on nongreedy users when greedy users belong to the minority users. We have investigated two cases: (1) without delay tolerance and (2) with delay tolerance.

Without delay tolerance
Suppose the traffic consists of greedy and nongreedy users. Let us define q as the traffic proportion of greedy users and $(1 - q)$ as that of nongreedy users. The term *greedy users* can be used if users are greedy in terms of (1) network capacity usage, or (2) call dwell time, or (3) both. Here, we have defined a user as greedy, if (1) the user's average call dwell time is 10 times longer than the average users and (2) the user requests immediate admission without delay. As the traffic volume of greedy users increases, heavier penalties are imposed on the nongreedy users. The call failure rate of nongreedy users increases sharply if $0.6 < t_a \le 1$, then it starts to saturate. In general, as the traffic volume of the greedy user increases, it places more adverse effects on nongreedy users.

Introduction of delay tolerance on nongreedy users
We have compared nongreedy users' performance for $q = 0.05$ and 0.1. When delay tolerance is introduced on nongreedy users, the call failure rate of greedy users increases

sharply if the total traffic volume is greater than 0.6 (i.e. $t_a > 0.6$). At full capacity, almost all greedy user calls are failed as its call failure rate reaches 0.95. It is interesting to note that further increase in delay tolerance for nongreedy users is more beneficial in the presence of more greedy users. This is shown in Figure 7.19, where g denotes greedy and ng denotes nongreedy users. It is worthwhile to note that when delay tolerance is introduced, the performance of nongreedy users improves significantly. However, further increase in delay tolerance, d_t, from $d_t = 1$ to $d_t = 2$, results in very little improvement in call success rates. Therefore, it suggests that a user benefits the most with a little tolerance in the delay, but unlimited delay tolerance fails to provide further improvement in call performance.

7.7.2 Reservation

In order to investigate the effect of reservation, we have considered three scenarios:

- A system with a small number of mobile users ($p = 0.3$),
- A system with a similar number of mobile and stationary users ($p = 0.5$), and
- A system with a large number of mobile users ($p = 0.9$).

For each system, the reservation rate, r, varies from $r = 5\%$ to $r = 40\%$. Here $x\%$ reservation means we have dedicated $x\%$ of the total capacity for the handoff traffics. The effectiveness of the reservation scheme is studied in terms of the new and handoff call failure rate. The relevant figures are shown in Figures 7.20 and 7.21. The effect of placing reservation criteria on handoff users is compared with the system without any admission criteria.

7.7.2.1 Without delay tolerance

New call blocking probability

For the system with a smaller number of mobile users (i.e. $p = 0.3$), the effect of putting reservation criteria on the handoff traffics is most dominant as the reservation rate r increases from $r = 20\%$ to $r = 40\%$. However, from $r = 5\%$ to $r = 20\%$, the effect of increased reservation rate on the new traffic performance is gradual. For the system with similar numbers of mobile and stationary users, (i.e. $p = 0.5$), the impact of reservation is not noticeable until $t_a > 0.8$. This is true even with 20% reservation. However, with 40% reservation, the new call blocking probability starts to increase even at $t_a = 0.5$. This is shown in Figure 7.20a. The negative impact of reservation on new traffic performance is more apparent as the total traffic volume reaches full capacity. However, if the system is highly mobile (i.e. $p = 0.9$), even with 40% reservation, it has a negligible effect on both new and handoff user performance. The relevant figures are shown in Figure 7.21a.

Handoff call dropping probability

For *less mobile* systems, the benefit of the reservation scheme is steadily increased as the reservation rate increases from 5% to 40%. Compared to the unreserved system, the handoff call dropping probability drops from 0.5 to 0.01, with 40% reservation. However, if

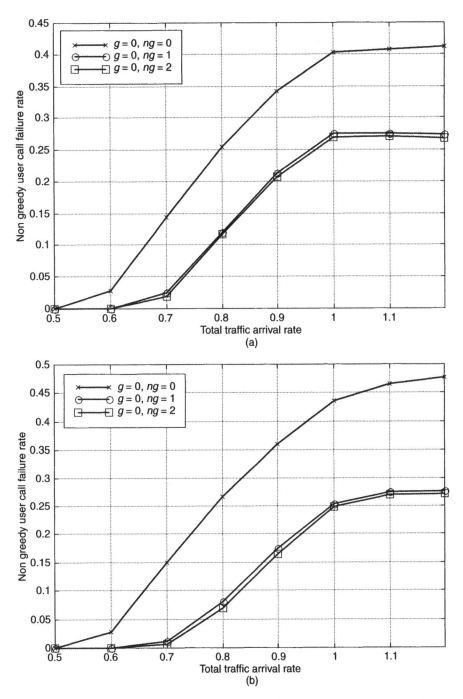

Figure 7.19 Introduction of delay tolerance on nongreedy users for (a) $q = 0.05$ and (b) $q = 0.1$

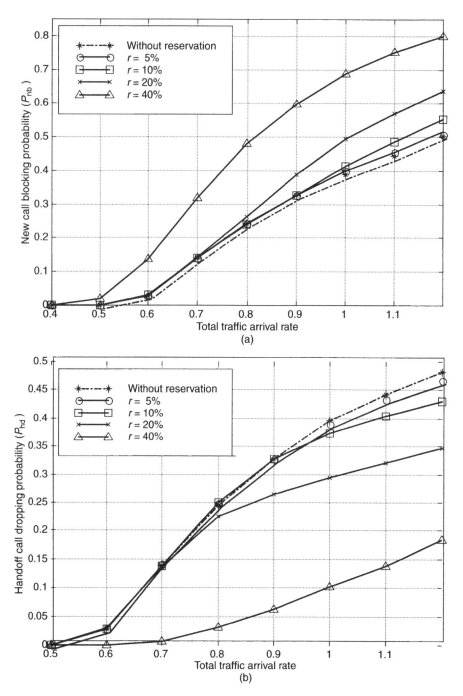

Figure 7.20 The effect of reservation with different reservation rate ($p = 0.5$): (a) new call blocking probability and (b) handoff call dropping probability

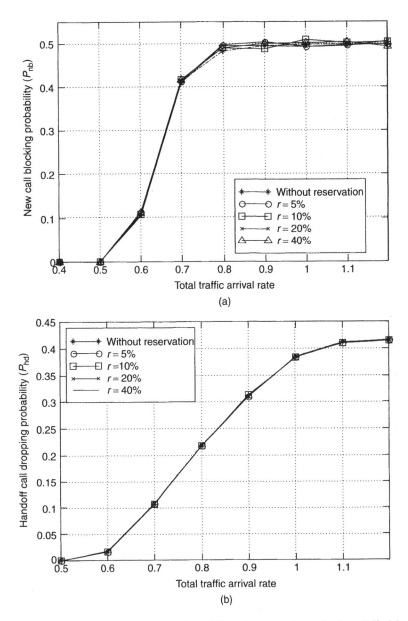

Figure 7.21 The effect of reservation with a different reservation rate ($p = 0.9$): (a) new call blocking probability and (b) handoff call dropping probability

the system has similar numbers of new and handoff users, 5% reservation has a negligible effect on the handoff traffics performance. Also, its negative impact on the new traffic is minimal. In order to achieve a similar level of improvement as in *less mobile* systems, a greater portion of total capacity has to be reserved for handoff users. It is worthwhile to note that the positive impact of reservation is more dominant as traffic reaches full capacity or in cases of congestion. This is shown in Figure 7.20b.

However, when the handoff traffics is predominant, that is, $p = 0.9$, reserving the resource for handoff users has very little effect on both new and handoff traffics performances. There is no apparent benefit of reservation. Both new and handoff traffics performances are not affected by the amount of reservation. This is shown in Figure 7.21b.

Overall, as long as the traffic proportion of nonreserved users is larger than that of reserved users, a reasonable to significant improvement can be achieved for reserved users. This applies even for a small increase in reservation rate. Here, increase in reservation guarantees a substantial improvement in reserved traffic performance.

On the other hand, if the reserved traffic is predominant ($p = 0.9$), the benefit of reservation is negligible. Reservation is ineffective and it is the least preferred option. However, reservation is very effective if the system operates near full capacity and QoS guarantees are required.

7.7.2.2 Introduction of delay tolerance

In this section, we have studied the effect of introducing delay tolerance on (1) new users only and (2) both new and handoff users. As in Section 7.7.1.2, ($n = x, n = y$) means the newly generated traffic can be placed in the queue up to x seconds before it is served and the handoff traffics can wait up to y seconds. If the waiting time, d_t, is longer than x or y seconds, a call fails.

Newly generated traffic only

The effect of introducing delay tolerance on newly generated traffic is studied in terms of new and handoff call dropping probabilities. The relevant figures are shown in Figures 7.22 to 7.25.

A system with a small number of mobile users ($p = 0.3$): Even with 40% reservation, if the newly generated traffic is delay tolerant, there is a significant improvement in the new traffic performance. Its benefit is more substantial for lower values of reservation rate. Further increase in delay tolerance in the newly generated traffic contributes to further improvement on the new call blocking probabilities. This is different from the system with $p = 0.5$ or $p = 0.9$, where most of the benefits from delay tolerance are obtained when $d_t = 1$. Further increase in d_t of the newly generated traffic fails to provide further improvement. In Figure 7.22, we compared the new traffic performance with $r = 5\%$ and $r = 40\%$.

If the reservation rate is small, the most dominant effect of delay tolerance appears at $d_t = 1$. Further increase in delay tolerance has very little effect on both new and handoff user performance. This is shown in Figure 7.23. However, with 40% reservation, if the newly generated traffic has a greater degree of delay tolerance, there is a noticeable decrease in the new call blocking probability. The delay-tolerant nature of the new traffic has greater effects on handoff traffics as the reservation rate increases.

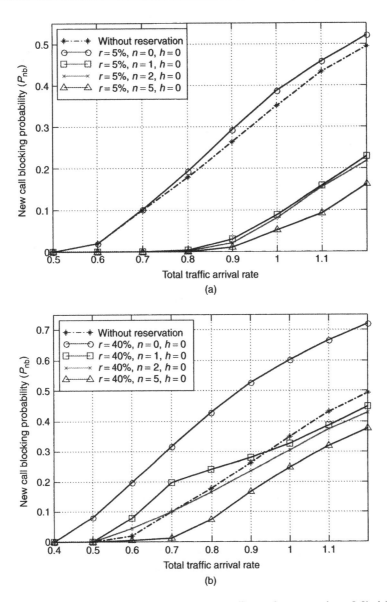

Figure 7.22 The effect of delay tolerance on new traffic performance ($p = 0.3$): (a) with 5% reservation and (b) with 40% reservation

A system with similar numbers of new and handoff users ($p = 0.5$): As the traffic proportion of newly generated users decreases from 0.7 to 0.5, the effect of reservation is not as dominant as in $p = 0.3$. Even with 40% reservation, if the newly generated traffic is delay tolerant (i.e. $d_t = 1$), the new call blocking probability is lower than the system without reservation.

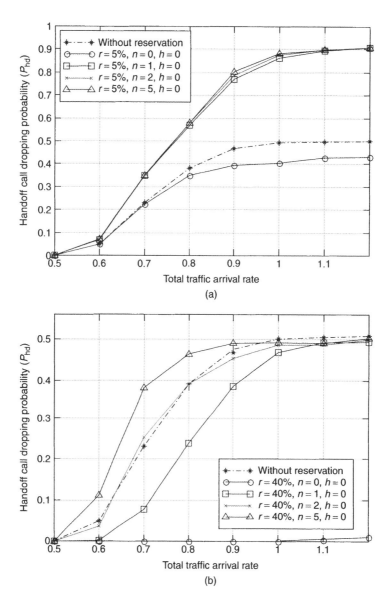

Figure 7.23 The effect of delay tolerance on handoff traffic performance ($p = 0.3$): (a) with 5% reservation and (b) with 40% reservation

Further increase in delay tolerance can achieve gradual improvement in the new traffic performance so that even at full capacity, it remains below 0.1. This improvement is more apparent if the reservation rate is high. Therefore, a larger delay tolerance in the new traffic is more appreciated for the system with a larger reservation rate. However, if the reservation rate is small, a small delay tolerance in new traffic can contribute a substantial improvement in its performance. Further increase in delay tolerance fails to provide further additional improvement. This is shown in Figure 7.24.

It is worthwhile to note that for smaller values of the reservation rate, for example, $r = 5\%$, introduction of delay tolerance on the newly generated traffic has profound effects

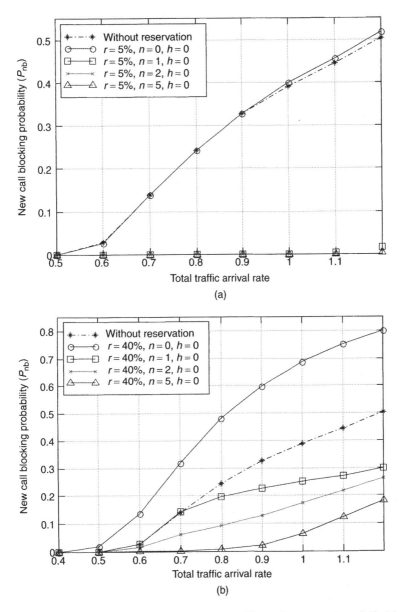

Figure 7.24 The effect of delay tolerance on new traffic performance ($p = 0.5$): (a) with 5% reservation and (b) with 40% reservation

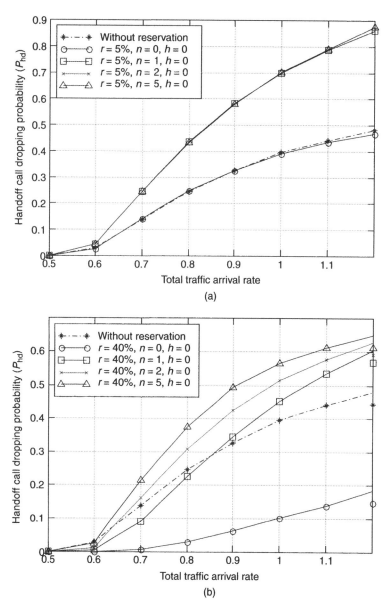

Figure 7.25 The effect of delay tolerance on handoff traffic performance ($p = 0.5$): (a) with 5% reservation and (b) with 40% reservation

on both new and handoff traffics performance. The new call-blocking rate drops to zero but the handoff dropping probability rises sharply. This is shown in Figure 7.25. If the newly generated traffic has greater delay tolerance (i.e. $d_t > 1$), it has a more negative impact on the handoff users as the reservation rate increases.

A system with a large number of mobile users (p = 0.9):   Finally, if the handoff users are predominant, in other words, if the system is highly mobile (i.e. $\lambda_h \gg \lambda_n$), the system is benefited the most with a small increase in delay tolerance in the newly generated users. Even with $r = 40\%$, the new call blocking probability drops to zero with $d_t = 1$. Further increase in delay tolerance is not necessary. Also, it is interesting to note that the handoff traffics performance is most likely to be affected when $d_t = 1$. Further increase in d_t has a negligible impact on the handoff user performance.

Overall, if the newly generated traffic is delay tolerant, there is a significant improvement in the new traffic performance no matter what the new traffic proportion is. However, it was the highly mobile system (e.g. $p = 0.9$) that enjoyed the most benefits. On the other hand, the delay-tolerant nature of the new traffic causes a drastic deterioration on the handoff traffics performance. This effect is more dominant (1) if the system is less mobile and/or (2) as the reservation rate increases. In addition, further increase in delay tolerance is more appreciated if (1) the system is less mobile and (2) the reservation rate is high.

Both new and handoff traffics

Now consider the case where both new and handoff users are delay tolerant. We have assumed that newly generated traffic has the same or a greater degree of delay tolerance. In general, as the traffic proportion of newly generated users increases, that is, $p < 0.5$, the benefit of further increase in delay tolerance on newly generated traffic diminishes.

A system with a small number of mobile users (p = 0.3):   When $r = 5\%$, the new traffic performance improves with further increase in delay tolerance on the newly generated traffic. Even with $(n = 1, h = 1)$, the new call traffic performance is better than the system without reservation. Also, the performance of handoff traffic is better than the reservation scheme alone, even if the new traffic has a greater degree of delay tolerance. However, in order to compensate the performance loss resulting from the reservation, further increase in delay tolerance is required in the new traffic to achieve a similar performance as in the system without reservation. This is particularly true if the reservation rate is large. For $r = 40\%$, even with $(n = 5, h = 1)$, the new traffic performance is worse than in the system without reservation.

For handoff traffics, when $r \leq 10\%$, its performance steadily worsens if the newly generated traffic has a greater delay tolerance. However, its effect tends to saturate around full capacity. For $r \geq 20\%$, introduction of delay tolerance is less effective. Further increase in delay tolerance of the newly generated traffic has very little impact on the handoff traffics performance.

When the reservation rate is high (i.e. $r > 20\%$), a larger delay tolerance in the newly generated users provides further improvement in new traffic performance with minimal negative effect on handoff traffics.

A system with similar numbers of mobile and stationary users (p = 0.5):   The effect of introducing delay tolerance in newly generated traffic has a more dominant effect when the number of mobile users is increased. The effect of a further increase in delay tolerance of the newly generated traffic is less dominant as the reservation rate increases. However, further increase in delay tolerance of the newly generated traffic contributes further improvement in new traffic performance regardless of the reservation rate. The loss of performance because of handoff traffics reservation is fully compensated if the reservation rate is less than 20%. However, if $r = 40\%$, further increase in delay tolerance on the new call traffic cannot compensate the performance loss due to handoff traffics reservation, if $t_a > 0.8$. Therefore, for a larger reservation rate, in order to compensate the performance loss caused by the reserved traffic, a greater delay tolerance on the newly generated users is required. For small values of the reservation (i.e. $r = 5\%$), an increase in delay tolerance of the newly generated traffic puts further adverse impacts on handoff traffics performance.

A system with a large number of mobile users ($p = 0.9$): As in previous cases, if the reserved traffic is predominant, reservation has negligible effect on both reserved and nonreserved traffic performance. If the newly generated traffic has a greater delay tolerance than the handoff traffics, a significant improvement in the new traffic performance can be achieved regardless of reservation rate. This is shown in Figure 7.26.

The performance of the handoff traffics, even with ($n = 5, h = 1$), is still better than the performance with reservation alone. Its performance steadily deteriorates as the newly generated traffic gets more delay tolerant.

Overall, if the reserved traffic is predominant and nonreserved traffic is more delay tolerant than the reserved traffic, nonreserved users enjoy the most benefits with reasonably less cost than reserved users. However, both can achieve a better performance.

Moreover, if nonreserved traffic is dominant, further increase in delay tolerance in nonreserved users helps to improve its performance with minimum impact on the reserved traffic performance. This is particularly true for the system with a large reservation rate.

7.7.3 Priority

In the previous section, we have studied the effect of reservation on the new and handoff traffics performance. Here, we have examined the effect of placing priority criteria on handoff users. The priority system performance is compared with the reservation system with various reservation rates.

7.7.3.1 Without delay tolerance

The new and handoff traffics performances are shown in Figures 7.27 and 7.28. The effect of placing priority admission criteria on handoff traffics is compared with (1) reservation systems and (2) the system without any admission criteria.

A system with a small number of mobile users ($p = 0.3$): Compared to the systems with similar or with larger number of mobile users (i.e. $p \geq 0.5$), placing a priority on handoff

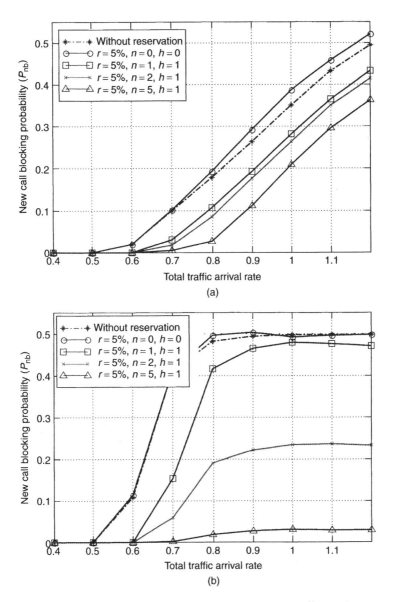

Figure 7.26 The effect of introducing delay tolerance on new traffic performance: (a) with small number of mobile users ($p = 0.3$) and (b) with large number of mobile users ($p = 0.9$)

traffics has less impact on new traffic performance. Compared to the reservation schemes, a priority scheme is more effective in guaranteeing the required service quality. With reservation, in order to obtain the same handoff traffics performance, 40% reservation is required. Although a priority scheme has profound negative impacts on the new traffic, its new traffic performance is still better than the 40% reservation system.

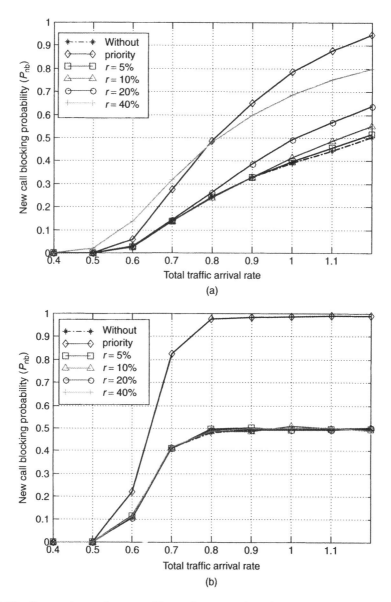

Figure 7.27 Comparison of new traffic performance in priority and reservation systems: (a) with a similar number of new and handoff users ($p = 0.5$) and (b) with a large number of mobile users ($p = 0.9$)

If keeping the handoff call dropping probability down to zero is the main concern, a priority scheme is preferred. Also, increase in reservation rate may help reduce the handoff call dropping probability, however, at the cost of substantial degradation of the new traffic performance.

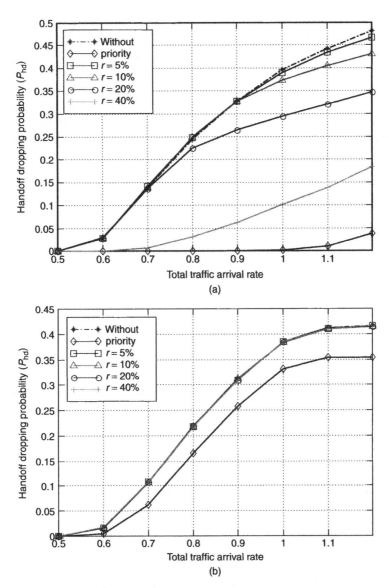

Figure 7.28   Comparison of handoff traffics performance in priority and reservation systems: (a) with a similar number of new and handoff users ($p = 0.5$) and (b) with a large number of mobile users ($p = 0.9$)

A system with similar numbers of new and handoff users ($p = 0.5$):   Again, in terms of the handoff traffics performance, a priority scheme is the most effective to guarantee the required service quality. Even in congestion, it remains below 0.05. However, for reservation systems, even with 40% reservation, the handoff call dropping rate fails to drop to zero. The interesting point is priority is even more effective in congestion (i.e. $t_a > 1.0$).

This is shown in Figure 7.28a. For new traffic, 40% reservation has more negative impacts on new traffic performance if $t_a < 0.8$. However, under heavy traffic flow, a priority scheme has more adverse effect on the newly generated traffic. Therefore, a priority scheme is a preferred option if $t_a < 0.8$.

A system with a large number of mobile users (p = 0.9):   If the handoff traffics is predominant (i.e. $\lambda_h \gg \lambda_n$), by placing a priority admission criteria on the handoff traffics, a small improvement can be achieved. However, the new call blocking probability almost doubles. The priority scheme is not as effective as in the above two systems. This is shown in Figure 7.28b.

7.7.3.2 Introduction of the delay tolerance

Suppose that the nonpriority users, that is, the newly generated users, are delay tolerant so that they can be placed in the queue if immediate admission request is denied. We have investigated the effect of introducing delay tolerance on (1) nonpriority users and on (2) priority and nonpriority users in terms of their performance.

A. Newly generated traffic only

New call blocking probability: By introducing delay tolerance on the newly generated users, the benefits obtained from the priority scheme are no longer available for handoff users. However, there is a substantial improvement in the new traffic performance. Also, this improvement becomes more substantial as the priority traffic volume increases. Further increase in the delay tolerance of the new traffic is only slightly beneficial if the system has less mobile users ($p = 0.3$). However, for a system with similar or larger number of mobile users (i.e. $p \geq 0.5$), further increase in delay tolerance fails to deliver further improvement in the new traffic performance. Both new and handoff traffics performances are unaffected. This is shown in Figure 7.29.

Handoff dropping probability: The effect of introducing delay tolerance is most dominant in systems with a small number of mobile users. Further increase in delay tolerance of the newly generated traffic has negligible effect on the handoff user performance. This applies to all the three scenarios we have considered in this section. The relevant graphs are shown in Figure 7.30.

   Without the introduction of delay tolerance, a priority scheme is the most effective in keeping the service quality of handoff users. However with a small introduction of delay tolerance on new traffic, the benefits obtained from the priority scheme are no longer available. The overall system performance is similar to the system without any admission criteria.

B. Both new and handoff traffics

From the previous section, we have seen that the users with a delay tolerance nature enjoy more benefits than the reserved or prioritized users. In this section, we have investigated the case where both new and handoff traffics are delay tolerant. As usual, we have assumed that new traffic has the same or a greater degree of delay tolerance. The relevant figures are shown in Figures 7.31 and 7.32.

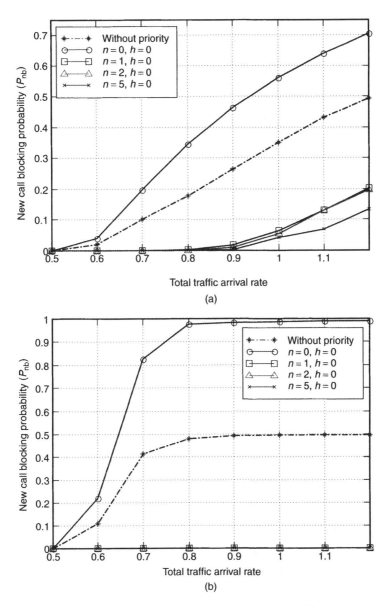

Figure 7.29 The effect of introducing delay tolerance on new traffic performance: (a) with small number of mobile users ($p = 0.3$) and (b) with large number of mobile users ($p = 0.9$)

A system with a small number of mobile users ($p = 0.3$): Unlike in previous cases, assuming both the new and handoff traffics are delay tolerant, it is possible to obtain a better performance than a priority scheme alone. For handoff users, just placing a priority is enough to achieve a zero handoff call-dropping rate. Also, further increase in delay tolerance in the newly generated traffic has no effect on the handoff traffics performance.

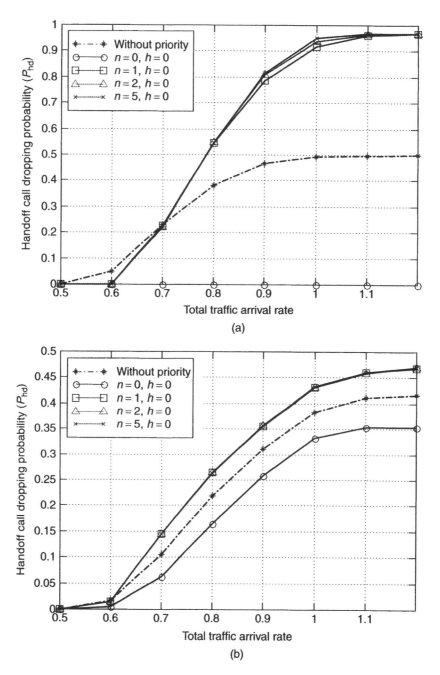

Figure 7.30 The effect of introducing delay tolerance on handoff traffics performance: (a) with a small number of mobile users ($p = 0.3$) and (b) with a large number of mobile users ($p = 0.9$)

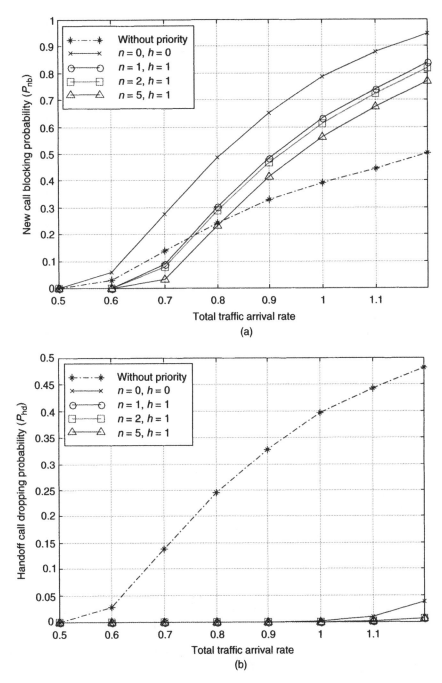

Figure 7.31 The effect of delay tolerance in a system with small number of mobile users ($p = 0.3$) on: (a) new traffic performance and (b) handoff traffic performance

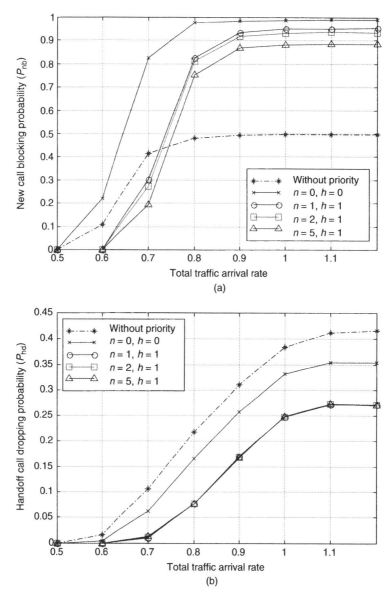

Figure 7.32 The effect of delay tolerance in a system with large number of mobile users ($p = 0.9$) on: (a) new traffic performance and (b) handoff traffics performance

However, it is beneficial for the newly generated traffic as the new call blocking probability is gradually reduced when the new traffic becomes more delay tolerant.

A system with similar numbers of mobile and stationary users ($p = 0.5$): By placing a priority on the handoff users, a heavier penalty is imposed on the newly generated users.

Even with ($n = 5, h = 1$), the new traffic performance is worse than the system without any admission criteria. For the handoff traffics perspective, a priority scheme is more reliable to deliver the guaranteed service especially when the traffic volume is high. As the new traffic gets more delay tolerant, the handoff call-dropping probability increased slightly but even at $t_a = 1.2$, it still remained below 0.05.

A system with a large number of mobile users ($p = 0.9$):   The adverse effect of placing priority on handoff traffics is more dominant. As Figure 7.32a shows, the new call blocking probability doubles when a priority scheme is employed. However, if both new and handoff traffics are delay tolerant, the new traffic performance is better than the system without priority as long as $t_a < 0.75$. When $t_a > 0.7$, P_{nb} starts to increase sharply and a further increase in delay tolerance offers very little improvement. Also, the handoff traffics performance is not affected by further increase in delay tolerance of the new traffic. Again, a priority scheme is more effective if the total traffic arrival rate reaches full or beyond full capacity.

In the case of handoff users (Figure 7.32b), employing a priority scheme provides initial improvement and if the handoff traffics is delay tolerant, it enjoys further improvement in its call performance. However, if only newly generated traffic is delay tolerant, both the priority and reservation schemes lose their merits and fail to provide any improvement in performance. Therefore, provided both new and handoff users share similar traffic characteristics, a priority scheme is a preferred option to reservation.

From this study, it is worthwhile to note that the system enjoys greater benefits if the system users are delay tolerant. Therefore, the system performance depends on both traffic management skills and traffic characteristics. Another interesting point is that a small increase in delay tolerance is all the system needs to boost its performance. Unlimited delay tolerance is most likely to fail to deliver further improvement. Considering that IP traffic is delay tolerant even for real-time applications (e.g. playback application), it has definite advantages over conventional real-time traffic.

7.7.4   Priority versus reservation

In Sections 7.7.2 and 7.7.3, we have investigated the effect of employing reservation and placing priority admission criteria on handoff users in terms of new call blocking and handoff call dropping probabilities. In this section, we discuss which scheme is more appropriate or effective to use under the circumstances examined in the previous cases.

7.7.4.1 Without the delay tolerance

If the traffic proportion of newly generated users is greater than the handoff users (i.e. $p < 0.5$), a priority scheme is more effective than reservation. However, as the volume of the handoff traffics increases, the priority scheme puts greater adverse impacts on the new traffic. As shown in Figures 7.27 and 7.28, the priority scheme is still the preferred option to reservation as it offers lower call failure rates to both new and handoff users, provided

$t_a < 0.8$. However, the effect of a priority scheme is more dominant as the traffic reaches full capacity. It is interesting to note that a priority scheme works even in congestion, that is, $t_a > 1.0$, where even 40% reservation fails to affect the system performance.

On the other hand, if the handoff traffics is predominant (i.e. $p = 0.9$), no performance improvement is obtained through reservation. Reservation fails to affect both new and handoff traffics performances. Although a priority scheme managed to achieve a small improvement in handoff user performance, it also caused a drastic degradation on new traffic performance. Overall, both reservation and priority schemes failed to deliver an improved performance. The system performance greatly depends on its traffic characteristics. Admission control is not effective and fails to achieve improved performances. In general, traffic management is most effective when it is applied on a smaller proportion of traffic.

7.7.4.2 Introduction of delay tolerance

A. Newly generated traffic only

Provided only the newly generated traffic is delay tolerant, its effect on the systems with reservation and priority is compared in Figures 7.33 through to 7.36.

New call blocking probability: When the newly generated traffic is delay tolerant, the new traffic performance of a priority system is similar to that of the system without any admission criteria. Here, it is interesting to note that the introduction of delay tolerance has less severe effects in reservation systems. Introducing delay tolerance on newly generated traffic has the most beneficial effects on the system with a large number of mobile users. Further increase in delay tolerance in the newly generated traffic is more effective in the system with a small number of mobile users. (i.e. $p = 0.3$). This is shown in Figures 7.33 and 7.34.

Handoff call dropping probability: For a system with a small number of mobile users, a priority scheme fails to provide a guaranteed service. This phenomenon is more dominant as the traffic reaches full capacity so that for $t_a > 0.8$, even 5% reservation provides better handoff traffics performance. This is shown in Figures 7.35 and 7.36. However if the handoff traffics is predominant, both the reservation and the priority schemes lose their merit. Its performance is similar to a system without any admission criteria.

Overall, the effect of introducing delay tolerance in new traffic has a more dominant effect on the priority system. In case of reservation systems, some of the benefits are still kept even if only the newly generated traffic is delay tolerant. It is more apparent if the reservation rate is high. Therefore, if the new traffic has advantageous characteristics such as delay tolerance, reservation is the preferred option to guarantee a minimum level of service.

B. Both new and handoff traffics

Figures 7.37 and 7.38 show, respectively, the new and handoff traffics performance if both are delay tolerant. Two cases are examined, (1) both traffic is equally delay tolerant ($n = 1, h = 1$) and (2) more practically, the newly generated traffic has a greater delay tolerance ($n = 5, h = 1$).

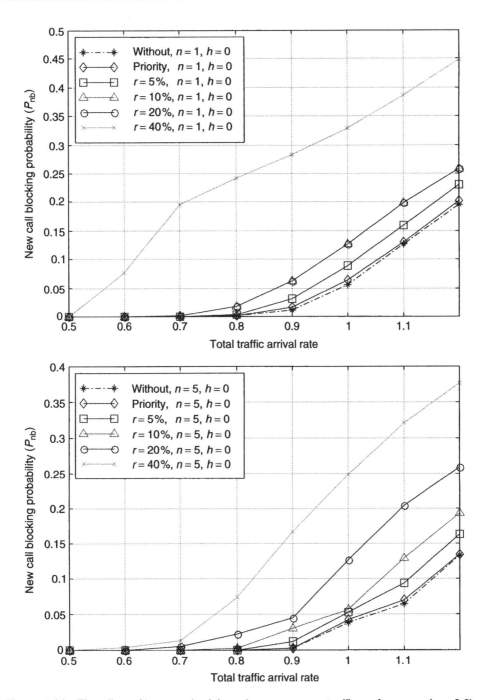

Figure 7.33   The effect of increase in delay tolerance on new traffic performance ($p = 0.3$)

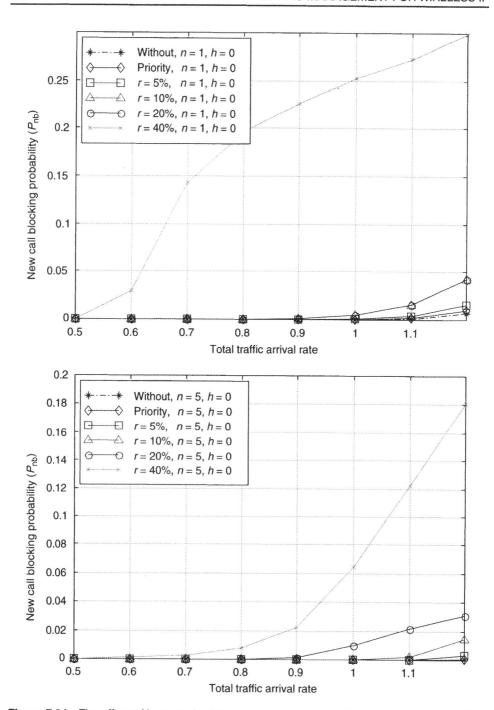

Figure 7.34 The effect of increase in delay tolerance on new traffic performance ($p = 0.5$)

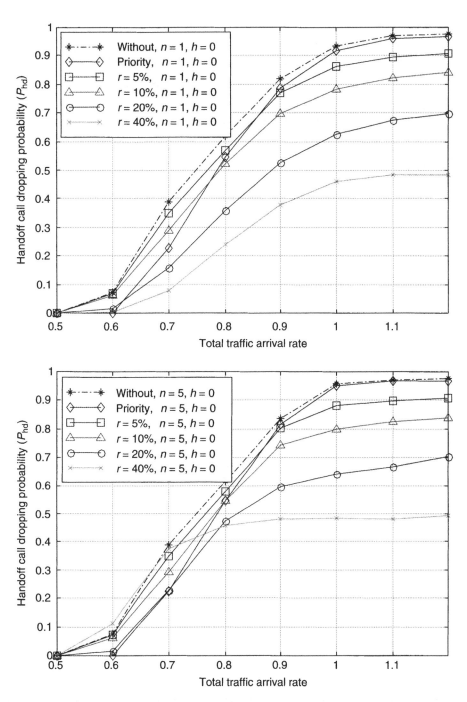

Figure 7.35   The effect of increase in delay tolerance on handoff traffic performance ($p = 0.3$)

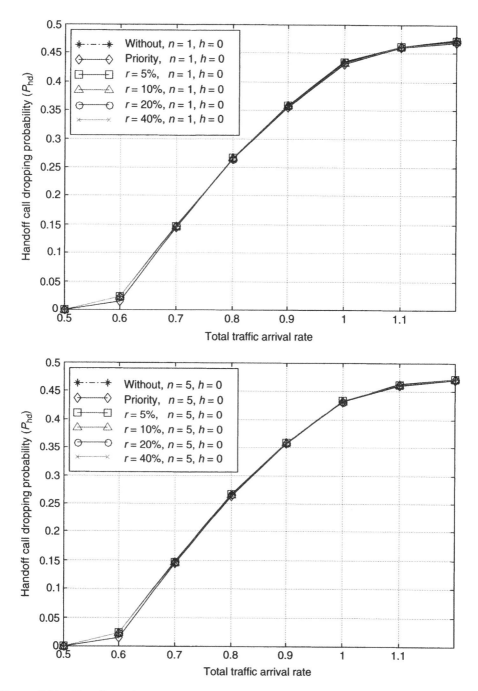

Figure 7.36   The effect of increase in delay tolerance on handoff traffic performance ($p = 0.9$)

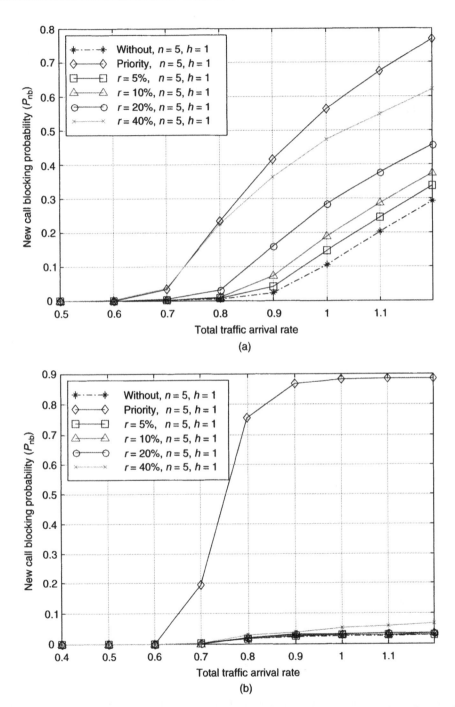

Figure 7.37 The performance comparison of new traffic for a system with: (a) similar number of mobile and non-mobile users ($p = 0.5$) and (b) large number of mobile users ($p = 0.9$)

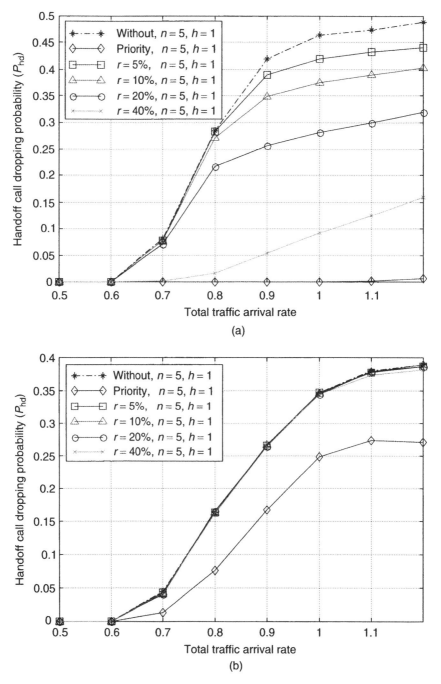

Figure 7.38 The performance comparison of handoff traffic for a system with: (a) similar number of mobile and non-mobile users ($p = 0.5$) and (b) large number of mobile users ($p = 0.9$)

New call blocking probability: Further increase in delay tolerance is more beneficial in reservation systems. As long as both new and handoff traffics are delay tolerant, a priority scheme has more adverse effects on the new traffic performance. However, if the handoff traffics (i.e. prioritized or reserved traffic) is predominant, only a priority scheme is effective in reducing the handoff call dropping probability. However, this improvement is not significant. Further increase in delay tolerance is particularly useful for a system with reservation. Although a reservation system fails to deliver a better handoff traffics performance, its new call blocking probability drops significantly, as the new traffic becomes more delay tolerant.

Handoff call dropping probability: In terms of the handoff traffic performance, a priority scheme is the preferred option to reservation as long as both new and handoff traffics are delay tolerant. Further increase in the delay tolerance has negligible effect on handoff traffic performance under prioritization. However, with reservation systems, the handoff traffic performance degrades slightly if the newly generated traffic becomes more delay tolerant.

Overall, whether the system is highly mobile or not, prioritization is a preferred option to reservation. However, if only the new traffic is delay tolerant, reservation is a preferred option to priority in order to reduce its profound negative impact on handoff traffic performance. Further increase in delay tolerance on new traffic is more beneficial in reservation systems. This benefit is substantial as the reservation rate increases.

7.8   SUMMARY AND CONCLUSIONS

In this chapter, we have examined two of the most common admission criteria for handoff traffic in wireless IP networks, (1) reservation and (2) priority. Since most of the real-time traffics in IP networks are delay tolerant, we have investigated the effect of delay tolerance on overall system performance. Throughout this chapter, we have assumed that newly generated traffic has the same or a greater degree of delay tolerance.

Overall, if the new and handoff traffics share similar traffic characteristics, a priority scheme is a preferred option to reservation. However, if the newly generated traffic has advantageous traffic characteristics such as delay tolerance, then reservation is preferred. Although both reservation and priority schemes fail to keep the service quality, between the two, it was the priority system that was affected the most. However, as long as both new and handoff traffics are delay tolerant, both reservation and priority systems work better than the system with just a reservation or a priority scheme. Also, the simulation shows that users benefit the most with a little tolerance in delay, but unlimited delay tolerance fails to provide further improvement.

In general, traffic management is least effective when it is placed on the larger proportion of traffic. Here, we have observed that the delay tolerance nature of handoff users plays a vital role in determining the user performance. The system performance greatly depends on its traffic characteristics. For $p = 0.9$, both reservation and priority schemes fail to influence the traffic performance. However, further increase in delay tolerance on newly generated traffic contributes a significant improvement in new traffic performance. Therefore, if one type of traffic is predominant, rather than employing traffic management schemes on that traffic, it is wiser to look at the aspect of the traffic characteristics for possible performance improvements. Traffic management is most effective when it is employed on the smaller proportion of traffic. In addition, it has minimal adverse effects on the rest of the traffic.

It is worthwhile to note that the system enjoys greater benefits from the delay tolerance nature of its users than from placing a reservation or a priority scheme alone. Therefore, the system performance depends on both traffic management skills and traffic characteristics. In order to achieve optimum performance, we need to consider possible benefits that can be obtained from both aspects.

REFERENCES

1. Trajkovic L & Neidhardt A, Effect of traffic knowledge on the efficiency of admission control policies, *Computer Communication Review* 1999.
2. Knightly E & Shroff N, Admission control for statistical QoS: theory and practice, *IEEE Network*, March/April, 20–29, 1999.
3. Misic J, Chanson S & Lai F, Admission control for wireless multimedia networks with hard call level quality of service bounds, *Elsevier Computer Networks*, **31**, 125–140, 1999.
4. Choi S & Shin K, A cellular wireless local area network with QoS guarantees for heterogeneous traffic, *Mobile Networks and Applications*, **3**, 89–100, 1998.
5. Peha J, Scheduling and admission control for integrated services networks: The priority token bank, *Elsevier Computer Networks*, **31**, 2559–2576, 1999.
6. Ayyagari D & Ephremides A, Admission control with priorities: approaches for multirate wireless systems, *Mobile Networks and Applications*, **4**, 209–218, 1999.
7. Soldatos J, Vajias E & Mitrou N, CAC and traffic shaping for performance control in ATM: the two-class paradigm, *Elsevier Computer Networks*, **34**, 65–83, 2000.
8. Guerin R & Peris V, Quality-of-service in packet networks: basic mechanisms and directions, *Elsevier Computer Networks*, **31**, 169–189, 1999.
9. Kim J & Jamalipour A, Traffic management and providing QoS in future wireless IP networks, *IEEE Personal Communications Magazine*, **8**(5), 46–55, 2001.
10. Zheng B & Atiquzzaman M, Traffic management of multimedia over ATM networks, *IEEE Communications Magazine*, **37**(1), 33–38, 1999.
11. ITU-T Recommendation I.371, Traffic Control and Congestion Control in B-ISDN, Geneva, August 1996.
12. Kim J & Jamalipour A, Measurement-based admission control for wireless IP networks, *2002 International Symposium on Performance Evaluation of Computer and Telecommunication Systems SPECTS 2002*, San Diego, Calif., 14–19 July 2002, pp. 587–591.

13. Sahinoglu Z & Tekinay S, On multimedia networks: self-similar traffic and network performance, *IEEE Communications Magazine*, **37**(1), 48–52, 1999.
14. Crovella M & Bestavros A, Self-similarity in world wide web traffic: evidence and possible causes, *IEEE/ACM Transactions on Networking*, **5**(6), 835–846, 1997.
15. Deng S, Empirical model for WWW document arrivals at access link, *Proceedings of IEEE ICC '96*, Dallas, Tex., June 1996, pp. 1797–1802.
16. Grossglauser M & Bolot J, On the relevance of long-range dependence in network traffic, *IEEE/ACM Transactions on Networking*, **7**(5), 629–640, 1999.
17. Grossglauser M & Tse D, A framework for robust measurement-based admission control, *Proceedings of ACM SIGCOMM '97*, Cannes, France, September 1997.
18. Guerin R, Ahmadi H & Naghshineh M, Equivalent capacity and its application to bandwidth allocation in high-speed networks, *IEEE Journal on Selected Areas in Communications*, **9**(7), 968–981, 1991.
19. Gibbens R, Kelly F & Key P, A decision-theoretic approach to call admission control in ATM networks, *IEEE Journal on Selected Areas in Communications*, **13**(6), 1101–1113, 1995.
20. Jamin S, Shenker S & Danzig P, Comparison of measurement-based admission control algorithm for controlled-load service, *Proceeding of IEEE ICCS 1997*, Kobe, Japan, April 1997, pp. 973–980.
21. Floyd S, *Comments on Measurement-Based Admissions Control for Controlled-Load Services*, Draft version (9 July 1996).
22. Jamin S et al., A measurement-based admission control algorithm for integrated service packet networks, *IEEE/ACM Transactions on Networking*, December 1996.
23. Xiao X & Ni L, Internet QoS: big picture, *IEEE Network*, **13**(2), 8–18, 1999.
24. Figueira NR & Pasquale J, Providing QoS for wireless links: wireless/wired networks, *IEEE Personal Communications Magazine*, **6**(5), 42–51, 1999.
25. Cheng L, QoS-based on both call admission and cell scheduling, *Computer Networks and ISDN Systems*, **29**, 555–567, 1997.
26. Naghshineh M & Wellebeek-LeMair M, E2E QoS provisioning in multimedia wireless/mobile networks using an adaptive framework, *IEEE Communications Magazine*, **35**(11), 72–81, 1997.
27. Paxson V, End-to-end packet dynamics, *IEEE/ACM Transactions on Networking*, **7**(3), 277–291, 1999.
28. Capone J & Stavrakakis I, Delivering QoS requirements to traffic with diverse delay tolerance in a TDMA environment, *IEEE/ACM Transactions on Networking*, **7**(1), 75–87, 1999.
29. Crow B et al., IEEE 802.11 wireless local area networks, *IEEE Communications Magazine*, **35**(3), 116–126, 1997.
30. Forouzan B, *Local Area Networks*, McGraw-Hill Higher Education, Boston, Mass., 2003.
31. Toh C-K, *Ad Hoc Mobile Wireless Networks—Protocols and Systems*, Prentice Hall PTR, Upper Saddle River, N.J., 2002.

8

Mobility in Cellular Networks

This chapter provides a complete overview on mobility models used in cellular wireless systems and location management techniques as the two main parts of mobility management required in mobile networks. In a wireless network, the users are basically assumed to be mobile, which means that they will change their network point of attachment frequently, irrespective of whether they are idle or active in terms of exchanging data with the network and other network users.

The user of a mobile cellular network may experience two types of mobility in the network. The first one is a terminal mobility that means the mobile device frequently changes its network point of attachment during movement and while an active session is ongoing. Continuous telephone conversation during a cellular user's travel time is an example of this type of mobility. Some cellular systems such as Global System for Mobile communications (GSM) also provide personal mobility, which is realized by the inclusion of a subscriber identity module (SIM) card in their systems. The user can remove the SIM card from one terminal and insert it into another GSM-compatible terminal and still receive the same type of services from the cellular network. Therefore, in addition to terminal mobility, here the user has access to a kind of personal mobility.

Therefore, the issue of mobility management in mobile networks, including cellular and wireless Internet protocol (IP), goes back to finding appropriate strategies that could enable the tracking of mobile's roaming patterns, a process commonly known as location management. As such, it is also of paramount importance, from the research point of view, to determine mobility models that could illustrate the users' movement pattern and the suitable network point of attachment at each time. These are the topics to be discussed in this chapter.

8.1 INTRODUCTION

Third-generation mobile communication systems evolve by orienting the integration of three essential domains: broadband, mobile, and the Internet [1,2]. This is an era of

The Wireless Mobile Internet: Architectures, Protocols, and Services. Abbas Jamalipour
© 2003 John Wiley & Sons, Ltd   ISBN: 0-470-84468-X

user-controlled technology in which the user specifies the type and the level of service he wishes to subscribe to and the price he is willing to pay. Thus, from the system development point of view, apart from appropriately configuring the mobile terminal, it would be of a great importance to ensure the availability of a reliable internetworking between various networks, with all networks attached to a common IP backbone.

In terms of location management, although additional problems and design criteria will emerge, for example, increasing security concerns in the version of an all-IP network, the underlying framework is the same. The questions narrow down to *when, where*, and *how* to perform a location update. With cellular technology coming of age, it seems valuable to study the range of existing techniques from which lessons can be learnt to provide essential guidance to the development of a more general solution for IP networks.

Developing an efficient location management technique is an important step in working toward the determination of an optimal solution to the problem of managing mobility. The biggest challenge in framing location management is to find the most favorable trade-off between the location updates load and the searching load; the two parameters that are frequently referred to as location registration cost and call delivery cost. Intuitively, one would assume that the load increases when searching is required to locate the present address of the destination mobile terminal. Conversely, more information load would result because of frequent updates if a more complete location information database is to be maintained. With the irregular nature of cell sizes in a cellular network, the behavior of mobile movement changes from cell to cell and from user to user. Thus, the need for designing an adaptive algorithm for tracking a roaming mobile becomes more imperative than ever. As a result, the number of relevant publications found in the literature is extensive. However, since some are referenced more frequently than others, it is easy to lose track of the complete set of available solutions. Despite the need for references, the number of publications that have actually provided an overview is small, leave alone attempts to identify the interrelations between developments. This observation provides the genesis of this chapter. It intends not only to give a complete overview of the existing developments for cellular networks, but also to provide a critical analysis of existing technologies. In the discussions, the main merits and demerits of the existing techniques will be summarized to indicate areas of possible improvements. This chapter is structured such that it not only provides a brief description of individual location management strategy but also highlights the interrelations between various proposals. The findings are significant not only to aid the basic operations of cellular networks including more recent developments of General Packet Radio Service (GPRS) but also to enhance various aspects of mobile communications.

The next section begins by highlighting developments of mobility models. In addition to a brief description of the operations, the merits and demerits of each model are critically examined. A list of specific location and paging techniques is compiled in Section 8.3 to clarify differences and similarities in the key design philosophy of various proposals. Through a critical evaluation of the designed operations, the significance of distinct features observed from each protocol is assessed and compared. Section 8.4 provides an analytical framework for the location management problem and then compares the characteristics of the commonly applied analytical models. Although there are other measures that are also important to evaluate the effectiveness of a location-tracking solution, a general comparison guideline is that the fewer the combined numbers of updates and paging, the better the location-tracking technique.

8.2 MOBILITY MODELS

To many, mobility modeling is simply making a model that characterizes the mobile users' roaming behavior. While this is true, its usage spreads over a wide range of applications; from the examinations of system efficiency in terms of handover, offered traffic, and signaling network dimensioning to the design of various paging and multilayer network management techniques. Given the desired blocking and/or forced termination probabilities, we need to be able to evaluate other significant design parameters such as call-dropping probability [3]. This is just an example in which mobility modeling would come into play. It provides information relating to mobile users' moving characteristics (in terms of call holding times and cell residence times), necessary for such a study [4–7]. Other than for general performance-tuning purposes, the availability of a suitable mobility model is also critical for developing a fairer billing mechanism. Differing from traditional telephony systems, statistical information regarding the probability of call completion and/or effective channel holding time (CHT) is essential to meet modern billing needs.

As in the case of location management, the availability of a realistic mobile-roaming environment is required before meaningful studies can be made. More specifically, by first analyzing the frequency at which a user shifts from one cell to another, it could then become possible to identify the most efficient updating and paging algorithms.

Research on the development of a realistic mobility model remains an interesting topic in its own right. Its importance lies in any operation that involves predictions; be it the anticipation of traffic demand in the operations of traffic management, or the forecasting of handoff likelihood. Its application is widely spread. Given the close relation between location management and other aspects of mobility management in general, a reliable mobility model also enhances specific designs involving resource management (e.g. call admission control strategies) and handoff management [8], just to name a few. Figure 8.1 illustrates the applications of a reliable mobility model.

Figure 8.1 Possible applications of the mobility models

The proper selection of an appropriate mobility model is just as important as the actual design of the location management technique for performance evaluation purposes. In order to sensibly assess the performance gains achieved by various proposed techniques over the existing standard, the mobility model applied for evaluation should reflect reality as close as possible. In this section, a diverse range of available mobility models is discussed in detail. The distinct features of each model will be highlighted in addition to a judicious examination of possible limitations in applications.

The definition of models describing mobile-roaming characteristics is complicated and diverse. To adequately describe the movement patterns, the model should reveal information about traveling direction and speed. The combined knowledge of both attributes gives specific details not only about the path of motion but also about the duration that a mobile spends at each location. Consequently, it is possible to select the location management scheme that promotes optimal performance on the basis of actually observed movement patterns.

While it is important to consider the actual movement patterns, the model will not mean much without a proper definition of network topology that details the dimensions and structures of the platform where the mobiles roam. Thus, in the first part of the discussion, an introduction is included to summarize some commonly assumed network topologies. Although some models are used more frequently than others in simulations, the discussion will give an overview of the available alternatives.

8.2.1 Topology models

In the description of a topology model, the term *regular* is used to describe networks comprising equally shaped cell entities regardless of the dimension of the frameworks. Conversely, when arbitrary cells are included in the network, the term *irregular* is used for the descriptions.

8.2.1.1 Regular

With individual cells in the framework sharing the same dimensions, a regular topology model provides the optimal cell layout for radio coverage. However, because of the actual geographical characteristics of cellular networks, it is not possible in reality to implement such cell arrangements. In fact, with further complications of varying transmitting powers and interference conditions, cells of arbitrary shapes and sizes are more commonly employed. Nonetheless, the incorporation of such a regular topology model has been used extensively in the literature for the evaluation of various location management techniques. The model's attraction is mainly due to the simplicity of implementation and its capability of providing some general comparisons between different algorithms. Among them, the one-dimensional mesh model has the simplest structure in which each cell will have two adjacent cells. Intuitively, a 2-D mesh configuration is formed when the one-dimensional model is extended to a two-dimensional one. The number of neighboring cells has thus increased from two to four. In some cases where diagonal movements are

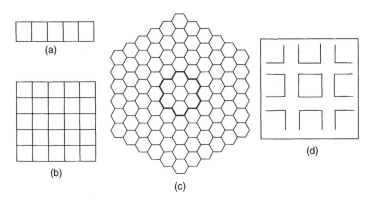

Figure 8.2 The commonly used topology models in cellular systems (a) 1-D mesh cells; (b) 2-D mesh cells; (c) 2-D hexagonal cells and (d) Manhattan topology

allowed, each cell will have eight possible directions of traversing. This, however, has been rarely evident from past analytical studies. An extension of the two-dimensional mesh cell topology is the Manhattan City model in which base stations are assumed to be located at the intersections of the streets. The most commonly used configuration in the literature is the two-dimensional hexagonal cell topology. Clearly, the cells are hexagonal in shape and have a maximum of six neighboring cells [9]. The actual probability of traversing will depend on the mobility model defined, which will be discussed later in this chapter. Figure 8.2 illustrates the graphical representation of the regular cell topology discussed.

The actual size of the cells can be appropriately defined according to the geographical characteristics and the roaming behavior of users in the networks. Specifically, in areas where a dense subscriber population is expected, smaller-sized cells will be necessary in order to have sufficient frequency replication to improve the capacity. On the other hand, when subscribers are found to have on average a higher traveling speed, bigger-sized cells will be more appropriate in order to reduce the number of updates that could incur during frequent cell-boundary crossings. Often, in areas where subscribers are more sparsely distributed, bigger-sized cells will also increase the coverage area. In general, there are terms specifically defined as *pico*, *micro*, and *macro*, to describe cells with magnitudes increasing from the smallest to the largest.

8.2.1.2 Irregular

The irregular topology model gives a more realistic measure of the actual cellular networks. The topology is irregular as the cells are neither regular in size nor consistent in the number of neighboring cells. While it might have the best approximation to the actual cellular systems, such an irregular topology model is rarely considered in the literature. In addition, the model varies in accordance to the specific network conditions and the computational cost associated with such implementation is significant.

There are a couple of irregular topology models proposed in the literature in an attempt to model a more realistic cellular system. In Reference [9], interrelations between adjacent cells in a location area (LA) are represented using a graphical computational algorithm. While the actual cells are represented by discrete nodes, vectors are used to illustrate the connectivity between them. A similar approach is proposed in Reference [10] for the evaluation of an information-based update scheme. Such a graph model, however, only shows the cells and their interconnections, but does not reflect actual information about cell sizes. For simulation purposes, a graph model can be generated on the basis of the assignation of an average node degree.

8.2.2 Movement models

There are a few possible approaches to categorizing various mobility models; the most significant differentiation among them is, however, the nature of the information revealed by the model. On the one hand, it is important to consider aggregate rather than individual movement behaviors. A suitable mobility model would have to be able to determine the trends of movements that best describe groups of users and thus form the basis for the design of an effective city infrastructure. Specific mobility measures may be based on socio-economic groups, geographical locations, or other measures, but the key feature is that the information will describe group behavior with individualism averaged. On the other hand, for the assignation of parameters in the implementation of specific location management techniques, the individual mobile movement behavior will play a more significant role. Specifically, the operation can be optimized for each distinct roaming characteristic observed from independent users.

Mobility models are classified under the category of individual movement, describing individual mobile movements as opposed to aggregate patterns. Depending on the time of the day or the day of the week, the transitioning behavior of the same user will differ. With the network topology predefined, such mobility models attempt to anticipate the mobile's traversing patterns between adjacent cells under various network scenarios. Within the discussions, we will further classify specific models according to their applications. Figure 8.3 illustrates a possible classification based on the correlation between distinct movements for individual mobiles.

On the one hand, there are mobility models that intend to give some very general descriptions of the movement patterns. These models often assume little knowledge prior to the transitions and are applicable when mobiles do not show distinct traveling patterns.

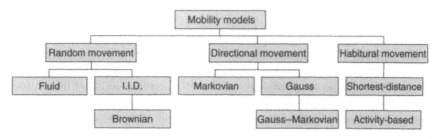

Figure 8.3 Mobility models

The desired level of randomness is incorporated in the movement by adjusting the probabilities of mobiles roaming to adjacent cells. The computation load required to establish such models is often small, and can be implemented virtually in all networks. On the other hand, there are more user-specific models proposed, such as the activity-based models and the shortest-distance models. Often, with the underlying assumption that the source and destination of the traversing path is known, these mobiles utilize individual and household activity patterns to describe the mobility patterns [11]. While the model may be able to give a more realistic description of the actual mobility patterns, the additional computational load required including data collection and analysis increases in direct proportion to the accuracy of the modeling.

The impact of mobility models on the performance of update schemes has been illustrated in References [12,13]. In the study, variations of standard and modified update strategies were applied to three different mobility models including fast movement, slow movement, and activity-based movement. With the call-arrival rate fixed for the three network scenarios, the simulation results demonstrated that the resultant operation costs for the update strategies differ with the varying mobility models applied. Effectively, the selection of an optimal update scheme also varies accordingly. The actual simulation details including definitions of network parameters are not clearly specified for the location management algorithms simulated. However, it appears that the dynamic scheme generally has better performances when the mobility pattern is either predictable where the movement pattern is traceable or the mobile has a high mobility rate in comparison to call arrivals.

8.2.2.1 Fluid model

The fluid model is an aggregate movement model. By averaging the mobility patterns for all mobiles, a fluid model is often used to describe the aggregate traffic. It is assumed that mobiles travel in a direction uniformly distributed over $[0, 2\pi]$. In addition, taking a circular region for example, the average number of site crossings (per unit time) N equals the product of population density (ρ), the average velocity (v), and the region circumference (πL) [14].

The biggest concern associated with the fluid model is that it is more accurate for regions containing a large population (due to the averaged values used for calculations). Thus, it is difficult to apply in situations where individual movement patterns are desired—more of an issue in studies of location management techniques.

8.2.2.2 Random movement model

The random movement model, an individual movement model, is perhaps the primary approximation that can be used to illustrate a mobile's roaming feature. The simplicity in the implementation comes from the lack of notion in directions. The model states that there is an equal probability to all adjacent cells regardless of the actual location of the current residence. Equivalently, the probability of the mobile moving forward is the same as its moving backward or in any other direction at every cell-boundary crossing [15,16].

Apart from the fact that such a general mobile offers limited options to distinguish individual mobiles, it reveals little information about the actual movement patterns. The model is commonly referred to as memory-less and has restricted implications in real cellular systems. Nonetheless, the scheme was sometimes applied in simulations to evaluate the performance characteristics of a designed location management technique under the worst possible roaming scenarios in which there is no correlation between adjacent movements in time.

8.2.2.3 Markov model (first order)

The Markov movement, an individual movement model, is one of the earliest models that was extensively used in simulations for the evaluation of various location management schemes. The model is more appropriate for pedestrian mobile users, for whom it is necessary to capture frequent stop-and-go behavior and common direction changes during movements [15,17]. In this model, a subscriber will either remain within a region (with probability q) or move to an adjacent region (with probability $1 - q$) at a discrete time t, according to a transition probability distribution. The model explicitly defines the probabilities in all possible directions of roaming. Differing from the basic random movement model in which the movements are uncorrelated, the Markov model allows adjustments to be made in traversing probabilities between adjacent movements in time.

Similar to what had been experienced with the random movement model, one of the limitations of this approach is that successive moves made by random determination are statistically independent of each other. Hence, there is no such concept of consecutive movements through a series of regions being considered in this model. In addition, although more realistic measures are now incorporated in the model, the definition of traversing probabilities is static. In brief, the statistical information is defined prior to the movement and remains the same throughout the roaming periods.

8.2.2.4 Finite-context model

A finite-context model is the more general term used to describe a Markov model of different orders. For example, the simplest possible Markov model of first order assumes that the movement patterns are describable by a time-invariant Markov chain. Consequently, the steady state probability of having a mobile to reside in a specific cell can be evaluated through the formation of balanced equations outlining the transitional characteristics between boundary crossings. Generally, the higher the order of the Markov model, the more the information is revealed about a mobile's roaming characteristics. Subsequently, the network is more certain about the predictions of the mobile's future residencies [10].

The finite-context model incorporates the concepts of trip and presumes that for each destination, there will be a particular path for the mobile to follow. Given that a certain level of correlation is assumed between adjacent movements in time, a history of the update centers recorded during previous updates is used to predict the mobile's future residency in terms of probability distributions. In addition, the level of uncertainty in the mobility model is measured by an entropy entity defined as the context.

Figure 8.4 illustrates an example of a digital search tree that is used to store a dictionary of contexts in a sequence of 'aaababbbbbaabccddcbaa' for a Markov model of second

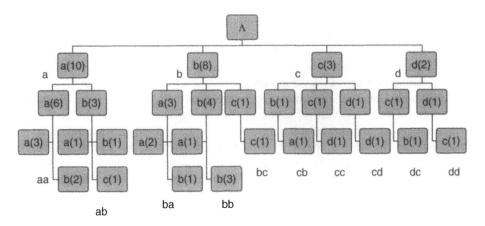

Figure 8.4 An example of a digital search tree for all contexts up to the second order

Table 8.1 The contexts along with the incurring frequencies for Markov models

Order-0	Order-1			Order-2	
a(10)	a | a(6)	c | b(1)	A | aa(3)	b | aa(2)	c | ab(1)
b(8)	a | b(3)	c | c(1)	A | ab(1)	b | ab(1)	c | bc(1)
b(3)	b | a(3)	c | d(1)	a | ba(2)	b | ba(1)	c | dd(1)
d(2)	b | b(4)	d | c(1)	a | bb(1)	b | bb(3)	d | cc(1)
	b | c(1)	d | d(1)	a | cb(1)	b | dc(1)	d | cd(1)

order. Starting from the root at level 0, each node represents a context and stores the information of the last cell that is recorded in the sequence. The presentation of the full context is completed with the inclusion of the relative frequency that the node appears, in the context of its parent node located one level up in the digital search tree [10].

Table 8.1 summarizes the contexts enumerating the roaming characteristics for the Markov models with varying orders of 0, 1, 2. Note that contexts with null information were excluded in the presentation for simplicity.

Clearly, a lot more information is revealed about the mobile's tendency to take specific routes when the order of the Markov model increases.

8.2.2.5 Gauss–Markov model

Although the adaptation of the Gauss–Markov distribution was first proposed to model the correlation between drift velocities in time [18], it was later shown that the same distribution can be utilized to model the correlation in traveling directions between adjacent movements [19]. It is proposed that while the mobility patterns are granularly tracked, the modeling parameters can be dynamically adjusted according to the variations observed in the actual movement characteristics. The main merit of applying a Gauss–Markov distribution is its flexibility to control prediction accuracy by adjusting the information feedback frequency. Consequently, less computation load is required to establish the modeling framework in comparison to the more mobile-specific activity-based model.

The Gauss–Markov model also assumes that the mobile will have a certain destination in mind, except that it is not necessary to define a specific traversing path. However, some correlation between the traveling directions at each boundary crossing is expected. Depending on the level of correlation, each movement will incur a change of direction in the range of $[\pi, -\pi]$ with reference to the last updated cell. Generally, a greater correlation between adjacent traveling directions can be seen with a smoother line.

In an ideal case in which a mobile is moving in a straight line, the distribution from the Gauss–Markov model will show the characteristics of a low pass filter (i.e. an almost flat curve). Conversely, when the correlation between the transverse directions decreases, a more abrasive change (and hence fluctuations in the moving directions) can be presented in the distribution model, which then approximates the characteristics of a high pass filter. This presented capability justifies the suitability of its usage.

Effectively, the Gauss–Markov mobility model can be considered as a more generalized version of the finite-context model. In addition, it is possible to increase the precision of predictions by occasionally sending dummy paging packets that function as training signals to increase the precision of the predictions. The performance gain will be further improved at the expense of increasing bandwidth consumption over the air interface.

8.2.2.6 Activity-based model

There are specific models proposed, such as various activity-based models that utilize individual and household activity patterns to describe the mobility patterns [11,12,13,20]. While the model might be able to give a more realistic description of actual mobility patterns, the additional computational load required including data collection and analysis increases in direct proportion to the precision of the modeling. Such a trade-off restricts its range of applications.

8.2.2.7 Shortest-distance model

The shortest-distance model operates on the basis of the underlying assumption that the network has the knowledge of the roaming mobile's source and destination. Subsequently, once the mobile enters the LA, until its final exit, the movements within the bounded registration are expected to follow the shortest path. To ensure that the number of cells traversed in the current LA is always a maximum, the probability of moving to a neighboring cell in one specific direction will depend on the previous movements within the LA. For the Manhattan city topology considered in References [21,22], the mobile has three options for its next movement at every intersection; going forward, turning right or turning left. On the basis of the assumption that the mobile will arrive at the destination through the shortest path, each time a turning is made, the probability of repeating the same operation in the next movement becomes zero. In other words, no return trip is considered during the mobile's movements. The basic design concept is very similar to that for the Gauss–Markov model. Although the purpose of utilizing the observed correlation

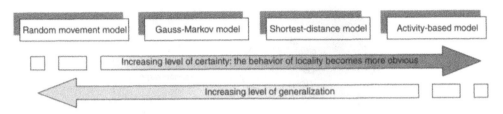

Figure 8.5 A general comparison between different mobility models

from previous traveling directions to predict future movements is the same, there seems to be more constraints involved in the application of the shortest-distance model in terms of traveling patterns.

Furthermore, the application of the shortest-distance model will incur a similar computation load to that of an activity-based mobility model. In reality, the proposed model is only realizable if the mobile acquires sufficient information about the geographical characteristics before its movements. It is possible to consider a combined operation of the shortest-distance model and the activity-based mobility model. Given the great similarities observed between the two models, an optimal performance is likely to be achieved at a reduced operational cost. Figure 8.5 shows a general comparison between different mobility models.

8.2.2.8 Mobility traces

Mobility traces record actual movement behavior for certain segments of the population and may be more realistic than mobility models. On a smaller scale, Reference [14] has collected movement traces within an in-building environment generated from a small section of the population. On a larger scale, the SUMATRA project has generated a set of traces for daily movements in the San Francisco Bay area for the duration of seven days. However, as the traces are of an extremely large population size, it is difficult to have a complete set of data incorporated for performance evaluation purposes [23].

8.2.3 Residence time models

Cell residence time is the main parameter used to identify mobility characteristics. It anticipates the time a particular mobile user spends on a cell (independent of being engaged in a call) before moving to another [3]. Thus, it provides a quantitative measure of the frequency of cell-boundary crossings and in turn, brings awareness about the necessity of efficient location and handoff management techniques.

For the cell-residence time, two parameters are separately defined corresponding to new calls and handoff calls. While the new call cell residence time (T_n) represents the length of time, a mobile terminal resides in the cell in which the call originated; handover call

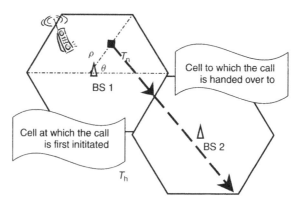

Figure 8.6 A graphical representation illustrating the difference in concept between a new call and a handover call

cell residence time (T_h) is the time a mobile resides in the handover cell before crossing to another cell. The main difference between the definitions of the two parameters is illustrated in Figure 8.6. Note that quantities of ρ and θ define the initial location of the roaming mobile.

The distribution of cell residence time is influenced by a number of factors. As well as the obvious parameter of user-mobility patterns (e.g. traveling speed, direction, and the paths a user follows), the sizes of cells (in terms of shape and radius) should also be taken into account.

Furthermore, as it is shown in Reference [24], the speed and direction distributions of the in-cell mobiles are different from those of the cell-boundary crossing mobiles. Reference [25] has taken the initiative to quantify the effects of cell residence distributions on cellular network performances in terms of call blocking, handoff failure, and forced termination probabilities. Thus, the importance of making the right assumptions on these parameters is obvious.

In the literature, two main approaches can be identified in modeling cell residence times. The first approach imposes assumptions on various system parameters. These include, but are not limited to, hexagonal geographic cell shapes, constant mobiles' speed, random distance traversed, and/or uniformly distributed traveling directions [26,27]. Although it could be a tedious process to characterize analytically the cell residence times using these modeling assumptions, Orlik and Hong [26,28] have both demonstrated the possibility of using this technique. An early work [26] (and many others) used negative exponential models (with the mean equal to η^{-1}) or the sum of exponential variants for dwell times. Other common distribution models include Erlang, Uniform, Weibull, and Deterministic; these, however, do not seem to be particularly relevant in modeling cell residence time [25].

However, as in reality cell shapes are often highly irregular in conjunction with the random nature of mobile characteristics, it seems somewhat impractical having to set certain constraints on the cell shape and/or distributions of the mobiles' migrating speed and directions. As a result, the second approach often attracts greater research interests as the cell residence time is modeled to capture the overall effects of cellular shape and user's mobility patterns [28]. In other words, from field tests, distribution models such as exponential distributions and lognormal distributions were able to give some close approximations [3]. In Reference [29], the suggested model traces mobiles in an environment in which their movement is governed by a set of random variables. It is shown that the generalized Gamma distribution provides the best approximation for the cell residence time distribution. The results are also confirmed in Reference [30].

Negative exponential distributions have in many ways shown themselves as being a strong candidate. Not only have they maintained the desirable Markovian property but the models were also general enough to accommodate a wide range of applications. Furthermore, a lot of credibility was gained through their simplicity in manipulating various mathematical expressions [26].

On the other hand, negative exponential distribution can only accommodate random variables for which the standard deviation does not exceed the mean. This somehow makes its implementation more restricted.

The generalized Gamma function has also attracted great attention as was very evident in more recent research works performed within the cellular network community. It is unfortunate that without the required memory-less property, the model cannot be used in the multidimensional birth–death framework. However, with its capability of representing large coefficients of variation, this model is still considered a favorable alternative to be employed [29].

The sum of hyper-exponentials (SOHYP) random variables is a very powerful distribution model due to its ability to represent a wide range of variation coefficients; from those less than unity (as in the case for exponential, Erlang models) and equal to unity, to ranges that are greater than unity [26]. However, its Laplace transform remains a complex rational function. This greatly increases the complexity of analyzing tasks. In addition, it remains unclear at this stage whether the model is in fact general enough for universal approximations.

The Cox model was in fact one of the earliest models in use for distribution purposes. It is general enough to cover other distribution functions such as Exponential, Erlang, hyper-exponential and SOHYP distributions. Thus, it can be qualified as the most general distribution model. The disadvantage is the rather complex mathematical equations that it involves. The complexity somehow makes any intended simulations to be less efficient [28].

Table 8.2 provides a comparison between these distribution model alternatives in terms of their mathematical approximations and applications. To complete our discussion, the parameters commonly used in modeling the mobility characteristics are briefly discussed in the following text. Although these might not have any direct impact on the problem of location tracking, their inclusion is essential in other aspects of mobility management.

8.2.3.1 Unencumbered session duration

Unencumbered session duration is the amount of time that the call would remain in progress if it could continue to completion without forced termination [31]. It represents the ideal

Table 8.2 Mathematical approximations to the residence time models

Model	Mathematical expressions
Negative exponential distribution	For new calls:

$$f_{T_n}(t) = \frac{8R}{3\pi V_{max} t^2} \left[1 - \sqrt{\left\{ 1 - \left(\frac{t V_{max}}{2R} \right)^2 \right\}^3} \right] \quad \text{for} \quad 0 \leq t \leq 2R/V_{max}$$

$$f_{T_n}(t) = \frac{8R}{3\pi V_{max} t^2} \quad \text{for} \quad t \geq 2R/V_{max}$$

For handoff calls:

$$f_{T_h}(t) = \frac{4R}{\pi V_{max} t^2} \left[1 - \sqrt{1 - \left(\frac{V_{max} t}{2R} \right)^2} \right] \quad \text{for} \quad 0 \leq t \leq 2R/V_{max}$$

$$f_{T_h}(t) = \frac{4R}{\pi V_{max} t^2} \quad \text{for} \quad t \geq 2R/V_{max}$$

R is the radius of a circle with equivalent area of the hexagonal cell and the traveling speed is uniformly distributed between 0 and V_{max} [29].

Generalized Gamma distribution

$$f_T(t) = \frac{\beta^{-\alpha} t^{\alpha-1}}{\Gamma(\alpha)} e^{-(t/\beta)}$$

$\Gamma(\alpha) = \int_0^\infty (x^{\alpha-1}) e^{-x} dx$ is the Gamma function defined for any real and positive values of a. The values of α and β vary for new calls and handoff calls [30].

Hyper-Erlang

$$f(t) = \frac{\beta^m t^{m-1}}{(m-1)!} e^{-\beta t}$$

β is the scale parameter, defined as $\beta = m\eta$ with m being the shape parameter and η representing the mean of the Erlang distribution [28].

case when there are an infinite number of channels and the handover procedure does not affect the duration of a connection, hence no handoff failure. Unfortunately, the number of radio channels is limited in reality and the duration of an actual call connection will depend on the network under consideration, for example, its traffic situation, channel availability, and so forth [28]. Hence, the formulation of the additional term *effective call holding time of an incomplete call* as opposed to *effective call holding time of a complete call*.

In the past, the unencumbered session time has often been assumed to be negatively exponentially distributed with the density function $f_c(t) = \mu e^{-\mu t}$ and a mean average call holding time equal to μ^{-1} [25,29]. With the increasing availability of various additional mobile services today (as opposed to purely voice telephone calls), it might be beneficial to consider a broader distribution model for unencumbered session times [24].

8.2.3.2 Channel holding time

In conventional telephone systems, handoff does not occur, and the channel holding time CHT is equal to the call duration. By contrast, in a cellular mobile network a call may experience a number of handoffs with the result that the CHT in a particular cell becomes a fraction of the total call duration. Intuitively, the CHT is the time during which a new or handover call occupies a channel in the given cell. Since the CHT is only one small portion of the cell residence time $f_r(t)$ and the call holding time $f_d(t)$, the CHT density function $f_h(t)$ can be written as

$$f_h(t) = \int_{t_r=t}^{\infty} f_r(t_r) f_d(t) dt_r + \int_{t_d=t}^{\infty} f_r(t) f_d(t_d)\, dt_d \qquad (8.1)$$

and is dependent on the mobility of the user. The CHT is a function of the system parameters such as cell size, user location, user mobility, and call duration [29].

Negative exponential distributions have been assumed to describe the CHT in most previous traffic analysis that models large and single-cell systems [32–34]. However, this assumption is not completely valid for personal communication networks. For these networks, Guerin [35] demonstrated that when the rate of direction change is low, the CHT is no longer exponentially distributed [36]. In fact, it was further demonstrated that only under the condition that the cell residence time is also distributed exponentially can the CHT be assumed to be exponentially distributed [37].

Khan and Fang [28,25] observed (using field data in two separate studies) that the CHT distribution for cellular telephony systems inherits a lognormal distribution. In the same way, Jordan [27] demonstrated that a mixture of Erlang distributions could also provide a better statistical fitting to the experimental data.

8.2.3.3 Average number of handovers per call

The average number of handovers per call represents the number of times a mobile crosses different boundaries during a call. Obviously, this should also be a random variable with its value being influenced by factors such as cell size, call holding time and other mobility parameters [29]. As the processing burden required in the system could be dramatically reduced by alleviating switching load, the aim is to have as few handovers as possible.

To summarize, Figure 8.7 gives an illustration of the relations between different traffic-related parameters outlined above.

8.2.4 Call-arrival models

As far as performance evaluation is concerned, not only is the information about mobile characteristics important but the knowledge of call rate is also essential to generate quantifying measures. It is important to note that the issue of location tracking becomes

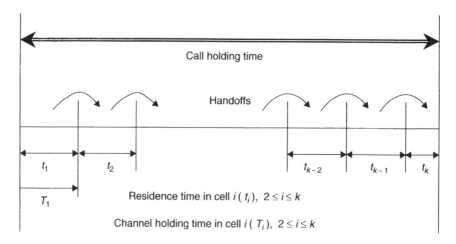

Figure 8.7   Relations between various mobility-related traffic parameters

a challenge because connection requests from other parties are expected for roaming mobiles, and hence the whole demand for mobile communications. Thus, for the same mobility rate, it is clear that the optimal frequency of the update should vary according to the rate of call arrivals. On the one extreme where call arrivals occur all the time, clearly a precise location tracking is essential to minimize the number of paging loads that would otherwise become necessary as time progresses. On the other extreme where there are no call arrivals, it will not be necessary to track the mobile. It is at the middle of the scale that efficient location management is essential. In brief, we need to find an optimal trade-off between the location update and the paging load such that a minimal operational cost is achieved. It is therefore necessary to determine a model that can approximate the call-arrival characteristics with reasonable accuracy. Subsequently, given a specific mobility model, the probability of having incoming calls during the time the mobile resides within a particular cell or area in some cases can be evaluated. Interestingly enough, the call-arrival rate is expected to be independent of radio technologies. In other words, the rate at which calls are received in a wired-network should be the same as in a wireless network. From basic queuing theories, calls are often modeled by Poisson distributions [9,15–17,22,38,39]. The same assumption should also apply to wireless networks. Thus, given a rate of λ_c, the call arrival is a memory-less process and has a time-varying probability distribution defined by

$$C(t) = \lambda_c e^{-\lambda_c t} \tag{8.2}$$

The only other information that would be necessary to optimize the operation is the relation between the mobility rate and the call-arrival rate, a characteristic often defined by call-to-mobility ratio (CMR). With the call-arrival rate assumed to be a Poisson distribution, the probability of call arrival in relation to the mobility rate is evaluated for an exponentially distributed mobility pattern. The analysis, however, can be appropriately modified to take into consideration different mobility patterns [40].

8.3 LOCATION MANAGEMENT SCHEMES

Mobility is no longer an exception, but a criteria that is to be complied with in today's telecommunications. An efficient location tracking mechanism is a crucial step in complying with the desired quality of service (QoS) metrics. In most conventional schemes in which the LA is fixed, the mobile is required to update the network when exiting the currently registered area.

For example, cellular networks assign each LA with a visiting location register (VLR), and thus, whenever the mobile moves out of the current location boundary, an update is due. In extreme cases in which a separate VLR is assigned at the cell levels, registration operations are performed upon cell-boundary crossings.

Although effective location management requires an optimal combination between update and paging operations, much of the research effort has treated the two key operations separately. Consequently, in the following sections, an overview is presented independently for the operations of update and paging.

8.3.1 Update strategies

The central aim of an update scheme is to define the time or location at which a new registration is required such that the network will at all times have a granular view of the mobile's location. Specifically, upon the detection of arrival of a new cell, a decision is made on whether a new registration is required depending on the actual location. Although the final effect will be the same, the actual operation details might vary.

There are, however, very few publications in the literature that actually compare the operations of the existing location management proposals. In studies that perform similar tasks [9,15,41,42], individual strategies are classified principally into *static* and *dynamic* schemes. Thus, a distinction is made on the basis of the nature of the database centers. The term static is used to describe specific techniques in which the assignation of LA is fixed independent of the individual mobile characteristics. Conversely, the term dynamic refers to update strategies where the formation of LAs may vary according to the actual mobile characteristics.

Such categorization is general and almost in some ways simple, as little additional information is revealed to reflect the more specific nature of an individual update technique. To avoid similar deficiencies in this chapter, update schemes are more carefully categorized to ensure their individualities are appropriately highlighted through their classification.

Thus, in this section, the individual scheme is classified according to the mechanism that is used in deciding the need for initiating an update operation. For most proposed update operations, the need for update is determined by a simple table lookup. Generally, the mobile terminals keep in their memory a list of cell identities (ID) retrieved from the network normally during the last registration operation. Upon the detection of roaming to a new cell, the mobile compares the current cell ID with that stored in the database. In some cases, a matching between the two suggests the need for an update, if the information maintained in the database provides details of the update boundaries; hence, an update is due when mobiles arrive at these locations. In other cases, the opposite condition applies, in which an update is due only when the current location has not been previously included in the record, or in other words, the mobile has moved out of the expected area. The more recent proposals, however, are designed to operate on the basis of the opposite philosophy. In these schemes, as the LAs are dynamically assigned according to the actual mobile movements, a new LA for the mobile will only become available upon the registration of a new update. Thus, an update is required when the mobile is detected to have reached one of those cells specified in the cache [43]. Any update that demonstrates this type of table lookup is classified under the category of *location area oriented*. The actual mechanism that was used to derive the set of cell IDs, however, varies significantly between different schemes.

There are, however, other schemes that demand for their update decision more operations than a table lookup. In these update strategies, additional computations are generally involved to evaluate the need for a location update in the mobile terminals. The concept of LA does not apply and the decision of an update depends mainly on the actual circumstances at the time a cell boundary is crossed. The term *non-location area oriented* seems to be the obvious choice for describing an update scheme under this category. Clearly, depending on the complexity of the operations, the required computation load and thus, power consumption at mobile terminals, will differ. The trade-off between the infrastructure expense and the achievable performance gain determines the suitability of incorporating this strategy into a given network scenario.

This distinction forms the basis in our classification of various location management schemes. Figure 8.8 classifies update algorithms based on the time when an update is due.

At the top level, the classification of update schemes can be made according to the nature of decision. In other words, while in some cases an update is performed when mobiles arrive at certain database centers, others register the new location upon exiting the defined area.

The discussions for each scheme are oriented around the questions of *when* to update, *where* to update, and *what* to update.

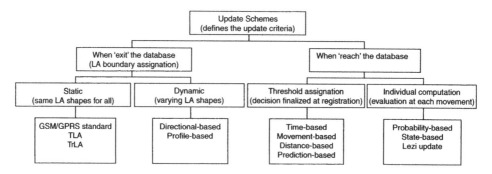

Figure 8.8 An overview of update scheme proposals optimized for individual mobile movements

8.3.1.1 Zone-based

Static update algorithms refer to the type of zone-based schemes in which the locations of the update centers are fixed for each network. Independent of an individual mobile's roaming characteristics, a registration is required whenever a mobile arrives at such cells [9,41]. While such schemes require little computational load to implement, the achievable performance gain is often limited. Clearly, without distinguishing the roaming characteristics of individual mobiles, it is difficult, if not impossible, to assign update cells such that the overall performance is optimized for all mobiles. To illustrate such deficiencies, consider the two situations in which the application of the static update algorithm is particularly infeasible. On the one extreme, when a mobile frequently passes through the selected reporting centers, a high update rate will result, thus incurring unnecessary operational expenses. On the other extreme, when a mobile does not roam into any of the selected reporting centers, no update will be registered and consequently a high paging load is likely to result upon call arrivals.

Recognizing such an inadequacy, strategies such as three-location area update are proposed to minimize the number of updates initiated by the repetitive motion characteristics observed from the movement patterns of a mobile. There are different methods to implement a profile-based update strategy, for example, a list of the most probable visiting locations can be defined for each mobile according to its movement history. Thus, an update at the reporting center will be necessary only if the specific update cell has not been previously compiled in the database [44].

8.3.1.2 Three-location area

In the three-location area (TrLA) update scheme, the mobile will have three neighboring LAs stored in the memory instead of only one, which is the currently residing LA for the general GSM/GPRS standard. Thus, for every occurrence of a boundary transitioning, the mobile checks whether a registration is required by comparing the obtained LA identification with the three LAs cached at the mobile node (MN). Classified also under the category of *update when exiting*, an update is due only when the mobile moves out from the big-location area (BLA) comprising of the three LAs. The information cached at the MN thus gets refreshed during the update operation. A simple two-step paging mechanism is applied in searching for the roaming mobile upon call arrivals. Clearly, the mobile will be located somewhere within the BLA defined by the update operation. Thus, during the first polling cycle, the last updated VLR is paged. The remaining VLRs are paged during the second polling cycle [45].

The actual mechanism used to select the additional LAs for caching is, however, not specified. It was not possible to determine whether some sort of prediction had been implemented on the basis of the available documentation. To a large extent, the scheme appears to be only a slightly varied version of the conventional static location update scheme.

The network is assumed to have a complete knowledge of the LA layout. Simulation results indicate that a performance improvement over the conventional GSM standard will only be evident if the paging delay constraint is allowed to be greater than one polling cycle.

Effectively, the proposed scheme suggests reducing the update cost by increasing the size of the update area. Although a two-step paging operation is incorporated, the saving is only equivalent to a special case of sequential paging with the complete update area being divided into two unequal-sized partitions. Thus, compared to a maximum paging load equal to a single LA, the maximum paging load for the proposed TrLA has increased by three times. The original challenge remains, and the significance of the new scheme needs to be better justified.

Furthermore, with additional information about the identification of neighboring LAs cached at the terminals and the network, the size of the database increases in direct proportion to the number of connecting subscribers. With mobile subscribers continuing to increase, it is likely that scalability issues will restrict the applications.

Discussions up to this point have considered only static assignments of the LA. Although the actual positions of the registration centers might be different for individual mobile users, the general shapes and sizes of the LAs remain the same. Hence, no specific distinction or consideration is given to individual mobiles that inherit different mobility characteristics. As a result, although performance gain over the conventional cellular standards might be evident, the extent of improvement is limited on an average.

To enhance operations, more user-specific LAs are assigned to reflect actual movement patterns. The ultimate goal is to define an update boundary that maximizes the number of transitions between cells before the mobile finally exits the LA. A large number of specific update strategies proposed under this category are based on the assignation of thresholds. The defined parameter will then be used to determine whether the update is necessary upon transitioning to a different cell. To enable a comprehensive comparison between different techniques, the operations for all schemes under the category of *dynamic update* is discussed within the same framework. Specifically, discussions will be structured to answer the particular questions of *how*, *what*, and *why*: 'How does the scheme operate?', 'What are the novelties introduced?', and 'Why is the proposal, or in some cases modification, significant?

8.3.1.3 Profile-based

As the name suggests, with the profile-based update scheme, a profile is maintained for each user in different time periods. Upon registration, the network assigns the mobile a list of regions where a high probability of residency is expected on the basis of what was learned from previous movements. A region can be a cell, or where appropriate, groups of cells. Mobiles are not expected to perform updates unless the region entered is not already included in the list. Thus, in extreme cases in which a region is used to represent a regular-sized LA, the operation turns into a modified version of the two location area (TLA) and the three-location area (TrLA) update schemes. This is possible, however, only if regular mobility patterns have been observed from past movement history [45].

For the systems to establish a reliable database describing the mobile's movements for different occasions, the subscriber is assumed to demonstrate a certain degree of consistency in movements. It was concluded in Reference [46] that when a medium-to-high predictability is observed from mobile movements, a lower location management can be obtained in comparison to other update schemes in which the boundaries are more generally defined. Other more specific analyses for the profile-based scheme can be acquired from Reference [40].

8.3.1.4 Probabilistic location

Classified under static update schemes, Reference [47] proposed a probabilistic location update scheme (PLU) in which the mobile registers with a probability of P that varies according to the call and mobility characteristics of individual users upon entering a new cell. Basically, the key conclusion obtained from the paper illustrates that as mobility increases (i.e. with decreasing CMR), the probability of needing a location update at the cell decreases. This somehow is complementary to justification in [19], which states that the more direct the mobility pattern is, the less the updating load that is required since the probability of predicting the correct location of a roaming mobile would be higher. Thus, in terms of categorizing the mobility characteristics, while one uses the mobility rate information (with respect to call arrivals), the other focuses on mobility directions. Both, however, aim at reducing the necessary updating loads by increasing the probability of accurate prediction.

8.3.1.5 Compression-based

Similar to the profile-based scheme, the compression-based update algorithm utilizes location probability profiles. The actual mechanisms that are used to establish the probability profiles are, however, different. While the former only requires a counter mechanism at the terminal end, the latter requires a lot more computation and analysis from both the network and mobiles, however, at the benefit of a more reliable profile database. Specifically, in the compression-based update, there is no concept of an LA definition. Thus, different from its profile-based counterpart in which a set of LAs is predefined according to the mobile's previous movement history, each cell is the equivalent of an LA on its own in the compression-based update.

To save on unnecessary memory requirement at the mobile end, the LeZi-update algorithm is proposed to be implemented on top of one or more threshold-based update schemes [10]. Thus, based on an always-update strategy, instead of triggering an update whenever the threshold is reached, the algorithm delays the update operation and attempts to process the information in chunks. At the time of registration, rather than sending information about the mobile's current residency, the past movement history having been encoded in a compressed form is registered at the network. A tree diagram is used based on the Ziv and Lempel compression algorithms. Thus, an update is registered only when the path is not yet recorded in the database. Clearly, the proposed update schemes will have an optimal performance gain only when regular mobility patterns become evident and the network is confident that the mobile's future movements will continue to show such predictability [10]. Effectively, the mobile and the system form an encoder/decoder pair. Considering that it is actually the movement history being reported during updates, this location-tracking strategy is considered more of a path-oriented than a zone-based solution. It should be noted, however, that the application of the scheme is based on the assumption that a mobile's movement pattern is generally repetitive and can be learned over time.

The fact that additional computation is required before a decision is made about the need for an update makes the compression-based update scheme appear to be similar to Reference [47]. In that case, the previous information based on residence time will be used to evaluate the probability of having call arrivals before the mobile exits the current cell. Clearly, with the call-arrival rate fixed, the longer the mobile resides in the area, the higher the possibility that the mobile can be located in the cell. Thus, in comparison to the compression-based scheme, the scheme described in Reference [47] will incur a lot more intelligence at the mobile terminals. This raises not only an issue of database conservation, but also a concern because of increased computation load.

8.3.1.6 Threshold assignation

A series of *threshold*-based update schemes represents some important and fundamental developments for basic user-specific update strategies. A specific parameter is assigned to the mobile by the network during registration; the quantity is then monitored continuously such that an update is performed when what is observed from the actual movement exceeds the quantity that is predefined by the network. The most commonly used parameters are time-, movement-, and distance-based update schemes.

A time-based strategy defines the frequency at which mobiles are required to register their new locations. At a defined interval T, the mobile compares its current location to the previously registered cell ID. An update is performed when it is found that both values differ. The implementation prerequisite for such a scheme is simple and requires only a timer at the mobile terminals. There are, however, certain challenges that need to be overcome before actual applications are realizable. It is true that the number of registrations can be controlled by the update duration T, but there is no guarantee over the effectiveness of such registration information. Clearly, when a mobile continues to engage in a repetitive movement pattern, a multiple number of registrations will incur without attempts to reflect the actual mobility patterns. These registrations are redundant and have minimal values to aid the paging operations. With paging unbounded, neither the cost of operation nor the QoSs can be controlled upon call arrivals [8,15,30].

Classified also under the category of threshold assignation update strategies, the movement-based scheme keeps track of a mobile's movements by counting the actual number of cell-boundary transitions. Specifically, for a defined threshold of M, an update is due whenever the number of cell transitions exceeds the defined constant. In comparison to its counterpart of a time-based update strategy, the information that is maintained about movement numbers minimizes the incurring of unnecessary updates that could possibly result from low mobility users when the threshold is quantified by time. In addition, the maximum paging area can be defined as it is certain that the furthermost point where the mobile can possibly reside upon call arrival will have a separation of M cells from its last registration. There are, however, other concerns that need to be addressed before the actual implementation is feasible in practical systems. Primarily, as the update scheme focuses more on the rate of traveling rather than the way of traveling, actual movement patterns of individual users are not well tracked by the network. Consequently, as the mobiles are asked only to trace the number of movements but not the actual cell residencies, any repetitive movements are unable to be detected by the system. Not only will the unnecessary updates create additional operational cost but the bounded paging area may also prove to be needlessly oversized, and thus incur further paging load. A potential solution is to invest additional database capacity in the terminals, thereafter; a counter is incremented only when the currently visited cell has not yet been recorded in movement history [9,15,41].

This solution, however, would increase the necessary intelligence at the MN, a consequence that is undesirable. An obvious solution is thus to assign a distance threshold in terms of cell numbers and to have an update registered only when the actual distance of traveling exceeds a predefined threshold D; hence the formation of a distance-based update strategy [16,17].

Among all these schemes, References [16,48,49] show that the distance-based scheme gives the best performance in terms of reduced update numbers over the conventional GSM/GPRS update schemes. One factor that contributes to such performance gains is that the effects of ping-pong movement patterns have actually been accounted for in the design of the system operations.

8.3.1.7 State-based

The state-based update strategy is one of the few classified under the category of *hybrid* techniques. The actual interpretations of the state are considered to be a variable, and can be uniquely defined for individual users. It is possible to combine operations of individual techniques to optimize the performance gain. For example, an update strategy combining the essential elements of time-based and movement-based schemes takes advantage of the movement-based scheme of defining a paging boundary while utilizing the merit of timing information to adjust the optimal threshold size. Subsequently, a further reduction in the update load can be expected with a minimal requirement of additional infrastructure.

References [38,39] analyzed a state-based update scheme in which the state is considered to be a combination of the current location and the time elapsed since the last update. On the one hand, the fact that the state can take any one or more parameters of the threshold-based update schemes makes it part of the LA oriented solutions. On the other hand, the need for additional computations to be performed at the mobiles after each cell-crossing, causes its linkage to the non-location area oriented category.

Reference [38] considers an algorithm *greedy* in which the decision of update is made at each cell boundary not necessarily to optimize the overall performance, but to minimize the operational cost for the current roaming interval only. To extend the application of the location tracking strategy, the level of greediness is adjustable by the introduction of an additional parameter α. With an allowable range of values defined between 0 and 1, α determines how far back previous roaming intervals should be taken into consideration for the minimization of the cumulative operational cost. An update is due only when the resultant paging cost will exceed the expected optimal.

Assuming a registration will be due at time $s + \tau$, given the current position, the elapsed time since the last update, and the past history, a state-based policy θ_g is generated to determine an optimal τ that minimizes the combined cost of paging and updates η. The extent of involvement of the past history in the optimization is controlled by α. The algorithm is said to be completely greedy when the optimal τ is assigned to minimize operational cost for the current roaming interval only. Effectively, an optimal registration area will vary as a function of time and will be assigned by the mobile each time a boundary crossing is detected.

To some extent there is a great similarity between Reference [38] and References [17,18] in terms of the method being used to predict the likelihood of residence. The biggest difference observed between the two, however, is the fact that while most computations are done at the mobiles in the former, a similar workload is imposed on the network in the latter. Consequently, with the expectation that Reference [38] will assume a mobile to have certain knowledge about its specific motion trajectories, equivalent assumptions of such information disclosure is not evident in Reference [17].

8.3.1.8 Load-adaptive threshold system

The load-adaptive threshold scheme (LATS) is also categorized as a hybrid update technique. In fact, this scheme is similar to that outlined in the state-based update strategy, in that, in addition to some predefined thresholds, the decision of performing an update is dependent on some additional parameters. In the load-adaptive threshold system, the extra consideration used to determine the need for an update is network loading. Upon entering a cell, the mobile compares its predefined threshold to that of the loading threshold generated by the cell. An update is thus due only when the need of the update defined by a priority level has exceeded that constrained by the loading conditions at the cell [50].

The application of LATS is most promising when the network is heavily loaded. With the maximum number of allowable updates constrained by the cell's loading threshold, the problem of location tracking can be managed without having to sacrifice other QoS metrics, for example, throughput.

8.3.1.9 Direction-based location

A recent publication [51] proposed a direction-based location update scheme with a line-paging strategy for PCS (personal communication services) networks. Basically, the scheme works as follows. Whenever the mobile enters a new cell, it determines whether a change of roaming direction has occurred since the last movement. An update will be registered only if the answer is affirmative, and hence the name directional-based location update scheme. Upon a call arrival, the last registered cell will be the first place the system looks at, the search then extends in both directions until the mobile is found. To set some upper bounds of paging loads, the search discontinues after reaching a time threshold T.

This estimation is based on the assumption that cells are regularly arranged so that each has unique identification in terms of cell coordinates. Mobiles are expected to roam mostly in a straight line with only occasional changes of direction that can be detected when the coordinate difference between adjacent movements is not the same as the previous differences. Because it is unlikely that mobiles always travel in an absolute straight line, there will be a fair amount of updates. As a result, this seems to contradict the goal of reducing the amount of location updates in designing an efficient location management technique. The other problem that would be encountered in the scheme proposed in Reference [51] is its complexity (i.e. heavy signaling and high computational load) that results from the necessary computation after each movement. As the scheme depends on the prompt detection of change of roaming direction by the mobile in order to make the corresponding paging strategy feasible, additional loading (and hence the necessity of power consumption) will be imposed on the mobile terminals. Consequently, the schemes appear to have optimal performances in a system whose call-arrival rate is a lot more frequent than its mobility rate. The application is thus restricted not only by the range of relevant mobile characteristics, but also the requirement of the system layout.

8.3.1.10 Kalman filter-based

A significant portion of movements is incurred with a specific destination in mind, it is thus reasonable to assume correlation between a mobile's past, current, and future locations. The purpose of including Kalman filter [52,53] in this scheme is mainly to predict the granularly traceable traveling directions, hence the next residency based on the past movement information obtained during update registrations.

Once the movement patterns of the immediate future are predicted by the Kalman filter with appropriate numerical values assigned for various directivity indices, a mobile-specific update boundary can be defined. Generally, a unit update often costs more than a unit paging. The optimal solution is to define the update boundary such that a call would arrive right after an implicit update is performed. The operational cost would therefore equate to that of a unit update cost. There are, however, certain difficulties that need to be overcome before one could guarantee that such a method works. Given that it is desirable to require as little additional intelligence as possible in achieving noticeable performance gains, the requirement of a precise prediction will need to be compressed as far as possible. The other alternative is to assign the update boundary just a little further from that of the expected time. Thus, upon call arrivals, paging signals will be sent in a sequence of reducing residency probabilities, predicted using information revealed about the time separations since the last registration time. It is thus possible to achieve an optimal operation in which, while minimizing the registration loads, the necessary paging signaling is strictly controlled [19].

The procedure of assigning the next update boundary upon registration is summarized in Figure 8.9.

As shown in the figure, the actual shape and size will depend on the actual movement patterns and the call-arrival characteristics respectively, for individual mobile users. Theoretically, the optimal solution would be to adjust the size of the update boundary according to the measured or predicted level of traveling directivity. However, as the update area increases, the number of maximum paging loads also increases. To minimize such dependency, an alternative solution is to fix the number of cells in one registration

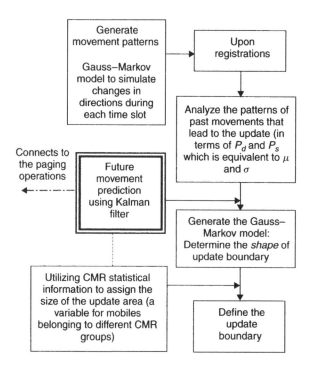

Figure 8.9 Procedures for assigning update boundaries

area, and to vary the dimensions of each (i.e. width and length) to reflect the traveling patterns. Specifically, while the size of the registration area is the same for mobiles inheriting similar call-to-mobility ratio characteristics, the actual shapes vary depending on their different mobility patterns.

Generally, the higher the probability of traveling in the main direction, the greater the certainty of locating the roaming mobile upon call arrivals, which justifies assigning a narrower registration area with a greater length. The ultimate goal is to maximize the number of movements in the LA before the mobile exits.

Figure 8.10 illustrates the differences between the assignation of a symmetrical and an asymmetrical update boundary. Though the asymmetrical update boundary can be of any shape, an optimal rectangular approximation will be shown to simplify the graphical presentation.

Clearly, the fact that the greater the correlation between transiting directions, the narrower the width of the update area can be because of a higher certainty about the mobile's movement patterns.

Finally, as an extension, what could be done is to dynamically adjust the size of the update area according to the observed CMR levels. Specifically, while the threshold is set to D first, it can be increased if no call arrives during the time that leads to the update. Subsequently, further reductions in the costs due to update can be achieved.

As a result of the asymmetrical update boundary definition, the mobile is required not only to keep track of the movement patterns, but also to record the set of update centers.

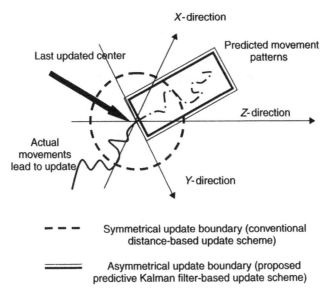

X-direction

Last updated center

Predicted movement patterns

Z-direction

Actual movements lead to update

Y-direction

‐ ‐ ‐   Symmetrical update boundary (conventional distance-based update scheme)

═════   Asymmetrical update boundary (proposed predictive Kalman filter-based update scheme)

Figure 8.10 Symmetrical versus asymmetrical update boundary

Consequently, it is expected that a slight increase in database size at the MNs becomes necessary in order to record the update cell identities. On the one hand, this appears to be the trade-off for an improved performance when compared to the existing symmetrical update boundaries.

On the other hand, given that cells are in reality randomly shaped (as opposed to hexagonal), even with a symmetrical update boundary, the mobile needs to explicitly record the information about individual cell identities. From this perspective, the additional database required will not cause any extra disadvantages than those already presented from the existing solutions.

8.3.1.11 Adaptive distance-based

The proposal is intended to uplift some of the unrealistic assumptions commonly imposed in the assigning of an update boundary. In this algorithm, an optimal update boundary is thus defined based on the assumptions of arbitrary cell topologies and general cell residence time distributions. Consequently, the implementation is no longer restricted by the structured cell configurations or the independent and identically distributed cell residence times. The concept of trip is also incorporated such that there might be a particular path for each defined destination [54].

To restrict the necessary computation load that results from the determination of appropriate threshold for all subscribers, it is possible to define a set of groups with significantly different mobile characteristics. Upon each registration, an appropriate group index is assigned to individual mobiles as a reference for future update operations. With the range of groups effectively identified, the average performance gain for all subscribers can be optimized with scalability concerns considerably catered to.

8.3.1.12 Dynamic location register assignation

An LA is dynamically adjusted in shape at each registration to ensure that the number of cells the mobile traverses in the area is maximized before an update incurs. On the basis of the shortest-distance model, an optimized LA is determined using a heuristic greedy algorithm. Generally, the iterative method starts by including only the last updated cell in the LA. Estimation is made to all cells on the perimeter of the current location to determine the mobile's next most probable residency. An extra cell is included in the LA at the end of each iteration. The algorithm continues until reaching the maximum LA that is predefined. Furthermore, to minimize the possible overheads that are likely to result from the advertising and storing of the irregular location area shapes, a separate heuristic algorithm is applied to determine the optimal dimensions of a corresponding rectangular location area. Simulation results reveal that such a rectangular LA approximation will give a comparable performance gain to what would otherwise be achieved from its irregular-shaped counterpart.

The evaluation of performance gain is currently based on the assumption of a Manhattan grid topology. Although it was suggested in this research work that the extension of the operations to an arbitrary cell topology would be equally straightforward, the amount of necessary computations seems to have suggested the opposite [21].

8.3.1.13 Predictive distance-based

The prediction of the mobile's future location is based on its location and velocity information registered during the update. Essentially, like the distance-based update scheme, with the actual traveling velocity considered in the assignation of optimal update boundary, the space-based scheme defines the update boundary in terms of the actual coordinates instead of in cell numbers. Part of the challenge is to determine an optimal LA. As a general rule, the shape of the assigned area should reflect the actual mobility patterns of the individual subscriber with the area size varying as a function of the rate of incoming calls. With the shape of the LA defined to optimize the number of cell transitions, the size should adjust to keep the paging cost per unit time constant. In other words, for a specific roaming characteristic, the more frequent the rate at which calls arrive, the smaller the LA should be. The actual implementation will depend on the observed traffic characteristics and network conditions, mainly the loading status [18].

8.3.1.14 Activity-based

Based almost on the same framework, is the proposal of an activity-based update scheme in which a personalized LA is defined for each subscriber based on its previous mobility history. For movements within the defined LA, the frequency with which each cell is accessed from its adjacent cells is measured along with the actual time of residency. An update is due when the mobile exits the current LA. A new LA is thus defined according to the previously gathered information, and cells are included in the registration area sequentially in the order of decreasing likelihood of residency until reaching the predefined maximum LA size. The procedure is recursive and stops when the LA reaches its maximum size.

The scheme is optimized for mobile characteristics in which regular mobility patterns are evident. Generally, the past movement history has demonstrated a consistency in the roaming area and the network is certain that the trend will continue in future movements. Utilizing the information observed from the consistency over movement patterns, the adaptive scheme can effectively reduce the necessary update loads [11–13].

Figure 8.11 summarizes the implications of various location updating strategies. It should be clear by this point that depending on the underlying assumptions and the simulating nature of individual mobility models, the application of the technique is not always suitable for all systems. Clearly, activity-based location management can only be available when there is sufficient information to have the relevant databases established. The strategy is very user-specific and is most apposite to represent daily activities that are highly consistent over a long duration of time with a periodicity measured in days or weeks.

8.3.2 Paging

Despite the fact that an efficient paging algorithm plays an equally important role in the update algorithm for the satisfactory operation of location management, specific research devoted to paging algorithms is less commonly evident. Such an observation is largely due to the increased restriction associated with design flexibility; not only because performance gain is greatly influenced by nonnegotiable delay constraints, but also a unit paging cost is often less costly than a unit update cost, as the bandwidth requirement is a lot smaller. To facilitate the discussions, Figure 8.12 summarizes the interrelations between different paging algorithms. The classification is made according to where and how polling signaling is sent during the paging operations. Thus, paging schemes are discussed to determine the locations and the order in which the paging information is distributed in searching for roaming mobiles upon call arrivals.

The operations of each paging scheme are discussed in more detail in the following text.

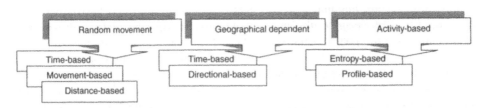

Figure 8.11   An overview of the implications of various location updating strategies

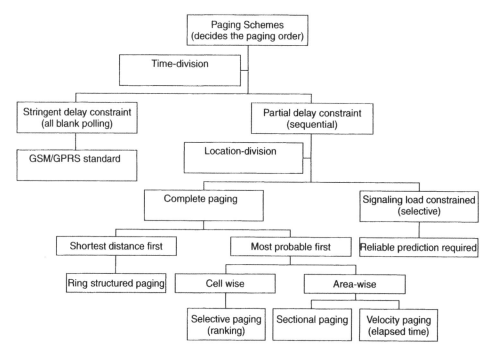

Figure 8.12   The paging schemes classified according to the nature of system definitions

8.3.2.1 Blanking polling

One of the main parameters used to quantify the performance of location tracking is the delay incurred in locating the roaming user. Depending on the nature of communications, the allowable delay constraints vary for real-time and non-real-time connection requests. Take multimedia transmissions for example. The range of acceptable delay is normally small, and hence, the mobile will be expected to be located within a shorter timeframe. Upon call arrivals, the whole LA where the mobile last registered is paged in one go. Assuming the mobile has been updated according to the defined technique, it is certain that its location is determined with a minimal delay. Such real-time services, however, come at the expense of a large polling-signaling load. Given that the complete area is to be paged during a single polling cycle, the paging cost grows proportionally to the size of the defined LA. Consequently, the operation defines the upper boundary of the incurring paging load. Thus, in order to achieve optimal performances, the actual boundary of the LA needs to be more carefully selected during the phase of location update. It should be obvious that a higher computational load can be expected because of the increasing precision found to be necessary. Nevertheless, blank polling is the technique that has been standardized for the GSM and GPRS systems. The algorithm results in the least delay and has the advantage of having the simplest implementation [9,41,46,55].

8.3.2.2 Sequential paging

The first possible saving in paging comes when multiple polling cycles are allowed during the paging operations. Once the delay constraint is relaxed, the complete LA can be partitioned into smaller areas, with polling signals sending sequentially to each of these areas. Through the assignation of a paging area, the boundary within which polling signals should be sent is defined. In general, sequential paging allows the size of the paging area during each polling cycle to be reduced, and hence, promotes possible bandwidth reservation. Clearly, the bigger the area, the higher the paging load will be during each polling cycle. In addition, it is possible to restrict paging load further by appropriately assigning the order in which the polling information is to be sent. Specifically, as long as the roaming mobile is located before the last set of the polling cycle is used, some savings in the resource utilization can be achieved. The reduced cost, however, is likely to result in a longer delay before the mobile's location is determined. Therefore, when delay constraint is set to unity, the evaluation represents an upper boundary on the average paging cost. Conversely, when delay constraint is set to infinity, the estimation gives a measure to the lower boundary of the paging cost.

In this section, several sequential paging techniques that are available in the literature are described in more detail. Depending on the actual movement patterns for individual mobiles, it is clear that there are certain directions where the probability of locating the roaming mobile is higher than in others, in fact, the better the prediction, the more the savings that can be achieved from the operation of sequential paging [9,56].

Shortest-distance-first paging

Shortest-distance-first paging has the simplest operational concept among all available alternatives. The paging starts from the cell where the last registration is performed, and progresses sequentially to cells of increasing separation from the last updated center. In a one-dimensional network topology, the polling signals are sent in linear fashion symmetrically from the last updated cell [51]. In a two-dimensional network topology, the term ring-structured paging is more commonly used to symbolize the sequence in which cells are paged. The scheme incorporates virtually no predictions, it simply assumes that the mobile has the greatest possibility of locating at the last update center, and the certainty reduces in cells that are further away from the center [56]. For a distance-based or movement-based update scheme, the maximum delay that can possibly incur will be equal to the size of the threshold. In scenarios where unlimited paging delay is not allowed, *rings* of cells will be grouped to comply with the paging constraint. Variations for the actual grouping should be appropriately assigned to optimize the performance gains.

Time-elapsed paging

It is also possible to consider the elapsed time since the last registration upon call arrivals as in the time-elapsed paging scheme. Assuming the mobile is traversing at a constant speed, it is expected that the longer the time elapse, the further away the mobile will be from its last updated cell. Thus, the sequence of paging is adjusted to reflect this anticipation. Although the underlying assumption is general and has only little modification from the basic shortest-distance-paging scheme, performance gain is possible depending on the actual mobility patterns as demonstrated in Reference [17].

Velocity paging

Velocity paging attempts to reduce the paging signaling by grouping users into different velocity classes according to the traveling speed registered at the time of update. Upon call arrivals, paging areas are generated from information gathered on an individual's velocity characteristics and the elapsed time since the last registration [18].

Highest-probability-first paging

Given that the time-varying probability distribution of user location is known, cells within the registration area are paged sequentially in the order of decreasing residence likelihood [38,39,57]. Upon call arrivals, the precise location of the roaming mobile would need to be determined within constrained delay times. Even with an asymmetrical update boundary in place, it is possible to further reduce the paging load by anticipating the distribution of residence likelihood at the arrival time of call requests. Figure 8.13 illustrates the relations between the occurrence of call arrival and update events in time. Note also the influences of CMR on the interarrival time between adjacent call requests. Clearly, the smaller the CMR, the greater the time elapsed since the last update (labeled as ▶ in the graph) upon a call arrival.

Given that the mobile is roaming at a speed known to the network, with information also known about the time advances since the last update, the location of the most probable residence should be anticipated with reasonable accuracy. Thus, it is justified to divide the complete update area into smaller paging sections, and to page each section in a sequential order of decreasing probability.

It is generally assumed that the mean of the distribution defines the most likely location of the roaming mobile, the probability of residence then decreases symmetrically on both sides away from the mean [38,39]. However, for such sequential paging to be implemented, the mobile needs not only to evaluate the cost paging at the point, but also to acquire information about conditional distribution on future locations.

8.3.2.3 Selective paging

The difference between sequential paging and selective paging is subtle, and thus, it is difficult to draw a clear distinction between the two operations. As was discussed earlier,

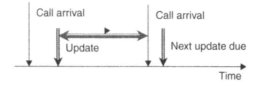

Figure 8.13 Interrelations between the location updates and call arrivals in the time domain

instead of restricting paging to be completed in one polling cycle, sequential paging allows only a partial area of reduced size to be searched during a single polling cycle. Depending on the actual formation of the partitions, it is likely that the roaming mobile is located before the complete LA is paged. The decreased signal requirement indicates a reduced operational cost. The saving, however, comes at the expense of increased paging delays. For certain mobiles in which the corresponding movement patterns are highly predictive, the granular traceable areas of residency can be anticipated with relatively high accuracy. It is, therefore, not necessary to page the complete LA. Thus, instead of sending polling signals to every cell within the registered LA, only parts of the complete LA require paging. Hence, the name *selective paging* is given, where partial areas are carefully selected to reflect the predicted information about residency probability. In some ways, it indicates a greater certainty about the prediction made in generating the dynamically adjustable paging areas [22,58].

Apart from the more general paging schemes that can be incorporated into any update schemes, there are some other more system-specific paging algorithms proposed in the literature. In Reference [22], paging operations are designed on the basis of the underlying assumption of a known update scheme and the corresponding shortest-distance model. Thus, given the call-arrival rate, the probability of having the mobile reside in any cell (l, m) is calculated and the evaluation ranked. With the number of partitions fixed by the allowable paging delay, given the size of a LA, the number of cells to be included in each partition can be appropriately determined. The complete LA is thus composed of smaller groups formed by associating cells in decreasing order of residence probability. Although the simulation results have shown that the performance gain over the conventional GSM standard is more significant than that achieved by other paging alternatives, the applications of such system-specific algorithms are more restricted.

8.3.2.4 Sectional paging

Sectional paging [59] functions similar to the schemes that are mentioned in Reference [51] in the sense that the directivity aspects of the movement patterns are taken into consideration. However, it allows at the same time a certain degree of freedom, specifically, directivity being in the sense of granular tracking rather than precise directional information maintenance. On the basis of the underlying assumption that a mobile will continue to travel in the same granular direction as it traveled prior to an update registration, information regarding the mobile's previous movement patterns was used to predict its future residency distribution. Subsequently, decisions can be made on the user-specific definition of the paging areas along with the paging order when a non-unity delay constraint is allowed. Therefore, the main difference between sectional paging and ring-structured paging comes from the way subsections are formed when the allowable paging delay is greater than unity. The ring-structured paging scheme groups cells according to their separation from the last updated cell with subsections paged in a sequential manner. Sectional paging groups cells with angular divisions with reference to the anticipated probability distributions. It aims to utilize the additional information made available about traveling directions, and to eliminate unnecessary paging costs via some appropriate predictions of the mobile's residence likelihood.

The complete operation of the proposed paging scheme comprises two parts. Firstly, the mobile is required to statistically analyze the pattern of movements upon registration and secondly, the network is given the responsibility to appropriately define the size of paging areas upon call arrivals. Figure 8.14 gives a concise illustration of the design details.

Briefly, once it is detected that an update has become necessary, the mobile will give an estimation of the granular direction of traveling or trend of moving. Statistically, this is an averaged quantity of all previous movements leading to the registration. To more explicitly quantify the correlation (in movement patterns) between chronologically adjacent registration updates, this measure is then compared with a previously cached value (statistically analyzed for past updates) to give a better prediction of the traveling patterns. Effectively, a matching definition of P_d and P_f will be projected to give an alternative presentation of the traveling trends. In this case, P_f represents the probability of moving forward with P_d denoting the probability of continuing in the dominant direction.

In the second stage, the network performs a one-off evaluation mapping the motion characteristics to the width of the sectional area according to various geographical conditions

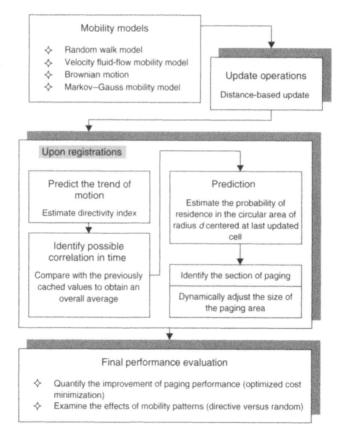

Figure 8.14 The sectional paging scheme

and specific user behaviors. Thus, for each evaluated value of P_d and P_f, a section boundary is selected to indicate the most probable residency distribution for the mobile in search. Upon call arrivals, where the location information is not already available, a search is carried out concurrently in all cells of the selected area. Generally, the greater the precision of the prediction, the fewer the number of cells required for paging and thus the better the system performance from the perspective of cost minimization.

It has been decided that one of the main design criteria of the sectional paging scheme is to minimize the required computations at the network while having performance improvement guaranteed. Given that only a simple lookup procedure is required at the network during call arrivals, this paging strategy will not only ensure that additional system intelligence is minimized, but also allow large fluctuations in mobile population to be accommodated.

Without restricting a specific mobility model to be applied in generating the desired movement patterns, Reference [56] has successfully demonstrated that even a slight relaxation of the paging delay (i.e. from unity to two) is sufficient to give some significant improvements to the paging performance in terms of cost minimization. Consequently, it is justified to consider only the simplest case in which the complete framework is partitioned into two sections when quantifying the improvements achievable by the sectional paging scheme. Figure 8.15 gives an illustration of the boundary selection concept for the sectional paging scheme.

Briefly, the bounded area will define the number of cells to be paged during the first polling cycle with the rest of the cells in the plane to be paged in the second polling cycle. The simulation is intended to show how, by adjusting the size of paging areas according

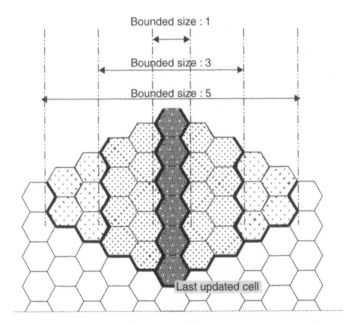

Figure 8.15 Concept of sectional paging: an illustration of the bounded size selection

to the online measures of the directivity information, the number of cells having to be included in each polling cycle is minimized. Theoretically, the more directivity the traveling pattern has, the higher would be the precision that the residency prediction would have, and hence, the performance would be optimized.

8.3.3 Final remarks

It is possible to consider a multimode operation in which the actual combination of update and paging algorithms can be dynamically adjusted according to the system loading measures at the time of registration. At any given instant of time, parameters such as CMR can be used to define the actual mode of operation.

Having discussed specific update techniques that are used to determine the time when an update becomes necessary, it is important to consider where the update signals are sent. For all strategies mentioned above, it is assumed that a registration is made directly at the home location register (HLR) where the updated user profile is maintained. Depending on where the roaming takes place, the time it takes to get a new update registered grows when the mobile is far away from the subscribed home network. To minimize possible delays, alternative locations for registering the update were suggested. The rest of the section gives a brief description of the available techniques.

8.3.3.1 Pointer forwarding scheme

The Pointer forwarding strategy eliminates the procedure of reporting to a HLR (subject to a location change) by setting up a forwarding pointer from the old visitor location register (VLR) to the new VLR [60,61]. It is noted, however, that depending on mobility, call arrival and the length of the pointer chain K, the improvement in system performance (and also cost) might not always be evident.

8.3.3.2 Location anchoring scheme

The Location anchoring scheme allows location changes to be reported to a local anchor that is periodically selected from the set of locally available VLRs. Hence, it reduces the necessary signaling traffic caused by location updates to the HLR [61,62]. In the static scheme, the serving VLR when the last call arrived is selected to be the anchor. Alternatively, a dynamic scheme can be used to select the anchor VLR. In such a case, the network also makes decisions on whether to change the local anchor every time the mobile makes a movement in addition to what has implemented for the static system. The resulting improvement varies according to the mobility and call-arrival characteristics.

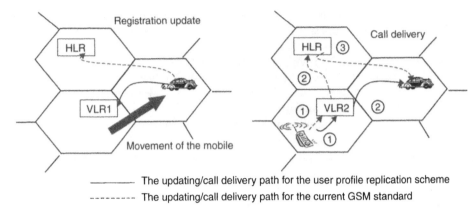

Registration update

Call delivery

Movement of the mobile

————————   The updating/call delivery path for the user profile replication scheme

----------   The updating/call delivery path for the current GSM standard

Figure 8.16   A graphical representation of the signaling transfers

8.3.3.3 *User profile replication*

For each call request, operational costs are associated with both the network and the callers. On one hand, it is important from the network's perspective to minimize the necessary searching cost in locating the roaming mobile within the registered update area. On the other hand, the caller also incurs expenses for lodging such connection requests; specifically, a database accessed locally will result in a shorter delay and consequently, a smaller cost than that incurred when a distant database is accessed. Although much attention has been focused on the specific method of sending polling signals within the LA that is registered in the network, the importance of minimizing the time to find the relevant LA to page in the first place should not be underestimated. Similar to what is experienced in the update operation, the question of where to send the query signals becomes crucial when the mobile is away from its subscribed network but is literally close to the caller mobiles.

The user profile replication scheme replicates users' records in multiple databases for easy access [63]. Very simply, whenever an update is made at the HLR, the network will update all the replicated databases. Thus, any database inquiry for a roaming mobile can be made locally before a possibly long-distant signaling message is sent to the HLR (Figure 8.16). Depending on the mobility rate and the call-arrival rate, the method may significantly reduce the signaling and database access overhead to compensate for the higher signaling overhead incurred during the phase of location registration.

8.4   ANALYTICAL FRAMEWORK FOR LOCATION MANAGEMENT

The effectiveness of individual update and paging techniques can be evaluated on the basis of the operational cost incurred within a fixed time period. In effect, for a predefined mobile characteristic and call-arrival rate, the operation costs resulting from the applications of different location management techniques can be assessed and compared. Given that good location management should be able to efficiently locate a roaming mobile when a call request arrives, it is equally viable to consider the statistical measures of the updates and paging load against the rate of call arrival when the sampling data involves a large range of mobile characteristics. This is possible as the rate of call arrival determines the number of calls within a defined time period.

Having studied the main location management techniques proposed in the literature, the chapter would not be complete without highlighting some of the general analytical frameworks to be used in the evaluation of the various location management schemes. It should become apparent to the readers now that the key parameters used to quantify the performance of specific location management techniques include the update load, paging load, and where applicable, the paging delay.

While the ultimate goal is the same in research work involving scheme evaluations, the actual analytical framework can have various representations depending on the approaches that are taken by the author. This section is devoted to comparing, and specifically to highlighting, the large similarities and strong resemblances among the available analytical systems. The main intention is to widen the analyzing scope and hopefully to inspire further techniques. In this section, we first describe the general expression used to estimate the total expected cost. Specific evaluation methods of the update and paging are then discussed separately in more depth.

8.4.1   Influential factors

The effectiveness of specific solutions to the problems of location tracking is mainly quantified by the costs that are incurred during operation. While in some the quantification is based on costs during call arrivals, in others the relative cost between update and paging is evaluated.

Other than the general acknowledgement of call arrival and mobility rate, specific network and mobile characteristics also have a direct impact on the actual performance measures. In order to optimize the overall performances, it is important to identify these parameters and to consider them when assigning system parameters to optimize performance gains. Obviously, some of the observed parameters will have a more crucial impact on the designed techniques than others. In this section, a list of commonly identified parameters has been compiled to extend the horizons in perceiving such location-tracking problems.

Given that many of the update strategies are, in some form or another, extensions to the basic distance-based threshold, the discussion of influential performance factors is oriented on the concepts of such a scheme.

8.4.1.1 Cost definitions

The definition of unit update cost has a significant impact on the overall operational characteristic, be it the selection of the optimal distance threshold or the switching between different modes of operations. In most network scenarios, a unit update is often more costly than a unit paging because of the amount of resources both wireless and wired systems require while having the new location registered properly. In certain cases in which the expense of an update operation becomes extremely high, unnecessary updates should be avoided at all times. Such additional caution taken during the implementation phase will affect the selection of the optimal threshold and thus, affect the overall performance gain.

8.4.1.2 Call and mobility characteristics

The rate at which the requests for call connections arrive plays an important part in the problem of location tracking. Clearly, in network scenarios where a mobile does not expect to receive any call connections during its time of roaming, the need for location registration is redundant. From the implementation point of view, the ideal threshold definition will be infinity, and thus the operation is equivalent to a *never update* strategy [9,41,47]. Although the occurrence is rare, in extreme cases in which calls are expected to arrive for the roaming mobile all the time, it will be necessary to set the update threshold small to avoid excessive paging load because the network is constantly required to obtain information about the mobile's whereabouts. As a general rule, the optimal threshold should decrease as the call-arrival rate increases.

In a busy urban environment with picocell topology, cell boundaries are crossed at a much higher rate than in a suburban network configured with macrocell topology. To ensure that the assigned threshold adequately reflects the characteristics of the specific network of interest, the rate at which a mobile traverses between boundaries should be considered to optimize the update operation.

The effects of mobility and call-arrival characteristics can be considered either separately or jointly.

8.4.1.3 Paging delay constraint

Although the impact of a paging delay constraint is generally seen in the paging operations, to optimize the overall performance, appropriate consideration of such a parameter taken at the assignation of update threshold will also ensure that a greater performance gain is achievable. For example, with the implementation of blanket polling, the higher the threshold, the greater the necessary paging load. Thus, a smaller threshold is often preferred over a higher alternative. However, when the paging delay constraint is relaxed, the range of feasible threshold increases. Consequently, optimally selected threshold as such is likely to maximize the overall performance gain.

8.4.2   Overall cost function

The total operational cost consists of two parts: the update cost and the paging cost. Although there are a few possible ways to model mathematically the cost function, the basic framework is the same. Intuitively, the challenge is to determine each part of the total cost that can be evaluated from the product of number and the unit cost, giving

$$C_{\text{total}} = U \cdot N_{\text{u}} + P \cdot N_{\text{p}} \tag{8.3}$$

Given a set of cost parameters, U and P, which respectively represent the unit update and paging cost, the real challenge is to estimate the numbers of each quantity in the process of cost evaluation N_{u}, N_{p}. There are a few alternatives to quantify such parameters. For example, References [21,22] express the cost relation by

$$c(k, \mu_{\text{a}}) = U \cdot u_k + P \cdot k\mu_{\text{a}} \tag{8.4}$$

For a location area containing k cells, u_k represents the update rate and $k\mu_{\text{a}}$ denotes the number of paging signals required for a call-arrival rate for μ_{a}.

The update rate is usually a function of the mobility pattern, the traveling speed, and the definition of the location update area. In this research work, the update rate is a measure of the time a mobile resides in the specific LA.

During a call, the location is reported to the network at each boundary crossing. The operation of mobility tracking is thus applicable between the interarrival of adjacent calls. On a comparison of various update schemes, it is thus common to evaluate the total cost incurred within this time interval. On the basis of the nature of the assessment, the study is categorized into various mobility models.

8.4.2.1 Sensitivity analysis

With predictions incorporated in many schemes, it becomes important to evaluate the impact that prediction accuracy has on overall performance, that is, the more sensitive the scheme, the higher the operational cost.

Apart from comparing the absolute operational cost, the range of variability in the resultant cost subject to other system parameters also gives a good indication of the stability of the performance gains. As part of the evaluation study, Reference [38] quantifies the performance gain of different location management techniques by examining the reduction in the variability of paging and registration cost under varying mobile characteristics. Generally, the smaller the cost standard deviation, the less sensitive the performance gain is to small changes in mobility indexes, and thus, the more reliable the location tracking strategy.

It should be clear that the purpose of location management is to determine an optimal trade-off between the update and the paging operations. Undoubtedly, while there are alternative methods available to quantify the performance gains, the general goal is the same, that is, to determine the best location tracking strategy that minimizes the operational cost. Having discussed the main characteristics of some commonly used mobility models and various update and paging strategies, it is now appropriate to examine the range of analytical models that are available for performance evaluations. In the following subsection, discussions are included along with basic descriptions of the analytical model utilized to evaluate the numbers. The purpose is to clarify the present state-of-the-art model, comparing the similarities and differences of specific models.

8.4.3 Update cost

Depending on the actual mobility characteristics, the quantifying parameters may be different; however, the common theme is the same, that is, to determine the frequency at which updates are performed. Intuitively, the general goal is to minimize the number of updates such that the cost from update operations is kept as low as possible. References [54,56,61,64] have quantified the efficiencies of update schemes by keeping a record of the number of times update registrations are required during the interarrival time of incoming calls. The update strategy that results in the least updates has the optimal performances for specific mobile behaviors. Alternatively, References [21,22] obtained similar evaluations by measuring the number of movements incurred for each update that was registered. Generally, the greater the number of boundary crossings before an update is due, the better and more efficient the location tracking strategy. To understand the basic concepts better, short discussions of each approach to the determination of update cost are included.

8.4.3.1 Markovian model-based analysis

Markovian movement patterns are generated on the basis of a slotted time model. At the beginning of each discrete time interval, the mobile transits to an adjacent cell with a predefined probability. Advancing from an independent and identical distribution model in which the transitioning probability to all adjacent cells is the same, a Markovian model allows assignations of varying probabilities in order to imitate better the characteristics of different movement patterns.

Earlier analysis assumes a one-dimensional system framework [17,18,65,66] in which each cell has only two adjacent cells. Thus, whenever a boundary crossing is initiated at the cell level, the mobile can move either to the right or to the left cell during each slotted time interval. With the transitional probability distribution also defining the likelihood that the mobile stays in the same cell, the simplest state machine needs only three states to describe the complete motion behavior. Figure 8.17 gives a general example of the mobile characteristics. In the illustration, the circles represent the states specifying the actions to

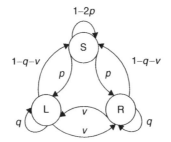

R   The mobile moves rightward in the next time slot
L   The mobile moves leftward in the next time slot
S   The mobile stays put in the next time slot

Figure 8.17   An example of the Markovian-motion state machine

take in the next time slot with the arcs indicating the probabilities of transiting from one state to the other [17].

At each instant of time, the mobile can be in any one of the states along with the transition probabilities specified in the state machine. For example, if at time slot t, a mobile is in state L, a leftward movement will occur in the next time slot $t + 1$ from its current location. In addition, the mobile will stay at state L with a probability of q, change to state R with a probability of v, or stay put as state S with a probability of $1 - q - v$ [15].

For a distance-based update strategy of threshold D, a registration area will consist of $2D - 1$ cells, which allow mobiles to move freely in the range $[-D + 1, D - 1]$ without having to register. Figure 8.18 shows a part of the corresponding Markov chain used to describe the complete motion model.

Each state will actually have two values, d denoting the distance from the last updated cell $d \in \{0, 1, 2, 3, \ldots\}$ and s denoting the next action to be taken $x \in \{R, L, S\}$. Let $Q_{d,s}$ denote the steady state probability of having the mobile reside d cells away from the last updated cell with state s. The complete Markov chain shows in two dimensions, indicating the transitional probabilities between the two values. To illustrate the basic concepts, Figure 8.19 shows an extract of the Markov chain which indicates the transitional behavior that contributes to the formation of the steady state of $Q_{0,R}$.

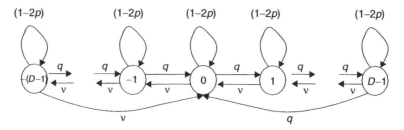

Figure 8.18 Markov chain-based motion mobility model

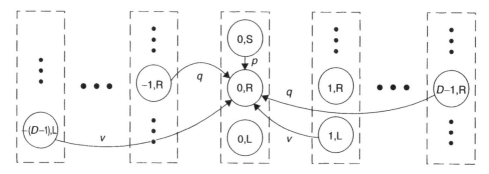

Figure 8.19 A graphical representation of the transitional information required to evaluate the steady state probability of $Q_{0,R}$

Mathematically, the motion model can be described by the set of balance equations shown in (8.5) to (8.12) [15].

$$Q_{0,R} = pQ_{0,S} + qQ_{D-1,R} + vQ_{-(D-1),L} + qQ_{-1,R} + vQ_{1,L} \tag{8.5}$$

$$2pQ_{0,S} = (1 - q - v)(Q_{D-1,R} + Q_{-(D-1),L} + Q_{-1,R} + Q_{1,L}) \tag{8.6}$$

$$2pQ_{d,S} = (1 - q - v)(Q_{d-1,R} + Q_{d+1,L}) \qquad 1 \le d \le D - 2 \tag{8.7}$$

$$Q_{d,R} = pQ_{d,S} + qQ_{d-1,R} + vQ_{d+1,L} \qquad 1 \le d \le D - 2 \tag{8.8}$$

$$Q_{d,L} = pQ_{d,S} + vQ_{d-1,R} + qQ_{d+1,L} \qquad 1 \le d \le D - 2 \tag{8.9}$$

$$2pQ_{D-1,S} = (1 - q - v)Q_{D-2,R} \tag{8.10}$$

$$Q_{D-1,R} = pQ_{D-1,S} + qQ_{D-2,R} \tag{8.11}$$

$$Q_{D-1,L} = pQ_{D-1,S} + vQ_{D-2,R} \tag{8.12}$$

With the set of steady state probabilities summed up to 1 (Equation 8.13), individual steady state probability can be obtained by solving the equations, giving (8.14) to (8.17).

$$\sum_{d=-(D-1)}^{D-1} (Q_{d,S} + Q_{d,R} + Q_{d,L}) = 1 \tag{8.13}$$

$$Q_{d,R} = \frac{p[(D - d)(1 - q + v) + 2(q - v)]}{D(1 + 2p - q - v)[D(1 - q + v) + 2(q - v)]} \qquad 0 \le d \le D - 1 \tag{8.14}$$

$$Q_{d,L} = \frac{p(D - d)(1 - q + v)}{D(1 + 2p - q - v)[D(1 - q + v) + 2(q - v)]} \qquad 0 \le d \le D - 1 \tag{8.15}$$

$$Q_{d,S} = \frac{(1 - q + v)[(D - d)(1 - q + v) + (q - v)]}{D(1 + 2p - q - v)[D(1 - q + v) + 2(q - v)]} \qquad 0 \le d \le D - 1 \tag{8.16}$$

$$Q_{0,S} = \frac{(1 - q + v)}{D(1 + 2p - q - v)} \tag{8.17}$$

An update is due when a mobile moves to the boundary cells with $Q_{D-1,R}$ or $Q_{-(D-1),L}$. Whether it is in the former situation in which the mobile is expecting a rightward move from its current location $D - 1$ or is in the latter situation in which the mobile is expecting a leftward move from its current location $-(D - 1)$, with the symmetrical threshold defined, the stationary probabilities for the two states are equal.

The expected number of updates transmitted in a time slot is thus equal to the probabilities of being in the two states $Q_{D-1,R}$ and $Q_{-(D-1),L}$ and can be approximated by

$$U_D = Q_{D-1,R} + Q_{-(D-1),L} = 2Q_{D-1,R}$$

$$= \frac{2p(1 + q - v)}{D(1 + 2p - q - v)[D(1 - q + v) + 2(q - v)]} \tag{8.18}$$

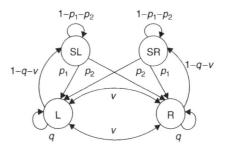

SR   The mobile stays put in the next time slot with the most recent move being rightward.
SL   The mobile stays put in the next time slot with the most recent move being leftward.

Figure 8.20   A modified Markovian-motion state machine

Clearly, the update rate is not only a function of the predefined threshold, but also of the actual transitional probability distributions. The probability of incurring an update decreases with increasing threshold and is in general an approximation to the ratio $q/(q + v)$.

Extending from the analysis of Reference [15], the effects of directional persistency across stops is examined in Reference [17]. Thus, instead of assuming that a mobile loses its sense of direction after stopping, two additional states are introduced to record the most recent move. Consequently, it is necessary to include a few more arcs describing the movement patterns. Figure 8.20 illustrates the modified Markovian-motion state machine.

The new definitions mainly include p_1, the probability of resuming motion in the same direction as that prior to stopping and p_2, the probability of resuming motion in the opposite direction from that prior to stopping. There are also possibilities for the mobile to remain staying put in the following time slot with a probability of $1 - p_1 - p_2$. The graphical representation of the Markov chain also becomes more complex resulting from the additional states. Figure 8.21 shows an extract of the transitioning behavior around the last update cell. As the update boundary is no longer symmetrical about the last update cell, $Q_{C,\cdot}$ now denotes the location of the center cell instead of $Q_{0,\cdot}$ as evident in the previous case.

While the size of a registration area remains the same as in References [15,48], the fact that the persistence across stops is now considered in the motion characteristics means the resulting steady state probability equations need to reflect the corresponding differences, giving [17]

$$Q_{C,R} = p_1 Q_{C,SR} + p_2 Q_{C,SL} + q Q_{D-1,R} + q Q_{-(D-1),L} + q Q_{C-1,R} + v Q_{C+1,L} \quad (8.19)$$

$$Q_{C,SR} = (1 - q - v)(Q_{D-1,R} + Q_{-(D-1),L} + Q_{C-1,R}) + (1 - p_1 - p_2)Q_{C,SR} \quad (8.20)$$

$$Q_{d,R} = p_1 Q_{d,SR} + p_2 Q_{d,SL} + q Q_{d-1,R} + v Q_{d+1,L} \quad d \neq -(D - 1), C, D - 1 \quad (8.21)$$

$$Q_{d,L} = p_2 Q_{d,SR} + p_1 Q_{d,SL} + v Q_{d-1,R} + q Q_{d+1,L} \quad d \neq -(D - 1), C, D - 1 \quad (8.22)$$

$$Q_{d,SR} = (1 - q - v)Q_{d-1,R} + (1 - p_1 - p_2)Q_{d,SR} \quad d \neq -(D - 1), C \quad (8.23)$$

$$Q_{d,SL} = (1 - q - v)Q_{d+1,L} + (1 - p_1 - p_2)Q_{d,SL} \quad d \neq D - 1 \quad (8.24)$$

$$Q_{D-1,R} = q Q_{D-2,R} + p_1 Q_{D-1,SR} \quad (8.25)$$

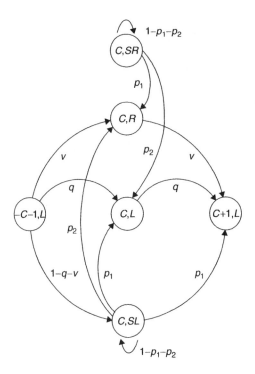

Figure 8.21 A modified Markov chain to present the motion model

$$Q_{D-1,L} = vQ_{D-2,R} + p_2 Q_{D-1,SR} \tag{8.26}$$

Other than modifications to some of the existing equations, note also the inclusion of extra balance equations in the determination of stationary state probabilities. In addition, as it is assumed that the forward direction after each update is by default a rightward movement, the state of $Q_{C,SL}$ will not exist in the modified motion model.

$$Q_{C,L} = p_2 Q_{C,SR} + p_1 Q_{C,SL} + v Q_{D-1,R} + v Q_{-(D-1),L} + v Q_{C-1,R} + q Q_{C+1,L} \tag{8.27}$$

$$Q_{(D-1),R} = q Q_{(D-2),R} + p_1 Q_{(D-1),SR} \tag{8.28}$$

$$Q_{-(D-1),L} = q Q_{-(D-2),L} + p_1 Q_{-(D-1),SL} \tag{8.29}$$

Furthermore, instead of evaluating $2Q_{D-1,R}$, the boundary conditions need to be separately considered for the determination of the expected number of update messages, giving

$$U_D = Q_{-(D-1),L} + Q_{D-1,R} = \frac{r}{(D-C)[(D+C)(1-r) + 2r - 1]T}$$

$$C \neq -(D-1), D-1 \tag{8.30}$$

where

$$T = 1 + (1 - q - v)\frac{1}{p_1 + p_2} \tag{8.31}$$

and

$$r = q + (1 - q - v)\frac{p_1}{p_1 + p_2} \qquad 0 < r \leq 1 \tag{8.32}$$

The additional term of $1/T$ comes from the explicit update that incurs when the predefined time period expires. The advantage of adding the concept of a time-based update in addition to the distance-based update operations is evident when mobiles remain in the same cell for a significantly long period of time. In that case, it is necessary to consider the mean holding time among cells.

Clearly, when $p_1 = p_2$ where it is assumed that the mobile loses its sense of direction after it stops, r and T are simplified forming

$$r = q + \frac{(1 - q - v)}{2} \tag{8.33}$$

$$T = 1 + \frac{(1 - q - v)}{2p} \tag{8.34}$$

If replacing C with 0, Equation (8.30) as expected becomes Equation (8.18) when Equations (8.33 and 8.34) are substituted.

$$\begin{aligned} U_D &= \frac{r}{(D - C)[(D + C)(1 - r) + 2r - 1]T} \\ &= \frac{2p(1 + q - v)}{D[D(1 - q + v) + 2(q - v)](1 + 2p - q - v)} \end{aligned} \tag{8.35}$$

Hence, the proof shows that additional parameters can be added to the basic Markovian model with only appropriate modifications to the corresponding balance equations. Specifically, the inclusion of additional states in the motion model allows individual movement patterns to be more accurately modeled, however, at the expense of increasing computational complexities.

With q fixed, r grows when the persistency p_1 increases and consequently, the update rate goes up. In order to minimize the resulting expected number of updates, it is important to relocate C such that an asymmetric distance-based position-update criterion is generated. As a rightward movement is assumed to be the forward direction, the idea is to move the update center as far as possible from the right end boundary cell. In the extreme case where a mobile shows a high persistence in motion characteristics, the optimal location for situating the center point C will be at $-(D - 1)$. Consequently, the update rate turns into

$$U_{\text{opt}} = \frac{p_1 + p_2}{(2D - 1)(1 + p_1 + p_2 - q - v)} = \frac{1}{(2D - 1)T} \tag{8.36}$$

In a more general form, however, the optimal C can be determined from the expression [17]

$$C_{\text{opt}} = \max \left\{ 1 - \frac{1}{2(1 - r)}, -(D - 1) \right\} \tag{8.37}$$

Simulation results included in Reference [17] have shown a reduction in the update rate with the implementation of optimal C. The success demonstrated in this work has since attracted huge research interests to explore the merits of implementing asymmetrical update boundaries. A brief section is included later highlighting specific methods for the determination of an optimal asymmetrical update boundary.

While the one-dimensional analytical model provides a good framework for the evaluation of system performances, it reveals limited information about mobile characteristics in a more realistic roaming environment. On the basis of the underlying structure, References [21,22,54,56,58,63] extend the analysis for a two-dimensional system with mesh and hexagonal network topologies. The discussions of the analytical framework are based on the developments of the existing tracking mechanisms. To highlight the effects of individual mobility parameters, the comparison is made against a reference system where the symmetrical update boundaries are assumed with mobiles demonstrating a random movement pattern. Figure 8.22 outlines the general framework of the discussions.

8.4.3.2 *Markovian model-based analysis for 2-D topology*

Generally, the number of updates is a function of the mobility rate and call-arrival rate. For a given CMR definition, assuming there are m cells traversing between intercall arrivals, the update rate is quantified by the probability that boundary cells are reached. Clearly, the higher the frequency of call arrival, the greater is the need for precise tracking of the mobile's

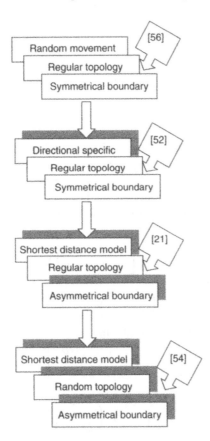

Figure 8.22 An outline of the discussion on the analytical framework

movements. The same general relation, however, does not necessarily apply to the measure of mobility rate. In fact, the number of updates required varies according to the actual mobility characteristics. Compared with what would otherwise be obtained from a movement-based update scheme of threshold M in which the update rate is simply M/m, the evaluation for the same parameter in the distance-based scheme becomes a lot more complex. The performance gain depends to a great extent on the actual roaming characteristics of individual mobiles. Generally, the greater the confidence about the predictions, the less the number of updates necessary to optimize the performance gains in terms of bandwidth consumption and delay compliance. Although reliable prediction may be possible for mobiles inheriting certain behavioral motion characteristics, anticipation of actual movement is not achievable in other scenarios where mobiles demonstrate less common traveling routes.

With the distance-based update strategy, update cost clearly increases with the number of times the distance threshold is reached. Given that there are m movements between call arrivals, the number of times the distance threshold is reached will determine the update cost. On the basis of the assumption of random movement patterns, Reference [56] proposes analytical models to study the cost of update and paging. The analytical models are significant as they provide an upper boundary to the performance gains that are achievable by dynamic update strategies over conventional GSM standards.

To evaluate the update cost during call arrival, there are two separate parameters to be quantified for a given threshold; that is, the probability of having m cell-boundary crossings during call arrival $\alpha(m)$, and the expected number of updates to be registered $E_u(m)$. Given then that the unit update cost is U, the update cost can be evaluated from

$$C_u = U \sum_{m=d}^{\infty} \alpha(m) E_u(m) \qquad (8.38)$$

Clearly, the definition of CMR will have a significant impact on the resulting total cost. Assuming call requests arrive following a Poisson distribution, Reference [40] provides a detailed framework to evaluate $\alpha(m)$ for a given cell residence time distribution CRT. Thus, for each specific CRT distribution defined, there is a corresponding $\alpha(m)$ derived to reflect the characteristics of the network concerned. For example, an exponential distribution will give

$$\alpha(m) = \begin{cases} 1 - \dfrac{1}{\rho}\left[1 - \left(\dfrac{1}{\rho+1}\right)\right], & m = 0 \\[3mm] \dfrac{1}{\rho}\left[1 - \left(\dfrac{1}{\rho+1}\right)\right]^2 \left(\dfrac{1}{\rho+1}\right)^{m-1}, & m > 0 \end{cases} \qquad (8.39)$$

as opposed to a chi-square distribution, giving

$$\alpha(m) = \begin{cases} 1 - \dfrac{1}{\rho}\left[1 - \left(\dfrac{1}{2\lambda_c+1}\right)^{1/2\lambda_m}\right], & m = 0 \\[3mm] \dfrac{1}{\rho}\left[1 - \left(\dfrac{1}{2\lambda_c+1}\right)^{1/2\lambda_m}\right]^2 \left(\dfrac{1}{2\lambda_c+1}\right)^{m-1/2\lambda_m}, & m > 0 \end{cases} \qquad (8.40)$$

where ρ is the CMR and is approximated by λ_c/λ_m.

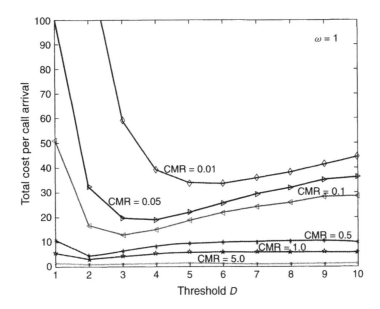

Figure 8.23 Impact of CMR, ρ, on the selection of threshold D

As a general rule, the selection of an optimal threshold depends on two factors: the mobility rate and the roaming directivity. These two parameters form an AND function for optimal system performance. To demonstrate the individual effect of each factor, Figure 8.23 shows the impact of CMR on the selection of optimum threshold D.

Generally, the smaller the CMR, the higher the mobility rate respective to the call-arrival rate and thus, the greater the update cost for a fixed threshold. Conversely, it is evident that the greater the CMR, the lower the expected update cost per call arrival. In general, an increasing CMR suggests a lower number of boundary crossings between call arrivals and thus, less updates will be required to maintain the reachability of the roaming mobile. The impact of CMR, however, seems to have diminished when increasing the threshold D. In fact, it is observed that when CMR is high (say greater than 5), the update cost is almost negligible for all values of the threshold D.

To anticipate an optimal threshold, earlier models assume that probability to all adjacent cells is equal. Thus, for a hexagonal network given in Figure 8.24, Figure 8.25 shows the state diagram used for the modeling of the transitional probability when the distance threshold is set to be D. Note that each state denotes the separation between the current cell and the last update cell.

Consider a more general form of the Markov model illustrated in Figure 8.26. If the mobile is currently residing in the state (or ring) s, the transitioning probabilities of going forward, sideways, and backward in any one step are denoted by $q_{s,s+1,D}$, $q_{s,s,D}$, and $q_{s,s-1,D}$, respectively, for an update threshold of D.

$$q_{s,s+1,D}^{(1)} = \frac{2s+1}{6} \tag{8.41}$$

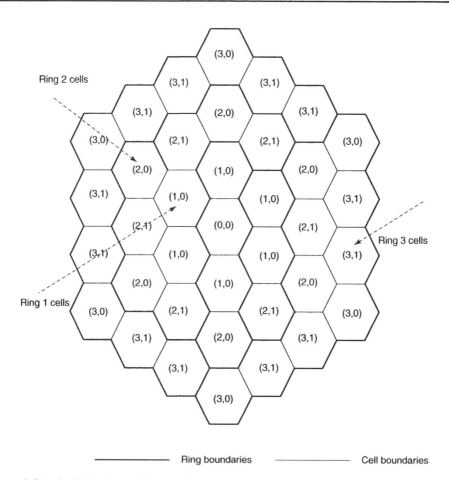

Figure 8.24 An illustration of ring topology

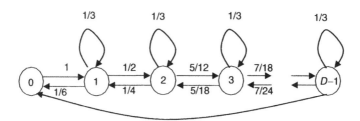

Figure 8.25 The state Markov model for random movement in a hexagonal topology

$$q_{s,s,D}^{(1)} = \frac{4s - 1}{3[4s - 1]} \tag{8.42}$$

$$q_{s,s-1,D}^{(1)} = \frac{4s^2 - 3s + (1/2)}{3s[4s - 1]} \tag{8.43}$$

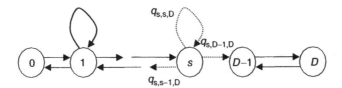

Figure 8.26   The state diagram illustrating the interring transition probabilities in a hexagonal cell

As the optimal threshold is selected on the basis of the distance traveled in terms of the number of cells, another way of determining the expected number of updates is to look at the probability of the mobile moving from state 0 to state D during the call's interarrival time. Thus, according to the transition probabilities derived in the preceding section, $E_u(m)$ can be evaluated as

$$E_u(m) = \sum_{k=D}^{m} q_{0,D,D}^{(k)} \tag{8.44}$$

where $q_{0,D-1,D}^{(k)}$ defines the probability of moving from state 0 to state $D - 1$ in k steps. Thus, if $k = m - 1$, there will only be one update during a call arrival (i.e. $E_u(m) = 1$) as it takes the whole m movements for the mobile to move from state 0 to state D. On the other hand, if $k = D - 1$, the probability of transiting to the next ring is found to be unity for every movement. In other words, it is guaranteed that every time the mobile makes D number of transitions, it will be reaching the predefined threshold ring for an update. Correspondingly, for k ranging from $D - 1$ to $m - 1$, the mobile wanders around between rings dependent on the transitional probability.

Although it is suggested in Reference [67] that the number of states required to represent the complete movement pattern can be reduced, the modeling remains based on the assumption of random movements. Thus, mobiles are expected to roam into all adjacent cells with the same probability regardless of their actual location. Given the pervasive usage of mobile devices in today's society, it becomes somewhat unrealistic to assume that mobiles always inherit memory-less movement patterns. Many of the movements have, in fact, demonstrated a traceable purpose that is often activity-oriented. Indubitably, it is imperative to consider such variability in the analytical models for a rational performance analysis.

The introduction of a *transitional directivity index* ω in Reference [58] is designed to fulfill such a requirement. Specifically, different transition probabilities are assigned for movements in varying directions. This in turn will allow for distinguishable measures to be made for varying mobile traveling patterns.

In this work, a new adaptive scheme in which an optimal distance-based update threshold is selected not only as a function of the CMR, but also as a transitional directivity index that was introduced to give some measures of the mobile's traveling patterns. Intuitively, instead of assuming that the mobile moves to all neighboring cells with an equal probability, it is now assumed in this framework that the outwards transition probability will have an additional factor ω. Consequently, to maintain equilibrium, the transition probabilities of moving sideways and backwards will also vary accordingly. It is therefore necessary to recompute the transitional probabilities between cells. Thus, for an update threshold of D, the general expressions derived for calculating the probability of entering adjacent rings from ring s are shown for the transitioning probabilities of going forward, sideways, and backward in Equations (8.45) to (8.47), respectively.

$$q_{s,s+1,D}^{(1)} = \frac{2\,\omega s + \omega}{6s} \tag{8.45}$$

$$q_{s,s,D}^{(1)} = \frac{2[(3 - \omega)s] - \omega}{3[4s - 1]} \tag{8.46}$$

$$q_{s,s-1,D}^{(1)} = \frac{2[(3 - \omega)s^2] - 3s + \omega/2}{3s[4s - 1]} \tag{8.47}$$

To illustrate the impact of ω on the resultant movement patterns, for a simple ring structure shown in Figure 8.27, the transitional probabilities to the neighboring cells for different values of ω are given in Table 8.3. The notations a, b, and c represent the movements of going forward, sideways, and backward, respectively.

Regarding the physical interpretation of the parameter ω, Table 8.4 provides a general guideline for the categorization of different mobile user groups.

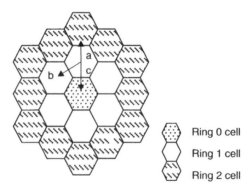

Figure 8.27   The simulation framework

Table 8.3 Impact of ω on the transitional probability

	Transition probability		
	$\omega = 0.5$	$\omega = 1$	$\omega = 1.5$
a	$\frac{1}{4}$	$\frac{1}{2}$	$\frac{3}{4}$
b	$\frac{1}{2}$	$\frac{1}{3}$	$\frac{1}{6}$
c	$\frac{1}{4}$	$\frac{1}{6}$	$\frac{1}{12}$

Table 8.4 Relations between ω and the inherited movement patterns

ω	Interpretation of the movement patterns
<1	Tendency of inter-ring movements (local area roaming)
$=1$	Random movement (nontraceable movement pattern)
>1	Tendency of destination-based movements

With the inclusion of a directional parameter, the basic concept used to evaluate the expected update rate is the same as before. Recall Equation (8.44) where the introduction of ω becomes significant, and the update number can be generally expressed by

$$E_{\mathrm{u}}(m) = \frac{2\omega(D-1)+\omega}{6(D-1)} \sum_{k=D-1}^{m-1} q_{0,D-1,D}^{(k)} \qquad (8.48)$$

Intuitively, the higher the value of ω, the more directive the traveling direction (i.e. more outwards), and thus, fewer boundary crossings are required before reaching the threshold state for the same mobility rate. Consequently, we end up having a scenario where the total update cost is not only a function of CMR and the threshold D [49,62,64], but also a function of ω, the parameter assigned to give a measure of movement directivity level. Therefore, without having to necessarily require much monitoring of the actual CMR variations, an optimal threshold can be selected dynamically according to the periodic feedback of ω estimates. The other alternative is to make $\alpha(m)$ a function of rings (instead of cell boundaries), and to make $E_{\mathrm{u}}(m)$ the expected number of updates for the m ring boundary crossings. That way, the operation can be effectively considered as a movement-based scheme with the expressions of probability functions $\alpha(m)$ derived not only as a function of CRT, but also with weight ω.

The idea of the proposed scheme is to adjust adaptively the distance-based threshold D only when the roaming mobile seems to have demonstrated a certain traveling direction or pattern. The key question this work tried to answer was to what extent does the directivity of the traveling characteristics affect the determination of an optimal threshold set up for cost minimization. Thus, if ω is found to be different from its previous values taken at the sampling time, D will be changed to ensure that the specific mobility patterns are taken into consideration. The focus is on anticipating the mobile's roaming characteristic using the estimated transitional directivity measures ω.

Figure 8.28 shows the impacts of ω on the selection of optimum threshold D.

Generally, for smaller thresholds, the performance shows that the predominant contribution is from the definitions of unit update cost. Thus, for roaming mobiles having the same CMR statistical characteristics, the cost of update becomes a function of ω. In other words, for the same number of mobile transitions, those that are estimated to have a more directive traveling pattern (i.e. higher ω), reach the same predefined threshold more quickly, thus resulting in greater cost because of the more frequent incursion of updates. Hence, the threshold is reached faster and consequently, incurs a higher updating cost to the network. Note also that the update cost is highest when the threshold equals 1. The need to have an efficient location management technique is reinforced, as

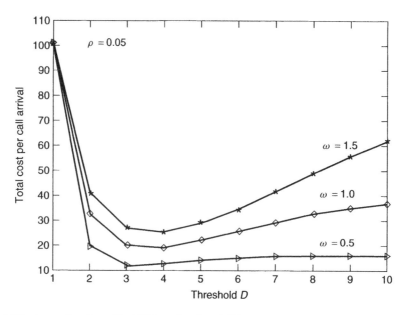

Figure 8.28 Impacts of ω with CMR, ρ, fixed at 0.05

a significant reduction in the update cost is evident even when the threshold is merely increased by one unit. The improvement in performance, however, stabilizes eventually with increasing thresholds.

An enhanced analysis

Clearly, for a distance-based scheme, the number of updates does not depend only on the number of movements, but also on the direction of movement, specifically, the probability of having the mobile roam toward the next ring-cell. Alternatively, it is possible to expand the expressions above to better illustrate the possible roaming characteristics. Briefly, for each update to occur, a minimum of D cell-boundary crossings, or a maximum of m movements are required depending on how does the mobile transit to the neighboring cells.

Consider the most general case in which a mobile inherits a random movement pattern; the number of updates can thus be evaluated by

$$E_u(m) = \left[\prod_{i=1}^{D} \left(\frac{2i+1}{6i} \right) \right] \left[\prod_{\substack{k=1 \\ j_k \in (1, D-1)}}^{A} \left(\frac{2j_k - 1}{6j_k} \right)^A \right] \left(\frac{1}{3} \right)^{m-2A-D} \quad (8.49)$$

The first term in Equation (8.49) takes into account the probability that the mobile transits to the next ring of cells after each movement. The actual probability varies according to the cell of residency. Clearly, a minimum of D movements will be all it takes to incur a new update in some cases. Although such a movement pattern is possible, the mobile is expected to inherit a strong correlation between traveling directions and hence, a restrictive movement pattern. It is thus more likely that reaching the update boundary requires more than D transitions. Clearly, apart from the basic D movements, there are $m - D$ movements in which the directions of transitioning are significantly different from their corresponding predecessors. In the extreme case in which a transition is made in the opposite direction to its most recent movement, the term *backward* is used to describe the moving characteristics. Assuming there are A units of such backward movements, the second term in Equation (8.49) takes into account the combined effects of these A transitions to the final pattern. In this expression, j_k refers to the ring of residence before the backward movement incurs. Apart from moving forwards and backwards, according to the definition of the network topology, it is possible that the mobile transits to an adjacent cell belonging to the same ring as the current cell. In this case, a *sideways* movement is said to have occurred. For a hexagonal cell topology, the transitioning probability is always equal to a third. Obviously, for every one backward movement incurred, there will be at least one other movement in the opposite direction required before the mobile is back on the main direction of traveling. Hence, for a total of $m - D - 2A$ units of sideways movements, the overall effects are considered by the last term in Equation (8.49). The resultant operational cost, however, will vary for different mobility patterns.

8.4.3.3 Modified analytical framework 2-D topology

In the following section, given that different assumptions are imposed for mobility patterns, the resultant modifications to the original analytical framework are compared. For the sake of simplicity in discussions, state transition diagrams are illustrated for all cases. The expected costs of update and paging can thus be evaluated from the corresponding transition matrices derived thereby.

One of the concerns raised over the operation of the basic analytical framework is the number of states that are necessary to represent the complete state information. Clearly, given that a random movement pattern is assumed, some states are actually the replicates of other states in a structured cell configuration. Recognizing this potential waste of computational resources, Reference [67] has proposed a new motion model intending to simplify the number of states required to capture the motion characteristics.

Generally, the complete cluster is divided into six equal pieces. Any two cells that have the same relative position on different pieces will be assigned with the same *type* number and are assumed to show the same roaming characteristics to their respective adjacent cells. Each cell is denoted by state (i, j), with i representing the mobile's current location in terms of cell separation from the last update and j indicating the type number the current cell is assigned to. As an example, Figure 8.29 illustrates the state diagram for a 4-subarea cluster based on the new approach of type classification.

Thus, equivalent to a threshold of D in a distance-based update scheme, for a D-subarea cluster with the new random walk model, the number of states required to illustrate the two-dimensional random walk will reduce to $D(D + 1)/2$ [67]. Compared with the

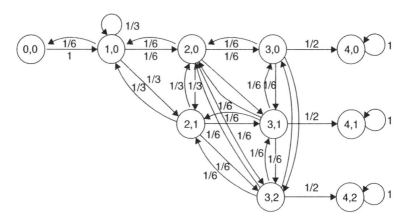

Figure 8.29 The state Markov model for the 4-subarea cluster

number of states $(3D^2 + 3D - 5)$ that would otherwise be required from the conventional random walk model in a hexagonal configured network, computational complexity requires modeling in which the transitional probabilities decrease significantly. It is proposed that the new random walk model will find applications in cellular networks mainly to determine the number of units visited before moving out of the bigger area. For example, it can be used to model the cell residence time distributions in macrocells overlapping microcells. It is thus possible to determine the number of smaller routing areas visited before the mobile moves to a new LA.

In Reference [51], a registration is performed whenever a change of direction is detected in the operations; the number of updates required is defined by the frequency at which changes of direction occurs in the movement pattern. While based on an embedded Markov chain, it is possible to modify the definitions of the transitional probabilities such that the additional features observed in the location tracking strategy are accommodated. Let each state denote the distance between a mobile's current location and its last update cell. On the basis of the assumption that the mobile moves in the same direction with a probability of q, either forward or backward, the corresponding Markov chain model can be illustrated as in Figure 8.30.

Different from the previous cases in which time-slotted models are used to represent the roaming characteristics of individual mobiles, in this framework, the probability of state transition is evaluated by the product of the mobility rate and statistical information about traveling directions.

Generally, in addition to the probability of call arrivals λ_c, the likelihood for the occurrence of an update is $\lambda_m(1 - 2q)$ for all intermediate states. For the boundary states, however, despite a transition in the same direction, a forward movement from state $D - 1$ or a backward movement from state 1 will also incur a registration at a probability of $\lambda_m(1 - q)$ based on the definition of system framework. Consequently, the update rate is a measure of the probability that the state 0 is reached from any of the three occasions; when a change of direction is detected, when the distance threshold D is attained, or when a new call has arrived. Summing up all the terms, the average update cost per unit

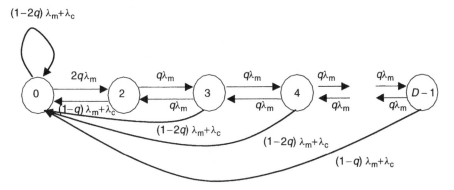

Figure 8.30 The state diagram illustrating the interring transition probabilities in a hexagonal cell

time can be evaluated by

$$C_u = \lambda_m U \left[(1 - 2q) \sum_{i=0}^{k-1} Q_i + (1 - q)Q_D \right] \tag{8.50}$$

where the steady state probabilities of Q_n, $n = 0, 1, 2, 3 \ldots$, are obtainable via the expressions derived from the Markov diagram.

$$Q_1 = \frac{(1 + \rho)(Q_0 - 1) + 2q}{q} - Q_D \tag{8.51}$$

$$Q_2 = \frac{(1 + \rho)Q_1 - 2q Q_0}{q} \tag{8.52}$$

$$Q_i = \frac{(1 + \rho)Q_{i-1} - q Q_{i-2}}{q} \quad \text{for} \quad 3 \leq i \leq D \tag{8.53}$$

where ρ is the call-to-mobility ratio and is approximated by λ_c/λ_m.

While the analytical framework provides some important measures for the efficiency of individual update schemes, the evaluations are often involved with certain unrealistic assumptions including structured cell configurations and symmetric random walk movement patterns. In terms of the modeling of the mobility rate, with an exponential cell residence time distribution commonly implied, the performance assessment reflects little of the individual mobile's roaming characteristics. It is thus important to consider specific tracking techniques that utilize the merits of defining irregular update boundary.

8.4.4 Optimal boundary assignation

The purpose of location tracking is to determine an optimal update boundary. The frequency at which an update is triggered depends not only on the movement patterns of a mobile but also on the appropriate assignations of an update boundary. Generally, a large threshold incurs fewer updates at the expense of increasing paging load when allowable delay is restricted at unity. A better attempt is made to assign the update boundary such that while keeping the maximum paging load constraint, the number of updates is reduced [21,38,54,56]. Where the selected thresholds result in a minimal operational cost, the specific set of boundary cells is referred to as optimal. If the purposes of an update strategy are to be summarized in one sentence, it can be said that it is about the determination of an optimal update boundary.

In the following sections, we examine the methods that were used to select such optimal update boundaries. Individual algorithms are categorized according to the specific parameters used to quantify the optimal performances.

Generally, the total operational cost expected is evaluated for all cells in the system framework and iteration algorithms are carried out to identify cells that comply with the optimal policy. The operation of searching for an optimal boundary is completed with such cells being included in the set forming the boundary cells. Although all iteration schemes have similar philosophies, the actual algorithm varies according to specific network characteristics.

8.4.4.1 Dynamic optimal LR assignation in 2-D topology

In Reference [21], the expected number of updates is evaluated by estimating the time the mobile roams within the assigned LA before incurring a registration upon its exit.

The analytical model is based on a Manhattan city street model in which base stations are located at the intersections of streets. Thus, instead of assuming time-slotted models, the mobile makes a transition at each intersection to one of the neighboring cells such that the shortest path is taken to reach the boundary cells.

At each intersection, the mobile has a choice of either staying in the same direction or taking a turn at a probability of P_s, P_r, P_l, that is, going straight, turning right and turning left, respectively, giving

$$\Pr(S) = P_s, \quad \Pr(R) = P_r, \quad \Pr(L) = P_l \tag{8.54}$$

With a shortest-distance model, it is assumed that the mobile will take a minimum number of steps to arrive at a boundary cell. The model thus neglects the possibilities of a return trip. Consequently, having to avoid backward movements, the transitional probability alters after each turn. As an example, assuming that the most recent turn Λ is to the right, the basic rules for modeling the transitional probabilities are

$$\Pr(S|\wedge = R) = \frac{P_s}{P_s + P_l}, \quad \Pr(R|\wedge = R) = 0, \quad \Pr(L|\wedge = R) = \frac{P_l}{P_s + P_l} \tag{8.55}$$

In all the cases, the probability of taking a particular path will be a product of individual transitions at each intersection. Thus, let $\Pr(v(i, j)|n)$ denote the probability of having a mobile reside in cell (i, j) after n movements, the statistical estimation of such a quantity can be obtained by

$$\Pr(v(i, j)|n) = \sum_{i=1}^{n} \Pr(X)_i \quad X \in \{S, R, L\} \tag{8.56}$$

For each transition, the direction of movement follows the relation

$$P_s + P_r + P_1 = 1 \tag{8.57}$$

It is noted that the initial values of P_s, P_r, P_1 are defined empirically according to the local traffic conditions in terms of flow rates out of and into each cell. Intuitively, the quantities of those probabilities are geographically dependent and have little relation to the individual mobile characteristics. The underlying assumptions are thus clearly different between the shortest-distance model and other mobile-oriented models such as Markovian movement patterns [21,22]. This observation proves the need to separate discussions on the analytical framework according to specific areas of applications.

As for the assignation of an optimal LA, irregular LA boundaries are assigned such that the number of cells traverse N_n in the specific LA before exiting is maximized. It is assumed that the service area has a dimension of $m \times m$, and that each cell in the topology has an absolute coordinate that does not change upon registrations. Given a specific source–destination combination, there is a corresponding matrix X defining the optimal LA boundaries. Specifically, an element $x_{i,j}$ equals to 1 when it forms part of the boundary set $R(A)$.

$$x_{i,j} = \begin{cases} 1 \\ 0 \end{cases} \quad \text{if cell } (i, j) \text{ is } \begin{cases} \text{assigned} \\ \text{not assigned} \end{cases} \tag{8.58}$$

Consequently, the distance threshold is defined in two dimensions by $D(\Delta x, \Delta y)$ in relation to the last update cell (α, β). The cells to be included in the optimal LA are identified utilizing an iterative greedy heuristic. The basic operations are briefly illustrated in Figure 8.31.

The iteration starts from the last update cell. For each of the immediate neighboring cells, the expected number of cells traversed by the roaming mobile will be recomputed assuming their inclusion in the collection of the boundary set. The cell that results in the highest number from each round will form part of the current registration area $O(n)$. The iteration algorithm continues until the assigned LA contains a maximum number of k cells as is defined by the network.

To evaluate the number of boundary crossings before an update is due is equivalent to determining the probability of moving out of any boundary cells $x_{i,j} = 1 \in R(A)$ into a cell on the perimeter of the existing boundary $B(A)$. From the assigned update boundary, it requires two steps in the evaluation of the number of traversed cells before exiting the current LA.

Firstly, the probability that the cell (i, j) is the last cell mobile station visits before exiting the LA can be evaluated by

$$\Pr(e(i, j)) = S(i, j + 1)\bar{x}_{i,j+1} + W(i + 1, j)\bar{x}_{i+1,j}$$
$$+ N(i, j - 1)\bar{x}_{i,j-1} + E(i - 1, j)\bar{x}_{i-1,j} \tag{8.59}$$

where

$$\bar{x}_{i,j} = \begin{cases} 0 \\ 1 \end{cases} \quad \text{if } x_{i,j} \text{ is } \begin{cases} 1 \\ 0 \end{cases} \tag{8.60}$$

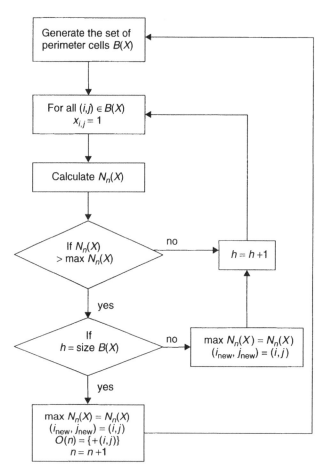

Figure 8.31 A graphical representation of the iterative greedy heuristic

As an example, for an irregular LA assigned in Figure 8.32, the probability that the mobile exits the current LA through cell (i, j) can be evaluated as

$$\Pr(e(i, j)|n) = \Pr(v(i, j)|n)p_1 + \Pr(v(i, j)|n)p_2 \tag{8.61}$$

With the underlying assumption of a shortest-distance model, it takes $(|i - \alpha| + |j - \beta|)$ movements for the mobile to reach an arbitrary cell (i, j) from the last updated cell (α, β). Thus, given that cell (i, j) is the last cell the mobile visits before exiting the current LA, the total number of cells traversed within LA will be

$$N_n = \sum_{(i,j)} (|i - \alpha| + |j - \beta| + 1) \Pr(e(i, j)) = \sum_{(i,j)\in R(A)} \sum_{m=i+j}^{\infty} (m + 1) \Pr(e(i, j)|m) \tag{8.62}$$

On the basis of the assumption of the shortest-distance model, it is possible to determine an optimal rectangular-shaped LA that gives a predefined cost ratio between a unit update

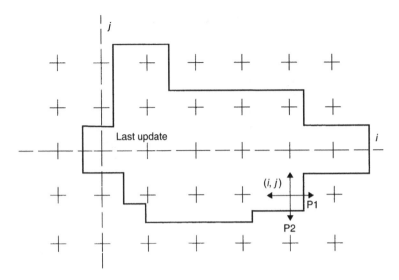

Figure 8.32   An irregular LA

and a unit paging. The measures of the update rate, however, will almost certainly be affected by the actual movement patterns, thus resulting in a varying update cost from what was originally expected from the initial analysis. To quantify the performance of such optimally assigned update boundary, the resultant update cost can be evaluated.

Let the cell residence time follow a Gamma distribution, the average time a mobile resides in a cell can be evaluated by [21,22]

$$\overline{T}_i = \int_{-\infty}^{+\infty} \left(\frac{-1}{\sigma_v \sqrt{2\pi L}} \cdot e^{\frac{-(L/T-v)^2}{2\sigma_v^2}} \cdot T^3 dT \right) \cong \frac{L}{v} + \frac{2L\sigma_v^2}{2v^3} \tag{8.63}$$

Assuming that each mobile has an equal probability to destine for any cells in the network. Each cell will thus have a probability P_{dest} of being the destination. Consequently, the average time a mobile resides in a cell will sum up to be

$$\overline{X}_i = \frac{1}{u_1} = \overline{T}_i(1 - P_{\text{dest}}) + \overline{T}_{\text{dest}} P_{\text{dest}} \tag{8.64}$$

where $\overline{T}_{\text{dest}}$ denotes the average time the mobile stays at the destination before roaming toward the next destination. In addition, it is assumed that the mobile incurs a zero delay at the intersection.

With N_n denoting the number of cells a mobile traversed before exiting the current LA, the average update rate will thus be

$$u_k = \frac{u_1}{N_n} = \frac{1}{\overline{X}_i \times N_n} \tag{8.65}$$

Intuitively, the greater the number of cells traversed within the assigned LA, the lower the update rate that will result, thus achieving a higher performance gain.

8.4.4.2 State-base paging/registration: a greedy technique

The duration between adjacent contacts with the network is of special concern to the operation of location tracking. It can define the time between two registrations, two paging operations and between a registration and a paging request. References [38,39] refer to this specific period as the roaming interval. Theoretically, it reveals information about the CMR characteristics. A greedy method is thus introduced to define a state-based update policy θ_g such that the update cells are assigned to optimize the performance of the current roaming interval. It is, however, possible to consider performances over previous roaming intervals by adjusting the level of greediness through the selection of α. Generally, given the expected cost of update and paging C_i and the current roaming interval d_i, the average per unit time cost is equal to

$$\eta_\theta = \lim_{n\to\infty} \frac{\sum_{i=1}^{n} C_{i|\theta}}{\sum_{j=1}^{n} d_{i|\theta}} \tag{8.66}$$

Upon entering a new call x_s after some time s, the greedy registration algorithm determines an optimal waiting time ι such that the expected cumulative per unit cost of registration and paging is minimized. An update is registered if the optimal time is equal to zero. Otherwise, the same procedure repeats when roaming to the next cell. Figure 8.33 summarizes the operation of the iterative algorithm.

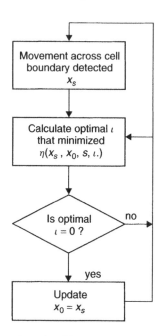

Figure 8.33 The greedy registration algorithm

Having obtained the framework that selects the update cells, it is important to study the method that is used to evaluate the cost. Essentially, the evaluation of the operational cost is based on the current location, the last known location, the time elapsed since the previous registration, and in some cases on past history. Given the current location at x_s, the expected cost associated with a registration due at $s + \iota$ time later can be evaluated by [25,38]

$$\overline{F}(x_s, x_o, \iota) = E_{x_{s+\iota}|x_s, x_o, \tau, s}[F(x_{s+\iota}, x_o, s + \tau)] \qquad (8.67)$$

where $E_{x_{s+\iota}|x_s, x_o, \tau, s}$ is the expected cost for the random variable $x_s + \iota$ given x_s, x_o, τ, s.

If on the one hand, a paging request arrives during the time $s + \iota$, the expected cost is contributed mainly by the paging operations. Given the current and last known locations, $F(x_s, x_o, t)$ defines the cost associated with the paging operations for a call arrival at time s. For a cell of area δ, the cost is determined by

$$F(x_s, x_o, t) = N(x_s, x_o, t)\,\delta \qquad (8.68)$$

where $N(x_s, x_o, t)$ gives a measure of the total number of cells searched. The average amount of paging load $\overline{N}$ decreases when a roaming mobile is searched in a decreasing order of probability. According to Reference [38], the minimum $\overline{F}(x_s, x_o, t)$ is achievable by

$$\min_{Y_n^*} \overline{F}(x_s, x_o, t) = \sum_{n=1}^{\infty} n p_{x_s|x_o}(Y_n^*|X_o)\,\delta \qquad (8.69)$$

Specifically, Y_n^* defines the order of searching with $p_{x_s|x_o}(Y_n^*|X_o)$ expected to be greater or equal to $p_{x_s|x_o}(Y_{n+1}^*|X_o)$.

With the call arrivals modeled by a Poisson process of rate λ_c, the probability distribution for the arrival of the next paging event will be $\lambda_c e^{-\lambda_c t}$. For a unit-paging cost defined to be P, the paging cost sums up to

$$C_p = e^{-\lambda_c \tau} + P \int_0^{\tau} \overline{F}(x_s, x_o, t)\lambda_c e^{-\lambda_c t} dt \qquad (8.70)$$

If on the other hand, no paging requests arrive during this specified time, a registration performed as originally planned, will incur registration costs with a probability of $e^{-\lambda_c t}$ giving an update cost of $Ue^{-\lambda_c t}$. Consider P to be the unit update cost with respect to the paging cost, the expected cumulative cost of paging and update becomes

$$\eta(x_s, x_o, s, \tau) = C_n + e^{-\lambda_c \tau} P \int_0^{\tau} \overline{F}(x_s, x_o, t)\lambda_c e^{-\lambda_c t} dt \qquad (8.71)$$

where C_n accounts for the total costs incurred during n most recent roaming intervals. With the level of greediness defined by α ranging between 0 and 1, the corresponding discount cost is evaluated by

$$C_n = \sum_{k=1}^{n} \alpha^k c_k \qquad (8.72)$$

Thus, when the algorithm is optimized only for the current roaming interval (e.g. $\alpha = 0$), C_n takes a null value.

To determine the expected per unit time cost, Equation (8.71) is divided by the total length of the roaming interval time yielding

$$\overline{\eta}(x_s, x_o, s, \iota) = \frac{C_n + P \int_0^\iota \overline{F}(x_s, x_o, t)\lambda_c e^{-\lambda_c t} dt + e^{-\lambda_c \tau}}{T_n + s + \dfrac{1 - e^{-\lambda_c \tau}}{\lambda_c}} \tag{8.73}$$

In addition to the current roaming interval, $s + \tau$, T_n represents the total duration of the n previous roaming interval durations t quantified by

$$T_n = \sum_{k=1}^{n} \alpha^k t_k \tag{8.74}$$

Thus, based on such cost estimations, an update is performed only when the expected cumulative per unit time cost of paging and registration is minimized. The state-based registration policy thus identifies a collection of points (x_t, τ) in which the optimal waiting time τ for a registration is equal to zero.

8.4.4.3 Adaptive distance-based location update algorithm

In Reference [54], the iteration goes through for each cell-boundary crossing that is expected to incur in the immediate future leading to the next registration. A decision of update is made according to the mobile's current state information $s = (i, j)$, in which i and j represent the location of the current cell and the most recent updated cell, respectively.

The selection is made by taking the smaller cost between the expected update and paging operations. Assuming calls arrive according to the Poisson distributions, on the one hand, if an update is performed at state (i, j), the expected total cost will be

$$v(i, j) = C_u = U + \int_0^\infty (1 - e^{-\lambda_c t})h(i, j)G(dt|i)$$

$$+ \sum_k \left[\int_0^\infty e^{-\lambda_c t} v(k, i) P(k|i) G(dt|i) \right] \tag{8.75}$$

Given cell i is the current cell of residence, $P(k|i)$ denotes the probability that k is the next cell of residence. In addition, with $h(i|j)$ represents the paging cost function, $G(dt|i)$ signifies the time differential to the cumulative distribution function of the cell residence time. On the other, the total cost to be expected in the absence of an update at state (i, j) will be

$$v(i, j) = C_p = \int_0^\infty (1 - e^{-\lambda_c t})h(i, j)G(dt|i) + \sum_k \left[\int_0^\infty e^{-\lambda_c t} v(k, j) P(k|i) G(dt|i) \right] \tag{8.76}$$

where $v(i, j)$ will denote the smaller cost between the two and is referred to as the minimum expected total cost between call arrivals.

On the basis of this concept, the value iteration algorithm is applied to obtain the stationary deterministic optimal policy $\delta^*(i, j)$ and the minimum corresponding cost expected $v(i, j)$. Where an update is expected to result in a minimum cost at state (i, j), $\delta^*(i, j)$ is defined to be unity. Conversely, when it is anticipated that no update will give a better performance with the current definition, $\delta^*(i, j)$ takes the value of 0. Figure 8.34 summarizes the main operation of the value iteration algorithm.

However, the network is required to maintain a mobility profile including the movement history and call history for each mobile user. Once the average mobility rate and call arrival is estimated from the profile, the optimal update policy is determined. Upon each registration, the set of boundary cells optimized for the given current location is

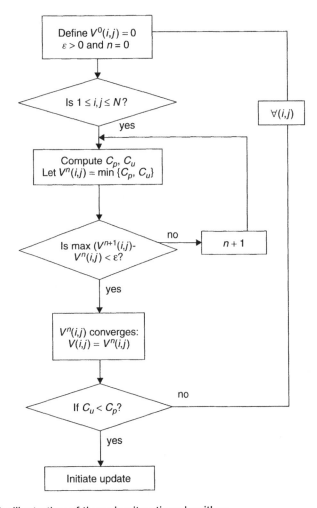

Figure 8.34 An illustration of the value iteration algorithm

downloaded from the network. Thereafter, the decision of the update will simply follow a table-lookup process.

Given that the optimal update boundaries are assigned off-line, the prediction relies greatly on a strong persistence in motion characteristics of a mobile. Consequently, the assignation of the optimal update boundary will have to be adjusted subject to changes in network structures and mobile characteristics.

The application is generally more restricted as the functioning of the proposed algorithm assumes importunate movement patterns over a longer period.

Clearly, regardless of the actual method, the selection of the optimal policy is a function of CMR characteristics and other cost parameters. Given that it is not always possible to estimate the call and mobility characteristics correctly, the sensitivity of individual update schemes to variations between the anticipated and actual mobile characteristics become an important measure to quantify the performance. It is possible to determine the relation between the change of the expected total cost and the variations in the actual mobile parameters; for example, the call-arrival rate, or the mobility rate.

8.4.5 Paging cost

If, on the basis of an underlying assumption of random movement patterns, the bigger the area enclosed within the update boundary, the longer the duration the mobile will remain in the current update area. Thus, the occurrence of a new update becomes less probable with an increasing size of the LA. However, the savings achieved in the update operations are abridged by the increasing paging load upon call arrival, that is, the greater the update area, the higher the number of cells required to be polled during the paging phase. Given the unavoidable trade-off between the two terms, the ultimate solution is thus to limit one cost and to minimize the other.

For the computation of paging cost, regardless of the actual method of paging, the analysis framework is the same for all variations of distance-based or movement-based update schemes [56,57,64,68,69]. Generally, the more certain the network is about the location of the roaming mobile, the fewer the paging signals that will be necessary to achieve the same goal.

8.4.5.1 Number of paging signals

Given a per unit paging cost of P, the calculation of the paging load N_{ave} comprises two parts, to estimate the probability of having the roaming mobile reside in subarea A_j (i.e. ρ_j), and to predict the number of cells φ_j to be paged thereby before the user is located. Specifically, the evaluation of such a cost can be defined by

$$C_p = P N_{\mathrm{ave}} = P \sum_{j=1}^{\eta} \rho_j \varphi_j \tag{8.77}$$

where η defines the allowable paging delay, and in a hexagonal network, it represents the number of subareas used to group a maximum number of $3D^2 + 3D + 1$ cells in a system of update threshold D. Conceptually, this simulates a hierarchical structure in which multiple cells are managed as a subarea. Thus, the methodology used to partition the LA into η subareas will play a dominant role in the evaluation of system performance.

Given each subarea A_j is made of a multiple number of cells, the probability of locating the roaming mobile in the subarea A_j is equivalent to the combined probability of finding the mobile in any of the cells $C_i \in A_j$. The alternative expression for the cost evaluation is thus

$$\rho_j = \sum_{C_i \in A_j} \pi_i \tag{8.78}$$

Intuitively, the number of cells embraced within the subarea (i.e. A_j) defines the number of elements to be included in the summation. Furthermore, as the paging cost is determined on a per call-arrival basis, it is essential to consider the rate of call arrival in the evaluation of the residency probability. To maintain the consistency in notations $\alpha(m)$ is used to represent the probability of incurring m cell-boundary crossings between call arrivals, as was the case for the update analysis. Thus, the evaluation of ρ_j can be expanded further, giving

$$\rho_j = \sum_{C_i \in A_j} \left(\sum_{m=0}^{\infty} \alpha(m)\gamma(C_i, m) \right) \tag{8.79}$$

where $\gamma(C_i, m)$ is a measure of the probability of mobile residing in cell C_i after m movement. Although the actual evaluation will require slight modifications for different paging schemes, it should be obvious that the quantity will depend on the movement rate and pattern of individual roaming mobile.

Moreover, with the subscript of the subarea indicating the order of paging, the roaming mobile will be located in the jth polling cycle if it is found to have resided in subarea A_j. Thus, the total number of cells that required paging could be evaluated by

$$\varphi_j = \sum_{i=1}^{j} n_i \tag{8.80}$$

where n_j represents the total number of cells embraced in the subarea A_j. Clearly, depending on the specific partition algorithm applied in the paging strategy, the formation of paging subareas will vary. Not only will the size of each subarea be different but also the order at which cells are paged are likely to be dissimilar. For example, on the one hand, in a ring-structure-based paging, each subarea would consist of a number of rings R_i. Assuming the mobile is residing in A_j upon a call arrival, the number of cells to be paged is therefore summed up to

$$\varphi_j = \sum_{i=1}^{j} \left(\sum_{R_k \in A_i} 6R_k \right) \tag{8.81}$$

On the other hand, for the sectional paging developed in Reference [59], the probability of location is considered according to the residence in each angularly divided section. Thus, the total number of cells requiring paging will be a measure of certainty in predictions. Such a quantity can be evaluated by

$$\varphi_j = D + \sum_{n=0}^{x-1} 2(D - n) \tag{8.82}$$

where x is the defined boundary size used to predict the most likelihood of residency and D is the update threshold. The main advantage of this scheme is that while paging delay is appropriately controlled, the number of paging signals is controlled to be at a minimum level.

Sectional paging versus ring-structure paging

To give a brief illustration of the possible improvements achievable by sectional paging, Figure 8.35 shows the simulation results when the definition of update threshold varies. Clearly, for a fixed section width, a higher paging cost would incur with an increasing update threshold. Thus, as a general design rule, the higher the update threshold, the wider the size of the sectional paging area should be in order to ensure a reliable prediction of the mobile's residency probability distribution. In summary, a sectional paging scheme is best suited for mobiles inheriting a high directivity in movement patterns under stringent paging delay constraints. Conversely, a ring-structured paging is the technique to use primarily when the mobile patterns seem to have shown a lack of specific traveling directions, and the movement pattern seems to be random.

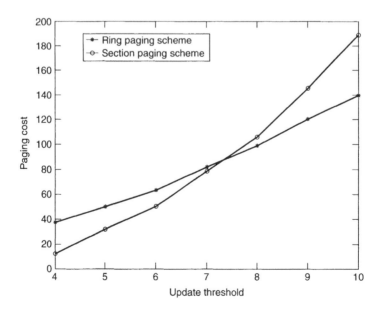

Figure 8.35 Performance comparisons for different update thresholds

8.4.5.2 Average delays

In quantifying the performance of a paging strategy, in addition to the estimations of paging load, the associated paging delay provides an important measure to the capability of individual scheme. Under a delay-constrained environment, the average delay associated with each paging operation can be evaluated by

$$L_{\text{ave}} = \sum_{j=1}^{\eta} j\rho_j \qquad (8.83)$$

The order of paging sequence follows the numerical order; hence, before the subarea A_3 is paged during the third polling cycle, subareas A_1 and A_2 have already been paged during the previous polling cycles. Clearly, the performance of L_{ave} is maximized according to the choice of n_j assigned for the set of subareas.

8.4.6 Partition algorithms

On the basis of the assumption that the probability of cell residency in the LA is known, there are different mechanisms available for the formation of paging subareas. Despite variations in the actual partitioning technique, the general goals are the same, that is, to decide on the size of each partition, and to assign cells in fulfilling the partitions, such that the number of paging load and the corresponding delay is minimized. Generally, according to the estimated probability, each cell is mapped onto a probability line indicating the location distributions at the time of call arrival. Figure 8.36 illustrates the relation between the defined parameters. Thus, given the number of allowable partitions η, the challenge is to determine the optimal partitioning algorithm such that the resulting paging operation is optimized.

In summary, the basic problem is twofold: firstly, to minimize the average paging load N_{ave} subject to delay constraints and secondly, to minimize the corresponding average delay L_{ave} over the set of polling strategies. Under the same delay constraints, the optimization of paging cost often has a greater priority than the average delay.

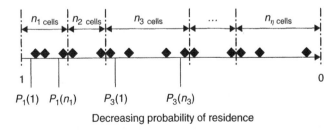

Figure 8.36   The probability line indicating the partitioning of paging areas

8.4.6.1 Shortest-distance-first partitioning scheme

For uniform location distribution, the mobile is assumed to have an equal probability of residing in any of the cells within the LA. Assuming the mobile resides in ring R_i, the number of cells requiring paging before locating the roaming mobile is equal to those bounded between the last update center and that of the R_i. The shortest-distance-first partitioning strategy simply groups cells according to the distance from the last update cell. Each subarea consists of one or more rings depending on the allowable paging constraint η. Generally, the closer the ring is to the last update cell, the sooner the corresponding ring-cells are paged. A minimal paging load incurs when the paging delay is unconstrained. In cases in which paging delays are constrained, it is likely that additional paging load will result depending on how polling cycles are scheduled among cells in the LA. Since the update threshold is not always evenly divisible by the number of allowable subareas, a partitioning scheme was proposed in References [49,56] such that the number of rings to be included in each subarea is approximately equal. Thus, assuming each subarea A_j will include rings embraced within b_j and e_j, respectively, they represent the indices of the beginning and the ending rings, giving

$$b_j = \left\lfloor \frac{jD}{\eta} \right\rfloor, e_j = \left\lfloor \frac{(j+1)D}{\eta} \right\rfloor - 1 \quad \text{for } 0 < j \le D \qquad (8.84)$$

as the first subarea will always include the cell of the last update, $b_0 = 0$ is true for all mobiles independent of actual call-arrival characteristics.

Finally, where additional updates are required to notify the network of specific movement patterns, the maximum paging load will decrease as a result of increased knowledge about the mobile's roaming behavior. For example, in the direction-based location update scheme as an update is due whenever the direction of traveling has changed from its last movement, the problem of tracking has thus effectively become a one-dimensional problem. Consequently, paging cost will be reduced to $2D + 1$ where D is the size of the threshold [51].

8.4.6.2 Selective paging scheme

The optimization problem is NP-complete. Thus, on the basis of a complete enumeration procedure over all possible N_{ave} and the corresponding L_{ave}, the optimum number of partitions and partition sizes subject to a defined delay constraint can be determined. The evaluation is, however, based on a shortest-distance mobility model with known transitioning probabilities [22].

Overall, simulation results demonstrate that a small number of partitions are sufficient to achieve a significant reduction in the paging cost with an acceptable delay performance. The finding is important as it demonstrates that the performance between paging load and the corresponding delay is not necessarily mutually exclusive. With appropriate arrangement, it is possible to find a convex in which the optimal performance between the paging load and the associated delay is optimized.

8.4.6.3 Highest-probability-first partitioning scheme

Reference [68] provides a comprehensive treatment of the delay constraints. On the one hand, dynamic programming is available for solving the optimal paging cost when given the maximum delay constraints or the weighted average delay constraints. On the other hand, when given the mean delay constraints, it is necessary to reformulate the constrained problems using continuous distributions. Thereby, the given discrete solution will only be a subset of the continuous solution, the analytically traceable solution will give an over bound approximation to the achievable performance gains. Where the scaling properties of continuous solutions applies, the minimum paging load increases proportionally to the size of LA under the same delay constraint.

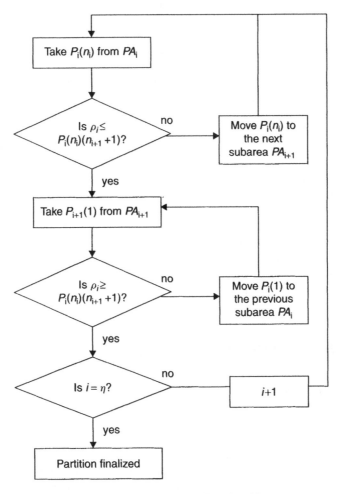

Figure 8.37   Implementation of the optimal partitioning algorithm

8.4.6.4 Optimal partitioning scheme

An optimal partitioning algorithm is proposed to minimize the average number of cells paged in locating a roaming mobile [57,68]. The formation of paging areas and the assignation of paging sequence are achieved according to a design rule that comprises of three conditions. Generally, in addition to the basic probability condition commonly evident in other partitioning strategies [22,69], a forward boundary condition and a backward boundary condition are required for the implementation of the optimal partition strategy.

Having mapped each cell on the probability line in the order of decreasing residence likelihood, initially, the cells are grouped into subareas such that the sizes of all subareas are approximately equal. As a result, each subarea will consist of at least $\lfloor N/\eta \rfloor$ number of cells. When the number of cells is not evenly divisible by the allowable number of partitions, an additional cell will add to the last $(N - D\lfloor N/\eta \rfloor)$ subareas. At the end of the first operation, each subarea will contain a number of cells listed in the order of decreasing probability. The cells of the smallest and the largest probability from each subarea are then tested for the backward boundary condition and the forward boundary condition, respectively. The optimal paging sequence can be obtained from the finalized partitions when all the conditions are complied with. Let $P_j(n_j)$ and $P_j(1)$ represent the cells with the smallest probability and the largest probability from the set PA_j in the subarea A_j; testing the backward and forward boundary conditions illustrated by Figure 8.37. Note that ρ_j defines the total probability of having the mobile reside in the subarea A_j.

Once the number of cells to be paged during each polling cycle is derived, the polling signal is sent according to the defined optimal order. In comparison to other paging schemes, the implementation of the partitioning scheme incurs the minimum computation load with a significant improvement over other paging strategies.

The proposed partitioning strategy is applicable to all mobile characteristics in which the location probability distribution can either be measured or derived. An important condition to ensure that the partitioning scheme works satisfactorily is that the distribution of ρ_i has to be finite. Thus, for some sufficiently large value of q, $P_z = 0$ with $z > q$. Where the paging delay is assumed to be unconstrained, the obtained paging load will give a measure to the absolute minimum.

8.5 SUMMARY AND CONCLUSIONS

Of increasing interest in the deployment of an all-IP network, it is significantly important to identify a location management technique capable of providing the required QoS measures in the world of wireless IP networks. In terms of the basic design criteria, a great similarity is evident between cellular systems and IP networks in their respective paths of evolution. In fact, the resemblance is so strong that it seems promising to reapply some of the well-developed operational philosophy in cellular technology to the vision of an all-IP network. The content of this chapter is intended to provide an overview to the existing mobility models and location management techniques in cellular networks.

Recognizing the great dependence between the design of a location management strategy and the assumption of the mobility model employed, in this chapter an overview has been included to highlight the commonly applied mobility models in the literature. To imitate the motion features, not only should the rate of movement be modeled with appropriate cell residency distributions but the traveling direction at each boundary crossing also needs to be specified. Consequently, unless appropriate justifications are given to the specific topology of application, the simulations will reflect little of the actual performance capabilities of individual location tracking methods.

Having introduced some of the commonly applied mobility models, a literature survey has been included in the chapter to compare the operational differences between specific location tracking and paging strategies. The central aim of a location management scheme is to define the time or location at which a new registration is required such that the network will at all times have a granular view of the mobile's residency. The discussions for each scheme have thus oriented around the questions of *when* to update and *where* to page in order to minimize the overall location tracking cost. Generally, better performances are achievable by tracking schemes that utilize the directional information of individual mobiles. Preference in certain directions may be simply due to each mobile user's behavior or may have resulted from specific geographical conditions.

To evaluate the capabilities of individual schemes, several analytical frameworks have been described in this chapter. Among a wide range of QoS parameters, we focused the study on the modeling of cost quantification. With the ultimate goal of determining the best trade-off between the information load and the searching load, the derivation of a common comparison framework will enable a performance comparison to be made between various strategies. In general, the Markovian movement-based cost model provides a good underlying analytical framework. While being capable of modeling the consistency between traveling directions, the analysis is straightforward and can be easily extended to include specific mobility features. Effectively, it has been illustrated that the challenge of location management can be considered as an optimization problem. In the operations of registration and paging, the optimization lies in the selection of an optimal threshold and the assignation of paging areas, respectively.

Developing an efficient location management technique is an important step in research toward the optimal solution to the problem of mobility. In order to provide an optimal solution for all users, a multimode technique should be implemented such that a different location tracking strategy is chosen to optimize the performance for the defined mobility characteristics and network conditions.

REFERENCES

1. Zeng M, Annamalai A & Bhargava V, A harmonization of global third-generation mobile systems, *IEEE Communications Magazine*, **38**(12), 94–104, 2000.
2. Lu W, Compact multidimensional broadband wireless: the convergence of wireless mobile and access, *IEEE Communications Magazine*, **38**(11), 119–123, 2000.

3. Fang Y, Chlamtac I & Lin YB, Modeling PCS networks under general call holding and cell residence time distributions, *IEEE/ACM Transactions on Networking*, **5**(6), 893–906, 1997.

4. Foschini G, Gopinath B & Miljanic Z, Channel cost of mobility, *IEEE Transactions on Vehicular Technology*, **42**(4), 414–424, 1993.

5. Meempat G & McDonald A, Mobile teleconferencing: design and performance of handoff management and session multicasting schemes, *Proceedings of IEEE ICUPC '98*, Vol. 2, 1998, pp. 1351–1357.

6. Yan J & Bhargava V, Performance evaluation of type-of-service based directed retry strategy in cellular mobile networks, *Proceeding of IEEE ICUPC '97*, Vol. 2, October 1997, pp. 676–680.

7. Morales-Andres G & Villen-Altamurano M, An approach to modelling subscribed mobility in cellular radio networks, *World Telecommunications Forum*, Geneva, Switzerland, November 1987, pp. 185–189.

8. van den Berg E, Zhang T, Chennikara J, Agrawal P & Kodama T, Time series-based localized predictive resource reservation for handoff in multimedia wireless networks, *Proceedings of IEEE ICC '01*, Vol. 2, Helsinki, Finland, June 2001, pp. 346–350.

9. Wong V & Leung V, Location management for next-generation personal communications networks, *IEEE Network*, **14**(5), 18–24, 2000.

10. Bhattacharya A & Das S, LeZi-update: an information-theoretic approach to track mobile users in PCS networks, *Proceedings of IEEE Mobicom '99*, August 1999.

11. Scourias J, Kunz T, Activity-based mobility modeling: realistic evaluation of location management schemes for cellular networks, *Proceedings of IEEE WCNC '99*, Vol. 1, 1999, pp. 296–300.

12. Kunz T, Siddiqi A & Scourias J, The peril of evaluating location management proposals through simulations, *ACM-Baltzer Journal of Wireless Networks*, **7**(6), 635–643, 2001.

13. Scourias J & Kunz T., A dynamic individualized location management algorithm, *Proceedings of IEEE PIMRC '97*, Vol. 3, Helsinki, Finland, September 1997, pp. 1004–1008.

14. Lam D, Cox D & Widom J, Teletraffic modeling for personal communications services, *IEEE Communications Magazine*, **35**(2), 79–87, 1997.

15. Bar-Noy A, Kessler I & Sidi M, Mobile users: to update or not to update? *ACM-Baltzer Journal of Wireless Networks*, **1**(2), 175–185, 1995.

16. Akyildiz I, Ho J & Lin YB, Movement-based location update and selection pagings for PCS networks, *IEEE/ACM Transactions on Networking*, **4**(4), 629–638, 1996.

17. Birk Y & Nachman Y, Using direction and elapsed-time information to reduce the wireless cost of locating mobile units in cellular networks, *ACM-Baltzer Journal of Wireless Networks*, **1**(4), 403–412, 1995.

18. Liang B & Haas Z, Predictive distance-based mobility management for PCS networks, *Proceedings of IEEE INFOCOM '99*, New York, March 1999.

19. Tung T & Jamalipour A, A Kalman-filter based paging strategy for cellular networks, *Proceedings of Minitrack on Quality of Service in Mobile and Wireless Networks HICSS '36*, Hawaii, January 2003.

20. Lui J, Fong C & Chan H, Location updates and probabilistic tracking algorithms for mobile cellular networks, *Proceedings of IEEE I-SPAN '99*, 1999, pp. 432–437.
21. Abutaleb A & Li V, Location update optimization in personal communication systems, *ACM-Baltzer Journal of Wireless Networks*, **3**, 205–216, 1997.
22. Abutaleb A & Li V, Paging strategy optimization in personal communication systems, *ACM-Baltzer Journal of Wireless Networks*, **3**, 195–204, 1997.
23. The SUMATRA Web site: http://www-db.stanford.edu/pleiades/SUMATRA.html.
24. Orlik P & Rappaport S, A model for teletraffic performance and channel holding time characterization in wireless cellular communication with general session and dwell time distributions, *IEEE Journal of Selected Areas in Communications*, **16**(5), 788–803, 1998.
25. Khan F & Zeghlache D, Effects of cell residence time distribution on the performance of cellular mobile networks, *Proceedings of IEEE VTC '97*, Vol. 2, Phoenix, Ariz., May 1997, pp. 949–953.
26. Hong D & Rappaport S, Traffic model and performance analysis for cellular mobile radio telephone systems with prioritized and nonprioritized handoff procedures, *IEEE Transactions on Vehicular Technology*, **VT-35**(3), 77–92, 1986.
27. Jordan J & Barcelo F, Statistical modelling of transmission holding time in PAMR systems, *Proceedings of IEEE GLOBECOM '97*, Vol. 1, 1997, pp. 121–125.
28. Fang Y & Chlamtac I, Statistical teletraffic analysis and mobility modeling of PCS networks, *IEEE Transactions on Communications*, **47**(7), 1062–1072, 1999.
29. Zonoozi M & Dassanayake P, User mobility modeling and characterization of mobility patterns, *IEEE Journal of Selected Areas in Communications*, **15**(7), 1239–1252, 1997.
30. Fang Y, Chlamtac I & Lin YB, Call performance for a PCS network, *IEEE Journal of Selected Areas in Communications*, **15**(8), 1568–1581, 1997.
31. Jabbari B & Fuhrmann W, Teletraffic modeling and analysis of flexible hierarchical cellular networks with speed-sensitive handoff strategy, *IEEE Journal of Selected Areas in Communications*, **15**(8), 1539–1548, 1997.
32. Del Re E, Fantacci R & Giambene G, Handover and dynamic channel allocation techniques in mobile cellular networks, *IEEE Transactions on Vehicular Technology*, **44**(2), 229–237, 1995.
33. Yoon C & Un C, Performance of personal portable radio telephone systems with and without guard channels, *IEEE Journal of Selected Areas in Communications*, **11**(6), 911–917, 1993.
34. Yum T & Yeung K, Blocking and handoff performance analysis of directed retry in cellular mobile systems, *IEEE Transactions on Vehicular Technology*, **44**(3), 645–650, 1995.
35. Guerin R, Channel occupancy time distribution in a cellular radio system, *IEEE Transactions on Vehicular Technology*, **VT-36**, 89–99, 1987.
36. Bolotin V, Modeling call holding time distributions for CCS network design and performance analysis, *IEEE Journal of Selected Areas in Communications*, **12**(3), 433–438, 1994.
37. Lin YB, Mohan S & Noerpel A, Queuing priority channel assignment strategies for handoff and initiated access for a PCS network, *IEEE Transactions on Vehicular Technology*, **43**(3), 704–712, 1994.

38. Rose C, State-based paging/registration: a greedy technique, *IEEE Transactions on Vehicular Technology*, **48**(1), 166–173, 1999.

39. Rose C & Yates R, Minimizing the average cost of paging under delay constraints, *ACM-Baltzer Journal of Wireless Networks*, **1**(2), 211–219, 1995.

40. Lin YB, Reducing location update cost in a PCS network, *IEEE/ACM Transactions on Networking*, **5**(1), 25–33, 1997.

41. Akyildiz I, McNair J, Ho J, Uzunalioglu H & Wang W, Minimizing mobility management in next-generation mobile systems, *Proceedings of the IEEE*, **87**(8), 1347–1384, 1999.

42. Araujo L & de Marca J, A comparative analysis of paging and location update strategies for PCS networks, *Proceeding of IEEE ICC '98*, Vol. 3, June 1998, pp. 1395–1399.

43. Jain R, Lin YB, Lo C & Mohan S, A caching strategy to reduce network impacts of PCS, *IEEE Journal of Selected Areas in Communications*, **12**(8), 1434–1444, 1994.

44. Pollini G & I C-L, A profile-based location strategy and its performance, *IEEE Journal of Selected Areas in Communications*, **15**(8), 1415–1424, 1997.

45. Garcia P, Casares V & Mataix J, Reducing location update and paging costs in a PCS network, *IEEE Transactions on Wireless Communications*, **1**(1), 200–209, 2002.

46. Xie H, Tabbane S & Goodman D, Dynamic location area management and performance analysis, *Proceedings of IEEE VTC '92*, May 1992, pp. 536–539.

47. Jeon W & Jeong D, Performance of improved probabilistic location update scheme for cellular mobile networks, *IEEE Transactions on Vehicular Technology*, **49**(6), 2164–2173, 2000.

48. Bar-Noy A & Kessler I, Tracking mobile users in wireless communications networks, *Proceedings of IEEE INFOCOM '93*, San Francisco, Calif., 1993, pp. 1232–1239.

49. Akyildiz I & Ho J, Dynamic mobile user location update for wireless PCS networks, *ACM-Baltzer Journal of Wireless Networks*, **1**(1), 187–196, 1995.

50. Naor Z & Levy H, LATS: A load-adaptive threshold scheme for tracking mobile users, *IEEE/ACM Transactions on Networking*, **7**(6), 808–817, 1999.

51. Hwang H, Chang M & Tseng C, A direction-based location update scheme with a line-paging strategy for PCS networks, *IEEE Communications Letters*, **4**(5), 149–151, 2000.

52. Kalman R, A new approach to linear filtering and prediction problems, *Transactions of Basic Engineering*, March, 35–45, 1960.

53. Haykin S, *Communication Systems*, 4/e, John Wiley & Sons, New York, 2001.

54. Wong V & Leung V, An adaptive distance-based location update algorithm for PCS networks, *Proceedings of IEEE ICC '01*, Helsinki, Finland, June 2001.

55. Lee H & Sun J, Mobile location tracking by optimal paging zone partitioning, *Proceeding of IEEE ICUPC '97*, Vol. 1, October 1997, pp. 168–172.

56. Ho J & Akyildiz I, Mobile user location update and paging under delay constraints, *ACM-Baltzer Journal of Wireless Networks*, **1**(4), 413–426, 1995.

57. Wang W, Akyildiz I & Stuber G, An optimal paging scheme for minimizing signaling costs under delay bounds, *IEEE Communications Letters*, **5**(2), 43–45, 2001.

58. Tung T & Jamalipour A, Adaptive location management strategy to the distance-based location update technique, *Proceedings of Minitrack on Quality of Service in Mobile and Wireless Networks HICSS '36*, Hawaii, January 2003.

59. Tung T & Jamalipour A, A novel sectional paging strategy for cellular networks, *Proceedings of IEEE Globecom '02*, Taipei, Taiwan, November 2002.

60. Jain R & Lin YB, Performance of an auxiliary user location strategy employing forwarding pointers to reduce network impact of PCS, *ACM-Baltzer Journal of Wireless Networks*, **1**(2), 197–210, 1995.

61. Chen I, Chen T & Lee C, Performance evaluation of forwarding strategies for location management in mobile networks, *The Computer Journal*, **41**(4), 243–253, 1998.

62. Ho J & Akyildiz I, Local anchor scheme for reducing location tracking costs in PCNs, *Proceedings of IEEE MOBICOM '95*, November 1995, pp. 181–192.

63. Krishnamurthi G, Chessa S & Somani A, Optimal replication of location information in mobile networks, *Proceedings of IEEE ICC '99*, Vancouver, Canada, June 1999.

64. Mao Z & Douligeris C, A location-based mobility tracking scheme for PCS networks, *Computer Communications*, **23**, 1729–1739, 2000.

65. Bar-Noy JA, Kessler I & Sidi M, Mobile users: to update or not to update? *Proceedings of IEEE INFOCOM '94*, Toronto, Canada, 1994, pp. 570–576.

66. Madhow U, Honig M & Steiglitz K, Optimization of wireless resources for personal communications mobility tracking, *IEEE/ACM Transactions on Networking*, **3**(4), 698–707, 1995.

67. Akyildiz I, Lin YB, Lai WR & Chen RJ, A new random walk model for PCS networks, *IEEE Journal of Selected Areas in Communications*, **18**(7), 1254–1260, 2000.

68. Wang W, Akyildiz I & Stuber G, An optimal partition algorithm for minimization of paging costs, *Proceedings of IEEE GLOBECOM '00*, Vol. 1, San Francisco, November 2000, pp. 188–192.

69. Rose C & Yates R, Minimizing the average cost of paging under delay constraints, *ACM-Baltzer Journal of Wireless Networks*, **1**(2), 211–219, 1995.

9

Transport Protocols for Wireless IP

Transmission control protocol (TCP) is the *de facto* transport protocol for today's global Internet. It performs at an acceptable efficiency over the traditional wired networks in which packet losses are usually caused by network congestion. However, in networks with wireless links in addition to wired segments, this assumption would be insufficient, as the high wireless bit error rate (BER) could become the dominant cause of packet loss, thus making TCP perform suboptima under these new conditions. TCP breaks the first rule that we have in a layered network, that is, the independency of a higher layer protocol from its underlying lower layers such as link layer and physical layer. TCP makes strict assumptions on the reliability of the lower network layers, probably because it has been designed for wired networks with such reliable channels. As the main reason for this poor performance for TCP, we may raise the fact that TCP cannot distinguish between packet losses due to wireless errors from those due to congestion. Moreover, TCP sender cannot keep the size of its congestion window at an optimum level and always has to retransmit packets after waiting for time-out, which significantly degrades the end-to-end delay performance too. In this chapter, we will raise the above issues in detail and look into techniques that could improve the situation. Such an improvement is a significant requirement for the future wireless mobile Internet.

9.1 INTRODUCTION

TCP and Internet Protocol (IP) are, respectively, the transport and network protocols in the TCP/IP reference model. TCP/IP is the most commonly used IP suite and therefore

The Wireless Mobile Internet: Architectures, Protocols, and Services. Abbas Jamalipour
© 2003 John Wiley & Sons, Ltd ISBN: 0-470-84468-X

for the future wireless IP network, in which the generated data of the Internet applications need to be transported over the wireless link, TCP is of a great importance. Nonetheless, another well-used transport protocol, that is, the user datagram protocol (UDP), which is mostly used for real-time multimedia applications such as voice over IP, is also very important for the wireless IP networks. However, there are distinguishing features of the two transport protocols. TCP provides a reliable data transfer, that is, the packets in a network that employs TCP will be delivered in order, without loss and without any error. On the other hand, UDP provides an unreliable transfer, which means that packets could be lost, received in different order, or with errors. But TCP employs congestion and flow control algorithms to provide such reliability that is not included in the UDP. As a result, the TCP users' data rates are limited but the UDP can push the data in the network and grab the available bandwidth as much as possible. This latter feature of the UDP makes it a favorite candidate for multimedia data transfer in which more bandwidth is required. Since the unreliable protocol UDP will be on top of the other unreliable network protocol (IP) in a UDP/IP network, higher layers of the network, such as application protocols, need to provide reliability to the multimedia applications in an UDP/IP network.

Most of the Internet applications in the future wireless IP networks, such as web browsing, e-mail, mobile banking, e-commerce, and file transfer protocol (FTP), however, need to use the TCP services, because of the requirement of a reliable data transfer. Because of this, in this chapter we will focus our discussions of the TCP performance in a wireless network. In the next chapter we will consider the network protocol IP to complete our discussion.

TCP, as a transport protocol, provides a reliable ordered communication of data streams by implementing a duplex protocol, time-outs, and sliding windows. It can work anywhere, regardless of the underlying network architecture. IP, as a network protocol, on the other hand is a connectionless, unreliable datagram service that by using information in its datagram headers can route packets in the network. So, the combination of TCP and IP in a TCP/IP network provides a reliable data architecture useful in case such reliability is needed.

TCP, with the features listed above, works well in the wired networks, in which the TCP was originally designed and optimized. In wired networks with low BER of 10^{-8} or less, the main cause of a packet loss is the network congestion, and the window-based TCP can accommodate this very well. However, in wireless networks with relatively high BER, around 10^{-3}, TCP performs poorly, owing to lack of distinguishability between the packet loss due to network congestion and the wireless channel errors. Therefore, some modification in the TCP/IP network is necessary for the future wireless IP networks in order to realize a higher bit rate.

In this chapter, we will first provide a very brief overview of the TCP and then discuss its new requirements for deployment in future wireless IP networks.

9.2 OVERVIEW OF THE TRANSMISSION CONTROL PROTOCOL

Transmission control protocol has been the topic of many books in the past three decades (e.g. see References [1–8]). Many researchers have used this topic to investigate the performance of the TCP in different conditions and within different networks, both wired and wireless. In order to give the reader the basic understanding of the TCP/IP networks and the TCP as one of the transport protocols within the TCP/IP, in this section we will review the main features of the TCP. We have tried to make this section as concise and as comprehensive as possible for the purpose of the topic of this book and the consistency in its contents. Nevertheless, the TCP description and implementation should be covered by a complete book, and therefore readers who are interested in more detailed discussion on TCP are referred to the references provided at the end of this chapter. TCP is defined in several IETF (Internet Engineering Task Force) RFCs (request for comments) including RFCs 793, 1122, 1323, 2018, and 2581 [9].

9.2.1 TCP/IP architecture

Internet can be defined as a connection of nodes on a global network using a DARPA-defined (Defense Research Projects Agency) Internet address. The protocol suite that consists of a large collection of protocols that have been issued as the Internet standards is referred to as TCP/IP (transmission control protocol/Internet protocol) [4]. TCP/IP was a result of protocol research and development conducted on the experimental packet-switched network ARPANET funded by DARPA. In contrast to the OSI (open system interconnection) reference model, which was developed by the International Organization for Standardization (ISO), TCP/IP has no official protocol model, but can be organized into five main layers of application, transport, Internet, network access, and physical. The network access layer can further be divided into two sublayers called *logical link control* (LLC) and *medium access control* (MAC). Information data processed in each application on a host computer should go through all these layers until it can be transmitted through the physical media on a local area network (LAN) and through intermediate routing and switching facilities on the wide area networks (WANs) and the Internet. Figure 9.1 illustrates the connections and the required protocol stack in a simple TCP/IP-based network. In the figure, communications between two hosts, A and B, on LAN A and LAN B, respectively, are provided with logical and physical connection through the Internet.

The two main components of any Internet-like data network that are shown in Figure 9.1 are the hosts and the routers. Hosts include any type of computer such as personal computers and workstations. Routers forward datagram packets between hosts and other routers when there is no common link (e.g. a bus) connecting them. A router operates at the network layer of the OSI model to route packets between potentially different networks. Another component that could be considered here is a bridge, which operates at data link layer and acts as a relay of frames between similar networks.

In order that routers perform their task, they use special procedures called *routing protocols*. Routing tables are built using these procedures and then a router can select a path for any given packet from a source host to a destination host. In the case of several routers between a source and a destination, routing will be performed on a *hop-by-hop* basis, in which each router finds the next node (router) for sending a given packet until the packet reaches its final destination.

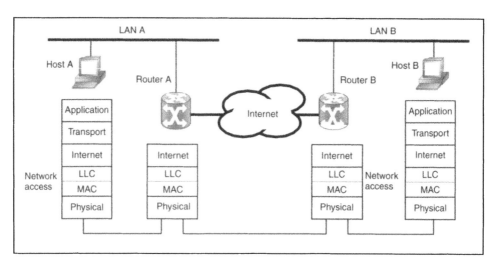

Figure 9.1 The Internet connectivity in TCP/IP networks

IP is the most widely used internetworking protocol at the Internet layer. An IP datagram includes a header and a payload. The payload of the IP packet contains all the higher layer headers such as TCP in addition to the application layer data. The header for the IP version 4 (IPv4) (i.e. the currently deployed version of IP) contains 20 bytes in addition to a variable size *options* field requested by the sending host. We will overview the IP and its header format in Chapter 10.

The transport protocol could be either TCP or UDP (as the most common transport protocols). As discussed earlier in this section, our emphasis is on TCP rather than UDP, and will be discussed shortly. UDP is defined in the IETF RFC 768 [9].

9.2.2 General features in TCP

TCP is an end-to-end, point-to-point transport protocol used in the Internet. Being a point-to-point protocol means that there is always a single sender and a single receiver for a TCP session. Being an end-to-end protocol, on the other hand, means that the TCP session should cover all parameters and transportations involved from the source host to the destination host. The latter is an important feature of the TCP and should never be forgotten during the analysis of any TCP/IP network or a protocol design.

TCP is a pipelined protocol. This means that the TCP packet data units (TCP-PDU), which are commonly named *TCP segments*, are logically enclosed in a pipe and thus they will be successively transported within the end-to-end TCP connections. This is one of the reliability features of the TCP, so that all TCP segments will be delivered to the receiver host in the same order that they have been transmitted by the sender host. This is of course logical, which means that even if the segments are delivered in a different order, TCP will make them in order before passing them to the higher layer protocol, that is, the application layer. Figure 9.2 shows the logical pipelining in TCP.

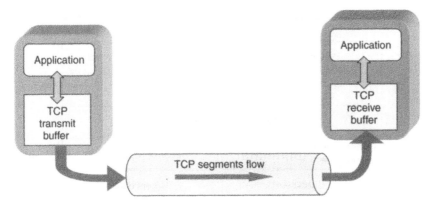

Figure 9.2   Pipeline configuration in TCP

There are buffers at both sides of a TCP connection. The TCP connection, however, is not seen by the network elements such as routers as they work at layers below the transport layer. These network elements just see the datagrams, that is, the IP layer packets.

TCP provides a means of full duplex data transfer. Therefore, a bidirectional data flow is available in the same TCP connection. TCP puts a maximum segment size (MSS) on its data. This MSS is usually less than 1500 bytes but in practical networks even smaller MSS is used, around 500 bytes.

TCP is a connection-oriented protocol. This means that before any data transfer could be started, a connection must be established through a process called *three-way hand-shaking*. During this process, the TCP sender and receiver come to an agreement in the establishment of a connection and set the relevant parameters such as MSS. This process involves exchange of several control messages. Such a signaling period before the exchange of data could sometimes put an unacceptable delay burden on the applications that are sensitive to delay such as real-time voice, and therefore is avoided in the UDP-type transport protocols.

TCP utilizes a complete flow control mechanism. By this method, TCP not only ensures that the sender host does not overwhelm the receiver host by sending too much data too fast but also ensures a fair bandwidth share among all TCP sessions concurrently used.

9.2.3   TCP segment structure

The TCP segment consists of a header and a payload. The payload includes the information data passed from the higher-layer application protocol for transmission. The payload has a variable size not greater than the defined MSS. The TCP header includes all information required for implementation of algorithms used in the TCP and the address information for the segment. An option field is included in the TCP header (which is usually not used) that can include specific information for a particular TCP connection. The existence of this field makes the size of the TCP header variable for different connections, so a header length field is also included in the TCP header, as shown in Figure 9.3.

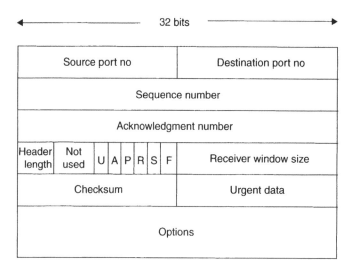

Figure 9.3 TCP segment header format

Sequence number and acknowledgment number field in the TCP header count the number of bytes transferred in the TCP connection for the purpose of flow control and reliable data transfer offered by the TCP. We will discuss these mechanisms shortly. Source port number and destination port number filed also provide correct pass of data to the applications. Note that IP is responsible for routing in the network and TCP is responsible for forwarding data to an application running inside a host. Checksum field is used for error detection and correction of the TCP segment header. Other bits used in the figure are used for connection establishment and sender–receiver synchronization, and so on [1].

9.2.4 TCP flow control

TCP utilizes a flow control mechanism in order that the sender host does not overflow the receiver host by transmitting too much data and too fast. Each TCP host maintains a receiving buffer with limited size. All data received from the IP layer come to this buffer before passing to the application layer. At each instant the buffer consists of two parts: the part that is filled with the TCP data already received and a spare part for accommodating new data. The size of the spare room is notified to the TCP sender through the receiver window size field in the TCP segment header. The TCP sender in response keeps the amount of transmitted, unacknowledged data less than the most recently received window size of the receiver. TCP uses the method of counting transferred bytes instead of segments. So in the beginning of a TCP session, a random number is used and then the transmitted bytes in each segment are biased by this number until all information data is transferred successfully.

By deploying the above flow control mechanism, TCP assures that the transmitting information data are never lost as a result of a full buffer at the receiver. The flow control is a mechanism to assure synchronization of writing speed by the sender and reading speed by the receiver. This compatibility arrangement in data rate speed used in TCP, however, could result in long delays in the transmission of data. For this reason, as mentioned earlier, delay-sensitive applications would prefer not to use TCP, despite its reliability feature.

9.2.5 TCP time-out mechanism

In order to avoid long delays when there is no response from the receiver in a TCP connection, a time-out mechanism is employed. Therefore, after each TCP segment transmission by a sender, a timer is set and it starts counting down. If the time expires but still there is no acknowledgement from the receiver, the TCP sender assumes that either the packet or the acknowledgment is lost, and so retransmits the same packet again until an acknowledgment is received.

The amount of time set at the timer is, however, of great importance. If the time expires too quickly, then premature time-outs will be generated during usual cases and thus unnecessary retransmissions will occur. On the other hand, if a long time is set for the timer, then TCP will slowly respond to the segment loss, which means longer delays in the transportation and overall end-to-end delay. Therefore, the TCP time-out must be set to be as optimum as possible.

TCP uses a mechanism to estimate the round-trip time (RTT) in the network, based on which the timer can be set accordingly. This will be done continually so that a variable estimation will happen. TCP collects information on the most recent RTTs and then makes an average value, calling it a sample RTT [2]. Estimated RTT is then computed in an iterative manner by using the following equation:

$$\text{Estimated RTT} = (1 - x) \text{ Estimated RTT} + x \text{ Sample RTT} \qquad (9.1)$$

This method is called *exponential weighted moving average* (*EWMA*) owing to the inclusion of the factor x. The method provides that the influence of the given sample decreases exponentially fast and puts more weight on recent samples instead. The typical value of x is 0.125. After computing the estimated RTT, the TCP timer is set equal to that value plus a safety margin, so that no unnecessary time-out would happen.

$$\text{Time-out} = \text{Estimated RTT} + 4 \text{ Deviation} \qquad (9.2)$$

where the *Deviation* is also computed iteratively using the EWMA method:

$$\text{Deviation} = (1 - x) \text{ Deviation} + x \text{ |Sample RTT} - \text{Estimated RTT|} \qquad (9.3)$$

9.2.6 TCP congestion control

Congestion in a network means that too many users send too much data for the connected network to handle. It has been an increasingly important problem in packet networks, so many researchers have devoted their time to handle this issue. TCP appreciates the fact that if the network becomes congested, no one can use the network resources at all and also the fact that when the network is congested, any additional transmitted packets would be lost because of lack of network resources such as the buffer space at the routers. So, in order to avoid further packet drop in such a situation, a congestion control mechanism should be implemented within the end host machines.

The congestion control employed in the TCP is different from other packet networks such as asynchronous transfer mode (ATM) in which an explicit feedback from the network assists in finding out a congestion situation. Such methods are called *network-assisted congestion control algorithms*. The congestion control used in TCP is an end-to-end congestion control and is not network-assisted. So there is no explicit feedback from the network layer to the TCP on congestion. The end systems need to find out a congestion situation in the network by using other factors such as experiencing longer-than-usual delay and more-than-usual packet loss in the network delivery of packets.

In order to control the congestion, TCP tries to limit its packet transmission rate until the congestion is recovered in the network. For this purpose, TCP maintains a congestion window of size W, which dictates the number of segments that could be transmitted by the TCP sender before the previously sent segments are acknowledged by the TCP sender.

Therefore, at each instant the TCP congestion window consists of two parts: the part that includes segments that have been transmitted but not acknowledged yet and the part that includes segments that could be transmitted without waiting for previous acknowledgments. If in any case all spaces in the congestion window are used, then the TCP sender has to stall until it receives acknowledgments for the previously sent segments. The segments that have been already sent but not acknowledged yet need to be maintained in the TCP congestion window in case a packet retransmission because of a packet loss or time-out is necessary.

By this method TCP controls the rate of transmission of the packets as well, and so control the congestion occurrence in the network. Therefore, the throughput of the TCP becomes a function of the size of the congestion window W as well as the round-trip time. If the throughput is measured in bytes per second, then with MSS bytes in each segment, the TCP throughput will be [2]

$$\text{TCP Throughput} = (W * \text{MSS})/\text{RTT} \tag{9.4}$$

The congestion control mechanism used in TCP allows probing for available bandwidth and ideally TCP transmits as fast as possible, that is, the congestion window is set as large as possible. So the TCP increases the congestion window size until a packet loss occurs (illustrating a congestion situation) and then decreases the congestion window size with the hope of recovering the network from the congestion.

On the basis of the above plan, TCP uses two phases during the congestion control. In the first phase, called the *TCP slow-start*, the size of congestion window increases by one segment per acknowledged segment after each RTT. So if the congestion window starts from 1, at the next RTT, the congestion window size becomes 2 assuming 1 segment has been acknowledged; at the second RTT, the size increases to 4 assuming 2 segments have been acknowledged; at the third RTT, the size increases to 8; and so on as a 2^n increase.

Therefore, the slow-start phase is not really slow but increases the TCP congestion window exponentially. This increase continues until a threshold level is reached when from that point the congestion window increases only by one segment linearly after each RTT, regardless of the number of acknowledged segments. The linear increase phase is called the *congestion avoidance* phase, and the slower increase in TCP congestion window size, that is, the number of segments that can be transmitted without acknowledgment (ACK), is reflected in the name of this phase.

The linear increase in TCP congestion window continues until a packet loss happens. At that time, the congestion window returns to its initial unity value and a new threshold is set equal to half of the congestion window size just before the time the packet loss happened. After that the TCP congestion window continues to progress in a similar way to what had been done before. An example of congestion control window progress is shown in Figure 9.4. In this figure it is assumed that initially a threshold of 16 segments is used and a packet loss happens at the transmission time of 8 segments. By that time the congestion window increases to 20 so that the new threshold is set to 10 segments for the next slow-start phase. The figure also shows that a second packet loss occurs at a time of 17 segments. Because of the shape of the curve shown in Figure 9.4, it is said that the TCP congestion control window has a saw-tooth behavior during its progress.

TCP has several different versions, the most commonly used in today's Internet being TCP Reno [10], TCP New Reno, and TCP Tahoe. The main difference among these versions is how they react to a packet loss event and how they recognize that a packet loss has actually happened. A detailed discussion on these TCPs is outside the scope of this book. As an example, a time-out illustrates packet loss in a TCP Tahoe, whereas a TCP Reno knows a packet loss when three duplicate ACKs are received. TCP Reno also skips slow start (fast recovery) after three duplicate ACKs but before the occurrence of the segment's time-out. TCP Vegas, another improved TCP [11,12], detects congestion even

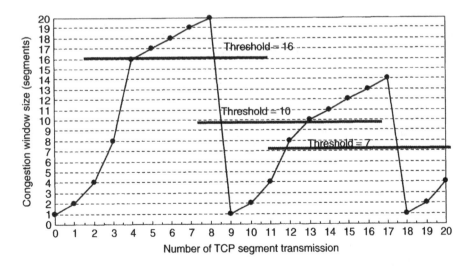

Figure 9.4   TCP congestion window progress

before a packet loss occurs by observing unusual increase in the RTT. By this method, the delay that results from changing the congestion window back to one is avoided and therefore a major improvement to the throughput of the TCP is achieved. Other types of early detection of congestion to improve TCP performance are also proposed in the literature (e.g. see Reference [13]).

9.2.7   Some conclusions on TCP

TCP congestion window progress is a kind of additive increase and multiplicative decrease. The congestion window increases very well but after a packet loss event, everything has to be started from the beginning. So in a network with a reliable physical layer, such as in a wired LAN, TCP should perform at very high efficiency.

TCP is also said to fairly share the link capacity with all users. So in a network in which N simultaneous TCP sessions are running, each connection will receive $1/N$ share of the total capacity. This can be investigated easily through the additive increase and multiplicative decrease mechanism used in the TCP congestion window size progress. Nevertheless, one can override this fairness simply by making multiple TCP connections at the same time or by using UDP as the transport protocol.

The TCP format on having slow-start and congestion-avoidance phases shows some effects in the delay performance of the TCP. It can be shown that the effect of slow-start in end-to-end delay performance is only substantial in high-speed networks and not when we use low rate links. This is because at high data rates, servers have to stall each time between each window because of the limitation of the TCP congestion control mechanism.

It can also be shown that the effect of slow start is most visible when the object size to be transmitted by the TCP is small or when the RTT is too long. These two cases can be expected because for sending a small object you still need to follow the phasing in the TCP and each step involves passing a RTT period. So when you want to send a small object or when the RTT is extremely long (such as in satellite links), using the TCP without any modification would cause some serious problems, both in terms of throughput and the end-to-end delay. Some of these issues will be discussed in Chapter 13.

To make a concise conclusion on the TCP, we may say that TCP provides a fair share link-capacity allocation to network users in terms of bandwidth and is a friendly approach in controlling the traffic load and thus the congestion problem in data networks. TCP performs this by employing congestion control and time-out mechanisms, both suitable and appropriate for the networks utilizing reliable and error-free channels, such as in a cable LAN. TCP has been developed and enhanced for many years and many applications use the TCP as their underlying transport protocol. However, all these have happened for wired networks and TCP has optimized its services on the basis of the assumptions generally applicable to wired networks. For the emerging wireless IP networks in which error-prone wireless channels are used, however, this will be a significant issue to see if TCP performs well or not. This will be our discussion from now on the end of this chapter.

9.3 TRANSMISSION CONTROL PROTOCOLS FOR WIRELESS CHANNEL

Because of the common usage of the TCP in Internet applications that require reliable data transfer, it is important to keep the TCP/IP protocol stack and also the network element structure as unchanged as possible even when mobility features required in wireless Internet are added to the network. However, TCP performs poorly in wireless networks running at high BERs and showing long delay as well as frequent and large delay variations. Therefore, a research challenge has been started in recent years on how the transport protocol (and particularly TCP) can be modified to be efficient even in error-prone and high-latency wireless channels, as it was in the wired Internet. The topic has made up many master and Ph.D. theses as well as numerous technical journal and conference papers in the last decade but the appropriate solution is yet to be discovered (see, for example, References [14–32]). This section is devoted to discuss this issue and to provide some numerical examples on the performance of TCP over the wireless channel.

9.3.1 Exploring the problem

Third-generation wireless networks are starting their services. These third-generation (3G) systems have promised to provide a range of Internet services in the mobile environment. For this purpose, they have been planned to use a packet core network (and eventually, an IP core network) in contrast to the circuit-switched network used in second-generation systems. This packet core network has been planned in order to provide service to the emerging packet-based applications, and in particular the Internet applications, more efficiently while it still can handle voice and other circuit-based applications, for example, by means of voice over IP techniques. 3G systems promised higher data bit rates, around 384 kbps to mobile users and up to 2 Mbps to indoor mobile hosts, than their second-generation (2G) counterparts.

Considering the dominant data traffic services promised in 3G systems and their connectivity with the backbone wired network, we could expect significant usage of the commonly used TCP/IP stack in these systems. This is due to the fact that many popular Internet applications, such as electronic mail, file transfer, web browsing, and remote network access, require a reliable data transfer, as the one provided by TCP, and that the vastly deployed wired Internet around the world has already adapted TCP/IP as its main protocol stack. In most situations, a mobile host will have some type of communication with a fixed host connected to the wired part of the network, as illustrated in the example given in Figure 9.5. Thus any extension of the wired Internet into the wireless environment should consider the usage of a similar protocol stack and also minimal change in the software deployed in the fixed hosts.

Mobile IP [33], defined in the IETF RFC 2002, tries to provide mobility features for the wireless and mobile Internet at the network layer. It modifies the, usually fixed, IP address of a host connected to the Internet into a virtual address form, namely, care-of address, so that the mobile host can move around and change its point of attachment

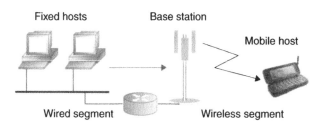

Figure 9.5   TCP packet flow in a heterogeneous wired/wireless network

to the network without violating the IP address configuration of the Internet and still maintain its connection. TCP, the transport control protocol of the TCP/IP stack, though not showing any modification requirement when the fixed network changes to a heterogeneous wired/wireless network, could actually implicate the performance of the Internet connectivity in wireless networks. The Mobile IP will be discussed in detail in Chapter 10.

TCP is the most commonly used protocol at the transport layer of the network stack in the Internet, originally developed for wired networks with low BER on the order of less than 10^{-8}. In this context, any wireless network with Internet service needs to be compatible with the protocol used in the wired network, that is, the TCP/IP. There are, however, some design issues in the TCP, which make it difficult to be used efficiently over wireless terrestrial and satellite links. Recently, there have been vast research activities comparing the performances of TCP in high-BER and high-latency channels (e.g. see References [16–21,23–31]) and modification proposals to improve its performance in terrestrial cellular and satellite wireless networks.

9.3.2   TCP performance expectation in wireless channel

TCP has been designed and tuned for networks in which segment losses and corruptions are mainly due to network congestion. This assumption might be invalid in many of the emerging networks such as wireless networks. The flow control mechanism used in TCP is based on time-out and window-size adjustment, which can work with high utilization in wired networks with low BER on the order of 10^{-8}. However, when the wireless channel is used (partially or totally) as the physical layer with a BER as high as 10^{-3}, it may perform inefficiently. The reason is that in the wireless channels the main cause for packet loss is the high BER and not the network congestion, as was assumed for wired networks. The low efficiency of the TCP in a wireless channel is a direct result of the fact that the TCP misinterprets the packet loss because of high error rate and because of congestion. Figure 9.6 illustrates this misinterpretation. On the other hand, in high-latency networks (such as cellular and satellite networks), adjustment of the window size could take a long time and reduce the system throughput.

TCP has the ability to probe unused network bandwidth by a mechanism called *slow start* and also to back off the transmission rate upon detection of congestion through the *congestion avoidance* mechanism. At the connection start-up, TCP initializes a variable called *congestion window* to a value of one segment. This variable determines the

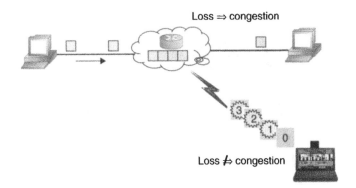

Figure 9.6 Wired network versus wireless network loss interpretations

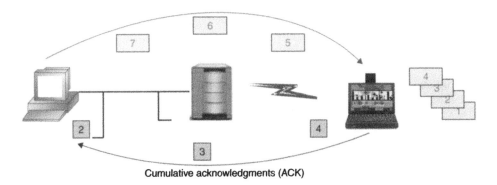

Figure 9.7 Cumulative acknowledgment in TCP

transmission rate of the TCP. The window size is doubled at every round-trip period and then increases linearly until a packet loss is experienced. At this time, the congestion avoidance phase is commenced, the window size is halved, and the lost packet is retransmitted. During this phase of the TCP, the window size is increased only linearly by one segment at each round-trip period and might be halved again upon detection of another packet loss. If the retransmitted packet is lost, the time-out mechanism employed in TCP reduces the window size to one. Since all these procedures are performed at the periods equal to round-trip delay of the channel, the system throughput could be degraded significantly where high-latency channels are involved. Figure 9.7 illustrates the transmission and acknowledgment exchange scenario in a wired plus wireless network.

As a result of the TCP behavior explained above, we cannot expect a very high performance for the TCP in wireless links. Figure 9.8 compares the performance of TCP Reno when it is used in a wireless LAN environment with that of the best possible performance in a wired network [23]. We keep this example as an indication of the poor performance of TCP in wireless network that should be addressed in future wireless Internet networks, but the reader may find it useful to get similar results for other types of the protocol and in other specific wireless networks.

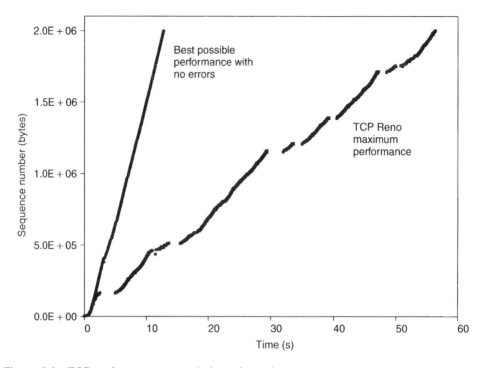

Figure 9.8 TCP performance over wireless channel

As a final note, let us provide a simple rule that can estimate the throughput of the TCP in a network that suffers from the wireless-type packet loss. This rule is based on the previously discussed Equation (9.4) provided for TCP throughput in a wired environment, that is, when the packet loss was only due to the network congestion. If there is packet loss other than that caused by network congestion, then a higher packet loss rate will result in a lower throughput, proportional to the square root of the packet loss rate. Also, a longer round-trip time in the network will result in a lower TCP throughput.

9.3.3 TCP enhancements

There are some modifications to the basic TCP that can be made so that the TCP can perform more efficiently in high-latency and error-prone wireless networks with Internet services. *Selective acknowledgment* (SACK) TCP [15,20], for example, is a method in which multiple losses in a transmission window can be recovered in one round-trip period instead of two in the basic TCP. SACK is effective when multiple TCP segments are lost in a single TCP window. This situation usually happens in networks with a large bandwidth-delay product and with high packet loss rate. In such a situation, the probability of multiple segment losses in a single window of data increases. As shown in Reference [20], in such networks, TCP SACK provides a superior performance compared with that of TCP Tahoe and TCP Reno.

TCP for transactions (T/TCP), another enhancement to TCP, also reduces the user perceived latency to one round-trip delay for short transmissions. In *TCP spoofing*, a router close to the base station is considered, which sends back ACKs for the TCP data. The responsibility for any segment loss in this method comes to the router. In another method, called *split TCP* [24,25], a TCP end-to-end connection is divided into multiple TCP connections (wired and wireless types) and a special *wireless TCP* connection is employed for the wireless link part. The method, which is sometimes called *Indirect-TCP(I-TCP)*, tries to separate packet loss over wired and wireless parts of the link (commonly occurring because of different reasons, that is, congestion versus BER) but asks for making a kind of violation in the semantics of the TCP as an end-to-end protocol. Figure 9.9 shows such a splitting mechanism.

Link-layer protocols are another alternative for improving the poor performance of TCP over wireless link (e.g. see Reference [22]). In these methods, usually forward error correction (FEC) or automatic repeat request (ARQ) methods are used to improve the performance. This method is illustrated in Figure 9.10. Independent timer reaction at link

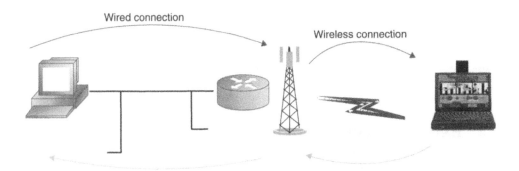

Figure 9.9 Splitting the TCP transmission path into two separate segments

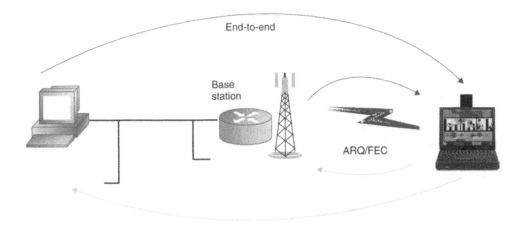

Figure 9.10 A link-layer approach to improve the transport-layer performance

and transport layers, which may result in unnecessary retransmissions, fast retransmission interaction, and large round-trip variations, are considered as major problems with link-layer approaches [19].

The last enhancement to the TCP for wireless channel that we will review here is called *Snoop protocol* [23]. In this method, the base station is equipped with a module called *snoop agent*, the function of which is to monitor the TCP packets transmitted from a fixed host to a mobile host and vice versa. The agent caches all these packets locally and in the case of receiving duplicate ACKs, retransmits the packets promptly and suppresses duplicate ACKs. The Snoop protocol performs retransmission of lost packets locally (at the base station) and hence avoids lengthy fast retransmission and congestion control at the sender side. By this method, end-to-end semantics of the TCP is maintained and performance of TCP is improved. The Snoop protocol is mainly used for the fixed host to mobile host direction, though an explicit loss notification (ELN) algorithm complementing the Snoop on the mobile host to fixed host direction has been later proposed in Reference [26]. A comprehensive comparison between the methods proposed for improving TCP performance over the wireless channel is given in Reference [19].

The research on modification of TCP to suit the wireless channel characteristics is ongoing and the interested reader may find it useful to check with the future related publications and also the IETF relevant working group activities [9]. In the following section, we focus our discussion on one of these modifications and provide numerical results and discussions for further exploring the topic.

9.4 EXPLICIT LOSS NOTIFICATION WITH ACKNOWLEDGMENT

The poor performance of TCP in error-prone wireless networks is mainly due to lack of explicit information at the transport layer as a result of a packet loss. This type of information was not required when TCP was developed since TCP had been designed to work in wired networks with low BERs and where the main reason for the packet loss was the network congestion. Other unusual reasons for the packet loss in these networks could be ignored without any difficulty in operation of the window-based and time-out-based TCP. For the wireless networks, if we can explicitly inform TCP the reason for a packet loss, then TCP will be able to maintain its throughput (i.e. not to reduce its congestion window size) if the packet has been lost not because of network congestion.

The methods reviewed in the previous section tried to improve the performance of TCP in wireless networks. But none of these algorithms actually lets the TCP sender know clearly whether the packet is lost because of wireless error or network congestion. This makes the TCP sender retransmit the packet as usual (or quicker than usual), subsequently being unable to keep the throughput high in the error-prone environment.

Snoop protocol [23] is a good scheme to improve the performance of TCP in a wireless network at fixed host to mobile host direction. But the Snoop protocol retransmits the lost packet like other link-layer solutions, not locally but through its snoop agent. The

Snoop protocol also suffers from not being able to completely shield the sender from the wireless losses.

Explicit congestion notification (ECN) method is another technique to improve the TCP performance in wireless links [32]. In this method, a TCP receiver informs the TCP sender of the network congestion explicitly through a bit called the *ECN-Echo flag*, when it receives an IP packet with the congestion experienced (CE) bit. Upon receipt of this information, the TCP sender reduces its congestion window.

On the basis of the performance improvements achieved in TCP Snoop and ECN protocols, a new protocol, namely, Explicit Loss Notification with Acknowledgment (ELN-ACK), is proposed that could remedy the limitations of the Snoop protocol [26–28]. In the ELN-ACK protocol implementation, it is required to make modifications to the structure of ACK packet, and the software part at base station, mobile host, and fixed host. These modifications, however, can be maintained at a minimum compared to other schemes. The method still looks at the throughput and delay performance improvement of the TCP at the fixed host to mobile host direction.

9.4.1 A new acknowledgment packet

In the ELN-ACK scheme a new form of acknowledgment packet called ACK_{ELN} is used. The sequence numbers of the four most recently lost packets judged by the mobile host and a bit called *the ELN bit* are included in the ACK_{ELN} acknowledgment packet. The purpose of the ELN bit is explicit indication of the reason for the lost packet. A '1' in the ELN bit indicates that the packet is lost in the wired network congestion, while a '0' in the ELN bit indicates that the packet is lost because of a wireless error. Therefore, the reason for a packet loss is explicitly informed to the TCP sender. The default value of the ELN bit transmitted by a mobile host is '1', that is, it is assumed that the corresponding packet was lost because of network congestion.

The ELN bit is judged at the base station. An ELN agent at the base station (to be introduced shortly) checks the information stored in the ELN bit to see if the packet has been lost before it arrived at the base station. If the agent finds that the packet was lost before it arrived at the base station, it retains the corresponding ELN bit at '1', otherwise it changes the ELN bit to '0'. After the ACK_{ELN} is processed by the ELN agent at the base station, it continues to transmit back to the fixed host. When the fixed host (the original sender) receives the ACK_{ELN}, the TCP sender will know the reason for packet loss from the ELN bit explicitly. A flowchart summarizing the ACK_{ELN} processing is shown in Figure 9.11.

9.4.2 A new agent at base station

Similar to the snoop agent used in the Snoop protocol [23], an ELN-ACK agent is introduced at the base station that has two main functions. One is to judge and store the packet loss information transmitted from the fixed host. Like ordinary wired networks,

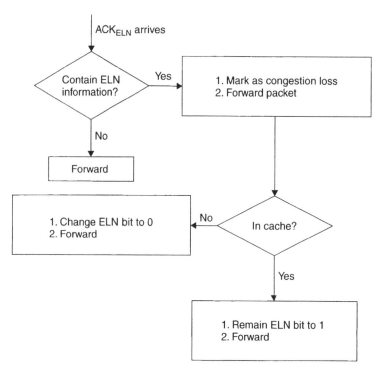

Figure 9.11   Acknowledge packet processing in the ELN-ACK technique

packets transmitted from the fixed host to base station may be lost because of congestion. If the base station receives a packet, which does not have an ordered sequence number, it will store the corresponding packet information in the ELN-ACK agent. Using the stored information, the base station can judge the reason for packet loss when it receives the ACK_{ELN} transmitted from mobile host. The second function is to judge the value of the ELN bit. When the base station receives an ACK_{ELN}, it will judge the lost packet on the basis of the stored information in the ACK packet. If it finds that the packet has been lost before arriving at the base station, it will fill the ELN bit with '1' to indicate the packet was lost because of congestion. If the lost packet has already arrived at the base station, it fills the ELN bit with '0' to indicate that the packet was lost in the wireless channel. Data processing procedure at the ELN-ACK agent is very similar to the one used in Snoop protocol.

9.4.3   Procedure at TCP sender

When the fixed host receives the ACK_{ELN}, it acts with the information stored in the ELN bit. If the ELN bit is '1', it means that the corresponding packet is lost because of wired segment congestion and thus it will proceed with the same procedure as in the window-based TCP algorithm. If the ELN bit is '0', it means that the corresponding packet is lost because of wireless error and thus it retransmits the packet immediately without any window reduction.

In the next section, the introduced TCP modification will be evaluated through computer simulation and at the same time the performance of the traditional wire-based TCPs will be examined when they are used in a wired-wireless network.

9.5 PERFORMANCE ANALYSIS

In this section, we will show numerically the poor performance of the traditional TCPs, used in today's Internet, while they are used in a heterogeneous network consisting of wired and wireless links. Performance of the proposed TCP enhancement in the previous section will also be compared to show how improvements of this type could achieve a more efficient backbone for the future wireless IP networks.

9.5.1 Simulation environment

Several experiments have been performed to measure the performance of data transfer from fixed host to mobile host. Figure 9.12 shows a simple network used for the simulations in this section to send TCP packets from a fixed host to a mobile host. The base station includes a finite-buffer drop-tail gateway, and the network consists of wired and wireless links. The ELN-ACK protocol has been implemented using C++ programming and the Network Simulator (NS-2) simulation package [34] has been used to simulate the TCP packet transmission in wired and wireless segments of the network. In the simulation, some parameters can be set to indicate different network conditions. These parameters are summarized as follows:

- Buffer size (B, packets) in the base station.
- Propagation delay (D, ms), which includes (1) the time between the release of a packet from the source and its arrival into the link buffer, (2) the time between the transmission of the packet on the bottleneck link and its arrival at its destination, and (3) the time

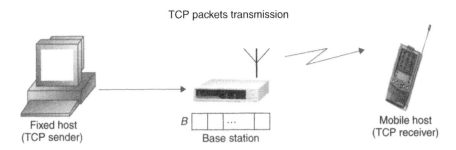

TCP packets transmission

Fixed host
(TCP sender)

B

Base station

Mobile host
(TCP receiver)

Figure 9.12 TCP simulation network

between the arrival of the packet at the destination and the arrival of the corresponding ACK at the source.

- The bandwidth (U, packets/ms) of the bottleneck link from base station to mobile host.

9.5.2   Throughput performance

The throughput performance, defined as the total number of original packets received by the receiver in a given period of time, of ELN-ACK, TCP Reno, TCP Tahoe, TCP Snoop, TCP Sack, and TCP Split have been investigated under different network conditions. The simulation results are shown in Figures 9.13 through 9.15.

In the simulation, first packet sequence trace of a bulk TCP transfer using the proposed ELN-ACK and the conventional (wired-optimal) TCP Reno has been considered. The simulation was performed under a typical wireless packet loss rate of 5%. It is found that in TCP Reno, when wireless errors occur, TCP throughput performance degrades significantly. In particular, it is observed that a coarse packet loss rate of about 5% led to a throughput performance degradation of a factor of 4.5 from ideal. A closer analysis of the packet sequence trace reveals the reasons for this poor performance. During the course of the transfer, packets are lost over the wireless link and need to be retransmitted. Every time the TCP sender detects the loss of a packet, it retransmits the lost packet, and also reduces its congestion window, ascribing the loss to network congestion. This is the correct interpretation for wired networks, but is usually an incorrect response in networks that have wireless links. As a result, the average TCP window size is small and time-outs are frequent. A stairslike packet transfer over time occurs in the process of the connection in TCP Reno due to these time-outs, which leads to degraded performance.

Figure 9.13 shows the throughout performance of TCP Reno, TCP Tahoe, TCP Split, TCP SACK, TCP Snoop, and the TCP with ELN-ACK under the condition that there is a buffer with a size of 5 packets at the base station and the propagation delay is 0.2 ms. The link bandwidth is set to 100 packets per ms for this simulation. On the basis of the results shown in this figure, the Snoop and the ELN-ACK protocols provide significant improvement when the packet loss rate becomes larger than around 0.3%. The throughput performance of the Snoop and ELN-ACK protocols, however, remains very close until a packet loss rate of 1%, but after that, the ELN-ACK performs better than the Snoop protocol. The better performance of Snoop and ELN-ACK compared to other TCP methods is clear since these two protocols provide better differentiation of the packet loss types over the wireless link (bit error–related packet loss) and over the wired link (congestion-related packet loss). However, the ELN-ACK protocol improves the throughput performance even more by sending information on the reason for packet loss to the TCP sender, whereas the Snoop protocol tries to handle all wireless-related losses at its snoop agent located in the base station. In other words, the ELN-ACK protocol adds extra features to the Snoop protocol and immunizes all packet loss even when the packet loss rate is high and the snoop agent cannot handle them. This is the reason for the better performance of the ELN-ACK compared to the Snoop protocol in high error bit rates.

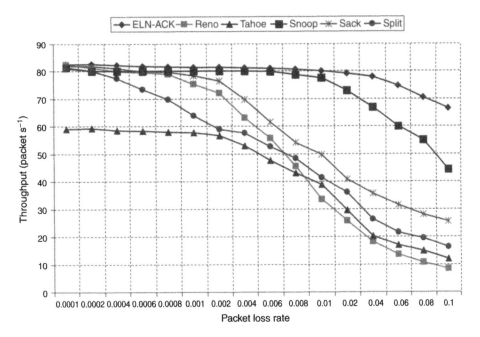

Figure 9.13 Throughput comparison for $B = 5$ packets, $D = 0.2$ ms, and $U = 100$ packets/ms

Figure 9.14 compares the throughput performance of TCP Reno, TCP Tahoe, TCP Split, TCP SACK, TCP Snoop, and the TCP with ELN-ACK protocols with the same conditions as used in Figure 9.13 but when the link has a smaller bandwidth. In this situation, packet contention rate is higher and thus the congestion-related packet loss becomes more important, and therefore the performance improvement of Snoop and ELN-ACK protocols is exhibited at higher packet loss rates compared to Figure 9.13.

With the same link bandwidth but with a larger buffer size at the base station, Figure 9.15 shows the throughput performance of different TCPs considered earlier. In this situation, ELN-ACK still performs the best compared to other schemes.

From simulations shown in Figures 9.13 through 9.15, it can be seen that the throughput of TCP Reno and TCP Tahoe drop sharply when the packet loss rate is increased to above 10^{-2}. Throughput of TCP Reno and TCP Tahoe drops to only 10%~20% compared with error-free wireless link, whereas the ELN-ACK scheme can keep the throughput as high as 80%~90% for error-free environment. There are significant performance benefits of using the ELN-ACK protocol. The main advantage of ELN-ACK is that it helps maintaining a large TCP congestion window at a high wireless error rate.

9.5.3 Delay performance

TCP Reno is the most popular type of TCP used in today's Internet. It contains a number of algorithms to control the network congestion while maintaining a good user throughput.

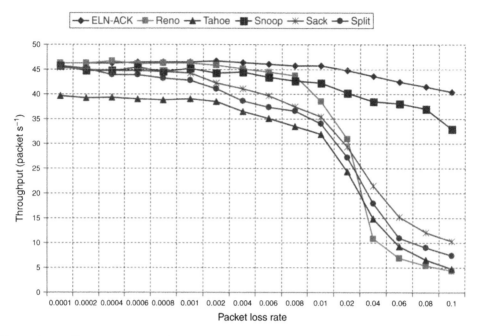

Figure 9.14   Throughput comparison for $B = 5$ packets, $D = 0.2$ ms, and $U = 50$ packets/ms

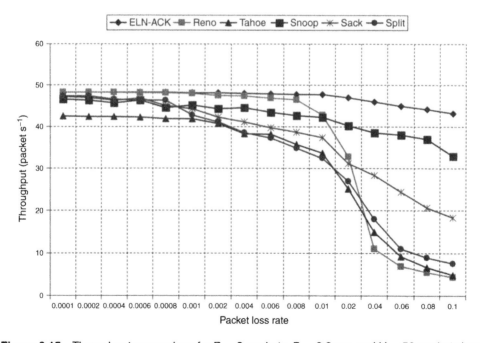

Figure 9.15   Throughput comparison for $B = 8$ packets, $D = 0.2$ ms, and $U = 50$ packets/ms

TCP Reno's fast recovery algorithm is optimized for the case in which a single packet is dropped for a window of data, but can suffer from performance problems when multiple packets are dropped because of the wireless error. In this section we illustrate the problem of TCP Reno and show the end-to-end performance degradation of TCP Reno in a high packet loss rate wireless channel. We also compare the simulation results of the TCP Reno algorithm with ELN-ACK to show the delay performance improvement of the TCP with ELN-ACK.

If the packet is successfully transmitted from a sender host to a designated receiver, the end-to-end delay is mainly determined by propagation delay, service time, and queuing at the base station. But if the packet is lost because of network congestion or wireless packet loss, the TCP sender has to retransmit the lost packet by performing a loss recovery process and awaiting time-out. As a result, the end-to-end delay becomes significantly long when a time-out happens.

Figures 9.16 to 9.18 show the delay of a 200-packet transmission using the TCP Reno and the ELN-ACK protocols. TCP Reno has quite good end-to-end delay performance in the absence of wireless error, as shown in Figure 9.16. The mean end-to-end delay is about 0.15~0.2 s. There are two packets with delays around 0.5 s; this is due to network congestion, and these two packets will be retransmitted by the loss recovery mechanism.

In Figures 9.17 and 9.18 the packet loss rate on the wireless link is 0.1; this means that in every 200-packet transmission there are about 20 packets lost in the wireless channel. On the basis of the simulation results, in TCP Reno the mean transmission delay is about 0.15~0.25 s and we can see that in 200 packet transmissions, there are 24 packets whose transmission delay is significantly above 0.2 s. These packets are lost somewhere (either because of network congestion or wireless error) in the network. Of the 24 retransmitted

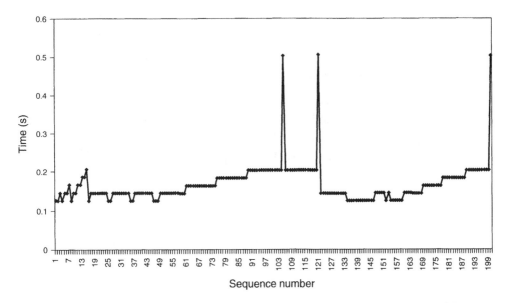

Figure 9.16   End-to-end delay for TCP Reno (without wireless error)

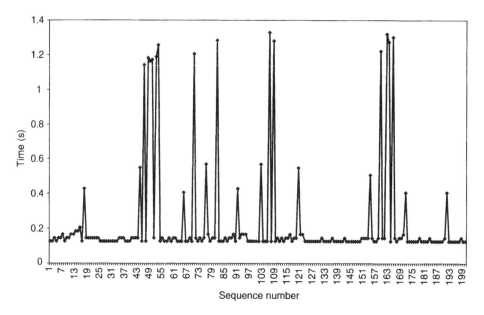

Figure 9.17 End-to-end delay for TCP Reno (wireless packet loss rate $= 0.1$)

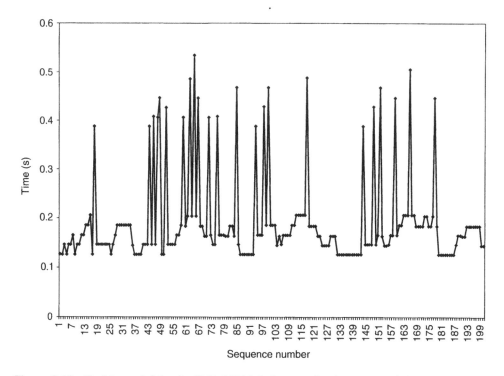

Figure 9.18 End-to-end delay for ELN-ACK (wireless packet loss rate $= 0.1$)

packets, 11 packets have the delay around 0.4 to 0.6 s; that means these packets are retransmitted by loss recovery mechanism without invoking time-out, 13 other packets have a delay around 1 to 1.4 s, which means that these packets are timed out. Because of the wireless packet loss, the TCP sender always has to wait for a time-out before retransmitting a lost packet. The ELN-ACK algorithm can efficiently avoid the time-out by retransmitting a lost packet immediately.

Figure 9.18 shows that there is no packet delay above 1 s in the ELN-ACK algorithm; all lost packets are retransmitted by loss recovery mechanisms or by fast retransmission. From Figure 9.18 we can find that the mean end-to-end delay for packet transmission is about 0.1∼0.2 s. There are 23 packets with end-to-end delay between 0.4 to 0.6 s. Most of these packets are lost in the wireless channel when it is first transmitted by the TCP sender. Unlike the TCP Reno, the TCP sender knows that these packets are lost because of wireless error and not because of network congestion. Thus, the lost packet can be retransmitted efficiently without incurring any window deduction, which avoids spending long idle time while waiting for the time-out.

9.5.4 Congestion window performance

The main reason for the occurrence of these time-outs in the TCP Reno algorithm is the small congestion window, which makes the TCP sender not to get enough duplicate ACKs in the procession and that the number of arriving duplicate ACKs is not sufficient to trigger a fast retransmission. The result is a time-out-driven retransmission that keeps the link idle for long periods of time. Figures 9.19 and 9.20 show the congestion window

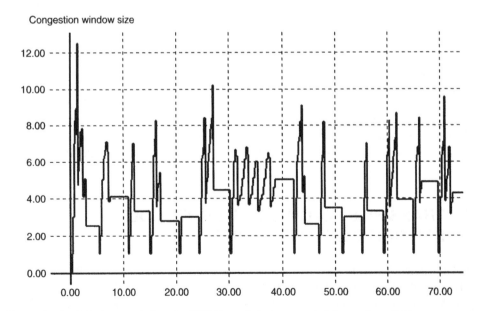

Figure 9.19 Window evolution for TCP Reno (wireless packet loss rate = 0.1)

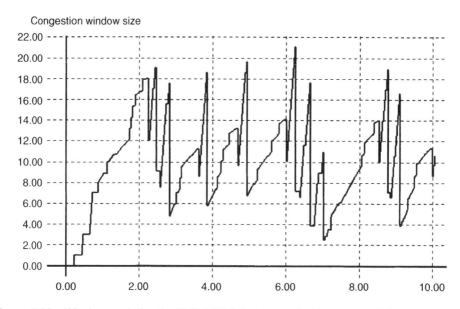

Figure 9.20 Window evolution for ELN-ACK (wireless packet loss rate = 0.1)

size in the procession of transmitting 200 packets for TCP Reno and TCP with ELN-ACK, respectively. From Figure 9.19 we can see that the window cannot be opened wide enough and is frequently reduced to one because of time-out. So in a high packet loss environment, the TCP Reno cannot efficiently transmit packets.

When there is no wireless packet loss, the only packet loss in transmission is due to network congestion. The TCP Reno sender retransmits the packet by using the loss recovery algorithm. The window size is halved when loss recovery happens, but no time-out happens because the congestion window is kept wide enough and there are sufficient duplicate ACKs transmitted back to trigger the loss recovery. The ELN-ACK performs similarly in the presence of wireless error, as shown in Figure 9.20.

From the above discussion, it can be seen that the ELN-ACK is an effective way to retransmit the lost packet quickly owing to wireless error, to keep the congestion window wide, and thereby to eliminate time-out and long idle time periods. Compared with TCP Reno, ELN-ACK algorithm significantly improves the end-to-end delay performance.

9.6 TRANSMISSION CONTROL PROTOCOLS FOR CELLULAR NETWORKS

Cellular wireless systems such as the second-generation General Packet Radio Service (GPRS) and third-generation Universal Mobile Telecommunications System (UMTS) and cdma2000 that provide data services such as Internet access have specific characteristics that determine the choice of transport protocol [35]. The first characteristic is their latency range. The cellular systems because of extensive processing delays at their physical layer, such as interleaving and other transmission delays at their radio access network, introduce high latencies. The typical values for RTT latency in these systems vary between a few hundred milliseconds and one second [35].

The data rates provided by the cellular networks are also different and usually asymmetric on uplinks and downlinks. A GPRS system, for example, has data rates of 10 to 20 Kbps in uplinks and 10 to 40 Kbps in downlinks. 3G systems will improve these figures to 64 Kbps in uplinks and 384 Kbps in downlinks in their initial implementations. Therefore, the bandwidth-delay product of the cellular networks will be between 1 and 5 kB for GPRS and between 8 and 50 kB for 3G. Such a link in a GPRS network is said to be long thin and in a UMTS network it is said to be long fat.

For both types of links in cellular networks, a good TCP performance will be possible by using large-size congestion windows. Loss recovery in long thin networks requires particularly a long TCP congestion window.

On the basis of these observations, in Reference [35] TCP SACK and TCP ECN are therefore recommended for cellular networks, both for long thin and long fat networks. In case the TCP SACK is not available, TCP New Reno [36] should be used in these networks.

Nevertheless, an appropriate TCP congestion window size selection has a significant role in the performance of TCPs in cellular network. The window size needs to be chosen in accordance to the cellular network bandwidth-delay product. In case the TCP specifications limit the choice of appropriate window size (e.g. as TCP limits the receiver window size to 64 KB), some other schemes such as the window scale option proposed in Reference [37] can be used.

The proposed TCP ELN-ACK scheme described in Section 9.4 and its performance evaluation presented thereafter illustrates a promising position for its introduction in the cellular data networks too.

9.7 SUMMARY AND CONCLUSIONS

While it is usually assumed that the efficiency of the higher-layer protocols are independent of their underlying protocol layer in a TCP/IP network stack, it is not really true in the case of the transport layer. If the traditional Internet's transmission control protocol is used in an error-prone wireless network, the congestion control algorithms deployed in the TCP cause an unacceptably low throughput and a large delay performance.

In this chapter, we have tried to explore the above fact by first outlining the techniques built in the TCP structure and then discussing their behavior under high BER and long delay conditions usually experienced in wireless networks.

We have provided a survey of the modified TCPs proposed in the literature in the past few years and then focused on a scheme in which the difference between a packet loss due to the network congestion and that due to a wireless channel error is recognized. Numerical results both on TCP throughput and end-to-end delay have been provided in this chapter to justify the poor performance of the traditional TCP in a wireless channel.

It is shown that some modification in the TCP is required if we look forward to a reliable wireless Internet in the future.

Nevertheless, it has been emphasized that the issue is yet to be resolved and still many researchers are working to improve the TCP performance. Since TCP relies on perfect assumptions of link and physical layers for the network (such as those usually available in wired networks), we can still keep TCP as it is and try to improve the performance and reliability at the lower layers of the network. Many researchers choose this approach and use FEC and ARQ techniques and similar methods to improve the performance of the wireless network without touching the congestion-control-based TCP. Cellular communication technologies such as GPRS and UMTS seem to take this approach in their wireless Internet services but on a long-term basis, enhancements in the old transport protocol would be necessary. This is because of the fact that whatever you do at the link and physical layers of the wireless channel, there are still some poor channel conditions that no lower layer protocol can improve.

REFERENCES

1. Stevens WR, *TCP/IP Illustrated*, Vol. 1, Addison-Wesley Longman, Reading, Mass., 1994.
2. Kurose JF & Ross KW, *Computer Networking: A Top-Down Approach Featuring the Internet*, Addison-Wesley, Reading, Mass., 2001.
3. Leon-Garcia A & Widjaja I, *Communication Networks—Fundamental Concepts and Key Architectures*, McGraw-Hill Higher Education, Boston, 2000.
4. Stallings W, *Data and Computer Communications*, Sixth Edition, Prentice-Hall, Upper Saddle River, N.J., 2000.
5. Comer DE, *Computer Networks and Internets*, second edition, Prentice Hall, Upper Saddle River, N.J., 1999.
6. Halsall F, *Data Communications, Computer Networks and Open Systems*, fourth edition, Addison Wesley, Reading, Mass., 1996.
7. Tanenbaum AS, *Computer Networks*, third edition, Prentice Hall, Upper Saddle River, N.J., 1996.
8. Comer DE., *Internetworking with TCP/IP: Principles, Protocols, and Architectures*, Vol. 1, Prentice Hall, Upper Saddle River, N.J., 2000.
9. Internet Engineering Task Force (IETF), Web site: http://www.ietf.org.
10. Padhye J, Firoiu V, Towsley DF & Kurose JF, Modeling TCP Reno performance: A simple model and its empirical validation, *IEEE/ACM Transactions on Networking*, **8**(2), 2000.
11. Brakmo LS & O'Malley SW, TCP Vegas: new techniques for congestion detection and avoidance, *Proceedings of ACM SIGCOMM '94*, October 1994.
12. Brakmo LS & Peterson L, TCP Vegas: end-to-end congestion control avoidance on a global Internet, *ACM Computer Communication Review*, **24**, 1995.
13. Floyd S & Jacobson V, Random early detection gateways for congestion avoidance, *IEEE/ACM Transactions on Networking*, **1**, 1993.

14. Floyd S, TCP and explicit congestion notification, *ACM Computer Communication Review*, **24**, 1995.

15. Mathis M, Mahdavi J, Floyd S & Romanow A, *TCP Selective Acknowledgement Options*, IETF RFC 2018, October 1996.

16. Chandran K et al., A feedback based scheme for improving TCP performance in ad hoc wireless networks, *Proceedings of ICDS '98*, 1998.

17. Kim D, Toh C-K & Choi Y, TCP BuS: Improving TCP performance in wireless ad hoc networks, *Journal of Communications and Networks*, **3**(2), 2001.

18. Xylomenos G, Polyzos GC, Mahonen P & Saaranen M, TCP performance issues over wireless links, *IEEE Communications Magazine*, **39**(4), 52–58, 2001.

19. Balakrishnan H, Padmanabhan VN, Seshan S & Katz RH, A comparison of mechanisms for improving TCP performance over wireless links, *IEEE/ACM Transactions on Networking*, **5**(6), 756–769, 1997.

20. Fall K & Floyd S, Simulation-based comparisons of Tahoe, Reno, and Sack TCP, *Computer Communication Review*, **26**(3), 5–21, 1996.

21. Xylomenos G, Polyzos GC, Metri P & Saaranen M, TCP performance issues over wireless links, *IEEE Communications Magazine*, **39**(4), 52–58, 2001.

22. Ayanoglu E, Paul S, LaPorta TF, Sabnani KK & Gitlin RD, AIRMAIL: A link-layer protocol for wireless networks, *ACM/Baltzer Wireless Networks Journal*, **1**, 47–60, 1995.

23. Balakrishnan H, Seshan S & Katz RH, Improving reliable transport and handoff performance in cellular wireless networks, *ACM Wireless Networks*, **1**(4), 469–481, 1995.

24. Bakre A & Badrinath BR, Handoff and system support of indirect TCP/IP, *Proc. Second Usenix Symp. on Mobile and Location-Independent Computing*, April 1995.

25. Bakre A & Badrinath BR, I-TCP: Indirect TCP for mobile hosts, *Proc. 15th International Conf. on Distributed Computing Systems (ICDCS)*, May 1995.

26. Balakrishnan H & Katz RH, Explicit loss notification and wireless web performance, *IEEE Global Telecommunications Conference (Globecom '98)*, Mini Conference, Sydney, Australia, November 1998.

27. Ding W & Jamalipour A, A new explicit loss notification with acknowledgment for wireless TCP, *The 12th IEEE International Symposium on Personal, Indoor and Mobile Radio Communication (PIMRC 2001)*, San Diego, Calif., September 30–October 3 2001.

28. Ding W & Jamalipour A, Delay performance of the new explicit loss notification TCP technique for wireless networks, *Proceeding of IEEE Globecom 2001*, San Antonio, Tex., November 2001.

29. Hu J-H, Yeung KL, Kheong SC & Feng G., Hierarchical cache design for enhancing TCP over heterogeneous networks with wired and wireless links, *Proc. IEEE Global Telecommunication Conference (Globecom 2000)*, San Francisco, Calif., November 27–December 1 2000.

30. Anjum F & Tassiulas L, An analytical model for the various TCP algorithms operating over a wireless channel, *IEEE Wireless Communications and Networking Conference (WCNC '99)*, New Orleans, 1999.

31. Prakash R & Sahasrabudhe M, Modifications to TCP for improved performance and reliable end-to-end communications in wireless networks, *IEEE Wireless Communications and Networking Conference (WCNC '99)*, New Orleans, 1999.

32. Perkins CE, *Mobile IP–Design, Principles and Practice*, Addison Wesley Longman, Reading, Mass., 1998.

33. Ramakrishnan K, Floyed S & Black D, *The Addition of Explicit Congestion Notification (ECN) to IP*, IETF RFC 3168, September 2001.

34. Network Simulator (NS-2) Simulation Tool, Web site. http://www.isi.edu/nsnam/ns/, 2000.

35. Inamura H, *TCP Over Second (2.5G) and Third (3G) Generation Wireless Networks*, IETF Internet Draft, draft-ietf-pilc-2-2.5g3g-10.txt, Work in progress, July 2002.

36. Floyd S & Henderson T, *The New Reno Modification to TCP's Fast Recovery Algorithm*, IETF RFC 2582, April 1999.

37. Jacobson V, Braden R & Borman D, *TCP Extension for High Performance*, IETF RFC 1323, May 1992.

10

Internet Protocol for Wireless IP

Network layer has a distinguishing role in realization of future wireless Internet protocol (IP) networks, and more generally, in any data packet network. The network-layer functionality could determine the efficiency of a wireless system and its performance in terms of quality of service (QoS) parameters. The main part of the network layer is the network protocol. In today's Internet, this is the IP that sits as the network protocol. Therefore, for the study of the future wireless Internet networks an in-depth understanding of the IP and recognition of its merits and drawbacks is of vital importance. This understanding will assist researchers in the field to find solutions for improving the IP toward its position within the future wireless IP networks. This chapter tries to provide such understanding by reviewing the current version of the IP, its next-generation format, and also the initiatives toward migrating the Internet into mobile environment.

10.1 INTRODUCTION

The Internet is probably most recognized by its simple but useful network layer. The network layer, which is sometimes referred to as IP layer because of the usage of the Internet protocol at this layer for the Internet, despite being only one layer of the multilayer TCP/IP model, has a significant role in providing Internet services to users.

The Internet had been developed originally through universities and governmental institutions as a kind of research project, and then started to provide services to the public, which is somehow on a free-of-charge format. This development was completely different from other telecommunications technologies such as telephony networks and television

The Wireless Mobile Internet: Architectures, Protocols, and Services.   Abbas Jamalipour
© 2003 John Wiley & Sons, Ltd   ISBN: 0-470-84468-X

broadcasting. The research nature of the Internet provided a free environment for the development of Internet services by the public. The main characteristic of the IP was that it could work independently from its underlying access technology, and thus the new development by the public had no significant effect on how the data originating from the Internet services was going to be transferred at the physical layer.

The new model used in the development of the Internet was brand new to the telecommunications industry and revolutionized computing, multimedia communications, and even the traditional telephony systems. The scalability of the Internet had a great share in making it so popular in a short period of time to the point that managing the network becomes unacceptably complex. The original free-of-charge service of the Internet was changing to a formal part of the telecommunications systems, which necessarily results in charging for providing the service.

The exponential increase in the number of subscribers to the Internet in all parts of the world has started research on new systems of Internet addressing. The increase in data rate speed provided by better physical media technologies also has initiated research on how the Internet routers can provide faster path selection and switching so that the total end-to-end latency of the network could be reduced. These new observations have finally resulted in a new generation of the Internet protocol.

In this chapter, we will first review the IP to see how it provides features such as scalability and an easy way of exchange of digital data without a geographical limitation. The IP version 4 (IPv4) as the version of the Internet protocol currently deployed is explained. We also show other protocols included in the network layer of the Internet.

Section 10.3 provides a comprehensive discussion on the next-generation Internet, or IP version 6 (IPv6), and explains the motives toward such a change in the IP. The transitional issues from IPv4 to IPv6 will also be discussed in this section.

In Section 10.4 the Mobile IP is addressed. How the fixed IP address used in the TCP/IP network can be used in a mobile environment is the subject of this section. The problems with the Mobile IP protocol and new research activities for improving the efficiency of the Mobile IP will also be described. Two other techniques to transfer the IP into mobile environment will be discussed in Section 10.5. Finally, we provide some concluding remarks in Section 10.6.

10.2   OVERVIEW OF THE INTERNET PROTOCOL

IP is the most widely used internetworking protocol at the network layer of a TCP/IP system. Network layer is available at all network entities, including end host, routers, and bridges. Note that this was not the case for the transport protocol (see Chapter 9 for details). Despite being a major part in network layer, the network layer, however, has more than just IP in its body. The three main sections of the network layer are as follows:

- Internet protocol (IP)
- Routing protocols
- Internet control message protocol (ICMP)

The IP protocol is responsible for (network or IP) addressing conventions, datagram (i.e. the network-layer packet) formatting, and packet handling conventions. Routing protocols are used for path selection within the network using routing tables. The common routing protocols in the Internet are RIP (routing information protocol, RFCs 1058 and 1723), OSPF (open shortest path first), IGRP (interior gateway routing protocol), and BGP (border gateway protocol). ICMP is used for error reporting and router signaling and is defined in RFC 792.

In this section, we overview some important features of the IP, again those that are relevant to the consistency of the contents of this book. Interested readers are referred to the numerous literatures available on the subject, some of them listed at the end of this chapter [1–9]. The materials provided here, however, require some basic knowledge on routing algorithms such as distance-based and link-state.

10.2.1 Hierarchical routing in the Internet

The Internet is a network of networks with tens of millions of end hosts, routers, and links. Management of finding a route within the complicated network mesh of the Internet is a task that can become very complex and confusing if appropriate methodologies are not adopted. In addition, there are many private and local networks within the Internet that want their networks to be administrated locally. Therefore, a hierarchical network management scheme would be the only choice in routing within the Internet.

The routers in the Internet are aggregated into separate regions called autonomous systems (AS) [2]. Therefore it becomes possible to define different routing algorithms for the routers residing in the same AS (intra-AS) and for the routing between pairs of ASs (inter-AS). Using this hierarchical method, the routers in the Internet can be categorized into those that are inside the same region or AS and communicate with other routers within the same AS and those that are connecting each AS to the rest of the Internet. We call the former type of routers local routers or simply routers and the latter type boarder or gateway routers. So, a gateway router on one side has the connection to its own AS domain and needs to use the routing algorithms used by all other routers within that AS and on the other side has the connection to the outside world and other gateway routers, and so needs to use the standard inter-AS routing protocols. Therefore, the gateway router protocol stack becomes dual stack to incorporate two different sets of protocols.

Intra-AS routing protocols are also called interior gateway protocols (IGP) and include RIP, OSPF, and IGRP as the most common protocols used in the Internet. BGP on the other hand is the typical example of an inter-AS routing protocol. Detailed discussions on these protocols can be found in Reference [2] and the references therein.

10.2.1.1 Routing information protocol

RIP is a distance-based routing protocol. It has been included in the Berkley software distribution UNIX in 1982. The number of hops is the distance metric in this protocol with a maximum of 15 hops. Each link is assigned a cost of one. Distance vectors are exchanged among neighboring routers every 30 s through an RIP advertisement.

The failure and recovery method in RIP is as follows. If there is no advertisement from a router for a period equal to 180 s, then it is assumed that the neighboring router or its link(s) is dead. A notice will be sent to the neighboring routers and those routers also send advertisements to their own neighbors with any update in routing vector, so the failure information is quickly propagated within the network. No further route is assigned through the failed router.

RIP routing tables are managed by an application-level process using user datagram protocol (UDP) as the transport protocol. Therefore, an application protocol is also necessary for the router, which in a usual situation does not go up to higher network layers.

10.2.1.2 Open shortest path first

OSPF is an open (to public) routing protocol that uses a link-state routing algorithm. Routing computations are based on the well-known least-cost-path Dijkstra algorithm [4]. Each node in the network has a topology map. Different from RIP, the advertisements in OSPF are sent to all nodes within the AS and not just to neighboring nodes.

There are some advanced features included in OSPF not included in RIP. All OSPF messages are authenticated and sent using TCP, and therefore a higher level of security than RIP is available in OSPF. Multiple same-cost paths are allowed in OSPF, whereas in RIP only one is allowed. For each link, multiple cost figures based on type of service are considered in OSPF. Integrated unicast and multicast and hierarchical OSPF for larger networks are also advantages of OSPF compared with RIP.

10.2.1.3 Interior gateway routing protocol

IGRP is a successor for RIP as a proprietary of CISCO. Like RIP it is a distance-based routing protocol. Several cost metrics such as delay, bandwidth, reliability, and link load are used in IGRP route selection. TCP is used to exchange routing information, adding the reliability of the protocol compared with RIP.

10.2.1.4 Boarder gateway protocol

BGP is the main inter-AS routing protocol used in today's Internet. BGP is a path-vector routing protocol. A path-vector routing protocol is similar to distance vector protocol, but rather than sending only the cost information, the entire path's information is advertised within the neighboring routers. So the routing advertisement includes not only showing the links to be used for routing packets but also explicitly notifying the intermediate routers. By this method, the use of a particular AS for the purpose of routing a specific packet is dictated, and in addition the traffic distribution among available links and paths in the network can be managed carefully.

BGP messages are sent using TCP instead of UDP used, for example, in RIP. BGP can be used for both intra- and inter-AS routing, so to differentiate the two, sometimes the terms internal BGP (IBGP) and external BGP (EBGP) are used.

10.2.2   Internet control message protocol

ICMP is used by hosts, routers, and gateway routers to exchange network level information. This information may include error reporting, an unreachable host, network, port, and protocol. ICMP may also be used for testing purposes in the network, such as for echoing a short message and its reply, where we want to check the availability of a network or a link. ICMP messages are carried within the IP datagram, so this protocol is a network protocol above the IP.

10.2.3   General features of Internet protocol

An IP datagram includes a header and a payload. Payload of the IP packet contains all the higher layer headers such as TCP in addition to the application-layer data. The header for the IPv4 (i.e. the currently deployed version of IP in the Internet) contains 20 bytes in addition to a variable-size 'options' field requested by the sending host. We discuss IPv4 in this section and leave the discussion on IPv6 (or next-generation IP, IPng) to the next section.

The IP header is the most significant part of the IP functionality. The most important parts of the header are the source address and the destination address. These are 32-bit IP addresses, as shown in Figure 10.1, assigned to each network interface of a node. A node with multiple interfaces, such as a router, then has more than one IP address. Each IP address has a network-prefix portion and a host portion. A network-prefix is identical for all nodes attached to the same link, whereas the host portion is unique for

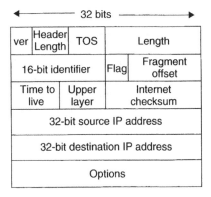

Figure 10.1   The IPv4 datagram header

each node on the same link. In the IPng, that is, IPv6, address fields are extended into 128 bits, which increases the available number of hosts in the network. Moreover, in IPv6, options are placed in separate optional headers that are located between the IPv6 header and the transport-layer header. This will speed up router processing of datagrams. In addition, other enhancements, such as address autoconfiguration, increased addressing flexibility for scalable multicast routing, and resource allocation that allows labeling of packets belonging to a particular traffic flow for special handling, are included in the new version of IP.

The most important task to be performed by the IP layer is routing. Whenever a packet is received by a node, a host or a router, for which the node is not its final destination (i.e. having a different destination IP address as the receiving node), the node must find out where the packet should be routed, in order to be closer to its final destination. Therefore, in the process of routing a packet, a forwarding decision must be made by each node. This decision can be made using an IP routing table, which is maintained at each node.

Each row of the routing table usually has four components, namely, target, prefix-length, next-hop, and interface. Whenever a node has a packet to forward, it checks for a matching between the packet's IP destination address field and the left-most prefix-length bits of the target field within the rows of the table. If such a match is found, the packet will be forwarded to the node identified by the next-hop field via the link specified in the interface field in that row. In the case of more than one matching, the packet is forwarded to the one that has the largest prefix-length. This will ensure that the next node is the node closest to the final destination. An entry in the routing table might be a host-specific route, with the prefix-length of 32, which can match with only one IP destination address; a network-prefix route, with a prefix-length between 1 and 31 bits, which match all destination IP addresses with the same network-prefix; or a default route, with a prefix-length of zero. This last route will match all IP addresses but will be used only when no other matching is found.

The routing tables might be created statically (manually) or dynamically. Usually, these routing tables are produced using one of the common shortest-path or least-cost algorithms such as Dijkstra or Bellman–Ford algorithms [4], widely used in other packet-switched networks. Because the Internet routing is based upon the network-prefix portion of the packet destination address, it greatly improves the scalability of the Internet.

10.2.3.1 Classful and classless addressing

Two types of addressing are possible in the Internet. The first one uses classes indicated as A, B, C, and D, as shown in Figure 10.2. As seen in the figure, the classes used are different numbers of bits in their network and host address portions. Class A starts with a 0 bit at the left-most bit position in its IP address, whereas classes B, C, and D start with 10, 110, and 1110, respectively. The remaining bits in the IP address for each class are used for separating host numbers. Therefore, each class can accommodate a limited number of hosts. On the basis of this figure, Table 10.1 lists the address allocation boundaries for each class.

The main problem with classful addressing is that it does not efficiently use the available IP address spaces, and especially with the increasing number of Internet hosts and routers,

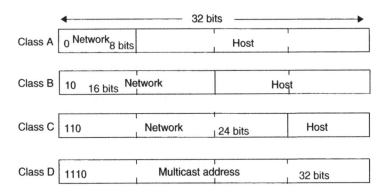

Figure 10.2 Classful addressing in the Internet

Table 10.1 Address allocation boundaries in each class

Address class	Address allocation from	Address allocation to
A	1.0.0.0	127.255.255.255
B	128.0.0.0	191.255.255.255
C	192.0.0.0	223.255.255.255
D	224.0.0.0	239.255.255.255

the space becomes more and more scarce. As an example, a class B network is allocated with 65 K IP addresses, and if there are only 10 K in that network, no other network could use the unused space in that network.

For this purpose, today's Internet uses a classless addressing method called classless inter-domain routing (CIDR) that allows an arbitrary size of the network portion in the IP address. Therefore, each IP address is shown in the form of *a.b.c.d/x*, where *x* specifies the number of bits used in the network portion of the IP address.

IP addresses can be set to a user manually by the network administrator or through an automatic method, called dynamic host configuration protocol (DHCP). DHCP allocates an unused IP address to a user upon receiving a request, for example, during the setup phase in a dial-up Internet connection.

Each Internet service provider (ISP) has access to a block of IP addresses for allocation to its users. Those addresses are managed by the Internet Corporation for Assigned Names and Numbers (ICANN), who has the authority to allocate IP addresses, manage domain name servers (DNS), assign domain names, and resolve disputes.

10.2.3.2 IP fragmentation and reassembly

The second four bytes in the IPv4 header are used for fragmentation (sometimes called segmentation) and reassembly of the IP datagrams. Fragmentation is used when the IP datagrams are too long for transmission. This method as we will see later, is disappeared in the next-generation IP, because it causes major processing delay and burden to the network routers.

Network links have a maximum transfer unit (MTU) indicator that shows the maximum length of a link-layer frame. In case an IP datagram is longer than this MTU, it needs to be split into smaller datagrams before it can be forwarded to the link layer. This is called an IP fragmentation. The opposite process at the receiving side of the network is called reassembly of the IP datagram portions into the original datagram. The 16-bit identifier, flags, and fragment offset fields in the IP header are used to make sure that the process of fragmentation and reassembly is performed without any information loss.

The length field in the IP datagram shows the size of the datagram being transmitted. For each datagram that needs fragmentation, a fragmentation identification number is assigned and will be carried within the header fields of all associated portions of that datagram. The last portion of the datagram is shown by a 0 flag in its header, whereas the previous portions use a flag of 1 in their header. The fragment offset is used to check for missing fragments.

Fragmentation and reassembly put extra and unnecessary burden to the network and thus it is better that they are avoided. One simple way is to ask the transport protocol, for example, TCP, to send shorter segments, so that even after the addition of the TCP header (20 bytes) and the IP header (20 bytes), the IP datagram is still short enough to be sent to the link layer.

10.3   INTERNET PROTOCOL VERSION 6

Sixteen years after introduction of IPv4 in 1978, Internet Engineering Task Force (IETF) [9] has started its activities toward development of the IPng. Sixteen years is a long period of time for the fast-growing IP technology and during that period many potential provisions have been adopted by network operators. Therefore, virtually a version 5 of the IP has been unofficially implemented in the network, so the IPng has been called IPv6. (See also References [10–12].)

10.3.1   IPv6 motivations

The initial motivation for changing the IP was that the 32-bit IP address space that has been included in the IP header was going to be fully allocated; some expect that this will happen by the year 2008. The 32-bit address field in the IPv4 header theoretically can provide 4.29 billion IP addresses, but in reality only 200 million addresses are useable. This number cannot accommodate the current Internet growth rate, and with the introduction of future Internet hosts such as cellular phones and embedded Internet, this number is definitely too small.

For the current needs a network address translator (NAT) server can fix the problem cosmetically by multiple usage of a single IP address. However, in the long term a more reasonable solution is required, even after disregarding other problems caused by the NAT approach in this solution, such as network security vulnerabilities. The IPv6 thus has been planned to have 128 bits in the address field giving 2^{1033} useful IP addresses to the Internet. It is said that this number will be sufficient if we want to give an IP address to each grain of sand found on the Earth.

There was, however, more to this initial motive in the development of IPv6. Firstly, when there is enough number of available IP addresses, manual device configuration or automatic DHCP for IP address would not be necessary, and therefore the future Internet will enjoy autoconfiguration. Secondly, the QoS could be better managed and provided with a better IP header design. Thirdly, some changes in the IP header format assists faster processing speed and datagram routing, enabling the future high-speed networks. Finally, the download delay of the web sites, which currently becomes a major problem with high-demand sites, could be shortened by the inclusion of the new anycast address. This means that the best server among some available replicated or mirror servers will be used for routing.

10.3.2 IPv6 header format

The IPv6 datagram header, different from IPv4, has a *fixed* length of 40 bytes. Therefore, there will be no option field as in IPv4 in IPv6. This will speed up the routing process at the intermediate routers in the network. The approach can be seen as a similar one used during the invention of asynchronous transfer mode (ATM) with fixed-size cells compared to variable-size packets in previous packet-switched networks, which has resulted in higher speed of the ATM. The header format of an IPv6 datagram is shown in Figure 10.3.

All fields related to the fragmentation and reassembly used in IPv4 have now disappeared in IPv6. It is simply because of this that IPv6 does not allow any fragmentation of the IP datagrams. With this method a major burden from the routers has been taken off and this can speed up the routing process and delivery of the data within the Internet. The task is, however, forced into higher layers in the network, most closely, the transport layer. Therefore, TCP in IPv6 networks has to limit the size of its segments to be passed to the network layer. Since TCP is implemented at the end hosts rather than at the router,

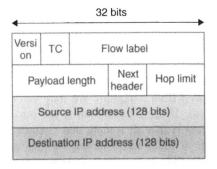

Figure 10.3 IPv6 datagram header format

it would mean a shift in complexity from the core network into the edge network. A similar phenomenon has been seen during the move from the circuit-switched telephony networks with simple end hosts (i.e. telephone sets) to the advanced packet-switched networks such as Internet with intelligent end hosts (i.e. digital computers). Now the end host computers will become even more advanced to do more tasks than in the past.

Source and destination address fields have 128 bits each. The payload length field shows the size of the data information part of the IP datagram, and the next header field provides inclusion of longer headers within the payload of the IPv6 datagram, which was already within the header's option field in the IPv4. The hop limit field in the IPv6 header is a down counter to avoid unlimited circulation of a single datagram within the network.

The traffic class field as an 8-bit indicator replaces the type of service field used in IPv4. This field can be used for treating different types of network traffic differently, to provide QoS allocation in the network. The flow label also identifies the datagrams into real-time and non-real-time traffics, thus making the multimedia traffic delivery in the future Internet easier and with a better quality than that provided in IPv4.

10.3.3   Internet protocol transition

Maybe one of the most critical things during the transition of an old system to a new one is how such a transition could be implemented. Specifically, for the Internet with hundreds of millions of nodes, end hosts, and networks, it will be impossible to turn off the network even for a short period of time, while the node protocols are upgrading. Therefore, for sometime we should think of having both IPv4- and IPv6-enabled nodes in the Internet, until all worldwide routers and hosts could be upgraded [2]. Similar to any system upgrades, two logical approaches are possible for the transition period of IPv4 into IPv6: dual-stack approach and encapsulation. Nevertheless, we need to consider the IPv6 datagram deliveries from an end-to-end point of view between a pair of source destination hosts.

10.3.3.1 Dual-stack approach

Assume that during an end-to-end path between a router at the source network and a router at the destination network, which is used for the delivery of an IPv6 datagram in the Internet, there is a network with nonupgraded routers still running the IPv4 protocol. In order to deliver the desired IPv6 datagram, we may use other alternative paths that do not include IPv4 networks. If such a selection is not possible or not economic, then what we can do? One method is that all routers that connect the outside network to the nonupgraded network of IPv4 router have included a dual network stack, on one side IPv6 and the other side IPv4. With this method, all IPv6 datagrams addressed to the IPv4 network are passed through this dual-stack input router and the router translates (formats)

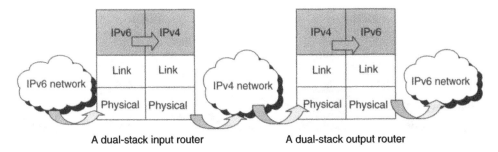

A dual-stack input router   A dual-stack output router

Figure 10.4   Dual-stack approach in transition between IPv4 and IPv6

the IPv6 header into IPv4, which can be delivered by the old network. Such a dual-stack input router is shown in Figure 10.4.

Each IPv6 datagram is passed through the dual-stack router and its header is reformatted in accordance with the IPv4 header format. This method should solve the problem. When the datagram goes out from the IPv4 network, it will be again reformatted as an IPv6 datagram by a dual-stack output router and then passed to the IPv6 network for future delivery in the Internet.

The method looks workable but we should consider the fact that in the IPv6 header there are some information that have no place in the IPv4. For example, the information related to the flow type in flow label field of IPv6 will be lost during the translation of IPv6 header into IPv4 header. If these information are not vital for the purpose of the delivery of data for a particular Internet service, then the dual-stack approach is fine. Otherwise, we should use the encapsulation approach.

10.3.3.2 Encapsulation approach

Encapsulation approach in the transitional period is easier in concept than the dual-stack one. It does not encounter any reformatting of the IPv6 header into an IPv4 header by the IPv4 network boarder routers. The method is as simple as putting the IPv6 datagram, including its header and payload, within the payload of an IPv4 datagram and leaving it to the nonupgraded IPv4 network for delivery. At the output port of the IPv4 network, the IPv6 datagram is decapsulated from the IPv4 datagram payload and passed into the new IPv6 network. The process of encapsulation and decapsulation of the IPv6 datagrams is illustrated in Figure 10.5.

In the process of encapsulation and decapsulation of the IPv6 datagrams, no IPv6 related information is lost, compared with the dual-stack approach in which the new information such as flow label were corrupted. This method is sometimes called tunneling and is considered as the promising approach during the transition period of upgrading all networks to IPv6.

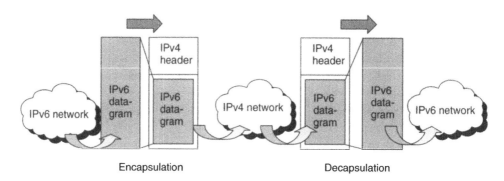

Figure 10.5   Encapsulation approach in transition between IPv4 and IPv6

10.3.4   Current status of IPv6

Despite all benefits considered in the IPv6 as discussed earlier, the progress in implementation of the new IP is not so good [13]. The main reason would be the little support for IPv6 in North America by the ISPs. This may be because of the fact that the biggest portion of the current IP address space is allocated to those areas. The shortage of the IP address therefore is mainly felt in Asian countries where the number of Internet users is growing very rapidly in recent years.

It is also correct that there is more demand in Asian countries because of the profusion of smart cellular phones and portable personal digital assistants (PDA) with Internet capabilities that require more IP addresses.

The main obstacles for the IPv6 progress are

- cost and effort required to migrate to IPv6,
- protocol's shortcomings, and
- perceived lack of need for standard's advantages.

The current version of the IP is working fine for many of its users and unless there is a common problem for the majority of those users, no one wants to do extra improvements, which essentially require capital funds. Indeed, there will be a huge cost and effort involved in any migration to a new protocol at the network layer.

The IPv6 despite its long history of development does not resolve all issues with the IPv4 and this would be another reason for the slow progress in its deployment in the Internet. More enhancements based on current and future requirements of the Internet still need to be included in IPv6. Apart from the above issues, there are some problems from both vendors and users in support of the new IP.

10.3.4.1 Vendor support

There is certainly very little support from the network vendors in the development of IPv6-compatible equipments required in the network, such as routers and switches. This problem accordingly is slowing down the process of migration to the new network. Some of the few developments in this way are introduced here.

IBM has developed UNIX equipment with the operating system and TCP/IP stack that supports IPv6 in 1997, called RS/6000 server. More recently OS/390 servers also support IPv6. CISCO systems IOS (Internetworking Operating System) routers are also developed to support IPv6. Microsoft developer's IPv6 technology in the Windows 2000 and the Internet Explorer bundled with Windows XP are also supposed to support IPv6.

Sun Microsystems support of IPv6 is seen in the Solaris 8 operating system and the Java Development Kit version 1.4. Several Japanese companies such as Fujitsu (GeoStream R940 router), Hitachi (GR2000 backbone router), Matsushita (IPv6 security gateway and router), NEC (IP8800/700 series switch), and Sony (PlayStation system with IPv4/IPv6 dual stack) have started their work on supporting equipment for IPv6 [13].

10.3.4.2 User support

Network vendors have started releasing IPv6 compatible products. But IPv6 will not gain support until ISPs and enterprises use the protocol in their equipment and software. Sequentially, enterprises are not going to activate IPv6 capabilities unless their business partners do so. This makes a long-delay loop toward deployment of IPv6 in the Internet.

Owing to a serious need for the allocation of more IP addresses to the ever-increasing number of Internet users (both mobile and fixed) in Asian countries, deployment of IPv6 networks are more active in the Asian-Pacific region. For example, a new IPv6 network has been developed from scratch in this region and the Japanese NTT OCN (Open Computer Network) has developed an IPv6 native gateway service (which is an IPv6 tunneling service) as the first global IPv6 backbone.

10.3.5 Wireless: direction for IPv6

Even if the current dominant fixed access of Internet can be handled by the IPv4 in most parts of the world, by the introduction of more mobile and portable Internet-enabled devices, it will be revealed that there is no choice other than full deployment of the IPv6 in the Internet. The number of mobile Internet devices such as PDAs, cellular phones, pocket PCs, and laptop computers will be growing in the near future at a rate not imaginable in the fixed Internet era a few years ago. At that time, the shortage of the IP addresses will be cleared for all countries including those that currently have access to many IP addresses. The number of Internet users will soon pass the one-billion level.

Network address translation schemes, such as NAT, are capable of a little cure for the IP address shortage problem. They could, however, act as the protocol translators (from IPv4 to IPv6 and vice versa) in the next few years during the transitional period. IPv6 networks will be developed and spread and direct access to those networks by upgraded hosts and routers and indirect access to them from nonupgraded networks and

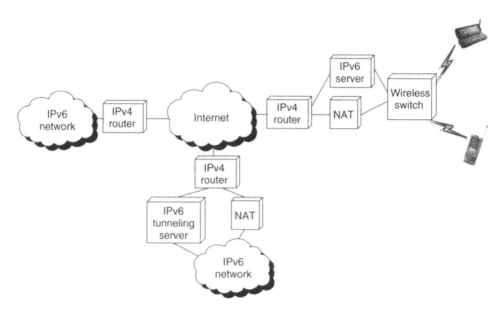

Figure 10.6   The wireless direction for IPv6

users through tunneling and dual-stack methods will soon become common. Figure 10.6 illustrates the above scenario.

10.4   MOBILE IP

We cannot conclude the chapter on the IP without a look at the Mobile IP, the protocol that was invented to resolve the address portability of the Internet. In this section, we will overview the Mobile IP protocol, originally introduced by Charles Perkins in the IETF RFC 2002 [14]. Since then many literatures and books have been written on the subject of Mobile IP (see, for example, References [15–26]), but it is yet to get a stable stand in the Internet. RFC 2002 was then updated to RFC 2290 [27] and RFC 2794 [28], and after that they were replaced by the RFC 3220 [29]. At the time of writing this book, RFC 3344 [30] was the most recent draft on Mobile IP. In the first two subsections, we will describe the Mobile IPv4 so that the reader becomes familiar with the original concepts, and after that, the new features provided in Mobile IPv6 will be outlined.

10.4.1   Protocol overview

As it was explained in the preceding chapter, TCP is an end-to-end protocol. This necessarily means that the TCP end hosts need to keep their IP addresses fixed during any single session. Such a fixed IP address can be renamed as the home address of the host, that is, an address that has been given to the host by his home network administrator. However, if the host wants to physically move to another network, then the IP address of the host needs to be changed. So, a new care-of address (CoA) is given to the mobile host (MH). This CoA could be interpreted as a temporarily allocated IP address while the host is visiting another (foreign) network.

Having defined these two types of addresses, Mobile IP protocol considers the *mobility* problem in the IP networks as a *routing* problem. Therefore, handling the mobility of an Internet host becomes the issue of how the packets addressed to a host could be routed to that host correctly and also how the host, as a visitor in a foreign network domain, could send packets using the foreign network resources. A router has to look after the visiting host in the foreign network, which the Mobile IP called a foreign agent (FA), and the home network resided router of the host in a similar way is called a home agent (HA). Figure 10.7 provides an overview to the Mobile IP protocol.

It seems that with simple adjustments and definitions given in the Mobile IP, the move of an Internet host between two different networks (or in general among several networks) has been resolved by appropriate routing mechanisms. For this purpose Mobile IP is sometimes referred to as a routing IP protocol. The Mobile IP is a solution to macromobility, that is, the handover between networks.

A binding, that is, a dynamic tunneling between the CoA and the home address is required during the delivery of packets to and from the visiting host. This is shown in Figure 10.7 and with more details in Figure 10.8.

When a mobile node (MN) moves from its home network to a foreign network, the home and visiting routers (i.e. HA and FA) make some signaling to authorize the MN to be in the visiting network and to use its network resources. Therefore, after each move, the HA knows where it should find the MN. Assume that a packet is addressed by a corresponding node (CN) to an MN. Since the MN could be at any location, CN sends the packet to the home network of the MN using the home address of the MN. The HA of the MN upon receiving the packet sends the packet to the FA router of the network that the MN is visiting at that time. The FA then forwards the packet to the MN accordingly. A reply or acknowledgment can then be sent from the foreign network via the FA to the CN. The process outlined above during the delivery of a packet to the MN in a Mobile IP network requires a triangle routing (as shown in Figure 10.8) and tunneling of the

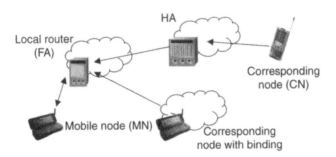

Figure 10.7 Mobile IPv4 protocol overview

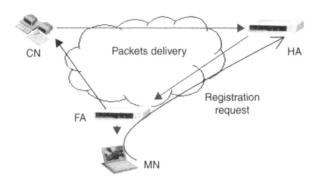

Figure 10.8   Packet flow in a Mobile IPv4 network

original packet for a different address outside the MN home network, that is, different from the MN's fixed address.

Therefore, in summary, the core operations involved in the Mobile IP protocol include agent discovery, registration, and packets tunneling. This is exactly what mobility management is defined to be, that is, to detect the MN's change of location, to register the new location with the HA (either directly or via FA), and finally to perform handover as the MN moves to the new network.

10.4.1.1 Registration

Upon detecting a change in location, the roaming MN acquires a new IP address, that is, the CoA, from either the received FA advertisement (FACoA) or the DHCP, a colocated CoA (CCoA). The MN then notifies the HA of the new location through the process of registration. This process is shown in Figure 10.8.

10.4.1.2 Tunneling and routing

Data packets from CNs are generally routed by default to the MN's home address. The HA attracts packets destined for those nodes that are away from their home network and redelivers them according to the corresponding CoAs being registered by each roaming node.

After the registration with the HA is complete, the mobility management protocols should secure a way for packets to be routed to the current point of attachment. The method used to forward data to roaming MN is known as encapsulation. Though Mobile IP assumes an *IP-within-IP* encapsulation methodology, as shown in Figure 10.9, other encapsulation mechanisms are applicable upon an agreement made between relevant network entities. Examples of these other alternatives are *minimal encapsulation* and *address resolution protocol* (*ARP*).

Minimal encapsulation uses the same principles as IP-within-IP, however, with a different header, which allows less bytes per header in datagrams. This header includes the

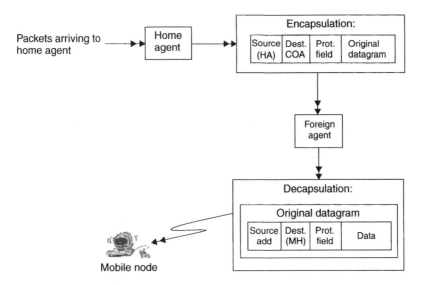

Figure 10.9 Mobile IPv4 tunneling with IP-within-IP encapsulation

original source address only when the tunnel source is different from the original source of the datagram.

ARP allows each host on the network to build up a table of mappings between IP addresses and link-level addresses. In other words, ARP is used to translate high-level addresses into physical hardware addresses. These mappings are timed out periodically and removed.

In Mobile IP, the HA will keep an ARP table for each of its MNs. Whenever a node on the home network broadcasts an ARP packet in an attempt to locate the MN, and the mobile node is away from home, the HA will supply its address so that packets will be destined to it. In order to update the ARP cache, the HA will broadcast gratuitous ARP to all the nodes on the home network, every time a registration is performed.

The tunneling methods described above will render the network slow, since each datagram will undergo extra processing at the HA. This problem is solved by the use of ARP broadcasts.

10.4.2 Performance issues in Mobile IPv4

The original Mobile IP protocol introduced in the IETF RFC 2002 encountered some inefficiencies, basically within three main categories according to each step of the mobility management process: location management, routing management, and handoff management. In this section we try to clarify those issues.

10.4.2.1 Location management

Referring back to the Mobile IPv4 operations, outlined previously, a serious inefficiency is widely evident in that a registration with HA is required at every handoff. This includes not only changes in networks (shown in Figure 10.10c) but also any change of links, a common scenario in a campus network in which one faculty is assigned a different link from the other (shown in Figure 10.10b). Such a registration requirement applies also to an even smaller scale of mobility, say from one point of attachment to another on the same link (shown in Figure 10.10a).

As a result, it is not hard to imagine the much-wasted resources that are associated by the frequent location updates arising from frequent movements of many MNs attached to the network at any instant in time.

Although the need of notifying the home network of mobile users' current locations is always present, it is questionable whether accurate location information is essential for MNs that are not active (i.e. MNs that do not exchange any data). Somehow, it seems logical to have separate mobility management techniques for idle and active MNs, therefore allowing variations in adjusting the update frequency at which MNs' movement notifications are sent.

The main problem then is how to find an adequate trade-off between the searching load and the information load. Load increases when searching has to take place to locate the current address of the receipt MN. Conversely, more information load would result (owing to frequent updates) if a more complete location information database was to be maintained.

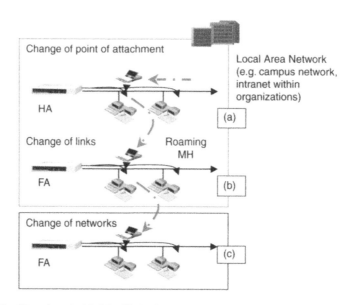

Figure 10.10   Situations in Mobile IPv4 where registrations with HA is necessary

10.4.2.2 Routing management

One of the biggest concerns in Mobile IPv4 is the inefficiency associated with the way packets are delivered to a roaming MN, namely, the triangle routing, an asymmetric routing with respect to topology. Specific concerns in this aspect are from both the user and the network.

From the user perspective, they are

- mobility related disruption (packet losses during handoffs), and
- high data latency (due to possibly distant HA).

From the network perspective, they are

- inefficient use of the link (or network) resources due to tunneling,
- high control overheads during frequent movement of an MN,
- support of QoS not straightforward, and
- reliability issues (heavy dependence on HA).

If the CN was to know, somehow, the MN's CoA, then it can tunnel the packets straight to the MN without having to bypass the HA. This is what is known as *Route Optimization* [15,19]. The main idea is to allow potential CNs to keep an updated mobility binding for the MN of interest. A binding associates each MN's home address with its current location, CoA, and is maintained by CNs in a binding cache. When a CN is to initiate communication with a roaming mobile, the location information is retrieved, and packets can be sent accordingly. Note that for security reasons, it is the HA's responsibility to provide binding updates (BU) to any concerned nodes upon the completion of an authentication process.

Even with route optimization, the packet-loss problem (during handoff) still remains unsolved. As a packet is routed to the receipt MN, there is a possibility that the packet arrives at the FA just after the MN leaves. Ideally, these packets should not be dropped but should be further redirected to the new FA (possibly by the previous FA).

One solution is to let the previous FA also maintain a binding cache for their formerly visited MNs. Thus, by encapsulation, misdirected packets can be redelivered, and hence promote a smooth handoff. Figure 10.11 provides a graphical illustration of the route optimization mechanism.

Though with route optimization, Mobile IP does seem to have an enhanced operation, there are, however, other complications that should be taken notice of, including possible inconsistency in cached bindings, disrupted data transfer while CN is obtaining new bindings, creating additional traffic load even when the moving MN is idle, and security issues such as sending bogus registrations by network attackers to CNs to cut all ongoing communications. Moreover, as resource saving would only become significant when the MN is far from the HA (and is near the CN), in most cases, the resources saved by direct tunneling is small in comparison to the authentication and key distribution necessary to ensure that the operations are performed securely.

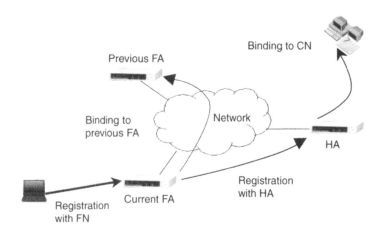

Figure 10.11   Route optimization mechanism in Mobile IPv4

10.4.2.3 Handoff management

Handoff is a process in which all information about a roaming MN is transferred from the old network to the new network to which the MN will be attached. In a cellular network, this would refer to the move from one cell to another cell, as shown in Figure 10.12. In the literature usually the term handoff is used for analog systems, whereas for digital systems the term handover is used. In this book, however, we use the two terms equally. While Mobile IP does seem to provide satisfactory performance for mobiles that are roaming among various networks, the cumbersome handoff operations become rather inefficient when the scale of movement is small.

Looking at the rapid growth in mobile communications in the last decade, there is a trend of ever-increasing traffic. Consequently, the channel being used, which has a limited bandwidth, will require a special protocol to limit the total capacity for each user. In other words, this will require smaller cells, which in turn will accentuate the need for seamless roaming. As the size of the cell decreases, frequent handoffs will become more of an important issue to be dealt with.

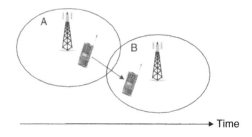

Figure 10.12   Concept of handover

Somehow, it seems logical to simplify the operations by separating the mobility management tasks depending on the nature of the mobile movement. From a network's perspective, such a distinction comes between intra- and internetwork mobility.

10.4.3 Mobile IPv6

Similar to the Internet protocol (IP) that found its way into a new generation, Mobile IP has also been amended and named Mobile IPv6 [20,22,31]. The main features of Mobile IPv4 that were discussed earlier apply to this new version, but some new features have also been added in accordance with the improved segments of IPv6. Maybe one of the most distinguishing features changed in Mobile IPv6 compared with Mobile IPv4 is the deletion of an extra agent, called foreign agent.

Since the IPv6 provides sufficient number of IP addresses to mobile users, only collocated CoA would be required in Mobile IPv6. In IPv6 new features such as neighbor discovery, address autoconfiguration, and the fact that any router may send a router advertisement (RA) are included so that the need for the Mobile IP FA is dismissed in Mobile IPv6. Route optimization becomes a mandatory part in Mobile IPv6.

The CoA of an MN can be used as the source address in the IP header for sending packets from the MN, since his home address is carried in a packet in the home address destination option. Therefore, in Mobile IPv6 there will be no need for reverse tunneling.

To decrease the overheads in Mobile IP tunneling, the MN's CoA is carried in the routing header option within the original packet, and therefore packets are not encapsulated in Mobile IPv6. Also the destination option used in Mobile IPv6 piggybacks the control messages and thus the need for separate control packets is dismissed.

10.4.4 Handover in Mobile IPv6

Three types of handover are considered in the Mobile IPv6 protocol:

- Smooth handover
- Fast handover
- Seamless handover

Smooth handover refers to a handover process with low probability of a packet loss. On the other hand, a fast handover is the one that encounters low delay during the process of handing over the information of a roaming MH. Seamless handover can then be considered as a handover that combines the features of both smooth and fast handovers and apparently is the most favorite type of handover.

In Mobile IPv6, mobile-controlled handover and network-controlled handover are possible.

10.4.4.1 Mobile-controlled handover

A mobile-controlled handover is shown in Figure 10.13. As the name indicates, the process is initiated by the MN roaming to a new network. The process involves four steps:

1. The MN starts the handover process by sending a special router solicitation (RS). This solicitation assists in finding the nearest point of attachment for the roaming node.
2. Previous access router sends back a proxy RA back to the MN.
3. Previous access router sends a handover initiate (HI) to the network. This signal informs the network that the node is going to perform a handover.
4. The new access router sends a handover acknowledgment (HACK) to the previous router, informing that it accepts the MN in its network.

10.4.4.2 Network-controlled handover

A network-controlled handover is shown in Figure 10.14. As the name indicates, the process is initiated by the network to provide roaming of the MN to a new network. The process involves three steps:

1. The previous access router sends a proxy RA on behalf of the new access router. This advertisement contains prefix and lifetime information required for the handover process.

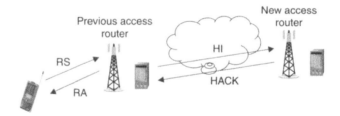

Figure 10.13   Mobile-controlled handover in Mobile IP

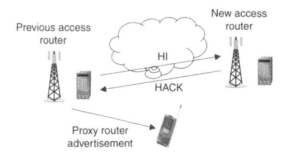

Figure 10.14   Network-controlled handover in Mobile IP

2. Previous access router sends an HI message to the new access router.

3. MN should finalize the context transfer at the new access router network.

10.4.5 Hierarchical mobility agent

After the discussions given in the previous parts of this section, it should be clear that there is a lot of signaling involved during the mobility management process in Mobile IP protocol. This is due to signaling to HA when it is far (in terms of intermediate hops and networks involved) from the MN. More signaling necessarily means more delay or higher latency; something that should be avoided in any data network and especially in future wireless IP networks in which the wireless channel already includes enough latency during data delivery.

A solution to the high latency problem considered in the new drafts of Mobile IP is to use a hierarchical arrangement of the routers, referred to as hierarchical mobility agents. This solution is illustrated in Figure 10.15. Different levels of mobility agents are considered in this architecture, including local mobility agents (LMA), regional mobility agents (RMA), and global mobility agents (GMA). The method tries to localize signaling to a visited domain rather than a long path from the network currently visited by the MN all the way to his home network.

Regional registration and regional BU are thus implemented in this hierarchical architecture. In theory, this type of hierarchy structure will definitely help in reducing the signaling involved for the mobility management in any mobile network, including Mobile IP network, and with more levels of hierarchy a better performance can be achieved. However, in practice, one or at the most two levels of hierarchy would be sufficient to provide a near maximum performance improvement.

10.5 CELLULAR IP AND HAWAII

In this section, we briefly discuss two other proposals on migrating IP into mobile environment: Cellular IP and HAWAII. They have been proposed after Mobile IP in response

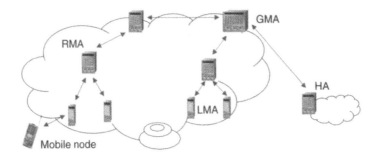

Figure 10.15 Hierarchical mobility agents in Mobile IP

to solve its inefficiencies in handling IP mobility, but have some similarities with the Mobile IP.

10.5.1 Cellular IP

Cellular IP [32,33] is specifically designed for a highly migrating MN during active data transfer where a minimum disturbance to ongoing data sessions becomes essential. To achieve optimal system operations, Cellular IP maintains two parallel mappings, paging cache (PC) and routing cache (RC) to separate paging and routing processes. PC, maintained only in selected nodes, is used for all MNs (either idle or active). As this only coarsely tracks the movement of MNs, information stored is useful for searching the roaming nodes.

Routing cache on the other hand, maintains an updated location database for active hosts. With a time-out interval approximating packet timescale, information stored is capable of routing high bit rate data. Once a packet has arrived for a roaming host in the network at the gateway router in the Cellular IP network, it is routed according to the routing information maintained in RC. In cases in which only PCs are available for the destination MH, arriving packets are queued in the gateway, while a paging packet, with zero payload, is sent to locate the roaming node. This process is shown in Figure 10.16.

The default route from each base station to gateway can be determined through various shortest-path algorithms. These include Bellman–Ford and Dijkstra's algorithms [4], just to name a few. For an active MH, RCs are maintained at all the nodes along the default route. For an idle MN on the other hand, in order to save unnecessary resources wasted on storing precise location information, PCs are updated only in selected nodes. To ensure that sufficient nodes are used to keep at least a coarse track of the roaming mobile, nodes that have branched out ports and are located at remote areas are often included in the selection (e.g. nodes N1 and N2 in Figure 10.16).

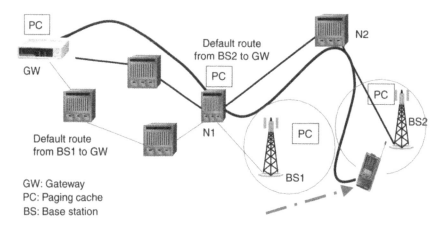

Figure 10.16 Cellular IP operation

Cellular IP has a flexible handoff support. There is no advance information necessary for each newly arrived MH to create or maintain PCs and RCs. Similarly, for every departing MH, no prejudice notifications are required. In short, this is simply a plug-and-play solution. Having said that, the selection of PC time-outs, RC time-outs, and also the repetition rates of paging and routing updates are crucial not only to minimize unessential waste of resources but also to ensure a seamless (soft) handoff.

There are quite a few advantages associated with the Cellular IP protocol. Among all, the simplicity in implementation seems to be particularly attractive. In addition, the superb network scalability, which allows Cellular IP to be deployed in distinct environments, gives network operators the extra capability to extend network sizes dynamically according to the demand growth.

In general, under the assumptions in which the MHs move frequently, Cellular IP does seem to give a better alternative than Mobile IP to accommodate local mobility. However, as they become less mobile, the margin of systems performance may no longer be significant.

Yet, there are other obvious deficiencies with Cellular IP. As all routing and paging information are cached with respect to the default route between the MN and the gateway router, packets from a roaming mobile are always sent to the gateway no matter what the actual destination address is. This operation becomes rather inefficient when two communicating parties are actually mobiles located within the same Cellular IP network. That is, despite the fact that two mobiles are physically close to each other, the transmitting packet between them still needs to be routed to the gateway located several hops away, before it turns back and is routed as an ordinary downlink packet. Figure 10.17 illustrates such a situation.

Moreover, as the only information that needs to be included in various control packets, mainly paging updates and routing updates, is simply the mobile's IP address (for identification purpose), various authentication processes will have to be realized to ensure secure operations. There are more recent works on Cellular IP within the IETF such as References [34,35].

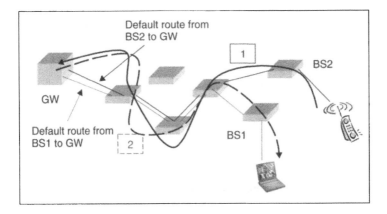

Figure 10.17   Routing path for mobiles located in the same network

10.5.2   HAWAII

Another similar alternative, but with further reduction in paging load is seen in HAWAII (Handoff-Aware Wireless Access Internet Infrastructure) [36–38]. As before, paging updates are sent to DRR, except this time, at a much-reduced frequency. This is achieved by further dividing the location area into smaller routing areas. Thus, instead of having to send paging updates upon moving to a new cell, HAWAII requires updates only when it crosses the routing area boundaries.

It is, however, interesting to note that in HAWAII, an increase in paging update time does not necessarily mean a reduction in signaling messages. In this case, although a paging update is sent only when shifting between routing areas, usual Mobile IP messages are still required from an MH during each handoff[1]. These frequent Mobile IP messaging packets, in comparison to the zero-payload control packets evident in Cellular IP, to some extent still waste the radio resources that are already scarcely available.

On the other hand, by splitting the registration process into two parts (from MH to base station and between base station and HA), the existence of the HAWAII network remains invisible to roaming nodes. This is particularly significant from the mobile's point of view.

Other than simply reducing updates frequency and minimizing high latency and disruption during handoff, HAWAII has also given better security and authentication measures for the mobile's intradomain movement. Figure 10.18 gives an illustration of mobility management in HAWAII.

In fact, as the protocol is built on top of IP, HAWAII is more like an improved cellular version of the Mobile IP. Hence, the strong similarity of control packets exchange is evident between both Mobile IP and HAWAII, though instead of having changes in point

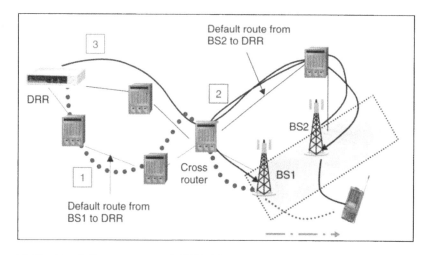

Figure 10.18   Handoff management in HAWAII

---

[1] HAWAII is triggered (within the domain) by Mobile IP registration messages.

of attachments (as well as changes of links) as in Mobile IP, handoff is referred to changes in base stations in HAWAII.

10.5.3 Cellular IP versus HAWAII

There are some similarities between HAWAII and Cellular IP. From the system's point of view, while a Cellular IP network is distinguished from normal Mobile IP networks by Cellular IP network identifier, HAWAII uses network access identifier (NAI) to recognize different HAWAII domains. In a similar manner, from operation's point of view, both establish and update host-based routing entries in only selective routers or nodes. Table 10.2 summarizes major similarities and differences for Cellular IP and HAWAII.

10.6 SUMMARY AND CONCLUSIONS

In this chapter, we have overviewed the main characteristics of the network protocol of the Internet, the IP, in its currently deployed version, IPv4, and in its next-generation format, IPv6. We have also overviewed the activities toward migrating the IP, originally designed for fixed networks, into the mobile environment by using the Mobile IP protocol. Issues and main features of the original Mobile IP protocol as well as new initiatives in this macromobility solution to the roaming problem between networks have been outlined.

In order to provide Internet users with services while they are moving, there are three alternative solutions. These solutions come within the application layer, the network layer, and the link layer.

The application-layer alternative tries to solve the mobility above the network layer. DNS is an example of an application-layer protocol that can address the mobility of the Internet users. Since DNS is capable of matching the alphabetical address of a server (e.g. a web site address) with its current numerical IP address, we may assume that during the movement of an Internet host, the database entries in the DNS is updated

Table 10.2 Cellular IP versus HAWAII

	Cellular IP	HAWAII
Similarities	• Maintain end-to-end connectivity with minimum disruption as mobile host moves • Reduced registrations to home agent • Improved tolerance to router and to link failures within network	
Differences	• Operations remain the same regardless of location of mobile host • No distinction between handoff and normal operations	• Different treatment for roaming within home and foreign domains • Path setup mechanism varies for power-up and handoff operations

regularly to illustrate the new IP address of that host at each time even after moving to another network and getting a new address. The problem with this method is that the DNS database-updating load becomes extremely high when there are frequent movements by the user. Although many Internet researchers tried to come up with a solution for modifying the DNS to accommodate the user mobility between networks, it appears that this method has a fundamental shortage in providing efficient user mobility. A new alternative to DNS for handling the user mobility at the application layer is under way within the IETF [9] under the title of session initiation protocol (SIP).

The link-layer alternative wants to make the user mobility invisible by the network layer. Therefore, similar to the application-layer approach using DNS capabilities, in this method an appropriate mapping between the host IP address and the link-layer address (e.g. an Ethernet address) is performed through the link-layer entities, such as the ARP. There are some limitations to this technique as the link layer has a close relationship (interface) with its underlying physical layer, therefore making the technique inapplicable for user mobility between different technologies. The scalability of the link-layer mobility techniques is also under question.

Our discussions in this chapter, however, were neither the application-layer mobility solutions nor the link-layer ones. The user IP mobility can be best addressed at the network layer, hence naming it a network-layer technique. At the network layer these are actual IP addresses that need to be changed when the user moves from one network to another. Therefore, there will be no address mapping of different types (i.e. server name and IP address in the application-layer methods and Ethernet address and IP address in link-layer schemes). However, the network-layer techniques could require mapping between the same-type IP addresses during the user mobility, as, for example, seen in the Mobile IP tunneling technique.

The discussion provided in the chapter together with the location management techniques and user mobility models introduced in Chapter 8 and the enhanced transport-layer protocols for the wireless channel outlined in Chapter 9 should provide a solid framework for the study of the mobility issues in future wireless IP networks.

REFERENCES

1. Stevens WR, *TCP/IP Illustrated*, Vol. 1, Addison-Wesley Longman, Reading, Mass., 1994.
2. Kurose JF & Ross KW, *Computer Networking: A Top-Down Approach Featuring the Internet*, Addison-Wesley Longman, Reading, Mass., 2001.
3. Leon-Garcia A & Widjaja I, *Communication Networks—Fundamental Concepts and Key Architectures*, McGraw-Hill Higher Education, Boston, Mass., 2000.
4. Stallings, W, *Data and Computer Communications*, Sixth Edition, Prentice-Hall, Upper Saddle River, N.J., 2000.
5. Comer DE, *Computer Networks and Internets*, 2/e, Prentice Hall, Upper Saddle River, N.J., 1999.
6. Halsall F, *Data Communications, Computer Networks and Open Systems*, fourth edition, Addison Wesley Longman, Reading, Mass., 1996.

7. Tanenbaum AS, *Computer Networks*, 3/e, Prentice Hall, Upper Saddle River, N.J., 1996.

8. Comer DE, *Internetworking with TCP/IP: Principles, Protocols, and Architectures*, Vol. 1, Prentice Hall, Upper Saddle River, N.J., 2000.

9. Internet Engineering Task Force (IETF), Web site: http://www.ietf.org.

10. Brander S & Mankin A, *IPng Internet Protocol Next Generation*, Addison-Wesley, Reading, Mass., 2000.

11. Gilligan R & Nordmark E, *Transition Mechanisms for IPv6 Hosts and Routers*, IETF RFC 2893, August 2000.

12. Deering S & Hinden R, *Internet Protocol, Version 6 (IPv6) Specification*, IETF RFC 2460, December 1998 (originally in IETF RFC 1883).

13. Lawton G, Is IPv6 finally gaining ground? *IEEE Computer Magazine*, **39**(8), 11–15, 2001.

14. Perkins C (Ed.), *IP Mobility Support*, IETF RFC 2002, October 1996.

15. Perkins C, Mobile-IP, ad-hoc networking, and nomadicity, *Proceedings of the 12th COMPSAC '96 (International Computer Software & Applications Conference)*, August, 1996, pp. 472–476.

16. Perkins C, *IP Mobility Support Version 2*, IETF Internet draft (work in progress), draft-ietf-mobileip-v2-00.txt, November 1997.

17. Perkins C, Mobile networking through mobile IP, *IEEE Internet*, **2**(1), 58–69, 1998.

18. Perkins C, Mobile IP, *IEEE Communications Magazine*, **35**(5), 84–99, 1997.

19. Solomon J, *Mobile IP: The Internet Unplugged*, Prentice Hall PTR, Upper Saddle River, N.J., 1998.

20. Perkins C & Johnson D, *Mobility Support in IPv6*, IETF Internet draft (work in progress), draft-ietf-mobileip-ipv6-13.txt, September 2000.

21. Gustafsson E, Jonsson A & Perkins C, *Mobile IP Regional Registration*, IETF Internet draft (work in progress), draft-ietf-mobileip-reg-tunnel-02.txt, March 2000.

22. Soliman H, Castelluccia C, ElMalki K & Bellier L, *Hierarchical MIPv6 Mobility Management*, IETF Internet draft (work in progress), draft-ietf-mobileip-hmipv6-02.txt, November 2000.

23. Bhagwat P, Perkins C & Tripathi S, Network layer mobility: an architecture and survey, *IEEE Personal Communications*, **3**(3), 54–64, 1996.

24. Jung P, New Internet service opportunities offered by Mobile IP, *Comec*, **76**(7–8), 8–13, 1998.

25. Gustafsson E, Jonsson A, Hubbard E, Malmkvist J & Roos A, *Requirements on Mobile IP from a Cellular Perspective*, Internet draft (work in progress), draft-ietf-mobiuleip-cellular-requirements-01.txt, April 1999.

26. Johnsson M, *Simple Mobile IP (SMIP)*, IETF Internet draft (work in process), draft-ietf-mobileip-simple-00.txt, March 1999.

27. Solomon J & Glass S, *Mobile-IPv4 Configuration Option for PPP IPCP*, IETF RFC 2290, February 1998.

28. Calhoun P & Perkins C, *Mobile IP Network Access Identifier Extension for IPv4*, IETF RFC 2794, March 2000.

29. Perkins C (Ed.), *IP Mobility Support for IPv4*, IETF RFC 3220, January 2002.

30. Perkins C (Ed.), *IP Mobility Support for IPv4*, IETF RFC 3344 August 2002.

31. Wisely D, Eardley P & Burness L, *IP for 3G, Networking Technologies for Mobile Communications*, John Wiley & Sons, Chichester, West Sussex, England, 2002.

32. Valko A, Campbell A & Gomez J, *Cellular IP*, IETF Internet Draft (work in process), draft-valko-cellularip-00.txt, November 1998.

33. Valko A, Cellular IP: a new approach to Internet host mobility, *ACM Communication Review*, January 1999.

34. Campbell A, Wan C-Y, Shelby Z & Gatzounas D, *Cellular IPv6*, IETF Internet Draft (work in progress), July 2001.

35. Shelby Z, *Cellular IP Route Optimization*, IETF Internet Draft (work in progress), July 2001.

36. Ramjee R, La Porta T, Thuel S & Varadhan K, *Hawaii: A Domain-Based Approach for Supporting Mobility in Wide-Area Wireless Network*, IETF Internet Draft (work in progress), 1998.

37. Ramjee R, La Porta T, Thuel S, Varadhan K & Salgarelli L., *IP Micro-Mobility Support using HAWAII*, IETF Internet Draft (work in progress), draft-ietf-mobileip-hawaii-00.txt, June 1999.

38. Ramjee R, La Porta T, Thuel S, Varadhan K & Salgarelli L, *Paging Support for IP mobility Using HAWAII*, Internet draft (work in progress), draft-ietf-mobileip-paging-hawaii-00.txt, June 1999.

Part III

Advanced Topics in Wireless IP

Chapter 11 INTERNET PERSPECTIVES ON WIRELESS IP

In view of merging the Internet research activities mainly carried out under the umbrella of the IETF and the research and standardization developments for the 3G systems dominantly supported by the ITU and its bodies including ETSI, 3GPP, and 3GPP2 toward the realization of a generic wireless IP network, these organizations have tried to complement the network functionality of each other. Therefore, in this chapter, the undergoing activities for that collaboration will be reviewed. The materials provided in this chapter can illustrate the main requirements of the future wireless IP networks consisting of the Internet initiatives at the network layer and the network and access technologies of the 3G wireless systems.

Chapter 12 MOBILE AD HOC NETWORKS AND FUTURE CHALLENGES

Ad hoc networks have attracted attention from the research community since the early nineties. Earlier research was focused on ad hoc routing, that is, on how routes can be discovered and how packets can be forwarded toward their destinations. Gradually over the years, other technical issues have become important too, such as media access control protocols, ad hoc multicasting, and support for TCP over ad hoc networks. The mobile ad hoc networks will definitely have a great share in future wireless IP networks. In this chapter, after providing a brief discussion on fundamentals in mobile ad hoc network, future research challenges for ad hoc mobile networks will be presented.

Chapter 13 SATELLITES IN WIRELESS IP

Satellite has been an important element of the telecommunications networks for many years, providing long-distance telephony and television broadcasting. The involvement of satellites in IP networks is a direct result of new trends in global telecommunications in which Internet traffic will hold a dominant share in the total network traffic and special features of high-capacity satellite channels will be discussed in this chapter. The large geographical coverage of the satellite footprint and its unique broadcasting capabilities as well as its high-capacity channels retain the satellite as an irreplaceable part of communications systems, despite the high cost and long development and launching cycle of a satellite system. In this chapter, the role of satellites in future wireless Internet networks will be discussed and several research issues will be explored.

11

Internet Perspectives on Wireless IP

In the line of converging the Internet research activities mainly carried out under the umbrella of the Internet Engineering Task Force (IETF) and the research and standardization developments for third-generation (3G) wireless systems dominantly supported by the International Telecommunication Union (ITU) and its bodies including the European Telecommunications Standards Institute (ETSI), the Third-Generation Partnership Project (3GPP), and the Third-Generation Partnership Project 2 (3GPP2), toward the realization of a generic wireless Internet protocol (IP) network, these organizations have tried to complement the networks of one another. As an important and practical perspective therefore, in this chapter, some of the results of these ongoing activities are summarized. The materials provided in this chapter by no means specify the final answers to the wireless IP architecture, as they are still evolving, but can illustrate some fundamental requirements of the future wireless IP networks, which will consist of the Internet initiatives at the network layer and the network and access technologies of the 3G wireless systems. The reader may find many of the elements discussed in this chapter to be included in the final version of wireless IP architectures as a result of the importance of the services they provide. Nevertheless, the reader is suggested to continually consult with the web sites of the relevant organizations referenced in this chapter for up-to-date information and possible changes that might be included in future.

11.1 PACKET DATA SERVICES

The IETF [1], originally the main standardization body for the wired Internet, in recent years has started to include mobility features within its request-for-comments (RFC) and

The Wireless Mobile Internet: Architectures, Protocols, and Services. Abbas Jamalipour
© 2003 John Wiley & Sons, Ltd ISBN: 0-470-84468-X

Internet drafts, as a response to the increasing demand on the Internet access while the users are on the move. Their research while started as a kind of separate research activity, by giving IP address mobility to the originally fixed IP addresses from those introduced in cellular networks, has recently been converging onto cellular telecommunications research mainly carried out within 3G standard bodies such as the ETSI [2], the 3GPP [3], and the 3GPP2 [4]. Many of the IETF Internet drafts and RFCs are now prepared as a joint work between the original Internet standards bodies and the telecommunications standards bodies, including the ITU [5].

In a particular example, 3GPP2 has recently produced several technical specifications on wireless IP architecture and details of network standards as a result of works within its TSG-P, wireless packet networking technical specification group. According to these specifications [6,7], for the packet data service in a mobile environment, two types of services would be provided:

- Local and public network access
- Private network access

Local and public network access services include the usual services that could be received from public data networks such as those offered by the global Internet. Public information search and data acquisition, file transfers, and electronic mail are examples of the public network services. Private network access services are generally identical (but not essentially) to those of local network and public Internet but may include additional services offered by a service access provider (SAP) to its own private IP network.

These services are provided either by Simple IP or by Mobile IP access methods. The two protocols try to make the IP address portable in the network so that the users can move around and still be connected to the network and receive online services.

In the Simple IP a user is assigned a dynamic IP address from the SAP to which the user has subscribed. The user maintains his IP address within a predefined network-dependent geographical area dictated by the SAP. Outside that area, the user would not be able to maintain the IP address. The Simple IP therefore provides an IP mobility feature within a limited area and a limited range of user mobility.

The mobile network access in Mobile IP is based on the IETF RFC 2002 [8], as described in Chapter 10 [9–18]. The user in this method will use either a static IP address or a dynamic IP address from his home network. The user has a wider mobility range when using the Mobile IP compared to the Simple IP, and is able to maintain the IP address when movement is within the International Mobile Telecommunications (IMT-2000) network or other mobile networks.

In case there are multiple IMT-2000 service providers, the mobile station (MS) must establish packet data sessions with the IMT-2000 network to ensure that the user receives services from them.

In general, for a packet data reference model, at least four functional layers are required [6], as shown in Figure 11.1:

- Access layer
- Data link layer

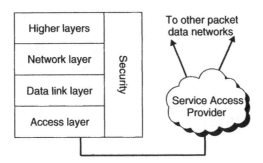

Figure 11.1   The packet data service reference model

- Network layer
- Security

These layers are briefly explained in the following sections.

11.1.1   Access layer

The MS receives the packet data services through a radio access technology. The radio access technology could be of, for example, TDMA (time division multiple access) or narrowband CDMA (code division multiple access) type used in second-generation cellular networks or wideband CDMA (W-CDMA) type used in 3G systems. The access layer also covers signaling standards, that is, those used for Simple IP and Mobile IP. Only a single packet data service (either Simple IP or Mobile IP) is supported. Differentiation will be required to be performed at higher layers.

The access network authenticates and authorizes the MS for access services. The access network also establishes a connection to the IMT-2000 network and initializes a data link layer session. After the establishment of this link layer session, network layer protocols are executed to establish the packet data session. Authentication is a process in which a user's identity is verified by the network. Authorization, on the other hand, is a process in which a particular user's right to access a specific service and information is verified.

11.1.2   Data link layer

IMT-2000 networks support two types of data link layers. The first one is the versions 1 and 2 of the Internet point-to-point protocol (PPP), originally defined in the IETF RFC 1172 [19] and then amended in many other RFCs including those in References [20–25]. In particular, the PPP supported here is the one in compliance with the RFC 1661 [23]. The PPP compression control protocol, introduced in the IETF RFC 1962 [24], is used to negotiate a PPP payload compression algorithm.

In the Mobile IP service, higher layers will not be reset when the MS reestablishes a PPP link connection to a new IMT-2000 serving area.

The second data link layer protocol that is supported by IMT-2000 is a simple data link layer protocol for version 2, as the one used in Reference [26].

11.1.3 Network layer

As mentioned earlier, two types of network access methods are supported: the Mobile IP and the Simple IP.

For local and public network access, the home agent (HA) of Mobile IP resides in IMT-2000 service provider network (SPN). Authentications and authorizations are provided either by the SPN or by a private network.

For private network access, the HA of Mobile IP resides in a private network and both authentications and authorizations are provided by the private network.

In case of Simple IP, for the local and public network access, the IP address is dynamically assigned from the serving network. For private network access, the process is the same with an inclusion of VPN (virtual packet network) software in the MS.

11.1.4 Security

Three levels of security are included in the packet data service in IMT-2000 for a MS. These are radio access security, IP network security, and user end-to-end security. A simple authentication and security layer (SASL) is proposed in Reference [27].

The radio access security is responsible for the MS authentication and also for supporting the air interface encryption. IP network security would be different in accordance to the network layer service used. For the Mobile IP, the foreign agent (FA) could be used to challenge to authenticate the MS. For Simple IP, either a CHAP (challenge handshake authentication protocol) [28–30] or a PAP (password authentication protocol) [31–37], both of which reside in the data link layer, could be used.

The user end-to-end security provides additional security measures by the user and could be considered as an optional security used in critical situations.

11.2 PACKET DATA SERVICES – A FUNCTIONAL MODEL

In general, the functions required to support the packet data services are [6,7]

- Home agent (HA)
- Packet data serving node (PDSN)
- Authentication, authorization, and accounting (AAA)

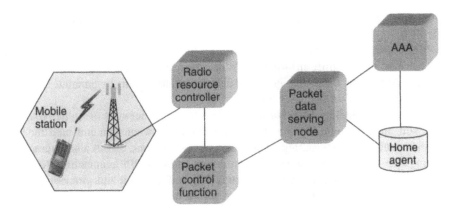

Figure 11.2 A functional model to support mobile packet data services

- Packet control function (PCF)
- Radio resource control (RRC)
- Mobile station (MS)

These functions are connected to each other in a pattern as shown in Figure 11.2. In this section, we briefly discuss each function.

11.2.1 Home agent

The definition and usage of HA in a Mobile IP network was discussed in Chapter 10. For the mobile data packet service in IMT-2000, the HA authenticates Mobile IP registration from an MS. HA redirects packets to the respective FA, and may establish, maintain, and terminate secure communications to the PDSN as a Mobile IP FA.

HA also receives provisioning information from AAA for users. It may also assign a dynamic home address for the MS.

11.2.2 Packet data serving node

The PDSN generally establishes, maintains, and terminates PPP sessions to MSs. In a Simple IP network, the PDSN also provides the IP address. FA functionality is also supported by the PDSN.

The PDSN initiates AAA functions to the AAA unit for the MS data session and may establish, maintain, and terminate secure communications to the HA or to the Mobile IP foreign-home authentication extension.

For Simple IP networks, PDSN maps the MS IP address with a unique link layer connection used to communicate with the PCF. In Mobile IP networks, PDSN maps the

MS IP address and the HA address with a unique link layer identifier to communicate with the PCF.

The PDSN also receives the user's profile from the AAA for the MS including differentiated services and security information. It also records the data usage and receives the accounting information from the PCF and then correlates them to generate accounting information to forward to the AAA unit.

Using a reverse tunneling, PDSN routes packets to the IP network or to the HA. It also interacts with the PCF unit for link layer connections between that unit and the PDSN on establishment, maintenance, and termination of connections. PDSN also interacts with the serving PCF unit and the target PCF unit to maintain a PPP connection. Monitoring the source addresses of packets received from a MS and marking and processing packets as necessary for the user's quality of service profile are also other tasks carried out by the PDSN.

11.2.3 Authentication, authorization, and accounting

The AAA unit is a major element in mobility and resource management in mobile data networks and is discussed in many literatures and standards (e.g. see References [38–42]). The tasks carried out by the AAA unit can be classified in accordance to the location of the unit, whether in SPN, or in home IP network, or in broker network.

11.2.3.1 AAA in service provider network

The main functions of AAA in the SPN are summarized in this section. The first one is to pass authentication requests from the PDSN to the MS's home IP network and authorization from the MS's home IP network to the PDSN. It also stores accounting information for the MS from the PDSN. AAA also provides the mobile user's profile (such as quality-of-service profile) to the PDSN when it is received from the user's home IP network.

AAA in the SPN may also assign a dynamic IP address for Simple IP service, and for the Mobile IP, interact with a previous PDSN to support the handoffs between multiple PDSNs where it does not involve the user's home IP network. In case of Mobile IP, AAA dynamically identifies a HA and assigns a user to that home agent.

11.2.3.2 AAA in home IP network

On the basis of requests from the local AAA, the AAA unit in the home IP network authenticates and authorizes the MS. This may involve providing authentication key information to the HA and the local AAA. This is used for a preshared key in an IKE (Internet key exchange) process [43] or for the mobile IP foreign-home authentication extension.

The AAA unit in home IP network provides a user profile and quality-of-service information to the corresponding PDSN. This information will assist in providing Internet quality of service based on the mobile user's subscription agreement. For Mobile IP, the AAA in home IP network dynamically identifies an HA and assigns a user to that home agent.

11.2.3.3 AAA in a broker network

A broker network is an intermediate IP network with an administrative domain that connects the mobile user via appropriate IP networks to the Internet and his home IP network. The AAA unit in a broker network forwards requests and responses between an SPN and the mobile user's home IP network without a direct association. Three modes of operation for a network broker would be possible [6]:

- *Nontransparent*: The AAA unit in the broker network examines requests and responses and creates new requests and responses. In this mode, the broker AAA assumes financial responsibility for the serving node.
- *Transparent*: The AAA unit in the broker network only relays the requests and responses without any process or making any new request or response.
- *Redirection*: The AAA unit in the broker network simply refers the service provider to another AAA unit.

The AAA unit in the broker network may optionally verify certificates when they are passed in the AAA requests between the home and the serving network of the MS.

11.2.4 Packet control function

Link layer's connection establishment, connection maintenance, and connection termination are provided by the PCF unit. The PCF interacts with the PDSN to support dormant handoffs, maintains the knowledge of radio resource status (number of active connections, available capacity, etc.), and buffers packets arriving from the PDSN when radio resources are not available or are insufficient.

The PCF also communicates with the RRC unit to request and to manage radio resources when relaying packets to and from the MSs. In case of a hard handoff, forwarding the serving PCF information to the target PCF to reestablish a new packet data session to PDSN is also performed by the PCF unit. The PCF maps the MS's identifier and connection reference to a unique link layer connection identifier used to communicate with the PDSN and also collects and sends air link–related information to the PDSN.

11.2.5 Radio resource control

The main function for the RRC unit is to establish, maintain, and terminate radio resources for the exchange of packets between the MS and the PCF unit. It also maintains the knowledge of radio resource status and broadcasts the packet zone identifier in the system overhead message.

Optionally, the RRC unit supports air interface encryption to the MS and authentication and authorization of the MS for radio access. Since the RRC unit has the direct and initial physical and logical connection to the MS, the above optional tasks are reasonable to be put at the RRC unit.

11.2.6 Mobile station

The MS establishes, maintains, and terminates a data link protocol to the PDSN. It requests appropriate radio resources from the network (through the RRC) and maintains the knowledge of radio resources for a packet session. Optionally, air interface encryption to the RRC and to the Mobile IP or the Simple IP functionality is also supported by the MS.

The MS buffers packets from the mobile applications when the radio resources are not available or are insufficient. Any change in packet zone identifier, system identifier, or network identifier should be detected by the MS and as a result, an origination message is sent to the RRC unit to initiate a dormant handoff. In case of Simple IP, the MS accepts a dynamically assigned IP address, whereas in case of Mobile IP, it uses a static home IP address or accepts a dynamically assigned home IP address.

11.3 ARCHITECTURE MODELS

On the basis of the Mobile IP and the Simple IP network access protocols for mobile users as predicted in the 3G IMT-2000, 3GPP2 proposed two architecture models as shown in Figures 11.3 and 11.4, respectively, for Mobile IP and Simple IP [6]. The main difference between the architecture models for Mobile IP and Simple IP is that in the latter case the HA is not required but the interaction with the AAA servers might be used in a roaming case.

The radio network (RN) consists of RRC and PCF units, described in the previous section. The MS has the access to a SPN by using an air interface to connect the RN. The access to SPNs is limited to one at each time. The service provider might be the user's home IP network or a visitor IP network.

Visitor location register (VLR) and home location register (HLR) are performing the mobility management procedures using appropriate signaling and VLR-HLR interactions using the air interface. HLR is the permanent location for storing the user's information and profile. But when a user is outside his home network, the HLR forwards the user's information and profile to a location register server (i.e. the VLR) in the network the user is visiting. Access service parameters are stored in the HLR and cached in the VLR, while the MS is registered in the SPN.

An open interface between the RN and the PDSN, called the R-P interface, is used. The interaction between the PDSN and the local and visited AAA and other servers are provided through the use of IP.

Figure 11.5 shows the protocol reference model for the Mobile IP user data transfer [6]. This figure is based on the architecture previously shown in Figure 11.3. The MS consists

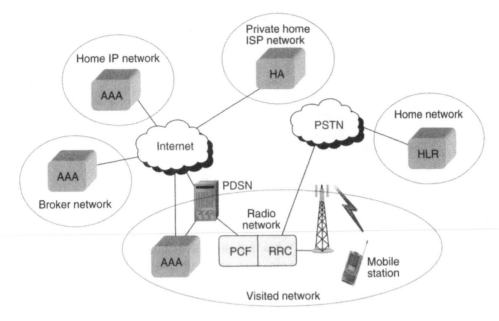

Figure 11.3 3GPP2 architecture for the Mobile IP

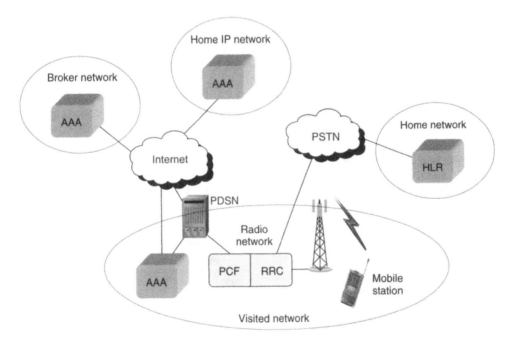

Figure 11.4 3GPP2 architecture for the Simple IP

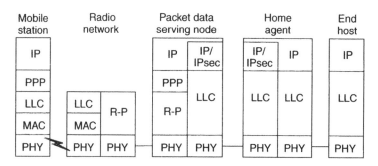

Figure 11.5 The protocol reference model for Mobile IP

of the air link physical layer, a medium access control (MAC) layer, a link layer control (LLC), a PPP, and an IP as its network layer protocol. The MS is accessed through the radio channel to the RN. The RN has a dual-stack architecture for communicating to the MS through radio channels on one side and to the packet serving node through cables on the other side. The interface between the PDSN and the RN, as mentioned earlier, is an R-P interface. Other network protocol stacks at the HA and end host are of usual configuration. For the Mobile IP control messaging and IKE, a similar protocol reference model could be considered with the inclusion of a user datagram protocol (UDP) layer on top of the IP layer, to exchange the short signaling of the key used in IKE [6].

For the Simple IP architecture, the protocol reference model is shown in Figure 11.6. The model is more simplified compared with the Mobile IP case due to the fact that there is no need for a HA in the Simple IP architecture. Other parts are similar to the Mobile IP case.

For the intraservice provider interfaces, the AAA protocol (client-server) is used between the PDSN and AAA. Another client-server AAA protocol is used between the HA and the AAA. The interface between the RN and the PDSN is an RN-PDSN or simply an R-P interface.

For the peer-to-peer interfaces between the home network and the visited IMT-2000 network, namely, the intrafamily networks, Mobile IP protocol is used between the HA and the PDSN. A peer-to-peer AAA protocol is used between one AAA server and

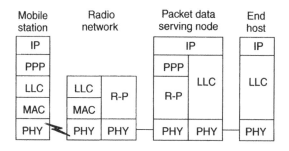

Figure 11.6 The protocol reference model for Simple IP

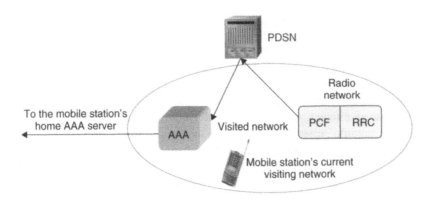

Figure 11.7 Accounting procedures in packet data services

another AAA server. Connection between the HLR and the VLR is provided by an ANSI-41 protocol.

The accounting process is summarized in Figure 11.7. RRC and PCF units first send information about the air link usage by the MS to the PDSN. The PDSN has an interface with the local AAA server that supports a reliable AAA protocol. Using this interface, the PDSN sends combined received information from the PCF and the RRC units with other IP data specific accounting information to the local AAA server. The local AAA server may optionally send the accounting information to the MS's home network or to the broker network. The local AAA server also must allow for the MS's home network to rerequest or repoll any previous accounting information if required. Accounting information is usually exchanged between the visited AAA server and the home AAA server, using standard encoding and decoding rules, for example, the accounting data interchange format (ADIF) [44,45].

11.4 SUMMARY AND CONCLUSIONS

In this chapter we have introduced some of the 3GPP2 activities toward the wireless IP network realization in line with the ongoing research in IETF. The network architecture models based on two network access protocols, Mobile IP and Simple IP [6,7], have been addressed and their network elements have been described. The reader should consider the information provided in this chapter only as some indicatives on the required architectural elements in future wireless IP networks. This is because of the fact that these standardizations are still far from being complete. For up-to-date information the reader should always consult respective standard bodies [1–5] and in particular keep an eye on new documents published by the 3GPP2's TSG-P, the wireless packet networking technical specification group.

To conclude this chapter, we need to include another part on mobility management, which is the main research topic on the migration of the IP into the mobile environment.

Mobility management in a mobile network covers two main parts: location management and handoff management. Location management is used for routing purposes as we need to find the actual location of an MS from time to time and to find its nearest point of attachment to the network, for example, a base station in a cellular wireless network. This topic has been covered in Chapter 8.

The handoff management is an important part of the mobility management in any mobile network because an efficient, reliable, and quick handoff technique is required to maintain and reroute an ongoing session while the MS moves from the coverage area of a base station to the next one. The mobility models described in Chapter 8 and the discussion on handoff in IP networks in Chapter 10 cover this part of the mobility management. Since even a short interrupt in transmission of data could cause loss of a huge amount of data, the efficiency of the handoff protocols and how to decide to initiate a handoff process will affect the performance of wireless IP network significantly.

In the 3GPP2 architectures for the wireless IP discussed in this chapter, we can observe two types of handoffs: a PCF-to-PCF handoff and a PDSN-to-PDSN handoff [6]. For the PCF-to-PCF handoff, a link-layer mobility management function is used to manage the change of an R-P session's point of attachment (i.e. a PCF), while maintaining the PPP session and the IP addresses. PCF-to-PCF handoffs may happen for an active or dormant MS.

A PCF-to-PCF handoff involves a PDSN selection, a new R-P session setup, and the teardown of the previous R-P session. Each PCF is uniquely identified in the network by the combination of a system ID (SID), a network ID (NID), and a packet zone ID (PZID).

For the PDSN-to-PDSN handoffs, the Mobile IP provides IP-layer mobility management functions that maintain persistent IP addresses across PDSNs. The MS will affect a PDSN-to-PDSN handoff by requesting its HA as per the specifications given in the IETF RFC 2002 with some extensions.

A PDSN-to-PDSN handoff requires active MSs and involves the establishment of a new PPP session, the detection of a new FA via the agent advertisement message, the authentication by RADIUS (remote authentication dial in user service) [46–49], and finally the registration with the HA. A complete discussion on handoffs can be found in Reference [6].

REFERENCES

1. The Internet Engineering Task Force (IETF), Web site: http://www.ietf.org.
2. The European Telecommunications Standards Institute (ETSI), Web site: http://www. etsi.org.
3. Third Generation Partnership Project (3GPP), Web site: http://www.3gpp.org.
4. Third Generation Partnership Project 2 (3GPP2), Web site: http://www.3gpp2.org.
5. The International Telecommunication Union (ITU), Web site: http://www.itu.int.
6. Third Generation Partnership Project 2 (3GPP2), *Wireless IP Architecture Based on IETF Protocols, Version 1.0.0*, Technical Specification 3GPP2 P.R0001, July 2000.

7. Third Generation Partnership Project 2 (3GPP2), *Wireless IP Network Standard, Version 3.0.0*, Technical Specification 3GPP2 P.S0001-A, July 2001.

8. Perkins C (Ed.), *IP Mobility Support*, IETF RFC 2002, October 1996.

9. Perkins C, Mobile IP, *IEEE Communications Magazine*, **35**(5), 84–99, 1997.

10. Perkins C, *IP Mobility Support Version 2*, IETF Internet draft (work in progress), draft-ietf-mobileip-v2-00.txt, November 1997.

11. Perkins C, Mobile networking through mobile IP, *IEEE Internet*, **2**(1), 58–69, 1998.

12. Solomon J & Glass S, *Mobile-IPv4 Configuration Option for PPP IPCP*, IETF RFC 2290, February 1998.

13. Solomon J, *Mobile IP: The Internet Unplugged*, Prentice Hall PTR, Upper Saddle River, N.J., 1998.

14. Gustafsson E, Jonsson A, Perkins C, *Mobile IP Regional Registration*, IETF Internet draft (work in progress), draft-ietf-mobileip-reg-tunnel-02.txt, March 2000.

15. Calhoun P & Perkins C, *Mobile IP Network Access Identifier Extension for IPv4*, IETF RFC 2794, March 2000.

16. Perkins C & Johnson D, *Mobility Support in IPv6*, IETF Internet draft (work in progress), draft-ietf-mobileip-ipv6-13.txt, September 2000.

17. Perkins C (Ed.), *IP Mobility Support for IPv4*, IETF RFC 3220, January 2002.

18. Perkins C (Ed.), *IP Mobility Support for IPv4*, IETF RFC 3344 August 2002.

19. Perkins D & Hobby R, *Point-to-Point Protocol (PPP) Initial Configuration Options*, IETF RFC 1172, July 1990.

20. Simpson W, *The Point-to-Point Protocol (PPP) for the Transmission of Multi-Protocol Datagrams Over Point-to-Point Links*, IETF RFC 1331, May 1992.

21. McGregor G, *The PPP Internet Protocol Control Protocol (IPCP)*, IETF RFC 1332, May 1992.

22. Simpson W, *The Point-to-Point Protocol (PPP)*, IETF RFC 1548, December 1993.

23. Simpson W (Ed.), *The Point-to-Point Protocol (PPP)*, IETF RFC 1661, July 1994.

24. Rand D, *The PPP Compression Control Protocol (CCP)*, IETF RFC 1962, June 1996.

25. Simpson W, *PPP Vendor Extensions*, IETF RFC 2153, May 1997.

26. Carlson J, Langner P, Hernandez-Valencia E & Manchester J, *PPP Over Simple Data Link (SDL) Using SONET/SDH with ATM-like Framing*, IETF RFC 2823, May 2000.

27. Myers J, *Simple Authentication and Security Layer (SASL)*, IETF RFC 2222, October 1997.

28. Simpson W, *PPP Challenge Handshake Authentication Protocol (CHAP)*, IETF RFC 1994, August 1996.

29. Zorn G & Cobb S, *Microsoft PPP CHAP Extensions*, IETF RFC 2433, October 1998.

30. Zorn G, *Microsoft PPP CHAP Extensions, Version 2*, IETF RFC 2759, January 2000.

31. Leech M, *Username/password Authentication for SOCKS V5*, IETF RFC 1929, March 1996.

32. Haller N & Metz C, *A One-Time Password System*, IETF RFC 1938, May 1996.

33. Haller N, Metz C, Nesser P & Straw M, *A One-Time Password System*, IETF RFC 2289, February 1998.

34. Newman C, *The One-Time-Password SASL Mechanism*, IETF RFC 2444, October 1998.

35. Kaliski B, *PKCS #5: Password-Based Cryptography Specification Version 2.0*, IETF RFC 2898, September 2000.
36. Zeilenga K, *LDAP Password Modify Extended Operation*, IETF RFC 3062, February 2001.
37. Zeilenga K, *LDAP Authentication Password Scheme*, IETF RFC 3112, May 2001.
38. Calhoun P, *AAA Problem Statements*, IETF Internet draft (work in progress), draft-ietf-aaa-issues-05.txt, January 2002.
39. Mitton D, St. Johns M, Barkley S, Nelson D, Patil B, Stevens M & Wolff B, *Authentication, Authorization, and Accounting: Protocol Evaluation*, IETF RFC 3127, June 2001.
40. Hardcastle-Kille S, *Mapping Between X.400(1988)/ISO 10021 and RFC 822*, IETF RFC 1327, May 1992.
41. Linn J, *Common Authentication Technology Overview*, IETF RFC 1511, September 1993.
42. Haller N & Atkinson R, *On Internet Authentication*, IETF RFC 1704, October 1994.
43. Harkins D & Carrel D, *The Internet Key Exchange (IKE)*, IETF RFC 2409, November 1998.
44. Brownlee N, *Accounting Requirements for IPng*, IETF RFC 1672, August 1994.
45. Glass S, Hiller T, Jacobs S & Perkins C, *Mobile IP Authentication, Authorization, and Accounting Requirements*, IETF RFC 2977, October 2000.
46. Rigney C, Rubens A, Simpson W & Willens S, *Remote Authentication Dial in User Service (RADIUS)*, IETF RFC 2058, January 1997.
47. Rubens A, Simpson W, Willens S & Rigney C, *Remote Authentication Dial in User Service (RADIUS)*, IETF RFC 2138, April 1997.
48. Aboba B & Zorn AG, *Implementation of L2TP Compulsory Tunneling via RADIUS*, IETF RFC 2809, April 2000.
49. Rigney C, Willens S, Rubens A. & Simpson W, *Remote Authentication Dial in User Service (RADIUS)*, IETF RFC 2865, June 2000.

12

Mobile Ad Hoc Networks and Future Challenges[1]

Ad hoc networks have attracted attention from the research community since the early nineties. The author himself was also deeply engrossed and interested in this area of research since that time. Earlier research was focused on ad hoc routing, that is, on how routes can be discovered and how packets can be forwarded toward their destinations. Gradually over the years, other technical issues become important too, such as media access control protocols, ad hoc multicasting, and support for transmission control protocol (TCP) over ad hoc networks. In this chapter, future research challenges for ad hoc mobile networks based on the author's own perspectives are presented. In particular, the issues discussed are (1) integrated ad hoc power management, (2) high-capacity ad hoc networks, (3) integration of ad hoc and wireless LAN technologies, (4) quality of service (QoS) support, (5) service discovery architectures, (6) forwarding models and incentives, and (7) address initialization, resolution, and reuse.

12.1 INTRODUCTION TO MOBILE AD HOC NETWORKS

In order to provide a self-reading literature on wireless Internet Protocol (IP) in this book, it has been decided to add a short introductory section on mobile ad hoc networks (MANETs), right before the advanced topics presented by Dr Toh in this chapter.

---

[1] This chapter (except for Section 12.1) is authored by C-K. Toh, Georgia Institute of Technology, GA 30305, USA. He is now the Director of Research, TRW Systems, CA.

The Wireless Mobile Internet: Architectures, Protocols, and Services.   Abbas Jamalipour
© 2003 John Wiley & Sons, Ltd   ISBN: 0-470-84468-X

Therefore, in this section we will review the basics in mobile ad hoc networking that should be sufficient for the readers to follow the discussions hereafter in the chapter. Readers who are interested in more details on ad hoc networks are referred to many good papers on this topic and in particular to a recent text written by Toh [1].

12.1.1 Wireless LAN

One of the extensions to the wired Ethernet is the wireless LAN, defined in the IEEE 802.11 standards [2–4]. Wireless LAN is becoming very popular in providing mobile Internet access in office and campus buildings owing to the ease in the movement of users while connected to the Internet. IEEE 802.11 standards define a set of medium access protocols to extend the wired Ethernet into the wireless domain. FCC (Federal Communications Commission) in 1985 modified the radio spectrum regulations for unlicensed devices, so that wireless LAN could operate within the ISM (industrial, scientific, and medical) bands, if the equipments operate under 1 W of power. Only in the United States the 902-MHz and 5.725-GHz bands can be used, whereas the 2.4-GHz band is available globally [4]. The usage of unlicensed ISM frequency spectrums simplifies deployment of a new wireless LAN with very few and low-cost equipments. Nomadic Internet access, portable computing, multihopping including ad hoc networking are some of the applications of wireless LAN technology. Depending on the standard, the wireless LAN can achieve a speed of up to 1–2 (IEEE 802.11), 11 (IEEE 802.11b), or 54 (IEEE 802.11a) Mbps, in an ideal situation and in good wireless channel conditions.

In principle, a wireless LAN domain can be provided easily through an access point (AP) cabled to the usual wired Ethernet in a LAN system. Therefore, the AP could be considered as a router or a hub connecting several end hosts to the LAN system. The only difference here would be that the end host will access the AP through wireless channels, rather than cables. Since each AP will give access to several end machines, some type of multiple access control has to be established by the AP to share the wireless channel among all end users. Spread-spectrum technology, both direct-sequence and frequency-hopping, are used for this purpose in the standard. More recently, OFDMA (orthogonal frequency division multiple access) is proposed for the wireless LAN at high data bit rates.

Each AP in a wireless LAN system can provide coverage to mobile Internet users in an area around a maximum of 500 m in radius. Therefore, by having multiple APs, it is possible to establish a cellular-like wireless LAN. In such a case, cellular-type issues, such as handoff and maximum capacity will become apparent. Figure 12.1 shows an illustration of a wireless LAN with two APs and several end machines. The users of a wireless LAN system can obtain an IP address through a DHCP (dynamic host configuration protocol) similar to a dial-up connection or by having a fixed IP address provided by their network administrator similar to a desktop user.

12.1.2 Ad hoc networking using the wireless LAN

The technology provided by the IEEE 802.11 allows users also to dynamically form a private network without the need for an AP [1]. Therefore, it is possible to make a

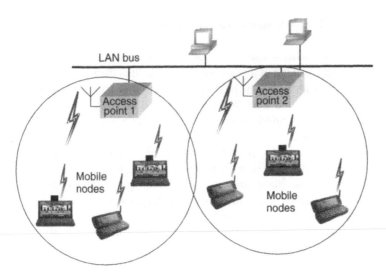

Figure 12.1   A basic illustration of a wireless LAN system

temporary network of computers, for example, during a meeting, where there is no server. All users will have the same level of the network hierarchy. The computers in this network can exchange their data files through the wireless LAN network, which could be isolated from the local wired (wireless) network. This is a very basic implementation of a MANET, which clearly does not have any infrastructure supporting it. Internet Engineering Task Force (IETF) has a working group called MANET that develops the RFCs and standards for this emerging technology. Figure 12.2 shows an ad hoc network with four mobile computers, which can be compared to the configuration previously given in Figure 12.1.

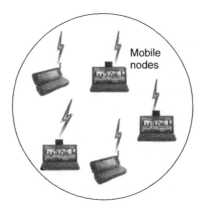

Figure 12.2   A basic illustration of an ad hoc network

12.1.3   IEEE 802.11 specifications

The IEEE 802.11 standard defines two types of services for the wireless LAN: basic service set (BSS) and extended service set (ESS). In the BSS a network of computers is established either with a central base station (AP) that can connect the users of the wireless LAN network to the other parts of the wired network or without a central base station, which provides an ad hoc network between several users without any access to other parts of the network.

Two or more wireless LANs that are using the BSS can be connected through any of the IEEE LAN standards such as Ethernet or Token Ring to make an infrastructure of wireless LANs, so that the system covers a larger geographical area, similar to the concept of cellular networks. This configuration is the ESS for the IEEE 802.11 standard. The wireless LAN illustration shown in Figure 12.1 was this ESS.

Two types of medium access control (MAC) are defined by IEEE 802.11: distributed configuration function (DCF) and point coordination function (PCF). DCF is the basic MAC protocol for wireless LAN and it is the only access for an ad hoc networking type of configuration. DCF is a contention access technique, which means that the wireless LAN users need to compete in getting a channel for data transmission. DCF is based on the fundamental Internet MAC protocol CSMA (carrier sense multiple access) with additional collision avoidance (CA), which makes it CSMA/CA [5,6]. One reason for using CSMA/CA in wireless LAN and not the usual CSMA/CD (CSMA with collision detection) used in wired LANs is that for the wireless media, detecting a collision is not as easy as in the case of wired systems. Also, in the case of wireless channel there is always a chance of getting involved into the *hidden-terminal* problem.

On the wired network, detection of another signal from a user can be performed by measuring the current signal power on the wire. However, in a wireless environment, it is possible that a user is in the range of the base station and thus visible to it, but outside the range of another user, who is also seen by the base station. This phenomenon is called the *hidden-terminal problem*. Therefore, when a user wants to transmit his packet over the radio channel, detecting the radio signal power would show only the presence of the other users in his range and not the hidden terminals. If the user transmits a packet and at the same time another hidden-terminal transmits his packet, both packets will be lost. The hidden-terminal problem is illustrated in Figure 12.3.

Thus, to avoid the hidden-terminal effect, the wireless MAC needs to add an extra packet exchange before a transmission to make sure that no one else is transmitting at the same time. Therefore, the base station in the wireless LAN acts as a server that allows a user to transmit or not after a request proposal.

The PCF is implemented on top of the DCF for time-sensitive transmissions in an infrastructure wireless LAN architecture. PCF uses centralized, contention-less polling access by utilizing a software called *point-coordinator* (PC) [4]. PC software is located at the base station and polls users one after another to avoid any contention for their transmissions. As the PCF runs over the DCF, the sensing process of the DCF is performed only once at the beginning of the PCF polling cycle.

The IEEE 802.11 defines three types of specifications for the physical layer, on the basis of frequency hopping spread spectrum (FH-SS), direct sequence spread spectrum (DS-SS),

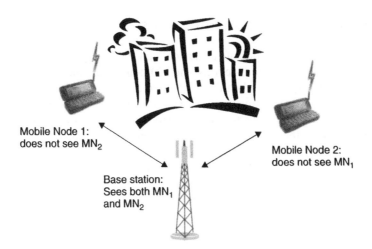

Figure 12.3 The hidden-terminal effect

and infrared communications. BPSK (binary phase shift keying) and QPSK (quadrature phase shift keying) were used as the modulation schemes in DS-SS specifications of wireless LAN for its early standard, for a bit rate of 1 and 2 Mbps, respectively. Other modulation schemes have been added later in IEEE 802.11b and IEEE 802.11a standards to allow higher bit rates of 5.5 and 11 Mbps in IEEE 802.11b and 54 Mbps in IEEE 802.11a. In the new standard IEEE 802.11b, the MAC and the logical link control (LLC) layer protocols are kept the same as in the original IEEE 802.11 and only the physical layer has been modified. For IEEE 802.11b, again DS-SS is utilized. Dynamic rate shifting is also allowed in IEEE 802.11b so that in a noisy environment the bit rate could be decreased from its highest 11 Mbps dynamically to 5.5, 2, or 1 Mbps.

12.2 INTEGRATED AD HOC POWER MANAGEMENT

While the CPU speed is advancing with time, battery power life has still not reached quantum leaps. Most mobile devices today are powered using batteries and hence the operational lifetime of these devices is limited to a few hours before requiring recharge or battery replacement. If there is an electrochemical limit on the battery capacity and its lifetime, then smart power conservation is necessary.

Ad hoc networking is enabled through a set of communication protocols. These protocols are designed to support ad hoc routing, media access, multicasting, and data transport. However, power issues may not necessarily be included in the design of these protocols. Traditionally, network protocols are designed to support communications, not power conservation. However, with the widespread use of mobile devices, it is crucial to optimize power usage to prolong the operation lifetime of these devices.

12.2.1 Device power consumptions

The overall power consumption of a device can be categorized into two major parts, namely, (1) communications-related and (2) non-communications-related. Power consumed by device display, keyboard, disks, memory, and CPU can be classified as non-communications-related. Innovations have already been made to improve on '*device*' *power consumption*, especially for the former. Protocol designers are beginning to look into embedding power-efficient features into communication protocols.

A major disjoint effort can be found in power-efficient protocol work. For example, proposals for power-efficient MAC protocol and power-efficient routing have been made. However, these protocols do not exhibit synergy in their power conservation operations, that is, they operate in a mutually exclusive manner. For example, while the routing protocol might be choosing a route comprising minimum number of nodes with sufficient remaining power, the MAC protocol might be aggressively initiating packet retransmission in response to the poor fading channel. Hence, power conserved by the routing protocol may be ruined by the underlying MAC protocol.

12.2.2 Power managements

Power management has to occur at the *device, protocol, and application layers*. Device power management is widely used in mobile computers today. More and more power-manageable hardware are designed and deployed. Advance power management (APM)

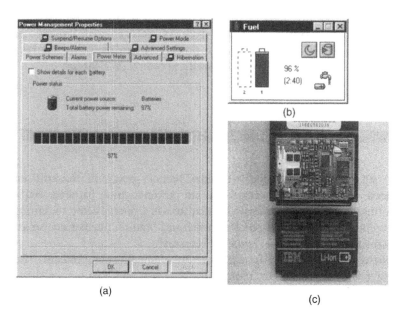

(a)

(b)

(c)

Figure 12.4   (a) Power monitor on Windows OS; (b) fuel indicator; and (c) smart battery logic in battery pack

tools are present to control power usage of a system on the basis of the system's activity. Figures 12.4a and 12.4b show the power management interface available on Microsoft Windows, while Figure 12.4c reveals the presence of smart battery logic in battery packs for laptop computers. Several power states are introduced so that the system can be placed in specific power saving modes as the system is left idle or unused.

Power conservation at the protocol levels occurs at the *data-link* [7–9], *network*, and *transport* layers. At the data-link layer, unnecessary retransmissions and collisions during channel access are avoided whenever possible. At the network (routing) layer, routes are selected on the basis of the remaining battery life of the nodes [10] and their route relaying loads [11]. Finally, at the transport layer, packet losses are handled in a localized manner whenever possible to conserve power. Avoiding repeated retransmissions during flow control could also conserve power. All these efforts, however, appear rather disjoint. Researchers have been working on power-efficient protocols at these layers independently. Power conserved at one layer does not necessary get conveyed down to the lower layers and vice versa. Hence, to achieve overall effectiveness in protocol power conservation, one has to strive for an integrated power management framework.

12.3 MAC PROTOCOL FOR AD HOC NETWORKS

At the MAC layer, dedicated slots and channels can be coordinated among nodes in a route to ensure that the QoS requirements on channel access are met. Since nodes can be mobile, it is crucial that nodes selected for the communication path have to be 'associatively' stable [11]. The absence of a centralized and fixed base station implies that channel access would not be entirely contention-free.

In an environment in which nodes share transmissions over a common channel, nodes supporting active routes should transmit more aggressively and neighboring nodes should back off and reattempt at a less frequent interval. This provides some form of QoS assurance so that the nodes in the route can transmit and forward packets within some bounded delay and bandwidth requirements.

The presence of asymmetric links [12,13] can make communications complicated. In MANETs, omnidirectional radios give rise to hidden terminals and to exposed nodes problems [1]. Directional antennas can alleviate some of these problems since signals can be directed in a specific spatial orientation. This feature also reduces the number of potential collisions in the channel. In sectorized systems, each sector is treated as a different cell. Hence, this allows further frequency reuse than what is possible in cellular systems.

Ad hoc networks may not be able to attain very high communication performance through the use of omnidirectional radios. Smart antenna technologies have advanced to a stage in which transmissions and receptions can be controlled electronically and spatially. Smart antennas are also very resilient toward multipath fading. Currently, there are two forms of smart antenna systems: (1) switched beam and (2) adaptive array. Switched beam antennas can be particularly useful when nodes are mobile. The structure of a switched beam antenna transceiver (SBAS) is shown in Figure 12.5. An SBAS system allows one

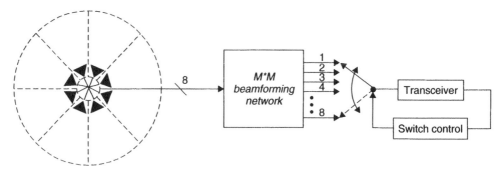

A switched beam transceiver uses an antenna array with eight elements

Figure 12.5   A switched beam smart antenna system

to selectively transmit and receive at/from a specific antenna sector/array element. This feature allows one to reduce the probability of packet collision and signal interference.

Unlike switched beam antennas, adaptive array antennas have the ability to effectively locate and track various types of signals to dynamically minimize interference and to maximize signal reception. This is achieved through the use of advanced signal processing techniques. By exploiting these features obtainable from smart antenna systems, the MAC protocol can further enhance link performance [14].

The challenge facing the design of smart antenna–based MAC protocol for ad hoc mobile networks is the ability to intelligently select appropriate sectors for transmissions and reception in order to counteract mobility, channel fading, asymmetric links, hidden terminals, and exposed nodes problems. Some recent work utilized Global Positioning System (GPS) information to aid antenna beam steering. However, this requires each node to be equipped with a GPS receiver. Another area worthy of research is power control for packet transmission and reception. With appropriate control, hidden terminal, exposed nodes, and packet collisions can be reduced.

12.4   QUALITY OF SERVICE SUPPORT FOR AD HOC

Supporting QoS in mobile networks presents great challenges. While roaming is an attractive feature to have for many mobile users, it is inadequate if their calls or connections are constantly dropped and restarted. In cellular networks, the core network is generally a wired network of switches and routers. The cellular base stations perform call admissions and coordinate channel access. Ad hoc networks, however, do not have a wired backbone. To support end-to-end QoS, all nodes in the route have to support the same notion and assurance of desired QoS.

QoS mapping is paramount toward achieving QoS assurance. QoS assurance is different from QoS guarantee. QoS has to be supported at MAC, routing, and transport layers. Most ad hoc routing protocols do not support QoS. Routing metric used merely refers to the shortest path or the minimum number of hops. However, bandwidth, delay, and packet loss (reliability or data delivery ratio) are important QoS parameters. Hence, mechanisms should be built in current ad hoc routing protocols to allow for *route selection* based on QoS requirements and QoS availability of the network over the selected route. It is desirable to have the capability to select the best route that fulfils QoS requirements.

In addition to establishing QoS routes in response to route requests, *QoS assurance during route reconfiguration* has to be supported too. Past research was focused on finding alternate partial routes quickly and in a localized fashion. However, QoS considerations need to be made to ensure that end-to-end QoS requirements continue to be supported. Better still, the same mechanism to derive QoS routes during route requests can be reused to support route repair operations. This ensures uniformity and consistency.

There is also a need to distinguish flows using the same route. In ad hoc wireless communications, *multiflow* and *multiroute* architectures exist. Multiflows could coexist over the same route. When this happened, a flow identifier is necessary. When multiflows occur over different routes from the source to the destination, they are less interdependent. The former is commonly referred to as *mobile trunking*. This is analogous to the scenario of having multiple virtual channels on a virtual path as in ATM (Asynchronous Transfer Mode) technology. Mobility over a mobile trunking path could, therefore, affect multiple data traffic flows concurrently. For the latter case, however, route rerouting could be initiated and handled individually and independently.

12.5   AD HOC SERVICE DISCOVERY ARCHITECTURES

Ad hoc mobile networks are self-organizing and adaptive networks. Devices of different forms and capabilities are networked together and hence, certain devices could act as clients, while others act as servers. This scenario resembles the client–server architecture found in distributed systems. However, what differs greatly is the presence of mobility, power, and bandwidth constraints in ad hoc mobile systems.

In the past, research work was focused on resource recovery in the Internet. With the vast information available in hosts scattered geographically across the Internet, intelligent mechanisms are needed for users to quickly and accurately locate and retrieve information from the network. The network is, therefore, viewed as the fast, rich, and distributed interconnection of information databases. Protocols proposed for such purposes include SLP (service location protocol), SUN Jini, salutation protocol, and simple service discovery protocol (SSDP) [1]. However, none of these protocols are designed for error- and delay-prone wireless networks.

The inclusion of wireless connectivity in nodes and routers results in wireless networks. Bluetooth [15] is one such network that differs from cellular networks since there are no requirements for fixed radio base stations or APs. Although Bluetooth has its own SLP, it is still only applicable to single-hop piconets or scatternet based on a master–slave architecture. The dynamic nature of ad hoc mobile nodes could render the use of centralized service directory agents (DAs) inappropriate (since it would result in poor performance).

In some service location architectures, *user*, *directory*, and *service* agents are used. The user agent (UA) is a software entity that searches for requested services on behalf of the client. DAs are used to act as a broker between the service provider (the server) and the service requester (the client). Service requests are intercepted by the DA, processed, and the outcome sent back to the requestor. Service providers, therefore, register their services to the nearest DAs. These registrations have to be performed at a sufficient frequency so that the service records in the DAs are kept up to date.

The performance of an SLP can be measured by:

1. *Service availability*: It defines what percentage of service requests sent by the clients is fulfilled by the presence of service providers in the network.

2. *Control overhead*: This concerns how much control overhead is incurred by the protocol.

3. *Speed of service access*: This refers to the time taken to access the desired service from the server.

4. *Speed of service query reply*: This refers to the delay incurred from the time the request is sent by the requester to the time a reply is received. Note that this reply could be sent by the service agent (SA) or the DA.

Research work on ad hoc service discovery is scarce even today. One such work [16] investigates centralized, distributed, and hybrid approaches toward service discovery. It was discovered that the hybrid approach is more suitable to ad hoc networks owing to the higher overall service availability with a lower incurred overhead. Further research is needed to derive new service discovery, location, and access paradigms.

12.6 FORWARDING MODELS AND INCENTIVES

An ad hoc network is a form of community network, that is, it relies on the willingness of ad hoc mobile hosts to forward and relay packets toward the destination. However, forwarding other hosts' packets can result in

1. dissipation of available battery power,

2. consumption of memory and CPU cycles,

3. possibility of security attack, and

4. consumption of user bandwidth over the air.

Figure 12.6 implies that some forms of *forwarding and rewarding models* have to be established. Policies can be programmed into ad hoc mobile devices so that such devices will only forward packets that fulfill certain criteria, such as the following:

1. Originator and "group membership' of the host that transmit the packet.

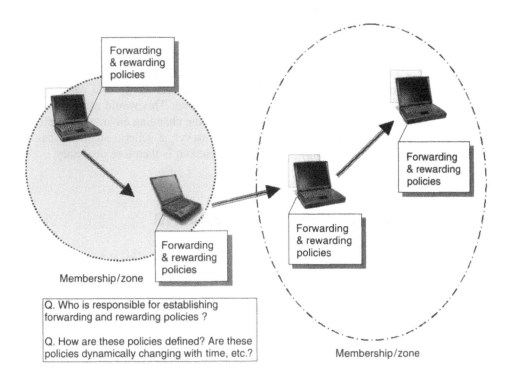

Figure 12.6 An illustration of forwarding and rewarding issues for ad hoc communications

2. Any mutual 'agreement' between the originator of the packet and the node that is pondering to relay the packet. Such agreement could include accumulation of credits (moneywise, internet usage membership, security agreement, mutual forwarding contract, etc.) for the node relaying the packets [17].

3. Packet zones, that is, only packets that originate from a certain network zone (or subnetwork) will be considered.

4. Urgency of the data to be relayed. This is familiar to domestic '911' calls where forwarding such data can save lives. Users may be much willing to forward such distress calls on a pervasive basis.

Clearly, many other factors can be taken into consideration to further refine forwarding and rewarding policies. An algorithm that takes all these factors into consideration and establishes these policies is needed. Who then should be responsible for establishing these policies? Should it be the telecommunications operators, service providers, or device manufacturers? Should such policies be established in a centralized or distributed manner? In the former scenario, users may submit their 'desires and restrictions' to service providers. The service provider then registers concerned devices as 'ad hoc mode enabled' and derives the forwarding and rewarding policies for them. Such policies can be programmed into the devices (via wireless links as in a mobile phone) or users might have to appear at certain establishments to have their devices configured. This, however, may be less favorable.

The distributed approach toward having the rewarding and forwarding policies established relies on devices communicating with each other and establishing the policies on their own. Users can specify and enter their desires into the device and can demand that a new forwarding and rewarding policy be established. This would also mean that such policies could dynamically change over time with the changing environment and the availability of network resources and battery life. However, a generic algorithm has to exist in the device to allow this to happen. Further research is therefore necessary.

12.7 AD HOC ADDRESSING AND NAMING

Ad hoc networks need some form of addressing so that hosts can be identified and packets can be relayed hop-by-hop and delivered ultimately to the destination. Ad hoc networks that do not need to be connected to the backbone Internet can be viewed as an isolated network. This implies that hosts in this network can practically take any unique address. However, even if the environment is a stand-alone ad hoc network, the following issues need to be considered:

1. *Address syntax*: Should addresses for ad hoc mobile hosts be classified into classes as in IP addressing and should it also contain the network and host portions? Will ad hoc networks contain subnetworks? How does one ensure uniqueness in addresses?

2. *Address initialization*: Who should initialize each host with the appropriate network address? Recall that such assignments have to be unique to each host in the network.

3. *Address conflicts*: When an ad hoc intranetwork migrates to the proximity of another, there is potential possibility of address conflicts. Under such circumstances, conflicts have to be resolved in a swift manner.

4. *Address resolution*: How would hosts in an ad hoc intranet know their destination nodes' address?

5. *Address reuse*: Once a node belonging to one intranetwork migrates away, there is a great possibility of reusing the 'lost' network address. Again, how can this migration be detected and the address freed and reused?

6. *Unreachable hosts*: How are unreachable hosts handled? Are ad hoc routers still capable of responding with Internet control message protocol (ICMP) messages?

Who should act as the address allocation agency? Is DHCP even possible or applicable? In addition to addressing issues, naming poses another great challenge. In the past, users utilized names for the ease of remembrance and identification. Names hide the specifics of numeric addresses from the users. The resolution of name to addresses is achieved through the use of name servers. Such servers are organized in a logical and hierarchical manner such that name-address queries are propagated to the upper level server if the local server is unable to resolve the query. Normally, the resolution can be achieved in a short time owing to the high-speed interconnection of servers.

For ad hoc mobile networks, would it be possible to support naming? How would a node be selected to act as the name server? What would happen when an assigned name server node migrates away? Could names reflect a better syntax to define the host and the environment surrounding it (or so-called 'domain')? How should we define the resultant naming space so that heterogeneous wired and mobile networks can be included? This could have serious implications for the tactical environment.

12.8 CONNECTION PRECEDENCE AND PREEMPTION

Ad hoc mobile networks are envisaged to provide data, audio, and video services to mobile users. In the defense era, provision of multimedia services is considered important. In addition, mobile users differ by their ranks, type of decisions, and resulting actions. Hence, a high-ranking official might want his connection request to be fulfilled, in view of the importance and the urgency of his actions. If the chosen route path is preoccupied, it might be necessary to allow the new connection request to preempt the existing connection. While the provision of this feature is particularly attractive for battlefield scenarios, it does require changes to underlying protocols.

For on-demand source-initiated routing protocols, if a new request with a higher precedence level originates at a source node that already has multiple routes active, then a check procedure has to occur. If the request results in a route path that is already congested, then decision has to be made to select an existing route to preempt in order to grant this request. For protocols in which route selection is performed at the destination, it is at this point that the destination node performs route preemption. All nodes in the preempted route have to be informed and their forwarding tables updated. The applications at both source and destination nodes have to be terminated and the user informed. This can be termed as *end-point* preemption. Figure 12.7 illustrates the process of preemption of an existing route by a new route in a MANET.

A follow-up of this event is the use of rerouting instead of having the connection dropped as a result of preemption. Rerouting will cause some form of disruption to existing data flows but it is still less annoying than dropping a connection. A disadvantage of initiating rerouting is that it could defer the preemption process, that is, resources tied down by the current route could not be released until an alternative route is found to complete the rerouting process. This could result in severe implications for the preempting user.

Route preemption could also be triggered by an intermediate node. Suppose an active route 'Q' exists on the first source node SRC1, N1, N2, N3, and the first destination node DEST1. Suppose another source node SRC2 initiates a route request toward a destination node DEST2. Suppose the chosen route 'W' is SRC2, N8, N7, N3, N5, DEST2. Hence, N3 is common to both routes. However, when N3 received the path setup message from DEST2, decision to preempt route 'Q' is already contained within the setup packet. Hence, N3 could initiate route 'Q' to be preempted by sending control packets to N3 upstream and downstream nodes on route 'Q'.

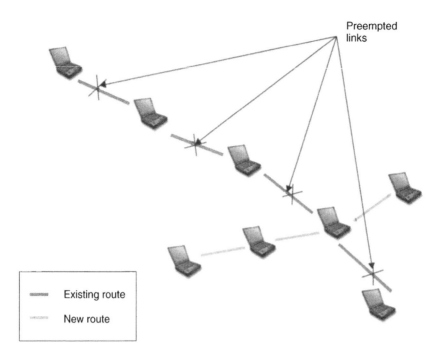

Preempted links

Existing route

New route

Figure 12.7 An existing route could be preempted by another upcoming route owing to nature of urgency and importance

Research is needed to investigate when and how preemption of communication paths can be supported in ad hoc mobile networks. Intelligent control of preemption activities can result in offering communications to those when urgently in need (hence fulfilling critical applications and requests) while at the same time allowing effective use of the network for data transport to mobile users. A network with connections preempted most of the time could render the network unusable! This demands further studies.

12.9 SUMMARY AND CONCLUSIONS

A new form of networking technology has evolved in which dynamic network formation can occur over a multitude of heterogeneous devices. Research into the area of ad hoc mobile networking has begun since the early 1990s. Gradually, issues related to routing and multicasting have been addressed. In this chapter, the technical challenges prior to the realization of a usable self-organizing and adaptive mobile network have been highlighted. While the infrastructure formation and data transport mechanism is essential, the provision of host/network addressing, security, QoS, and client/server services are crucial to mobile users. Discussions have been made on the use of ad hoc networking in intelligent transport highways, underground train station networks, pedestrian telecommunication networks, defense sensors networks, and so on. By further investigating these remaining challenges, we will be one step closer toward realizing and deploying ad hoc mobile networks and services.

REFERENCES

1. Toh C-K, *Ad Hoc Mobile Wireless Networks: Protocols and Systems*, Prentice Hall PTR, Upper Saddle River, N.J., 2002.
2. Crow BP, Widjaja I, Kim JG & Sakai PT, IEEE 802.11 wireless local area networks, *IEEE Communications Magazine*, **35**(9), 116–126, 1997.
3. IEEE 802.11, Web site: http://www.ieee802.org/11.
4. Forouzan B, *Local Area Networks*, McGraw-Hill Higher Education, Boston, Mass., 2003.
5. Stallings W, *Data and Computer Communications*, sixth edition, Prentice Hall, Upper Saddle River, N.J., 2000.
6. Comer DE, *Computer Networks and Internets*, second edition, Prentice Hall, Upper Saddle River, N.J., 1999.
7. Singh S & Raghavendra CS, PAMAS—Power aware multi-access protocol with signaling for ad hoc networks, *ACM Computer Communications Review*, July, 1998.
8. Talucci F & Gerla M, MACA-BI (MACA by invitation)—A wireless MAC protocol for high speed ad hoc networking, Proceedings of IEEE ICUPC, 1997.
9. Tang Z & Garcia-Luna-Aceves JJ, Hop-reservation multiple access (HRMA) for ad hoc networks, Proceedings of IEEE INFOCOM Conference, 1999.
10. Toh C-K & Shih C-H, Maximum battery life routing to support ubiquitous mobile computing in wireless ad hoc networks, *IEEE Communications Magazine*, **39**(6), 138–147, 2001.
11. Toh C-K, Associativity-based routing for ad hoc mobile networks, *Journal on Wireless Personal Communications*, **4**(2), 1997.
12. Kim D-K, Toh C-K & Choi Y-H, LAWS: Location-aware long-lived route selection for mobile ad hoc networks, *IEEE Electronic Letters*, September, 2000.
13. Kim D-K, Toh C-K & Choi Y-H, On supporting link asymmetry in mobile ad hoc networks, Proceedings of IEEE Global Communications Conference (GLOBECOM 2001), San Antonio, Tex., November 2001.
14. Kim D-K, Toh C-K & Choi Y-H, ROADMAP: A reliable and robust ACK-driven protocol for wireless ad hoc networks, Proceedings of IEEE Military Communications Conference (MILCOM 2001), October 2001.
15. Bray J & Sturman CF, *BLUETOOTH: Connect Without Cables*, Prentice Hall PTR, Upper Saddle River, N.J., 2001.
16. Guichal G & Toh C-K, Performance evaluation of centralized and distributed service location protocols for pervasive wireless networks, Proceedings of IEEE Personal Indoor and Mobile Radio Conference (PIMRC 2001), San Diego, Calif., September, 2001.
17. Buttyan L & Hubaux JP, Enforcing service availability in mobile ad hoc WANs, Proceedings of ACM/IEEE MOBIHOC Workshop, August 2000.

13

Satellites in Wireless IP

A satellite has been an important element of telecommunications networks for many years, providing long-distance telephony and television broadcasting. The involvement of satellites in Internet protocol (IP) networks is a direct result of new trends in global telecommunications in which Internet traffic will hold a dominant share in the total network traffic, and the special features of high-capacity satellite channels will be discussed in this chapter. The large geographical coverage of the satellite footprint and its unique broadcasting capabilities as well as its high-capacity channels make the satellite an irreplaceable part of communications systems, despite the high cost and long development and launching cycle of a satellite system. In this chapter, the role of satellites in future wireless Internet networks will be discussed and relevant research issues will be explored.

13.1 INTRODUCTION

In this chapter, we will review the satellite communications systems and introduce a new era for satellite communications toward broadband satellite systems and satellite-for-the-Internet systems. This means that the satellite is changing its traditional role from being simply a relay in space to becoming an active element similar to a switch or a router in terrestrial networks. We will start the chapter with a short historical overview of satellite communications and then provide up-to-date information on new broadband and Internet satellite systems. We will briefly review third-generation (3G) wireless cellular systems, in which Internet access is considered, in order to show the role and contribution of satellites in these systems and thus in the mobile Internet. Satellite applications within the 3G wireless terrestrial systems as well as in the global Internet will be discussed. Several implementation topics including mobility and location management that are common in satellite and terrestrial mobile networks will also be discussed. We will then

The Wireless Mobile Internet: Architectures, Protocols, and Services.   Abbas Jamalipour
© 2003 John Wiley & Sons, Ltd   ISBN: 0-470-84468-X

open the discussion on topics on satellite transport of Internet traffic and the challenging issues that need to be resolved. Finally, we will conclude the chapter with a concise but complete discussion on the future perspectives of satellites in the global Internet connectivity problem.

13.2 OVERVIEW OF SATELLITE COMMUNICATIONS

A satellite is one of the oldest components in the telecommunications systems. For almost one half of a century, satellite networks have provided long-distance communications services to the Public-Switching Telephone Network (PSTN) as well as television broadcasting. These services are particularly best justified by the large footprint coverage of the satellite and to this date, there is no substitute for satellites in this field. In these types of service, a satellite acts as a communications repeater or relay (in accordance to whether the transmitted signal is digital or analog, respectively) that communicates with ground stations and resolves the problem of transmission of electromagnetic waves between different parts of the world that are not in the line of sight of each other. A noteworthy achievement in satellite communications is the formation of INTELSAT (International Telecommunications Satellite Organization), which in 1964 established a means of fixed-satellite service among nations [1].

13.2.1 Mobile satellite services — First generation

In the 1980s, satellites were being deployed for the first time in mobile telecommunications by providing direct communications to maritime vessels and aircrafts. The first major development in this area was the INternational MARitime telecommunication SATellite organization (INMARSAT) system. In 1982, INMARSAT started a new era of satellite communications, called *mobile satellite services*, or MSS. The INMARSAT used a geostationary satellite system using L-band (1.5–1.6 GHz) to provide telecommunication services mainly to ships. In the first generation of MSS, INMARSAT defined five standards: Standard A (1982), Standard B (1993), Standard C (1991), Standard M (1992/93), and Aeronautical Standard (1992). Different worldwide telecommunications services including voice, facsimile, and data were considered in these standards. While INMARSAT A and B are mostly considered as the service to ships, INMARASAT C is planned to provide service to small craft, fishing boats, and land mobiles. INMARSAT continues its worldwide services as one of the most reliable satellite communications systems.

Although INMARSAT remains as the most distinguishable satellite system of its kind, there were other MSSs developed during the *first-generation mobile satellite systems*, such as QUALCOMM in North America (1989), ALCATEL QUALCOMM for Europe (1991), and the Japanese NASDA system (1987).

13.2.2 Mobile satellite services — Second generation

Reduction in size and cost of user terminals was the motive for second-generation (2G) MSS being introduced, around 1985. In this generation, interconnection of satellite systems with terrestrial wireless systems has also been considered. In 1995, INMARSAT defined its mini-M standard with worldwide voice, data, facsimile, and telex services at 2.4 Kbps. American Mobile Satellite Corporation (AMSC), NSTAR of Japan, European mobile satellite (EMS), and several others are included in the 2G MSS.

Satellite systems have always faced unavoidable long propagation delay and large transmission power requirements. Consideration of small-size user terminals and direct radio communications between users and satellites (i.e. without using a ground station) led to the idea of using satellites in lower-altitude orbits than the geostationary orbit. Among possible orbit selections, low Earth orbit (LEO) satellites with an altitude between 500 and 1500 km and medium Earth orbit (MEO) satellites with an altitude between 5000 and 13,000 km were considered [1]. The altitude selection given above assures that the satellites reside outside the two Van Allen belts to avoid the radiation damage to the electronic components installed in the satellites. The use of these nongeostationary satellite systems for commercial purposes started a new era in mobile satellite communications. Use of spot beam antennas in these satellites produces a cellular type structure within coverage areas and hence a frequency reuse scheme can be applied, making the system a high-capacity cellular-like network on the ground with satellites as the base stations (BSs) in space.

LEO and MEO satellite systems, due to their shorter distance to the Earth, solve the problem of long propagation delay and high power consumption, but introduce new challenges to the communications industry. Since the satellite is closer to the Earth, compared to a geostationary satellite, it is not possible to employ just three satellites to cover all parts of the world as in the case of geostationary satellite systems. Therefore, for LEO and MEO, a constellation of satellites on the order of tens of satellites is required. This means more complexity and of course higher cost to the satellite system, which eventually must be passed on to the users. Many LEO and MEO satellite systems were proposed in the early 1990s in North America and around the world and obtained frequency spectrum licenses. Only a few of these systems were completed and became operational, including IRIDIUM (1998) with 66 satellites and GLOBALSTAR (2000) with 48 satellites. However, financial problems associated with the high cost of LEO systems forced IRIDIUM to cease its operation in the year 2000. Besides higher network complexity and more expensive control management requirements of nongeostationary satellite systems, LEO and MEO satellites also have shorter lifetimes than satellites in geostationary systems. This means more frequent satellite launch requirements and higher maintenance cost to the satellite system.

The operational failure of the advanced but complex IRIDIUM satellite system revealed that although the technology for implementing a mobile satellite phone system is available, it is not possible to compete in cost and services of such a system with the fast-growing terrestrial cellular systems and the new Internet services using LEO satellites. The roaming capability between different 2G cellular networks in different countries and those considered in the 3G wireless systems are quite adequate to provide telecommunications services to the majority of the world population at lower costs and better quality (e.g. delay) than what can be achieved through satellite systems. The new trends in the telecommunications industry in transmitting data traffic and Internet traffic at high speeds over wireless channels could not be matched by satellite systems. The IRIDIUM system, for example, could provide short data services at the very low data rate of only 2.4 kbps.

Satellite systems, however, maintain their unique feature of broadcasting. *Satellite broadcasting* has been a success for a long time and continues its dominance for long-distance coverage and service to highly populated telephony networks. If this unique feature of satellite systems can be incorporated into the new trends in the telecommunications industry toward high-speed Internet access, then a new era of satellite communications technology will have begun. Broadband satellites are being developed for this market. Recent global antiterrorism activities have introduced new hopes for the IRIDIUM system, thanks to the system's complete global coverage even to locations where no other terrestrial or satellite ground station telecommunication infrastructure is available.

13.2.3   Broadband satellite systems

Broadband satellites [2–5] are referred to as systems that can provide high data rate transmission on the order of 1 Mbps and above. Digital video broadcasting (DVB) systems such as Eutelsat, SES, and INTELSAT, proprietary systems such as Spaceway, Astrolink, and iPSTAR, and proposed systems such as Teledesic, SkyBridge, WEST, Celestri, and so on are among such broadband satellite systems. Standardizations of these satellite systems are ongoing [6] in order to reduce the cost and increase the applicability, similar to the way in which terrestrial cellular systems have developed and have become successful. In this standardization, multicasting is also considered as a strong feature. Geostationary satellite systems are becoming the main interest of these services. Some of the applications of broadband satellite systems are shown in Figure 13.1. This figure illustrates how satellites can interconnect geographically distant networks through land gateways. The system shown in this figure is designed to provide access to the Internet contents in one place by users of many other networks. Each network usually includes a caching system for fast local multicast to its Internet users.

Broadband satellite systems can be categorized according to their specifications and capabilities. This could be based on the frequency bands of operation (C band 4–8 GHz, Ku band 10–18 GHz, Ka band 18–31 GHz, and higher bands V and Q), the orbit altitude and hence the satellite lifetime, power requirements and antenna size, usage of bent pipe or onboard processing (OBP) technologies, global or regional coverage of the system, satellite total capacity and user capacity, use of intersatellite links (ISL), number of supported terminals and required gateways, protocol used in the satellite system such as TCP/IP, DVB, asynchronous transfer mode (ATM), and so on, use of open or proprietary standards, total number of satellites in the system, and the total cost. Most new designs of satellite systems include OBP and onboard switching (OBS) facilities so that the satellite node changes its simple role of relaying into being an active element in the network. An example of a functional satellite system that includes OBS is shown in Figure 13.2. In this figure an ATM-switch like satellite is shown.

There are many regulatory and standard bodies currently involved in the development of issues related to the satellite communications industry. Regulatory bodies include WRC, Federal Communications Commission (FCC), ITU, ERO, and many national and regional regulatory organizations. Standards are mainly developed in Internet Engineering Task Force (IETF), European Telecommunications Standards Institute (ETSI), TIA, and ITU.

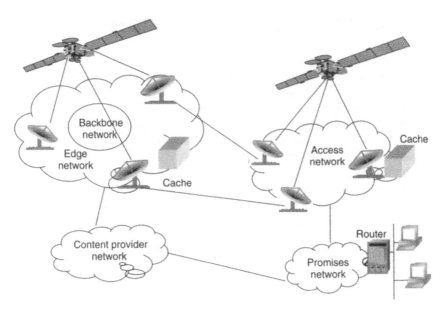

Figure 13.1 Applications of broadband satellites in interconnecting different networks

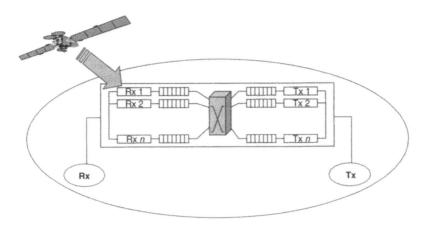

Figure 13.2 An example of satellite with onboard processing and onboard switching facilities

As a conclusion to this section, we must say that satellite systems have long development cycles compared to terrestrial systems and usually have less funding, and fewer engineers are involved in their development. Moreover, they compete over a more limited market than cellular systems. Most satellite systems are still proprietary and interfaces are not public, which in turn prevents competition. The standards for satellites will ensure interoperability and real competition and will be required for a broader consumer market. Therefore, in order to see further development in satellite systems, a widely acceptable standardization is vital.

13.3   SATELLITE FOR THE GLOBAL INTERNET

New multimedia and Internet services demand more cost-effective high-quality and high-speed telecommunications technologies and architectures. The primary issue is how it is possible to expand the current global Internet infrastructure so that the quality of service (QoS) can be improved from the current best-effort service and how high-speed access can be achieved. In this context, satellites can play an important role in expanding the Internet infrastructure using the large coverage area feature and in providing high-speed data transmission through a high-bandwidth capacity channel. Satellites however would not perform this task as an isolated network but would rather use an efficient integration with current terrestrial networks. So instead of having an IP network in the sky, as suggested in earlier proposals on some satellite IP networks, a combination of terrestrial and satellite networks would be a solution to the future high-speed Internet.

In a global Internet infrastructure, satellites could be used for many purposes. They can be used to connect geographically distant segments of the network or to interconnect heterogeneous networks. Satellites can provide direct telecommunications services to aircraft, ships, and isolated local networks on the ground and even to individual users. Flexible and quick deployment of bandwidth by satellite systems make them easily approachable by densely wired networks when required, as a good backup and supporting network.

13.3.1   Connection architecture of satellites

Figure 13.3 shows two different options for the satellite payload that can be used in satellite-based Internet architectures. In Figure 13.3a the satellite is used as a reflector in space connecting separate network segments through ground gateways. In Figure 13.3b, however, the satellite acts as an active component of the network that can utilize routing and switching processing. The satellites used in Figure 13.3 can be on any of the altitudes explained in Section 13.2; that is, geostationary or nongeostationary (LEO or MEO) or a combination of different altitudes. The satellites shown in Figure 13.3b, in addition to having connection to the ground gateways, are also employed in intersatellite links so that network connectivity can be created in the sky independently. This method should be considered as an important option in a future satellite-based Internet architecture. The method requires higher cost for the system and more complicated routing management. If special facilities are included in the mobile stations on the Earth, both methods can provide direct Internet connectivity to remote users without any other alternative terrestrial telecommunications infrastructure. A summary of the above satellite-based Internet architecture and current proposals of this kind can be found in Reference [7].

13.3.2   Application of satellites

A satellite node can also be used as a high-speed downlink for home Internet access. In this method, a home or office user with a satellite receiver, usually used for satellite

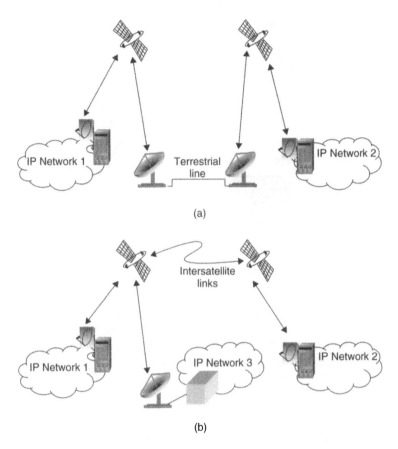

Figure 13.3 Two different payload options for satellite-based IP architectures: (a) bent-pipe architecture and (b) onboard processing satellites

television, can download the Internet contents at a very high data rate through the satellite downlink channel. A simple architecture of such a satellite-ground high-speed Internet is shown in Figure 13.4. In the architecture shown in this figure, the user first connects to his Internet service provider (ISP) using a normal dial-up connection. The dial-up connection forms a low-speed data communication (e.g. a usual 56-kbps connection) mainly in order to send requests to the Internet servers at the local ISP site. All Internet contents can then be forwarded to the customer through the high-speed satellite downlink upon receiving the request. The downlink can send the data to the user at speeds of one to a few megabits per second using digital video broadcasting satellites or other types of satellites. This method is especially appropriate for video-on-demand and other type of real-time Internet applications in which many users located in the same region want to retrieve the same contents over the Internet. The asymmetry in the Internet traffic that usually results in up to 10 times more data traffic on a typical Internet downlink connection compared to the uplink makes this method to be of special interest and application. Currently, this method is competing with other high-speed Internet access for home users including cable modems

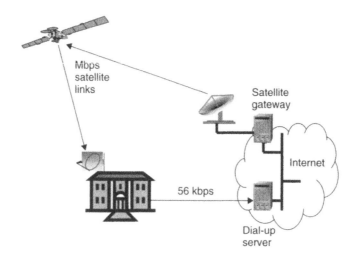

Figure 13.4   An architecture for satellite high-speed Internet access

and asynchronous digital subscriber line (ADSL) technologies. Some prototypes of these satellite Internet systems for home users have already been developed and demonstrated in Europe and other parts of the world [8,9]. With some modifications it is possible to extend the coverage of this type of Internet access to mobile users on the ground and also during long-distance flights and to ships.

13.4   SATELLITE IN THIRD-GENERATION WIRELESS NETWORKS

With the increasing popularity of portable computers and the expanding Internet capabilities of mobile phone handsets, a large demand for mobile computing has been generated in the past few years. Thus, instead of restricting data connections to be maintained always at a fixed position in the network, mobile users will be provided with equivalent multimedia and IP services. There is no doubt that the trend is toward a global mobile networking environment. In such a network, broadband satellites can be considered as an integral part of the network interconnecting the fast-growing terrestrial cellular and wired networks.

Broadband satellite networks for Internet access are the new generation of satellite networks in which Internet-based applications and services will be provided to users regardless of their degree of geographical mobility [2,3]. The main difference from conventional satellite networks will be that the new satellite networks will support high data rate transmission and broadband services and in particular the Internet. The Internet is the most rapidly growing technology and many new applications such as electronic commerce find their way through the Internet. Therefore, it is not surprising that broadband satellite networks focus on the Internet-based applications for their primary services, although voice and low bit rate applications still remain in the list of network services. ATM will be the envisaged switching mode for future broadband satellites due to its support of a variety of traffic such as constant and variable bit rate and QoS support [2]. Nevertheless, IP routing is considered as another alternative for these satellites due to lower cost and for being friendly to the Internet traffic.

In the sphere of terrestrial networks, there are at present two possible approaches for establishing the task of mobile computing: cellular-based and IP-based solutions [3]. Intuitively, while a cellular-based solution enhances the current mobile communications by extending the capacity for data and multimedia transmissions, an IP-based solution allows for user mobility by maintaining all ongoing Internet connections even in the presence of frequent handoffs or changes in the network point of attachments. In the forefront of these technologies, 3G wireless systems are being considered.

Third-generation wireless communications (3G) systems evolve by orienting the integration of three essential domains: broadband, mobile, and Internet (IP). In such a milieu, the increasing feasibility of virtual connections allows mobile users not only to roam freely between heterogeneous networks but also to remain engaged in various forms of multimedia communications. Whether it is geographical coverage, bandwidth, or delay, it would then be up to the users to decide when and how to switch from one access network to another depending upon the availability and appropriate cost/performance considerations, and thus, advance toward an era of all-IP-based communications. Consequently, it will be necessary to implement the 3G system as an universal solution that prompts transparent user roaming (among different wireless networks) while delivering the widest possible range of cost-effective services [10].

International Mobile Telecommunications (IMT-2000) is a unified 3G mobile system that supports both packet-switched and circuit-switched data transmissions with high spectrum efficiency, making the vision of anywhere, anytime communications a reality. Basically, it is a collection of standards that provides direct mobile access to a range of fixed and wireless networks [11]. The general idea was to make the development of 3G wireless technologies a gradual transition process from a circuit-switched to a packet-switched. As an example, for the GSM (Global System for Mobile communications), in order to have the system enhanced with improved services (by means of increased capacity, coverage, quality, and data rates), the evolution to 3G was made possible through the incorporation of an intermediate stage called GPRS, the General Packet Radio Service.

On the basis of the enhanced core network of GPRS, the Universal Mobile Telecommunications System (UMTS) was designed to be the backward-compatible 3G standard for GSM. UMTS supports multimedia services with extended intelligent network features and functions. As a first step of the integration, UTRAN (the UMTS terrestrial access radio network) will coexist with GSM access networks. The idea was to develop the UMTS core network by gradually incorporating the desired UMTS features to the GSM/GPRS core network [12].

For satellite systems, the situation is somehow different. The most apparent difference is that the market for satellite systems is much more limited than their cellular counterparts. Therefore, it would be difficult to assume the same approaches for satellite systems. Instead, satellite systems can incorporate their global coverage feature for the enhancement of the 3G terrestrial networks. Satellites can establish a high-speed backbone network to

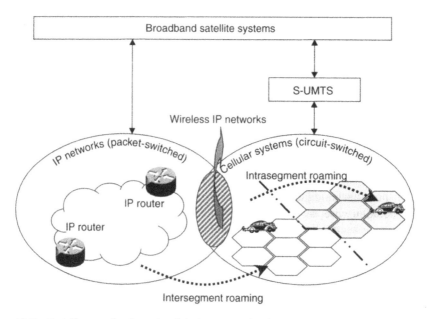

Figure 13.5   Satellite applications in global communications networks

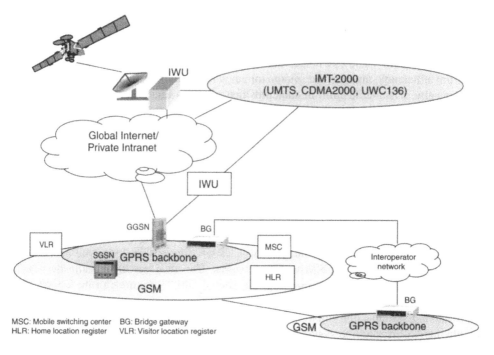

Figure 13.6   Interconnection of different terrestrial and satellite networks through interworking units

support the terrestrial networks and also to use their broadcast nature to deliver Internet content at high speeds directly to a group of users.

Satellite UMTS (S-UMTS), for example, is considered as a component of 3G networks [13]. The satellite segment of the network connects through appropriate interworking units (IWU) to the ground segments. An illustration of this incorporation of satellites in providing mobile Internet connectivity is shown in Figure 13.5. IWU for the satellite has similar functionality as the gateways used to interconnect 2G and 3G networks for interoperation of these networks during the transition period from 2G to 3G as well as the gateways used for interconnection of different operator networks of the same kind (e.g. GSM). Such a concept is shown in Figure 13.6.

13.5 TECHNICAL ISSUES FOR SATELLITE-BASED INTERNET IMPLEMENTATION

After the overview on satellite communications and 3G wireless networks and introducing the role of satellites within the 3G network architecture in previous sections, in this and the following section we look at some specific but important issues for mobile satellite networks that also apply to terrestrial and cellular networks.

13.5.1 Mobility management

It is widely agreed that to allow seamless user mobility, several considerations are necessary to ensure smooth transitions between different wireless technologies. Ultimately, mobility management is the key to enable successful convergence between wireless communications and computing. Often, mobility management is interpreted as a process that simply routes packets from one point (the source) to the other (the intended destination). However, such an assumption becomes inadequate as more and more unsolvable issues gradually become apparent. Given its complexity, there seems to be an inevitable need to redefine the previously overlooked issue—*the mobility problem.*

Very briefly, mobility implies adaptability: the capability of maintaining any established network connections by accommodating different system characteristics when a mobile user roams within and/or between networks. More specifically, mobility refers to the initiation of a handoff process, not only when moving between cells (as in a cellular wireless environment) but also when roaming from one wireless network (e.g. satellite) to another (e.g. GPRS). Depending on the level of the network stack from which a movement is considered, mobility can be classified into three categories, namely, air-interface mobility, link-level mobility, and network-level mobility.

Air-interface mobility is perhaps the most common case in which a handoff takes place between two adjacent BSs or access points (APs) within a radio access network. One can envisage this scenario as a pedestrian walking across microcell boundaries while being engaged in a conversation through voice or data transmissions. Link-level mobility goes up one level in the network hierarchy and is concerned with maintaining a point-to-point protocol (PPP) context across multiple radio access networks. The transitions, however, would still be within the same domain and technology. On the highest network level (among the three categories), network (or IP) mobility provides network-level mobility between different access networks (including wireless). Basically, this involves a change in the mobile's domain- (or location-) related IP address due to either (1) a change in radio access technologies or (2) a transition from one network operator to another. Note that in the latter case, the two networks involved might be implemented by the same access technology. Figure 13.7 attempts to illustrate the differences by listing the hierarchy of concern in the three cases. Note that the overall structure of a subnet can be considered to consist of three distinct stacks, with each stack being developed depending on the specific technology (or network architecture) under consideration.

Most issues related to mobility are associated either directly or indirectly with service delivery. By and large, it involves, but is not limited to, the process of routing management, handoff management (including resource management), and also QoS management. Having said that, each operation has its own set of predefined actions. Given that it might be possible to incorporate some of the specific techniques used in satellite systems to enhance the complete operations in a 3G network, a brief discussion will be given in the next few sections to frame this part of the mobility problem.

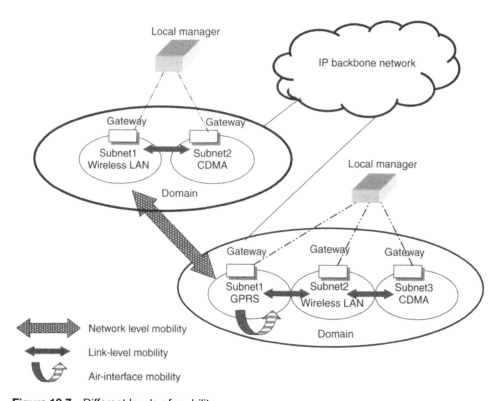

Figure 13.7   Different levels of mobility

13.5.2 Location management

Obviously, mobility is managed largely through the process of location management. This action involves not only storing and/or retrieving information from the location database but also sending paging signals whenever necessary to locate a roaming user. Although the need to notify the home network of the mobile users' current location is always present, it is questionable whether accurate location information is essential for mobile nodes (MNs) that are not committed to any data transmissions. Somehow, it seems logical to have separate mobility management techniques for idle and active MNs, and thus, to allow variations in adjusting the updating frequency at which the MNs' movement notifications are sent [14].

13.5.3 Routing management

One issue that relates closely to the provision of global roaming is the establishment (or management) of roaming agreements between various networks. As a mobile user roams across various geographical and/or network boundaries, appropriate global roaming agreements between networks (or among ISPs) will also have to be established [15]. In fact, the incorporation of satellites is a particularly significant example of such operations. In scenarios where a limited users population (or terrain conditions) has made it infeasible to implement wireless terrestrial technologies, the availability of satellite systems would instantly form an alternative access medium for a dual-mode handheld terminal.

13.5.4 Handoff management

A quality handoff management is particularly important for any real-time transmissions. As continuity plays a crucial part in grading the service quality for such a communication purpose, it is worth exploring the factors that would have an impact on handoff performance.

Mobility implies the necessity of MN handoffs. It is the process of reassociating the roaming mobile with a designated entity (in the new network) to maintain the much needed service continuity. Handoffs are performed at two layers; in the link layer (Open System Interconnection (OSI) Layer 2, which maintains link connectivity) and also in the IP layer (OSI Layer 3, which maintains network access). Physical connection to a BS can often be assumed to be seamless and almost instantaneous. The term network access denotes an MN's capability to exchange traffic in its current subnet without compromising its permanently allocated identity (IP address). An MN is said to have network access when its current subnet location corresponds with its registered network AP [16].

Successful handoffs are also crucial to ensure continuity of ongoing data connections (hence the provision of seamless roaming). However, to appreciate various coexisting network standards, the decision on the necessity of a handoff should be made on the basis of underlying network characteristics and specific application scenarios. This is particularly the case for intertechnology roaming (e.g. overlaying networks of Wireless LAN and GPRS), where the system characteristics might be significantly different. Essentially, a trade-off analysis among the resultant throughput, data rate, latency, and disruption measures would be beneficial in such instances, to determine the actual essentiality of a handoff action. In this respect, the availability of resources has a direct influence on the number of successful handoffs. Thus, specific issues with regard to resource management, such as channel allocation schemes and call admission controls, should all be carefully considered.

13.5.5   Quality of service management

QoS management is another significant area that has, in recent years, gained a tremendous research interest both at academic and commercial levels. In particular, with the gradual replacement of voice traffic by data traffic (and multimedia transmissions), a proper implementation of suitable bandwidth allocation mechanisms is crucial to allow successful provision of satisfying customer services. Apart from this, even the possibility of having a network capable of maintaining multiple, concurrent QoS flows (for various applications running simultaneously) would also be advantageous. In addition, the users should be given the opportunity to alter or renegotiate (when desired) the predefined service level specifications (SLS) with the corresponding providers through a continuous monitoring process of customer requirements [17].

Finally, there is a need to set up necessary SLS between networks. This is important as it allows user mobility to be managed independently of the access and backbone networks (e.g. broadband ISDN (B-ISDN) or GSM), while maintaining a certain quality level that has been specified by any one particular mobile user.

13.6   MOBILITY MANAGEMENT IN SATELLITE AND TERRESTRIAL NETWORKS

In the previous section, we have discussed some important aspects of mobility management. MSSs using nongeostationary orbits such as LEO and MEO have very similar characteristics to cellular networks and thus these issues are common between both the networks. The main similarity is that most of these systems use the cellular concept of increasing the total system capacity through a cellular-like coverage area arrangement introducing similar handoff issues as those involved in cellular systems. There is, however, a major difference between the proposed scheme in satellite systems and what exists in the sphere of cellular networks. The key operational concept that differentiates the specific operations of mobility management in the two systems is the 'entity' being considered as the moving object. While the former encounters *mobile* movements within a fixed network architecture, the latter incurs *satellite* movements in reference to fixed MNs. Essentially, this suggests that the mobility management technique will be different.

Furthermore, while the prediction of a mobile's deterministic location is relatively easy to obtain (given the traveling characteristics, particularly speed of the LEO satellites), such certainty is not guaranteed in cellular systems. In other words, the difficulties encountered in cellular networks do not seem applicable to its satellite-mobile network counterparts. As a result, appropriate modification of the existing terrestrial-based solutions will be necessary before similar operations are suitable for applications on satellite-incorporated 3G systems. Generally, it would be conceptually a lot easier to anticipate satellite movements than mobile movements. Besides, the rate of call arrival would not be essential in the latter case (i.e. paging seems to be less of a problem for satellite applications).

13.6.1   Satellite networks

The use of LEO satellites is the most favorable for its high traffic capacity and reduced user power requirements both in satellites and in the ground terminal. However, as individual LEO satellites rotate relatively fast along the Earth's surface, handoff becomes a particular concern in coping with the nonstationary nature of the coverage area. Depending on the relation of the two satellites involved in the handoff operations, three types of handoff are classified. Basically, intrasatellite handoffs are used to describe changes between spot beams under the management of the same satellite. With the increasing involvement of network management, intersatellite handoffs indicate handoffs between satellites and link handoffs incur because of changes in the connection pattern of satellite footprints (or satellite network topology). As an example of the latter scenario, such handoffs occur when links to adjacent orbits are turned off when the concerned satellite moves near the polar region. Thus, the task is not only to utilize the available frequency spectrum efficiently but also to minimize unnecessary forced termination of connections due to handoff failures. In other words, it would be essential to at least attempt to anticipate user motions and to reserve the resources accordingly for the predicted residual time. A brief literature survey indicates that there are two major prioritization techniques that were designed specifically for such purposes: (1) use of guard channels and (2) queuing of handoff requests when the resources were not currently available. Consequently, the operation of call admission control also becomes important as it decides whether sufficient resources would be available to accommodate the newly arrived transmission requests [18].

13.6.2   Cellular networks

Cellular networks focus more on the efficient operations of location management specifically for idle mobile users. Thus, although the basic problem of managing mobility is the same, the actual emphasis on the system development is different for satellite and cellular systems. In fact, because of the movement of the LEO satellites, definitions of location area (LA) cannot be fixed even for the duration of a connection. Consequently, it is difficult to reapply some of the existing solutions from one system to the other (i.e. from cellular to satellite and vice versa). However, there are certain aspects in which the 'approaches' might be useful to seek alternative solutions for the open issues identified. For example, in terms of routing, Uzunalioglu [19] has developed a protocol aiming to reduce the frequency rerouting attempts during a link handoff.

Basically, target probability is defined to quantify the estimated duration of residency of a mobile terminal on one particular ISL. During the route establishment of a new call, only links that can demonstrate a lifetime greater than the target probability will be considered to form segments of the route. Though it might not seem obvious, this idea is similar to the predicting method used in location management operations in cellular networks, specifically, in the sphere of sequential paging where the optimal sequence is selected according to the probability of residence in individual subsections (or subareas). Thus, while acknowledging the fact that the prediction method would have been easier in the satellite systems (because of the fact that its motion is deterministic and predictable), the goal of determining efficient operations in both systems is the same.

13.6.3   Handoff management versus location management

Consequently, it becomes necessary to identify more closely the differences (or relations) between the operations of handoff and location management. Clearly, handoff management is significant only when the mobile is active; specifically, it is about the appropriate reservation of resources (such as bandwidth) along the roaming path of a mobile user while being engaged in a call connection. Its efficient operation is important to ensure that the various aspects of the QoS requirements (e.g. throughput versus forced call termination) are satisfactorily complied. Location management, on the other hand, is mainly for users who are currently idle but are expected to receive calls (or become active) while they frequently change their point of attachment to the network. In essence, only sufficient location information (about the mobile) is maintained so that the network could loosely track the mobile's movement and subsequently incur a minimal paging (or searching) load when the precise residency is required. Consequently, it would be correct to conclude that the predicted information for handoff needs to be more reliable than that desired for efficient location management. On the basis of this observation, it seems potentially viable to combine (at least to some extent) the operations of the two management processes of handoff and location.

13.7   SATELLITE TRANSPORT OF THE INTERNET TRAFFIC

Broadband satellite networks are being developed to transport high-speed multimedia and in particular Internet traffic through high-capacity satellite channels to network segments as well as to individual users. As in the case of any other wireless network designed to deliver Internet traffic, broadband satellite networks need to connect to the backbone wired Internet on the ground. TCP (transmission control protocol) is the most commonly used protocol at the transport layer of the network stack in the Internet, originally developed in wired networks with low bit error rate (BER) on the order of less than 10^{-8}. In this context, any wireless network with Internet service needs to be compatible with the protocol used in the wired network, that is, mainly the TCP/IP. There are, however, some design issues in the TCP/IP, which makes it difficult to be used efficiently over the wireless and the satellite links. Recently, there have been many research activities comparing the performance of TCP in high-BER and high-latency channels and modification proposals to improve its performance in terrestrial and satellite wireless networks [20–24].

13.7.1 TCP imperfections

TCP has been designed and tuned for networks in which segment losses and corruption of performance are mainly due to network congestion. This assumption might be invalid in many of the emerging networks such as wireless networks. The flow control mechanism used in TCP is based on time-out and window-size adjustment, which can work with high utilization in wired networks with low BER on the order of 10^{-8}. However, when the wireless channel is used (partially or totally) as the physical layer with a BER as high as 10^{-3}, it may perform inefficiently. The reason is that in the wireless channels the main cause for packet loss is the high BER and not congestion as it is in wired networks. The low efficiency of the TCP in a wireless channel is a result of the fact that the TCP misinterpreted the packet loss because of high error rate and congestion. On the other hand, in high-latency networks (such as satellite networks), adjustment of the window size could take a long time and reduce the system throughput.

TCP has the ability to probe the unused network bandwidth by a mechanism called *slow start* and also to back off the transmission rate upon detection of congestion through the *congestion avoidance* mechanism. At the connection start-up, TCP initializes a variable called *congestion window* to a value of one segment. This variable determines the transmission rate of TCP. The window size is doubled at every round-trip period until a packet loss is experienced. At this time, the congestion avoidance phase is commenced, the window size is halved, and the lost packet is retransmitted. During this phase of the TCP, the window size is increased only linearly by one segment at each round-trip period and might be halved again upon detection of another packet loss. If the retransmitted packet is lost, the time-out mechanism employed in the TCP reduces the window size to one. Since all these procedures are performed at periods equal to the round-trip delay of the channel, the system throughput could be degraded significantly where high-latency channels such as geostationary satellites are involved. Therefore, the high-latency satellite channel combined with the slow increase of the TCP congestion window size, results in the underutilization of the satellite high-capacity channel.

13.7.2 TCP enhancements

There are some modifications to the basic TCP that can be made so that the TCP performs more efficiently in high-latency satellite networks with Internet services (e.g. see

References [21–24] and references therein). Some of the methods discussed in Chapter 9 for improving TCP performance over wireless cellular networks are also applicable to the satellite channel. *Selective acknowledgment* (SACK) TCP [25], for example, is a method in which multiple losses in a transmission window can be recovered in one round-trip period instead of two round-trip periods as in the basic TCP. *TCP for transactions* (T/TCP) also reduces the user-perceived latency to one round-trip delay for short transmissions [26]. In *TCP spoofing* [21], a router close to the satellite link is considered, which sends back acknowledgments for the TCP data. The responsibility of any segment loss in this method belongs to the router. In another method, called *split TCP*, a TCP connection is divided into multiple TCP connections and a special *satellite TCP* connection is employed for the satellite link part.

Another alternative for delivering Internet traffic through broadband satellite networks and simultaneously providing QoS is to use IP over ATM or ATM protocols. In this regard, the IP will provide the availability of various Internet applications, whereas the ATM protocol supports the connection between two end-user terminals with a guaranteed end-to-end QoS. An example of such protocol combinations has been proposed for the Astra Return Channel System (ARCS), a geostationary multimedia satellite system using the *Ka* band on the return channels and the *Ku* bands on the forward channels [27].

In conclusion to the above discussion, we can say that the use of basic TCP in future broadband satellite networks will impose significant problems especially in the case of short transmissions (compared with the channel delay-bandwidth product). For the geostationary satellite links, the major problem with the TCP is the long round-trip time, whereas in the case of nongeostationary satellite networks, the round-trip delay variation or jitter becomes more dominant. In both situations, the burst error nature of the satellite channel and the high BER require more sophisticated flow and congestion control mechanisms that can separate the segment loss because of network congestion or because of high channel error rate.

13.8 SUMMARY AND CONCLUSIONS

In this chapter, we summarized the satellite communications from a networking point of view in order to see the role of satellites in future mobile and fixed IP networks. The historical summary provided in the first section of this chapter revealed that despite the high initial investment and maintenance cost of satellite systems, satellites will remain as an irreplaceable component for long-distance communications and multimedia broadcasting. In recent years, with the progress in optical communications and an increasing number of transoceanic cables, it may be mistakenly thought that cable will replace the satellite for long-distance communications. However, the satellite's easy and quick deployment of additional capacity in any part of the world provides a distinct advantage over the deployment of cable systems. Improvement in cable television also could not replace a satellite's broadcasting feature, especially because of the satellite's large footprint and simpler deployment.

When it comes to high-speed Internet access to the home, office, ships, aircrafts, and mobile users, again satellite systems show its unique features. The global Internet needs expansion both in the geographical domain and in the data transport capacity. Satellites would be the main telecommunications component, if not the only one as in many terrain circumstances, which can promise such expansion. The satellite's huge onboard channel capacity and large coverage area are sufficient to provide future deployment of new systems. A very handy example would be the efforts toward realization of in-flight Internet access to passengers using satellite networks by major aircraft companies and airlines [28]. Satellites will soon bring inexpensive Internet access to long-distance flights and using voice-over IP techniques will make a huge reduction in the cost of phone calls from and to airplanes.

For high-speed Internet access to the home and to small office users, currently ADSL and cable modem are the two leading technologies. With the new digital video broadcasting satellite systems in North America and Europe, however, these technologies found a need to compete with the satellites. The number of subscribers to satellite high-speed Internet access is increasing and getting closer to the number of subscribers to the other two technologies and this number is expected to increase even more rapidly by the introduction of inexpensive satellite receivers in the next few years.

Satellites have an even larger contribution in IP networks than to individual access as discussed above. A satellite node can be an intelligent ATM switch or an IP router in the sky interconnecting segments of the backbone networks on the Earth. Similar to the conventional usage of satellites in PSTN, satellites can play an important role in future packet-switched networks including the public Internet. The 3G wireless networks and beyond consider Internet and multimedia traffic to have the dominant share of the network traffic load, and satellites have already shown their role in the completion of any terrestrial mobile network. An example of S-UMTS was given in this chapter to outline the role of satellites in future mobile communication systems. Satellite ground stations acting as an interworking unit can solve the roaming issue between heterogeneous wired and wireless terrestrial networks, expanding the telecommunications to its ultimate universal stage.

Some important technical implementation issues concerned with a global IP network have been discussed in this chapter. Mobility management has been revisited and redefined and location, handoff, routing, and QoS managements have been discussed. All these issues are current research topics in mobile and satellite communications. For the high-latency satellite channel, as well as the error-prone wireless channel (including both satellite and terrestrial), the need for improvement in transport protocols currently employed in the Internet has been discussed and state-of-the art research activities toward improvement of TCPs have been reviewed. Note that other researchers are also currently working to improve the error probability of the wireless channel using forward error correction schemes and sophisticated coding algorithms. Although these works are of great importance in the establishment of a better quality wireless channel, we should not forget that there are always situations in which the wireless signal-to-noise ratio is too low and no coding scheme can improve it. Therefore, a better solution would lie in the higher layers of the network including the transport and network layers in which enhanced flow control algorithms speed up the data rate and the throughput of the wireless channel.

REFERENCES

1. Jamalipour A, *Low Earth Orbital Satellites for Personal Communication Networks*, Artech House, Norwood, Mass., 1998.
2. Jamalipour A, Broadband satellite networks–the global IT bridge, *Proceedings of the IEEE*, Special issue on Multidimensional broadband wireless technologies and services, **89**(1), 88–104, 2001.
3. Jamalipour A & Tung T, The role of satellites in global IT: trends and implications, *IEEE Personal Communications Magazine*, Special issue on multimedia communications over satellites, **8**(3), 5–11, 2001.
4. Farserotu J & Prasad R, A survey of future broadband multimedia satellite systems, issues and trends, *IEEE Communications Magazine*, **38**(6), 128–133, 2000.
5. Chitre P & Yegenoglu F, Next-generation satellite networks: architectures and implementations, *IEEE Communications Magazine*, 37(3), 30–36, 1999.
6. Neale J, Green R & Landovskis J, Interactive channel for multimedia satellite networks, *IEEE Communications Magazine*, **39**(3), 192–198, 2001.
7. Hu Y & Li VOK, Satellite-based Internet: a tutorial, *IEEE Communications Magazine*, **39**(3), 154–162, 2001.
8. Minei I & Cohen R, High-speed Internet access through unidirectional geostationary satellite channels, *IEEE Journal on Selected Areas in Communications*, **17**(2), 345–359, 1999.
9. Clausen HD, Linder H & Collini-Nocker B, Internet over direct broadcast satellites, *IEEE Communications Magazine*, **37**(6), 146–151, 1999.
10. Zeng M, Annamalai A & Bhargava V, Harmonization of global third-generation mobile systems, *IEEE Communications Magazine*, **38**(12), 94–104, 2000.
11. Mohr W & Konhauser W, Access network evolution beyond third generation mobile communications, *IEEE Communications Magazine*, **38**(12), 122–133, 2000.
12. Steele R, Lee CC & Gould P, *GSM, cdmaOne and 3G Systems*, John Wiley & Sons, Chichester, West Sussex, England, 2001.
13. Priscoli F, UMTS architecture for integrating terrestrial and satellite systems, *IEEE Multimedia*, **6**(4), 38–44, 1999.
14. Wong V & Leung V, Location management for next-generation personal communications networks, *IEEE Network*, **14**(5), 18–24, 2000.
15. Solomon J, *Mobile IP: The Internet Unplugged*, Prentice Hall PTR, Upper Saddle River, N.J., 1998.
16. Fikouras N, Malki K, Cvetkovic S & Smythe C, Performance evaluation of TCP over Mobile IP, Proceedings of the PIMRC '99, Osaka, Japan, September 1999.
17. Mehrotra A & Golding L, Mobility and security management in the GSM system and some proposed future improvements, *Proceedings of the IEEE*, **86**(7), 1480–1497, 1998.
18. Akyildiz I, NcNair J, Ho J, Uzunalioglu H & Wang W, Mobility management in next generation wireless systems, *Proceedings of the IEEE*, **87**(8), 1999.

19. Uzunalioglu H, Probabilistic routing protocol for low earth orbit satellite networks, Proceedings of International Conference on Communications (ICC '98), Atlanta, Ga., June 1998.
20. Goyal R, Jain R, Goyal M, Fahmy S, Vandalore B & Kota S, Traffic management for TCP/IP over satellite ATM networks, *IEEE Communications Magazine*, **37**(3), 56–61, 1999.
21. Partridge C & Shepard TJ, TCP/IP performance over satellite links, *IEEE Network*, **11**(5), 61–71, 1997.
22. Henderson TR & Katz RH, Transport protocols for Internet-compatible satellite networks, *IEEE Journal on Selected Areas in Communications*, **17**(2), 326–344, 1999.
23. Minei I & Cohen R, High-speed Internet access through unidirectional geostationary satellite channels, *IEEE Journal on Selected Areas in Communications*, **17**(2), 345–359, 1999.
24. Xylomenos G, Polyzos GC, Mahonen P & Saaranen M, TCP performance issues over wireless links, *IEEE Communications Magazine*, **39**(4), 52–58, 2001.
25. Mathis M, Mahdavi J, Floyd S & Romanow A, TCP Selective Acknowledgement Options, IETF RFC 2018, October 1996.
26. Braden R, T/TCP - TCP Extensions for Transactions Functional, IETF RFC 1644, July 1994.
27. ASTRA Return Channel System, System Description Documentation, Societe Europeenne des Satellites, Document No.: ARCS.240.DC-Eoo1-0.2, issue 0.2, May 1998.
28. Karlin S, Take off, plug in, dial up, *IEEE Spectrum*, August, 52–59, 2001.

Acronyms

2G	second generation (wireless cellular systems)
3G	third generation (wireless cellular systems)
3GPP	Third-Generation Partnership Project
3GPP2	Third-Generation Partnership Project 2
AAA	authentication, authorization, and accounting
ACK	acknowledgment
ADIF	accounting data interchange format
ADSL	asynchronous digital subscriber line
AGCH	access grant channel
AMPS	Advanced Mobile Phone Systems
AMSC	American Mobile Satellite Corporation
AN	access network
AN	access node
ANSI	American National Standards Institute
AP	access point
APM	advance power management
ARIB	Association of Radio Industries and Business, Japan
ARP	address resolution protocol
ARQ	automatic repeat request
AS	autonomous system
ATM	asynchronous transfer mode
BA	behavior aggregate
BCCH	broadcast control channel
BDT	Telecommunication Development Bureau
BER	bit error rate

The Wireless Mobile Internet: Architectures, Protocols, and Services.   Abbas Jamalipour
© 2003 John Wiley & Sons, Ltd   ISBN: 0-470-84468-X

BGP	border gateway protocol
B-ISDN	broadband ISDN
BLA	big-location area
BMC	broadcast/multicast control (layer)
BPSK	binary phase shift keying
BS	base station
BSC	base station controller
BSS	base station subsystem
BSS	basic service set (IEEE 802.11)
BSSAP	BSS application part
BTS	base transceiver station
BTSM	BTS management
BU	binding update
CAC	call admission control
CAMEL	customized application for mobile networks enhanced logic
CBR	constant bit rate
CC	call control
CCCH	common control channel
CCH	control channel
CCITT	International Telegraph and Telephone Consultative Committee
CCoA	colocated CoA
CDMA	code division multiple access
CDPD	Cellular Digital Packet Data
CE	congestion experienced
CELP	code excited linear predictive
CEPT	Conference of European Post and Telecommunications
CHAP	challenge handshake authentication protocol
CHT	channel holding time
CID	cell identification
CIDR	classless inter domain routing
CLI	calling line identification
CLNP	connectionless network protocol
CMR	call-to-mobility ratio
CN	core network
CN	corresponding node
CoA	care-of address
CPCH	common packet channel
CPU	central processing unit
CS	circuit switching
CSD	Circuit Switched Data
CSMA	carrier sense multiple access
CSMA/CA	CSMA with collision avoidance
CSMA/CD	CSMA with collision detection
CWTS	China Wireless Telecommunication Standards Group

DA   directory agent
DAB   direct audio broadcasting
D-AMPS   Digital APMS
DCCH   dedicated control channel
DCF   distributed configuration function
DCH   dedicated channel
DCS1800   Digital Cellular System (at 1800 MHz)
DECT   Digital Enhanced (aka European) Cordless Telecommunication
DHCP   dynamic host configuration protocol
DiffServ   differentiated services
DNS   domain name server
DS-CDMA   direct sequence CDMA
DSCH   downlink shared channel
DSCP   DiffServ code point
DSL   digital subscriber line
DS-SS   direct sequence spread spectrum
DTAP   direct transfer application part
DVB   direct video broadcasting
DWDM   dense WDM
EBGP   external BGP
ECN   explicit congestion notification
ECSD   Enhanced Circuit Switched Data
EDGE   Enhanced Data rates for GSM (aka Global) Evolution
EFR   enhanced full rate
EGPRS   Enhanced GPRS
ELN   explicit loss notification
EMS   European Mobile Satellite
ESS   extended service set
ETSI   European Telecommunications Standards Institute
EWMA   exponential weighted moving average
FA   foreign agent
FACCH   fast associated control channel
FACH   forward access channel
FBm   fractional Brownian motion
FCC   Federal Communications Commission
FCCH   frequency correction channel
FCCH   frequency correction channel
FCFS   first-come-first-served
FDD   frequency division duplex
FDM   frequency division multiplex
FDMA   frequency division multiple access
FEC   forward error correction
FGN   fractional Gaussian noise
FH-SS   frequency hopping spread spectrum

FM	frequency modulation
FOMA	Freedom Of Multimedia Access
FR	frame relay
FTP	file transfer protocol
GEO	geostationary earth orbit
GGSN	gateway GPRS supporting node
GMA	global mobility agent
GMSK	Gaussian minimum shift keying
GPRS	General Packet Radio Service
GPS	Global Positioning System
GSM	Global System for Mobile communications
GSM	Group Special Mobile
GSM-MAP	GSM mobile application part
GTP	GPRS tunneling protocol
HA	home agent
HACK	handover acknowledgement
HAWAII	Handoff-Aware Wireless Access Internet Infrastructure
HI	handover initiate
HLR	home location register
HSCSD	High Speed Circuit Switched Data
HTML	hypertext markup language
HTTP	hypertext transfer protocol
IANA	Internet Assigned Numbers Authority
IBGP	internal BGP
ICANN	Internet Corporation for Assigned Names and Numbers
ICMP	Internet control message protocol
IESG	Internet Engineering Steering Group
IETF	Internet Engineering Task Force
IGP	interior gateway protocol
IGRP	interior gateway routing protocol
IKE	Internet key exchange
IMT-2000	International Mobile Telecommunications
IN	intelligent network
INMARSAT	INternational MARitime telecommunication SATellite organization
INTELSAT	International Telecommunications Satellite Organization
IntServ	integrated services
IP	Internet protocol
IP2W	IP to wireless
IPng	next generation IP
IPv4	IP version 4
IPv6	IP version 6
IS	intermediate system
ISDN	Integrated Service Digital Network
ISL	intersatellite link

ISO	International Organization for Standardization
ISOC	Internet Society
ISP	Internet service provider
ITU	International Telecommunication Union
IWF	interworking function
IWU	interworking unit
LA	location area
LAN	local area network
LAPD	link access protocol for the D channel
LATS	load adaptive threshold scheme
LEO	low earth orbit
LLC	logical link control
LMA	local mobility agent
LRD	long range dependence
MAC	medium access control (layer)
MANET	mobile ad hoc network
MAP	mobile application part
MBAC	measurement-based admission control
MC-CDMA	multicarrier CDMA
MDBS	mobile data base station
MD-IS	mobile data intermediate system
MEO	medium earth orbit
M-ES	mobile end system
MExE	mobile execution environment
MH	mobile host
MHF	mobile home function
MM	mobility management
MMPP	Markov modulated Poisson process
MN	mobile node
MNLP	mobile node location protocol
MNRP	mobile node registration protocol
MS	mobile station
MSC	mobile switching center
MSF	mobile serving function
MSS	maximum segment size
MSS	mobile satellite system
MT	mobile terminal
MTP	message transfer part
MTU	maximum transfer unit
MWIF	Mobile Wireless Internet Forum
NACK	negative acknowledgements
NAT	network address translation (aka translator)
NID	network ID
NLSP	network layer security protocol

NNI	network-to-network interface
OAM	operating and maintenance
OAM&P	operations, administration, management and provisioning
OBP	onboard processing
OBS	onboard switching
OCN	Open Computer Network (NTT, Japan)
OHG	Operator Harmonization Group
OS	operating system
OSA	open service architecture (UMTS)
OSI	Open System Interconnection
OSPF	open shortest path first
PAP	password authentication protocol
PBAC	parameter-based admission control
PC	personal computer
PC	point coordinator
PCCH	paging control channel
PCF	packet control function
PCF	point coordination function
PCH	paging channel
PCM	pulse code modulation
PCN	packet core network
PCS	Personal Communication Services
PCS1900	Personal Communications Systems (at 1900 MHz)
PDA	personal digital assistant
PDC	Personal Digital Cellular
PDCP	packet data convergence protocol (layer)
PDH	plesiochronous digital hierarchy
PDN	packet data network
PDSN	packet data serving node
PHB	per-hop-behavior
PHS	Personal Handy phone System
PHY	physical (layer)
PLU	probabilistic location update
PN	pseudonoise
PPP	point-to-point protocol
PS	packet switching
PSK	phase shift keying
PSTN	public switching telephony networks
PZID	packet zone ID
QoS	quality of service
QPSK	quadrature phase shift keying
RA	router advertisement
RACH	random access channel
RACH	random access channel

RADIUS	remote authentication dial in user service
RAN	radio access network
RF	radio frequency
RFC	request for comments
RIP	routing information protocol
RLC	radio link control (layer)
RMA	regional mobility agent
RN	radio network
RNC	radio network controller
RNS	radio network subsystem
RR	radio resource
RRC	radio resource control (layer)
RSVP	resource reservation protocol
RTT	radio transmission technology
RTT	round trip time
SACCH	slow associated control channel
SACK	selective acknowledgment
SAP	service access provider
SASL	simple authentication and security layer
SAT	SIM application toolkit
SBAS	switched beam antenna transceiver
SC-CDMA	single-carrier CDMA
SCCP	signaling connection control part
SCF	service capability feature
SCH	synchronization channel
SCP	service control point
SCS	service capability server
SDCCH	standalone dedicated control channel
SDH	synchronous digital hierarchy
SDO	standards development organization
SG	study group
SGSN	serving GPRS supporting node
SHCCH	shared control channel
SID	system ID
SIM	subscriber identity module
SIP	session initiation protocol
SLA	service level agreement
SLP	service location protocol
SMG	special mobile group
SMS	short message service
SNDCP	subnetwork-dependent convergence protocol
SNR	signal-to-noise ratio
SOHYP	sum of hyper-exponentials
SPN	service provider network

SRD	short-range dependence
SRNS	serving radio network controller
SS7	signaling system number 7
SSDP	simple service discovery protocol
SSP	service switching point
S-UMTS	satellite UMTS
T/TCP	TCP for transactions
TC	traffic class
TCH	traffic channel
TCH/F	full-rate traffic channel
TCH/H	half-rate traffic channel
TCP	transmission control protocol
TD-CDMA	time-division CDMA
TDD	time division duplex
TDM	time division multiplex
TDMA	time division multiple access
TD-SCDMA	synchronous time division CDMA
TE	terminal equipment
TES	transform-expand-sample
TM	traffic management
TOS	type of service
TR	technical report
TrLA	three-location area
TS	technical specification
TSAG	Telecommunication Standardization Advisory Group
TTA	Telecommunications Technology Association, Korea
TTC	Telecommunication Technology Committee, Japan
UA	user agent
UDP	user datagram protocol
UE	user equipment
UMTS	Universal Mobile Telecommunications System
UTRA	Universal Terrestrial Radio Access
UTRAN	UMTS Terrestrial Radio Access Network
UWC	Universe Wireless Communications consortium
VBR	variable bit rate
VC	virtual circuit
VHE	virtual home environment
VLR	visiting location register
VLSI	very large scale integrated
WAE	wireless application environment
WAN	wide area network
WAP	Wireless Application Protocol
W-CDMA	wideband CDMA
WDM	wavelength division multiplexing

WFQ	weighted fair queuing
WG	working group
WLL	wireless local loop
WML	wireless markup language
WSP	wireless session protocol
WTLS	wireless transport layer security
WTP	wireless transaction protocol
WTSA	World Telecommunication Standardization Assembly
WWW	World Wide Web

Index

The Wireless Mobile Internet: Architectures, Protocols, and Services. Abbas Jamalipour
© 2003 John Wiley & Sons, Ltd   ISBN: 0-470-84468-X

About the Author

Abbas Jamalipour (a.jamalipour@ieee.org) has been
with the School of Electrical and Information Engineering at the University of Sydney, Australia, since
1998, where he is responsible for teaching and research
in wireless data communication networks and satellite systems. He holds a Ph.D. in Electrical Engineering from the Nagoya University, Japan. In addition to
authoring the current book, he has authored the first
technical book ever written on networking aspects of
LEO satellites, entitled *Low Earth Orbital Satellites
for Personal Communication Networks*, published by
Artech House, Boston, 1998; a chapter in the presti-
gious *Wiley Encyclopedia of Telecommunications and
Signal Processing* edited by John Proakis 2003, and
another chapter in the book *Next Generation Wireless
Networks* edited by Sirin Tekinay, Kluwer Academic Publishers, 2001. He has authored
more than 80 papers in major journals and international conferences and has conducted
technical courses and tutorials at major international conferences and universities worldwide. He has served in technical program committees of several major international
conferences and has organized and chaired many technical sessions and panels at international conferences including a symposium in IEEE Globecom2001. He is currently the
vice chair to the Satellite and Space Communications Committee and the Asia Pacific
Board, Coordinating Committee Chapter, IEEE ComSoc. He has organized several special issues on the topic of 3G and beyond systems as well as broadband wireless networks
in IEEE magazines and journals. He is a technical editor to the IEEE Wireless Communications Magazine and a senior member of the IEEE, and a member of several technical
institutions such as the International Union of Radio Science (URSI), the IEICE and SITA
of Japan.

Printed and bound by CPI Group (UK) Ltd, Croydon, CR0 4YY
16/04/2025

14658550-0003